The Next Twenty-five Years

The Next Twenty-five Years

Affirmative Action in Higher Education in the United States and South Africa

∾

EDITED BY

David L. Featherman, Martin Hall, and Marvin Krislov

THE UNIVERSITY OF MICHIGAN PRESS
Ann Arbor

2013   2012   2011   2010   4   3   2   1

A CIP catalog record for this book is available from the British Library.

Library of Congress Cataloging-in-Publication Data

The next twenty-five years : affirmative action in higher education in
the United States and South Africa / edited by David L.
Featherman, Martin Hall, and Marvin Krislov.
p.   cm.
Includes index.
ISBN 978-0-472-11705-5 (cloth : alk. paper) —
ISBN 978-0-472-03377-5 (pbk. : alk. paper) —
ISBN 978-0-472-02155-0 (e-book)
1. Education, Higher—United States.   2. Education, Higher—South
Africa.   3. Affirmative action programs—United States.
4. Affirmative action programs—South Africa.   I. Featherman, David L.
II. Hall, Martin, 1952–   III. Krislov, Marvin, 1960–

LA227.4.N497   2009
379.2'60973—dc22   2009024924

Contents

Conclusions

Preface

In 2003, the United States Supreme Court heard two cases in which white plaintiffs sued the University of Michigan, arguing that the University's admissions policies violated the Constitution by considering the race and ethnicity of applicants among other factors. These cases raised the issue of affirmative action in university admissions for the first time at the Supreme Court level since *University of California Regents v. Bakke* in 1978. In 1990, the South African government released Nelson Mandela from prison, marking a new stage in the country's transformation. In an effort to overcome the legacy of apartheid, that country, too, has considered race in determining access to higher education. This procedure in university admissions has not yet been challenged in South Africa's Constitutional Court.

In *Grutter v. Bollinger,* a majority of the Supreme Court accepted the University of Michigan's argument that student body diversity was a compelling interest under the equal protection clause, and thus justified the limited use of race-sensitive admissions policies. The Court found that the law school's admissions policies, which relied on subjective evaluation, were holistic and satisfied the "narrow tailoring" prong of the law. On the other hand, in *Gratz v. Bollinger* a majority of the Court rejected the University's undergraduate admissions process as numbers-driven and mechanistic. The Court thus clarified that race-sensitive admissions policies could be permissible, but would be carefully scrutinized by the courts.

Writing for the majority in *Grutter,* Associate Justice Sandra Day O'Connor noted that "race unfortunately still matters." Yet she stated that "race-conscious admissions policies must be limited in time." In her much-discussed phrasing, Justice O'Connor wrote:

> It has been 25 years since Justice Powell first approved the use of race to further an interest in student body diversity in the context of public higher education. . . . We expect that 25 years from now, the use of racial preferences will no longer be necessary to further the interest approved today.

Justice O'Connor's speculation—and expectant hope—about the American future resonated beyond the United States and gave impetus to this book—specifically to its title and framing question about "the next 25 years." What justification can be found for affirmative action in American higher education—and, by inference, in other higher-education systems, such as South Africa's? Or to put it another way: Will a nation's compelling interest in achieving an integrated, diverse set of leaders still require the use of race-sensitive considerations in admissions? Justice O'Connor's speculation takes on even greater significance in the aftermath of the 2008 American presidential election, in which a candidate of biracial parentage and African American heritage, Barack Obama, captured widespread voter support across racial, economic, and gender lines.

These questions prompted a binational conversation about the future of affirmative action in higher education, hosted in 2005 initially by the University of Michigan and subsequently by the University of Cape Town, under the sponsorship of the Andrew W. Mellon and Spencer Foundations. As documented more fully in the introduction, these two public universities found their respective experiences—and, importantly, their policy outlooks—enlightened by each other's national debates about the ramifications of race, gender, and economic inequalities. Each introduced the other to insightful and contentious debates about the use of race-sensitive policies, debates that challenged any easy consensus either for or against affirmative action as a necessary means to consensually valued ends. The chapters of this book emerged from that conversation, either as more fully developed versions of arguments originally made at the conferences or as newly commissioned statements that were sought to round out this collection. The authors write from perspectives of social science, history, educational policy, and the law and span both countries. We see the book as opening up a transnational dialogue as our two countries, and many others, struggle with allocating the opportunities provided by selective higher-education institutions.

As our book went to press, both South Africa and the United States were undergoing profoundly important, albeit quite different political transitions. In South Africa, the controversial but constitutionally guided replacement of President Thabo Mbeki prior to the end of his term stirred up political uncertainty, largely the result of defections and expulsions from the ruling party, the African National Congress (ANC). Meanwhile, America elected its first black president. The significance of these events to the respective democracies cannot be overstated. Their timing, and the timing of this book, suggest a new phase in the conversation about affirmative action as public policy.

We coeditors wish to acknowledge with deep gratitude the encouragement and financial support of the Mellon and Spencer Foundations, and especially their presidents, William G. Bowen and Michael McPherson, respectively. Harriet Zuckerman, executive vice president of the Mellon Foundation, enabled us to extend Mellon's support toward the production of this book and its copublication by the University of Kwa-Zulu Natal

Press. We also wish to thank our colleagues at the University of Michigan and the University of Cape Town, and especially President Mary Sue Coleman and Vice Chancellor Njabulo Ndebele, for hosting the pivotal conferences that inform our work and that of our contributors.

We also wish to thank several invaluable colleagues for their support in translating the disparate conference papers into a coherent book. Jim Reische, a freelance editor and formerly on the staff of the University of Michigan Press, might legitimately be considered a fourth coeditor. He took on the heroic tasks of reformatting conference materials, editing chapters, and negotiating with authors over the economy of words. Jim made our work as senior editors manageable. We also thank Catherine Rector and Raye Holden, among others on our staff, who helped us reach our goal. Finally, we are fortunate to have worked closely with the University of Michigan Press, and especially its director, Philip Pochoda, and our editor, Melody Herr. Their guidance and encouragement, together with critical input from two reviewers, helped us refine our message and reach our audience more effectively. Finally, many of our individual authors sought out colleagues who read and critiqued preliminary drafts. Those names are far too numerous to include, but their contributions are nonetheless valued and enormously consequential; we and our authors remain humbly in their debt.

David L. Featherman
Martin Hall
Marvin Krislov

Foreword

Mary Sue Coleman

I was 10 years old and living in Georgia when the U.S. Supreme Court handed down its historic 1954 ruling in *Brown v. Board of Education,* making it illegal for America's schools to segregate children by race. In their landmark decision, the justices unanimously quashed the long-held notion of "separate but equal" education. I lived in a county where 50 percent of the residents were African Americans. And yet I only saw black children working in fields or local stores. I had no idea where the black families of my community actually lived, learned, or worshipped. At school, my classmates were white. At the movie theaters, black children my age sat in the balcony, absent from my view, both physically and intellectually.

Meanwhile, half a world away, in a part of the globe that most American children of my generation were only vaguely aware of, South Africans were engaged in a struggle of their own against an oppressive apartheid regime. In what seem like uncanny similarities to America's Civil Rights era, the year 1954 saw bus boycotts in Cape Town and nationwide protests against South Africa's segregated Bantu Education system. This was no coincidence: South Africa's leaders were acutely aware of events in the United States, and there was some exchange of ideas and encouragement. So it may come as no surprise that in South Africa, like America, people's hopes for justice and racial equality turned on the axis of education.

The mid-1950s in South Africa offered brief glimpses of hope for a more equal and just future, but this hope was tinged with a bitter awareness of institutional racism's destructive power. In the Georgia of my childhood, too, the hope for equality was quashed by the reality of prejudice. Responding to the *Brown* ruling, Georgia governor Herman Talmadge vowed to keep white and black children apart even if it meant facing down federal troops. And his successor, Governor S. Marvin Griffin, was just as firm. "I will maintain segregation in the schools," he promised, "and the races will not be mixed, come hell or high water."[1] It would be 10 years before the state satisfied the high court's order that black and white children should share classrooms.

A half century later, I find myself leading one of America's most respected public universities, an institution deeply proud of its historical openness to students from all backgrounds. The University of Michigan was one of the first public universities to enroll women and African Americans, and has long welcomed international students, as well.

In this time when America is quite radically reconsidering both the form and extent of its commitment to racial equality, it is, therefore, so appropriate that Michigan should join with our South African colleagues in hosting a broad-ranging assessment of how far we've come, and where we should go from here. We are, once again, at pivotal moments as nations.

As in 1954, our two countries are exploring and experiencing education's role in fostering racial equality.

In America, the evolution of this culture of equal access has recently taken an unexpected turn. Almost 50 years after *Brown,* the Court reaffirmed the essential legitimacy of affirmative action through its 2003 rulings in both *Gratz v. Bollinger* and *Grutter v. Bollinger.* Both decisions endorsed the compelling nature of the University of Michigan's goal of building a diverse student body, and the decisions in those cases offer important guidance regarding how universities can permissibly seek to achieve that compelling goal. While upholding the flexible, individualized, and holistic policy used at the University of Michigan Law School in the *Grutter* case, the Court found in *Gratz* that the mechanistic assignment of a quantifiable value to race was not an appropriate admissions practice.

Most importantly, Justice Sandra Day O'Connor, writing for the majority in *Grutter,* recognized that "race . . . still matters" in our society, although she expressed the hope that within 25 years after the rulings, our society would have progressed to a degree that public institutions of higher education would no longer need to factor race into their admissions decisions in order to achieve racial diversity.

The Supreme Court's decisions were heralded as an overwhelming victory for affirmative action in university admissions, in large part because *Grutter* marked the first time that a majority of the Court had not only upheld the compelling nature of the diversity interest, but had also endorsed the specific tools used by a university to achieve that interest. In fact, after the decision, the University of Texas, which had previously been precluded from considering race as a result of a 1995 Fifth Circuit decision (*Hopwood v. Texas*), decided to resume consideration of race in its admissions processes. Moreover, the Supreme Court recently reaffirmed in the 2006 *Parents Involved in Community Schools v. Seattle Public Schools / Meredith v. Jefferson County Board of Education* decision, that one "government interest [it had] recognized as compelling . . . is the interest of diversity in higher education upheld in *Grutter,*" which the Court described as "not focused on race alone," but as "encompass[ing] 'all factors that may contribute to student body diversity.'"

For the University of Michigan itself, however, *Grutter* was, sadly, a fragile victory. In late 2006, the voters of Michigan amended our state's constitution to outlaw any consideration of race, gender, or national origin in university admissions. While the law, known as Proposal 2, affects admissions programs at all of the state's 15 public universities and 27 public community colleges, the University of Michigan was clearly singled out by the amendment's proponents for its very public defense of affirmative action before the Court. In banning certain forms of affirmative action in public employment, education, and contracting, Michigan's citizens joined the electorates of California (Proposition 209 in 1996) and Washington (Initiative 200 in 1998). Florida had also abolished its public universities' affirmative action programs, albeit through a gubernatorial order rather than a ballot initiative.

As someone who stood on the Supreme Court steps cheering a ruling that benefited all students, I find this backlash disheartening. But it has also firmed our resolve: we must find effective ways to build college campuses that are rich with the experiences and knowledge of students, faculty, and staff of different ethnicities, family histories, and personal backgrounds. Achieving diversity in public higher education is, to quote Justice O'Connor, "a question of national importance." And as our dialogue with our South African colleagues—a dialogue captured in all its richness and complexity in the book you hold before you—demonstrates, the question does not end at our national borders.

In the wake of the *Brown v. Board of Education* ruling, the Georgia Legislature vowed to end public education completely before allowing the public schools to be integrated. The prospect of schools being shuttered appalled and horrified my parents, who wasted little time moving their young family to Iowa, a progressive state known for its public education system.

The irony was that my classmates and teachers and professors were largely white and from the Midwest. Grinnell College, where I earned my undergraduate degree, maintained a student exchange program with LeMoyne College (today LeMoyne-Owen College), a historically black college in Tennessee. In talking with a LeMoyne student about her life in Memphis, I was dumbfounded when she voiced her anxiety about entering a movie theater and sitting in the "wrong" section. Going to the movies? Scary? How could there be a wrong section?

This small but important exchange taught me how much we can, and need to, learn from people of different backgrounds. It is the reason why I believe that affirmative action is so essential, and successful, in improving the learning environment. In today's society, there is no other tool as effective as affirmative action for seeing that our student bodies and our faculties reflect the world around us.

"It is not enough just to open the gates of opportunity. All our citizens must have the ability to walk through those gates," President Lyndon Johnson told graduates of Howard University in 1965. "This is the next and the more profound stage of the battle for civil rights. We seek not just freedom but opportunity. We seek not just legal equity but human ability, not just equality as a right and a theory but equality as a fact and equality as a result."[2]

As a female scientist, I know firsthand the struggles of seeking equal access to opportunities. At Grinnell I was one of 10 chemistry majors, half of whom were women. And yet not one of our professors was a woman. The situation was the same when I went on to graduate school at the University of North Carolina, where half of the biochemistry students were women but all of the instructors were men. There was simply a dearth of female role models for aspiring women scientists like myself in the 1960s, and I know it played a direct role in some of my classmates' decisions to leave the academy.

We know from sound social science research that affirmative action enhances the learning environment for all students. For 17 years, Patricia Gurin, a professor at Michigan and a contributor to this volume, has studied the influence of diversity on students' experience. Her findings have been consistent: diversity in all its forms—racial, geographic, socioeconomic, or otherwise—contributes to students' critical thinking skills. "Students who had experienced the most diversity in classroom settings and in informal interactions with peers," she writes, "showed the greatest engagement in active thinking processes, growth in intellectual engagement and motivation, and growth in intellectual and academic skills."[3]

Perhaps the most encouraging finding from such research is that graduates carry the lessons learned from a diverse college environment into their subsequent relationships with people from different backgrounds. What greater skill can we teach our graduates? Such studies demonstrate the power of diversity to disrupt the patterns of segregation that continue to be a stark fact of American life.

When the University of Michigan went before the Supreme Court, we were joined by two particularly powerful allies in our arguments for affirmative action. The corporate community and America's military leaders made it clear that their institutions would no longer be the best in the world without affirmative action to recruit and retain corporate employees and military troops. In other words, affirmative action—and the resulting diversity it brings—has the power to transform social institutions.

This is powerful testimony. When multinational corporations such as 3M, General Motors, and Microsoft argue that affirmative action and, consequently, a diverse pool of employees is a direct factor in their success, it sends a strong message. One need only hear the words of A. G. Lafley, the highly successful CEO of Procter and Gamble: "All the data I've seen in 30 years of being in business—and all of my personal experience at P&G over the last 23 years—convince me that a diverse organization will out-think, out-innovate, and out-perform a homogenous organization every single time."[4]

Spreading resistance to affirmative action, in Michigan and elsewhere, poses a daunting challenge to universities' public mission. But we can also learn lessons from those who have gone before us. Perhaps most importantly, we know we cannot travel the path followed by our peers in the state of California, as they came to terms with Proposition 209.

In 1995, the University of California Board of Regents voted to ban affirmative action in admissions, an action that was followed the next year by a statewide referendum applying the same ban to all public bodies. Any meaningful consideration of race, gender, or ethnicity in public education, public employment and public contracting went right out the door.

Yet, even as they banned affirmative action, the UC Board of Regents also directed UC administrators to achieve a diverse student body. Affirmative action had been a critical tool for this purpose, and without it administrators found themselves struggling to recruit underrepresented minority students, particularly at the University's highly selective Berkeley campus.

University officials worked hard to retool their efforts to admit minority students. Faculty and administrators strengthened their outreach to high schools. The university system shifted its emphasis from aptitude tests to achievement tests. It intensified its reviews of admissions applications, and asked students to share more information about the obstacles they had faced in preparing for college. The system opened its doors to the top-performing 4 percent of students from all California high schools, and took in more transfer students from California community colleges.

It has been a massive, lengthy undertaking, overseen by thoughtful leaders. Unfortunately, it hasn't worked. The premier higher-educational system in California—the most racially and ethnically diverse state in the country, which sustains the fifth-largest economy in the world—is educating fewer and fewer underrepresented minority students.

A systemwide study undertaken by the University of California's Office of the President in 2003 documented what critics of Proposition 209 had long predicted: a "substantial decline" in the proportion of entering students who were African American, American Indian, or Latino. At the Berkeley and Los Angeles campuses—highly selective research institutions—the data were bleak. Between 1995 and 2002, the total freshman enrollment of African Americans, Latinos, and American Indians plunged by 56 percent at each campus.[5]

We simply cannot allow such a decline at Michigan. We must—and will—make it clear to students and their families that diversity is a core value of public higher education. We want a mosaic of students, and we will always work to attain it, using every available legal means, because it is the right thing to do for any public university committed to academic excellence.

Proposal 2 bans some forms of affirmative action. It does *not* ban the pursuit of broad diversity. This is a message we must convey again and again. America's universities—and particularly its public universities, with their unique role in our society—must never lose track of that fact. Our persistence and our unwillingness as educational leaders to accept anything less than broad diversity on our campuses send a strong message in this country.

As president of the University of Michigan, I have an important political advantage over my peers who led the campuses of the University of California at the time of Proposition 209's passage: the support of my Board of Regents, eight men and women elected by state voters. My predecessor, Lee Bollinger, enjoyed the same support as the University took its first steps to respond to legal challenges of our admissions policies. Where the UC regents initiated the end of affirmative action in their admissions system, UM's regents have stood with their president in advocating the value of affirmative action as a tool to achieve the educational benefits of a diverse student body. This is invaluable support in speaking out about diversity and its importance.

We must dedicate ourselves to creating educational opportunities for historically excluded or underrepresented groups, while building student bodies that foster an exciting and interesting mix of young men and women, who each bring something unique to the learning environment. We seek not only students with perfect grade point averages. We want strong grades, of course, but we want something more. We want to reflect the richness of the world on our campuses, and to keep the doors of opportunity open for all. Our academic excellence and our diversity are intertwined.

An open, tolerant society does not occur without institutions that lead. I admire the commendable, often heroic efforts of South African educational leaders like Njabulo Ndebele—and his predecessors, Stuart Saunders and Mamphela Ramphele—in facing down apartheid's proponents and overturning its devastating legacy at the University of Cape Town. At the University of Michigan, we are pursuing initiatives that we already know produce a diverse student body, including holistic reviews of student applications; outreach to middle- and high-school students; and the creation of campus offices and programs that support diversity. Our peer universities across the country are developing programs of their own: some out of necessity and others in anticipation of the challenges that are almost certainly on the way.

For more than 40 years, affirmative action has opened American society to all citizens, including racial minorities that had long been excluded from access to such fundamentals as education and fair employment. In South Africa, similar programs have for almost 15 years been providing similar access to the formerly excluded black majority. If America's public universities do not produce graduates of all backgrounds, this country will stumble as a global leader. If South Africa's universities do not, the country will lose its grip on the important advances it has so recently won. Either way, our nations would be burdened with unequal societies, struggling to produce educated workforces equipped to compete in the global economy.

Justice O'Connor's words in her *Grutter* decision, although written with reference to the United States, are just as applicable to South Africa, or for that matter any other democracy struggling to achieve the goals of full equality and diversity: "In order to cultivate a set of leaders with legitimacy in the eyes of the citizenry, it is necessary that the path to leadership be visibly open to talented and qualified individuals of every race and ethnicity."

It is our charge, and our obligation, to keep that path visibly open.

Mary Sue Coleman
President, University of Michigan

NOTES

1. "Ruling Tempers Reaction of South," *New York Times,* May 18, 1954.

2. Lyndon B. Johnson, *Public Papers of the Presidents of the United States: Lyndon B. Johnson, 1965,* vol. 2 (Washington, DC: U.S. Government Printing Office, 1966).

3. *Gratz, et al. v. Bollinger, et al.,* 97-75231 (E.D. Mich.) and *Grutter, et al. v. Bollinger, et al.* 97-75928 (E.D. Mich.) (1999).

4. *Grutter v. Bollinger,* Amicus brief of 3M, Abbott Laboratories et al., United States Court of Appeals for the Sixth Circuit, 2001.

5. *Undergraduate Access to the University of California after the Elimination of Race-Conscious Policies,* University of California Office of the President, Student Academic Services, 2003.

Foreword

Njabulo S. Ndebele

I have never been entirely comfortable with the use of the American phrase *affirmative action* in the South African context. Despite our common histories of colonialism and racism, the phrase does not sit comfortably with South African conditions. I have similarly struggled with expressions such as *disadvantaged communities* and *underprepared students*. Such phrases create powerful realities that influence the political choices of those who resort to their explanatory power.[1] The primary hazard of such expressions is that they create tensions between sociology and politics: one must always be fully aware of the context in which they are being used. The failure to recognize this tension can be devastating.

There are many definitions of "affirmative action." Most share at least two attributes. The first is an assumption that the overwhelming majority of Americans has enjoyed liberties and opportunities that have been intentionally, and even systematically, denied to demographic groups such as women and minorities. Affirmative action is, in this understanding, a special effort to correct the wrongs of history. This is a general, philosophical assumption.

The second common feature is an expectation that private and public institutions develop policies extending membership and its opportunities to the excluded groups. Specifically, these institutions must devise employment and admission processes that "favor" the victims of discrimination over the rest of society.

In the United States, affirmative action has meant the creation of opportunities that help minorities—including African Americans, Hispanics, and Native Americans and women—to advance within a social, political, and economic environment that has historically denied these groups a decisive influence. Affirmative action is in this sense an essentially accommodative, if concessionary, policy. Its essential thrust is to "bring in" under prescribed conditions those previously "left out."

But it would be a mistake to end here. The primary, and perhaps progressive, thrust of "affirmative action" is corrective. It reminds Americans that they should have been far more visionary, far more compellingly inclusive, when they declared that "all men are born equal." Of course, we all know that America fell short of this ambition for much of its history. It is never easy to correct a failure that should have been addressed so long ago.

With American social, economic, and political life now so thoroughly established, corrective policies may seem like too little, too late. For the "marginal" groups that are its intended beneficiaries, affirmative action may be experienced not as an arrival, but as an endless trial. The continuing legal challenges to affirmative action policies induce reactions ranging from anxiety to insecurity to incipient revolt.

Each successful deflection of one of these challenges boosts the confidence of affirmative action's supporters, normalizing the policy's intent. But as long as the structural conditions that keep marginal groups in poverty persist, affirmative action will be inadequate. Thus, America finds itself in one of those situations for which democracies are best suited: incremental progress, often accompanied by a great deal of public tension, but without any promise of resounding success.

The public drama of America's apparently simple bipartisan politics obscures an increasingly complex and diverse array of social experiences, which have not as yet been integrated into the political culture. In such a situation, conscience will tend to substitute for politics. This is precisely how one finds oneself in a perpetual state of "good things being done," without ever achieving definitive outcomes.

All of which suggests that, while affirmative action may be a valuable tool for raising Americans' awareness of their social-justice obligations, it has not compelled the United States to fundamentally reorganize itself in the short to medium term around an emancipatory project capable of assigning minorities a place in the formal political structure.

In contrast, I have experienced affirmative action in South Africa as a process by which previously oppressed, as opposed to disadvantaged, South Africans continuously seek to extend the boundaries of freedom through a demand for enhanced and meaningful participation, with the ultimate goal of redesigning the social, economic, and political landscape. Rather than being concessionary, South Africa's affirmative action is fundamentally invasive, albeit in a constitutionally mediated way. It is the continuation by constitutional means of what could have been a violent revolution. Long-term political objectives will, in the short to medium term, override sociological ones.

For South Africans, the challenge of affirmative action is to learn how to live with the agonies and ecstasies of life within the shared space imposed by the South African Constitution. Life in that space involves the recognition that those who were previously oppressed and now find themselves at the center of national life cannot act from a sense of entitlement; that the new culture of rights is also to be enjoyed by the past beneficiaries of apartheid. Newly enfranchised South Africans voluntarily imposed limitations on the means by which they could pursue their emancipatory goals.

Where the goals of American affirmative action seem always to be receding into the horizon, the goals of the South African struggle for liberation may already have been formally achieved. But they will not be easily enjoyed. It is in the effort to enjoy them that a new society will be created. This is precisely where the American struggle for affirmative action yields its greatest lessons. The now-famous case of *Grutter v. Bollinger* highlights the tensions inherent in a democratic system. For us, in South Africa, this reckoning comes early enough in the life of a new democracy.

It is up to the past beneficiaries of apartheid to participate in a constitutionally regulated social change. They can do so by developing a new sense of self-interest that includes the concerns of the now-dominant previously oppressed, who are still on the long journey of development. If they do so, then development stands a real chance of becoming a cooperative process, leading to a new, overarching sense of nationhood. Social negotiation deepens social bonding, no matter how conflictual the interaction might be.

America's and South Africa's respective experiences of affirmative action underscore the importance of context. If it were applied in South Africa, American-style affirmative action would signal containment within a world that was intended to be overthrown violently, but will now be changed over managed time. Whereas that same policy of affirmative action in the United States will offer South Africans lessons on how to manage change within a constitutional democracy.

The cardinal role of universities in both societies seems to speak for itself. Certainly for South Africa, what I have called the "space of negotiation" is a space of intense interaction. It is the space of what academics sometimes call "rigorous practice." The process of negotiation has the immense potential to generate new knowledge, if we can recognize it for what it is. Then affirmative action will be seen in America for what it has always been in South Africa: an emancipatory political action, not an accommodative truce.

The South African vision goes far beyond creating and enhancing opportunities for marginal social groups, to the quest for a new society. For example, the remarkable increase of black students in higher education over the last 12 years is an irreversible process. This rapid change would not have been possible without the advent of democracy in 1994. With the numbers in place and likely to continue growing, we must now focus on the quality of teaching, learning, and researching. The quality of institutional life will be a vital factor in nurturing young talent for work in society at large, or to stay and enrich the academic world.

The constitutional recognition of academic freedom gives South African universities an immense opportunity to deepen intellectual and academic work, while at the same time remaining publicly accountable. The tension between academic freedom and public accountability provides us with one of the opportunities for that "rigorous practice." I expect the intensity of that interaction to increase as easy assumptions about the future give way to the tough thinking and action that will be required to stay true to that vision.

The intellectual project that brought the University of Cape Town and the University of Michigan together in two memorable debates and discussions in 2005 and 2006 highlights another vital dimension of the struggle for human emancipation. Accommodative policies at the global level are highly unlikely to result in sustainable solutions. The requirements of "rigorous practice" at the global level have become far more complex than the current structures of global governance can accommodate. Universities have no option but to deepen their global consciousness and interests so that they can positively influence the process by which the world is being reshaped.

It has indeed been a privilege to work with remarkable intellectuals from both our remarkable countries, which I have often thought of as twins born at different times: so much that we share, and so much that is different, all held together by the strong bonds of mutually reinforcing experience.

Njabulo Ndebele
Former Vice-Chancellor and Principal
of the University of Cape Town

NOTE

1. N. S. Ndebele, "Maintaining Domination through Language," *Academic Development* 1, no. 1 (1995): 3–5.

The Next Twenty-five Years

Introduction

Twins Born at Different Times?

 ❧

David L. Featherman

Universities Actively Shape the Future

 ❧

Universities are wellsprings of new knowledge and technologies, guiding us toward comprehension and directing our energies to change the world. Such innovation—whether achieved through the arts, sciences, humanities, or the professions and technology—is the source of higher education's indisputable economic benefit to society. Universities also anchor democracies by serving as a fair broker, analyzing new ideas and contrasting them against their predecessors in a constant and progressive evaluation. These are the indirect routes by which universities foster social change.

Universities also act more directly as agents of change, serving both public and private interests. Their graduates create the economic and political benefits that putatively serve all citizens in a democracy. It is one measure of their greater creativity and productivity that university graduates typically earn a premium in the marketplace, relative to those without a higher degree. And this premium—in relative income and perhaps also in comparative social standing—is what propels social mobility. This is one of the foremost private benefits of higher education. But higher education's contribution to social mobility is also a public good: It offers intergenerational hope and inspires commitment in political democracies, even those where economic inequalities in the parental generation are large and might otherwise cause parents to despair of their children's futures.

Nevertheless, because universities actively shape the future and generate private as well as public goods—at one and the same time—they are publicly accountable to act justly in fulfilling their mission. Their burden of justice is a double one. On the one hand, they must bear the standard of excellence. Universities cannot advance the horizon of knowledge, cannot craft productivity-driven economies, and cannot expound their vision of an improved human condition without admitting and graduating the students most able to realize these ends. To do less while asking for the special benefits of public support—minimally, public tolerance of the special freedoms of inquiry that protect its faculty and students from political censorship—would be unjust. On the other hand, universities must simultaneously carry the banner of equity. They cannot make admissions choices that affect opportunities for social mobility, cannot train the next generation of their nation's leaders without paying scrupulous attention to the consequences of their actions. To do less would also be unjust.

This might seem like a daunting commission. But the world requires still more of universities. They must act wisely, subjecting themselves to careful scrutiny and self-criticism, assessing their commitment to both excellence and equity, and evaluating their contribution—as measured in the accomplishments of their faculty and graduates—to the public interest. And they must explain to the public what they have learned in this ongoing process. This is what universities do—they expand knowledge but also the capacity in themselves and in wider society to use that knowledge in shaping the future. They also must actively build public understanding of that mission as being in the public interest. Again, to do less as agents of change would be unjust. To do less is to risk losing public support.

Shaping the Future Wisely and Affirmatively

In proposing the just and wise course for higher education in the twenty-first century, this book tackles one of the most vexing challenges facing universities worldwide—the question of affirmative action. Affirmative action is the fulcrum point in the balance between excellence and equity. Affirmative action is about the "race question," but much more. It is about the ineluctable obligation of universities to shape the future. Affirmative action fulfills the public mission of universities by constituting student bodies and faculties wisely—balancing the double burden of excellence and equity and achieving the maximum good for a nation's economic and democratic future. In this sense, affirmative action is about deliberatively transforming legacies of history—for example, of slavery or apartheid—in order to shape the future justly and wisely. So conceived, affirmative action might base its rationale more on anticipating the future than on rectifying an unjust past.

Reframing the Affirmative Action Debate in Higher Education

Affirmative action is a much contested public policy, as will be elaborated subsequently and in several ensuing chapters. Without attempting to cover the full contours of that debate, *The Next Twenty-five Years* seeks to shape the conversation. To do so, it draws upon the experiences and reflections of scholars, educators, and public officials in two nations—South Africa and the United States. The book's underlying premise is that comparison between these two unfolding democracies—one ongoing for over two hundred years and the other in existence for less than two decades—will yield greater insights for enlightening the debate than would assessment of each by itself. The main goals of this comparison are an enriched perspective and a freshly insightful comprehension of the transformative mission of higher education—in anticipating and shaping the future of each nation—and of the role of affirmative action in doing so. Candidly, the book advocates on behalf of affirmative action, although as the arguments and points of view unfold across various authors and in the context of two historical moments in different nations, the basis and qualifications of advocacy differ in important ways. This is part of the richness of comparative analysis for enlightening the debates in both nations and for taking fresh perspectives in each with reference to the other.

Setting the Context of "Twins Born at Different Times"

ᠺ

In Njabulo Ndebele's preface, he likens South Africa and the United States to "twins born at different times." The rich metaphor is evocatively suggestive and potentially misleading. This introduction deploys Ndebele's metaphor rhetorically, deliberately, and cautiously, to leverage insights across historical contexts that are undeniably different. How could two nations conceived in different historical moments be likened to twins? Clearly Ndebele perceives some basis of consanguinity, if not literal, then rhetorical—a kinship, even if born of different circumstances, that makes these two places especially referential, as one twin is so often for the other.

This introduction delves into six possibilities of that inferred kinship to set the mind to work in the "as if" world that is the space of all metaphors. Thus, what follows is a thought experiment: Think about South Africa as if it were the United States, and vice versa. Think about the experience of one as if it were about to be or has been that of the other. What can be learned by Americans or South Africans about the rationale for affirmative action in higher education by these transpositions? And with fresh insights about each nation, what can be said about the future of affirmative action, the usefulness of it as one tool used by universities in shaping the future over the next 25 years or longer?

Here are at least six ways these "twins"—surely not identical—contemplate and compare their historical moments, past and present.

Both Countries Are Constitutional Democracies

With authoritative clarity in her chapter with Stewart Schwab, retired associate justice Sandra Day O'Connor of the United States Supreme Court delineates the constitutional protection of equal opportunity, as inscribed in America's Bill of Rights. In South Africa, the Constitution and incorporated Bill of Rights, adopted by Parliament in 1996, declare equal protection without regard for race, gender, language, or sexual orientation. The corresponding protection, while less decisively inscribed, was adopted in the United States over the course of a century after the ratification of the U.S. Constitution. Aware of the historical lessons of the American experience, drafters of the South African Constitution and Bill of Rights took a more comprehensive approach from inception. But that drafting also occurred immediately following the dismantling of apartheid and the astonishingly peaceful transition to a nonracial parliamentary democracy in 1994. Accordingly, justice in the South African Constitution included not only provisions for procedural equality but also the hope that this would be realized as substantive equality. To paraphrase Judith February in her chapter, the constitutional framework explicitly embraced "fair discrimination" as a legitimate means of rectification—by the state and by others—on behalf of those individuals and groups who had experienced negative discrimination under apartheid, and who were made unnaturally unequal by it. The aim was equitable outcomes as redress, not just equal opportunity.

Each country's constitution was the product of unique historical context, to be sure. The Americans were seeking to establish a postcolonial federalist state in which freedoms and rights of citizenship—framed in the language of free men "naturally equal" at birth and of individuals' inalienable rights—were contrasted against the British monarchy. Freedom was paramount to the Americans, including freedom from an overbearing state that could infringe on an individual's rights and fortunes. But history would not allow the South Africans to create such a passive state nor to protect individual rights while denying restorative justice for historically excluded groups. The need to overcome the legacy of colonialism and four decades of the apartheid state's discrimination on behalf of whites over blacks would not allow it. So while South Africans protected individual rights and freedoms, they also sought redress of former official state policies that overtly discriminated against racialized groups, most explicitly blacks, by requiring processes leading to equity in life outcomes, as well as procedural law. The new democratic state was to use all legal means, including affirmative action as a constitutionally protected remedy, to achieve not only procedural but also substantive justice.

In contrast with the United States, in South Africa affirmative action became an explicitly legal, constitutional remedy to rectify race-based inequities of the former apartheid state. Further, affirmative action was a policy strategy toward building a democratic, multiracial nation in which justice and equity were guaranteed to groups (e.g., blacks) as well as individual citizens. Because of this, "affirmative action" in South Africa is generally conceptualized as "the pursuit of equity." The justification for affirmative action—for the pursuit of equity—was both rectification of the past and diversifying the future talent pool of the nation. In her subsequent chapter, Judith February observes that few legal challenges to affirmative action have gained traction in South African courts so far. Whereas the U.S. Constitution's focus on procedural, rather than substantive, justice—that is, on equality of opportunity and equal rights rather than on equity and rectification—has made affirmative action far more contentious, and left it vulnerable to legal challenge. Indeed, one impetus for this book was the U.S. Supreme Court's decision in *Grutter v. Bollinger,* in which the plaintiff challenged the use of racial preferences in the University of Michigan Law School's admissions process. The Court ultimately permitted certain race-sensitive considerations in the admissions process, based on the argument that the nation had a compelling interest in a future leadership elite of diverse composition. Rejecting any legal argument framed by rectification for past injustice and exclusion, the Court did admit the value of diversity among students and faculty—for example, individual differences by race, culture, economics, and consequential early life experiences as contributions to the milieu of a learning community.[1] But the Court's verdict in the parallel *Gratz v. Bollinger,* challenging the University's undergraduate admissions policies, made it clear that these race-sensitive considerations were to be strictly limited in nature and extent. The result has been a move in many states—including Michigan—for constitutional amendments that will preclude public institutions and state governments from using race or gender as a consideration in access to state-funded institutions and services.

These amendments, based upon successful voter referenda, indicate apparent public doubt about the appropriateness of race and affirmative action in the formulation and implementation of public policy. Even in South Africa, increasing controversy over affirmative action—for example, in admissions and hiring decisions at the University of Cape Town—suggests growing doubt about the legitimate use of race in public policymaking, and about affirmative action's efficacy as a means to achieve equity and a deracialized or nonracial society, even where its provisions are inscribed in a nation's constitution.

Both Countries Are Racially and Ethnically Diverse

For at least three centuries, immigrants and colonists populated what were to become South Africa and the United States. In the latter, indigenous peoples—including tribal nations with formal governance—outnumbered the initial inflows from Europe. These native peoples and nations were over-taken by westward expansion, defeated in warfare, decimated by epidemics of European diseases, and finally resettled into reservations without many prospects for economic self-sufficiency and sustainability. The agricultural economies of the colonial era and the young United States were augmented by labor from the Atlantic slave trade, transported from West Africa via the Caribbean. Asian immigrants attracted by increased settlement and com-merce in the American West, including the construction of the transconti-nental railroads, became an active economic link to East Asia, as well. In the decades immediately before and after the turn of the twentieth century, im-migration fueled the rapid growth of America's population, especially in its coastal receiving cities. So great were the strains on the young nation, on its integrating fabric of popular democracy and its teeming and nearly un-governable cities, that commentators and politicians worried that Amer-ica's experiment with democracy might falter and implode under the pres-sure of rapid diversification within a context of a still consolidating, governable society.

Of course, America did not implode, and during most of the twentieth century a vibrant federalist nation consolidated second-, third-, and fourth-generation ethnic Americans who had fought in two world wars as a united people. If united in war, they were not otherwise fully amalga-mated into a society where ancestry and race no longer mattered. After decades of restricted immigration and an extraordinary mid-twentieth-century fertility boom that lasted two decades and fueled a lasting con-sumer-driven economy, America's twenty-first-century population is once again growing and diversifying, thanks to recent immigration from Central and Latin America, the Caribbean and Asia, as well as to the very high fer-tility of first-generation immigrant families, especially those from Mexico. Once again, America's national discourse is focused on the challenges of di-versity born of immigration: low domestic fertility is driving demand for immigrant labor, posing a challenge to America's cultural and linguistic co-herence. And this time around, the challenge is coming in the midst of globalization, in which communities of new immigrants can remain ac-tively attached—linguistically, culturally, economically, even residen-tially—to their home communities. Assimilation as "an American" can be highly contingent and diversely expressed.

This complex historical evolution has required that American diversity be tallied across categories of racial and ethnic ancestry. Doing so is funda-mentally a social and political task without guidance from modern biology. That is, postgenomic advances in molecular and population genetics have yet to characterize racial or ethnic categories in definitive genotypic terms. Many biologists doubt this will be possible scientifically.[2] Instead, race and ethnicity are fundamentally cultural and social "phenotypes" constructed principally out of popular beliefs about the essential similarities and differences among groups, and from the resulting social dynamics within diverse human communities. That is, in everyday life, racial and ethnic categories become socially and psychologically "real" even if they are not biologically "real." For example, they define who can interact comfortably with whom; who is to be emulated or despised; who is a trusted friend and who a hated enemy. When used by the state, these socially defined categories determine which groups have legal standing or full rights of citizenship, and which might have neither.

Article I of the United States Constitution framed the late-eighteenth-century basis upon which states could count individuals from certain groups as "people of the United States" for purposes of political representation. A slave was counted as only three-fifths of a person; "Indians, not taxed" (on tribal lands) were not counted at all. In the first decennial census of 1790, dominant nativist beliefs about superiority of "White" Europeans over "Black" and "Red" races entered naturally into the federal statistical system as tallied categories. Ever since that moment, race has been a socially constructed political reality as well as a demographic statistical category in American society. ("Free white females" were tallied in 1790, for purposes of representation, even though the right to vote for women was not granted until the twentieth century.) To be sure, the question of "who counts" in the decennial census—which groups are tallied separately from others—is still the subject of heated debate. So, too, are the official definition of race and the question of its distinction from ethnic ancestry. Perhaps most heated of all are the disputes over who gets to decide these questions.

Following the civil rights legislation of the 1960s—including voting rights and fair housing, the Office of Management and Budget (part of the executive branch of government) promulgated new guidelines for federal statistical agencies' tracking of compliance and enforcement. Race took on new political and legal significance during the civil rights era, and intermediary organizations representing racial and ethnic minorities demanded detailed and accurate accounting of their constituents. At roughly the same time, survey research techniques for ascertaining race were beginning to adopt self-reporting strategies in their questionnaires and self-identification techniques in their interviews. Agencies such as the Bureau of the Census experimented with different forms of questions and question sequences that putatively captured the most accurate counts across an enlarged number of racial and ethnic combinations. (The ordering of questions—race before ethnicity versus the opposite, for example—did produce different tallies.) Arguments that self-identification gave more credence to the self-constructed nature of race, over the socially imposed type, were often countered by race-based groups themselves, who asserted that socially constructed categories mattered vitally in the fight to ensure that equal protections—for jobs, housing, education, health care, and voting, as well as affirmative action to remedy past discrimination—were being achieved. Just prior to the 2000 decennial census, which ultimately used self-identification and allowed a person to select more than one race, a representative of the National Association for the Advancement of Colored People (NAACP) commented:

> We support the right of individual self-identification and support self-determination in defining one's racial makeup. But the census may not be the correct place to make such a personal statement, particularly in light of the fact that repercussions in census numbers impact the lives of many people. Provisions of the Voting Rights Act, for example, are specifically directed at correcting past discrimination (particularly in the Deep South) where African-Americans were denied their constitutional rights. With some figures showing 70 percent of African-Americans as possibly fitting into a multiracial category, will we be able to identify black voters in terms of fair representation?[3]

South Africa is similarly struggling with the challenge of understanding and documenting its diversity in terms of race and ethnicity. While the country's history of immigration and centuries of European colonization must be factored prominently into our understanding of its publicly acknowledged diversity, the still-fresh memories of the apartheid state and its hyperracialized policies trigger controversies over how to categorize and tally South Africans. Race was never any more biologically real in South Africa than in the United States; neither was it any less real in social, political, and behavioral terms. Apartheid made that dreadfully clear, by forcefully separating the lives and life chances of blacks from those of whites. The National Party—which ruled South Africa from 1948 to 1994—transformed previously taken-for-granted discrimination and segregation under colonial rule into a politically and legally enforced reality with far-ranging implications, right up to the line between life and death. The Population Registration Act 30 of 1950 and its amendments required that all South Africans be classified by officially recognized racial categories and registered as such. While that act was repealed in the formally nonracial South Africa, these categories continue to be used in public policy discourse and for tallying progress in remedying apartheid's adverse impacts on those who were victims of discrimination. As in the United States, some argue that in doing so official government policy—and universities seeking to redress historic racial exclusions—only perpetuate a racialized society and, in South Africa, the legacy or mentality of apartheid-type classification.

In South Africa, the notion of "races"—sometimes also referenced as "population groups"—encompasses four basic categories: Africans, Coloureds, Asians (sometimes known as Indians), and Whites (formerly known as Europeans). Certain ethno-linguistic groups, such as Zulu, Xhosa, and Afrikaner, are also distinguished, but usually as subcategories of "official" races. The term *non-white,* or, more commonly, *black,* is used to refer to all races set apart from "white." Throughout this book, these terms appear, signifying not only their historical significance but also their contemporary use in public and scholarly discourse, acknowledging the controversies in doing so.[4]

The histories of both the United States and South Africa are marked by white dominance.[5] Yet, perhaps contrary to expectations, this common tradition of white rule has moved them along divergent tracks. In America, whites were a demographic majority and politically dominant in the nineteenth and twentieth centuries, periods of immigration from Europe. That potent combination has permitted a larger role for ethnicity in the civic culture. Subsequent migrations from Asia, Mexico, and the Caribbean have greatly diminished the historic white, European ethnic majority, which had already amalgamated into a more general category of white Americans though extensive intermarriage.[6] In South Africa, on the other hand, colonizing whites of European ancestry—from 1652 onward, the Dutch, Germans, French Huguenots, and English—were always a demographic minority. Recognizing this, they set aside many of their ancestral animosities by the mid-twentieth century to cooperate in creating a racially exploitative and separatist state. Notwithstanding liberal whites' robust protests against the National Party's exploitative and brutal policies, after 1948 the officially defined races dominated ethnicity as the axis of diversity, the apex being the apartheid state. Herein lies the difference: White Americans unquestionably practiced their own forms of racial exploitation and apartheid with respect to Native Americans and African Americans, but historically they were never at risk of being overtaken, either demographically or politically. Ironically, increased immigration and high fertility rates among Hispanic Americans are bound to end white demographic dominance in the United States, and could alter the landscape of race-based politics, as well. In effect, American whites of European ancestry are becoming more like their counterpart whites in South Africa—a racial minority. That transformation is likely to affect the politics of affirmative action, as well as the politics of immigration.

Each Country Has Experienced Episodes of Race-Based Conflict and Subjugation

Indigenous peoples in both South Africa and America were overcome by European colonists beginning in the seventeenth century, through combat and exposure to foreign diseases. The Khoesan were depleted by war and disease and displaced by traders and farmers, as were American Indian tribes of the east coast and plains. Slavery and indentured servitude were common in both countries and vital to their colonial and postcolonial economies. For example, America imported West African slaves to pick cotton and serve plantations. Indigenous Bantu-speaking communities of South Africa were subjugated by conquest and became indentured as farm labor, supplemented in the sugar cane fields of Natal Colony by indentured subcontinental Indians. Both countries practiced forms of racial apartheid originating in European beliefs—often based upon biblical interpretation—in the "natural" superiority of the white race over darker-skinned peoples. In the United States of the late twentieth and early twenty-first centuries, "apartheid" became an unofficial but also unsubtle manifestation of persistent, even widening economic inequality based in "market-driven" residential segregation, whereas in South Africa, the National Party formalized apartheid as state policy after its ascent to power in 1948. The legal and quasi-legal enforcement of these laws by militia and police steadily rendered the lives of Africans, Coloureds, and Asians "naturally" unequal, as the officially defined races were separated and dissected over four decades.

Africans were forcibly removed from white farms, excluded from cities, and isolated in designated rural or suburban Bantustans, away from the sources of economic opportunity. As described subsequently in this book by Jonathan Jansen, local schools offered "Bantu Education" consisting of limited vocational training taught by instructors with inadequate preparation, resources, and remuneration. African workers were destined to labor in the gold and diamond mines or to provide menial labor and service work in cities far removed from their homes. The trip between home and work often took days: transportation was at best irregular, and at worst dangerous. A series of Pass Laws and permits regulated the flow of migrant workers to urban employment and "temporary" residences in squatters' shacks—makeshift villages with perhaps one potable water tap and no sewers—and later to new townships adjacent to white-controlled cities like Johannesburg, Durban, and Cape Town. Except for a minority of laborers who qualified to bring their families to the matchbox brick houses of the new urbanized townships, working men and boys lived apart from their spouses and relatives. Those left behind—many of whom were unable to seek, let alone find, work outside of marginal tenant farming or labor on white-owned farms at meager wages—subsisted on the scraps from a poorly developed informal economy, remittances, and the state old-age pensions paid largely to widows. Africans held no political franchise; they possessed neither voice nor means of exit against the force of police and security agents.

Over time, government policies favoring the development of urban economies created a demand for wage labor. This development benefited the small generation of Africans who had earlier been permitted to migrate. It helped even more the growing number of children born in towns and cities, who could remain and be educated there, albeit in racially separate schools. Meanwhile, the unemployed, landless Africans left behind in the Bantustans sunk deeper into grinding rural poverty.[7]

Conditions became somewhat less repressive for Coloureds and Asians. Education and health services were expanded and improved in the 1960s. The state created separate chambers of Parliament to represent Coloureds and Asians after 1983, and their communities were relocated or displaced far less frequently than the Africans'. Coloureds and Asians were able to stay involved in the rapidly growing urban economy, albeit in delimited sectors, and at wages and benefit levels well below those afforded to Whites. Such differential treatment of the various black groups (Africans, Coloureds, and Asians) exemplified the National Party's broader policy of divide and rule. African labor unions were banned, as were oppositional political parties such as the African National Congress (referred to throughout this book as the ANC). Leaders were forced into exile in other parts of Africa, or abroad, particularly in Britain. Extralegal police and security forces used paid informers, assassins, torture, and so-called dirty tricks (including middle-of-the-night raids on the homes of politically liberal blacks and whites) and planted misinformation to foment distrust within and between communities, disrupting nascent coalitions of political resistance.

While the apartheid state officially ended with the April 1994 election of the ANC to power, it had been weakening since the late 1980s, as signaled by the unbanning of labor unions for Africans, the recognition of the ANC as a political party, and the release of Nelson Mandela from prison. What remained was a legacy of "naturally unequal" life consequences for races made "natural" by apartheid's design. Some analysts would argue that the legacy also includes a continuing "apartheid mentality" that affects not only whites but also the ANC's governing style.[8]

Each Country Has Undergone Experiences of Racial Liberation and of Emergent Civil and Human Rights

These historic experiences are intertwined in the common legacy of passive resistance shared by the American civil rights movement and the South African freedom and liberation movements.

Following one of the deadliest single battles in the American Civil War, the Battle of Antietam, Abraham Lincoln warned that all states still in rebellion against the Union as of January 1, 1863, would have their slaves liberated, "as an act of justice, warranted by the Constitution, upon military necessity." The Emancipation Proclamation relied not on a social justice argument, but on Lincoln's presidential prerogative to seize enemy property used in rebellious warfare against the United States. Only in 1865, after the Union victory, did the Thirteenth Amendment officially ban slavery and involuntary servitude as permissible practices on American soil. And it took two additional constitutional amendments to end, at least officially, the enslavement and disenfranchisement of African Americans: the Fourteenth, ratified in 1868, which extended the rights of due process and equal protection under the law to all citizens and residents of the United States, especially former slaves; and the Fifteenth, ratified in 1870, which banned race-based voting qualifications. The southern states parried each of these amendments with a series of laws and de facto policies designed to sustain the practices of segregation and race-based servitude.

During the period 1876 to 1965, the southern and even some northern border states continued to adopt the Jim Crow laws that mandated a "separate but equal" policy that in practice actually relegated African Americans to inferior status, undercut their rights of citizenship, and compromised their equal protection. In 1913 President Woodrow Wilson allowed the federal government to sanction and practice racial segregation in the armed forces, a move that was mirrored across America in the further segregation of public accommodations, hospitals, schools, and residential communities, and in the denial of equal access to such simple amenities as a seat on a public bus or a clean public restroom. And following World War II, progressive legislation such as the so-called GI Bill that financed postsecondary education and home loans for returning veterans systematically advantaged whites over African Americans.[9]

The growing civil rights protests over these inequalities and injustices—some violent because of reactive police brutality or instigated by the Ku Klux Klan, but by and large peacefully inspired by leaders such as the Reverend Martin Luther King, Jr.—culminated in profound change by 1965. Many historians have emphasized the vaunted 1954 Supreme Court decision in *Brown v. Board of Education* as the turning point. That decision was followed by a wave of progressive federal antidiscrimination legislation, as well as a series of executive orders issued by Presidents Kennedy and Johnson in the 1960s, as David Garrow describes later in this volume. Chief among these legal changes were the Civil Rights Act of 1965, the Voting Rights Act of 1965, the Open Housing Act of 1968, and the Equal Employment Opportunity Act of 1972. The latter laid the foundation for a broad if ambiguous federal affirmative action policy.

Thus, remedies for constitutionally sanctioned slavery and race-based (as well as gender-based) discrimination erupted during two relatively brief periods, in the mid-nineteenth and mid-twentieth centuries. However, as happened with the Reconstruction-era legislation, so, too, have popular resistance and inconsistent federal enforcement blunted the antidiscrimination provisions of the civil rights and Great Society eras. The American democratic experiment in the twenty-first century still cherishes local control and states' rights, often more so than the intervention of the federal state to remedy inequalities, let alone achieve equity. In some sense, it took America some 200 years to seek remedy—at least formally, by constitutional amendment and federal legislation—for the unnatural inequities of slavery and Jim Crow.

In contrast, South Africa's peaceful democratic transition from state-sanctioned suppression of the black majority has been grounded in a philosophical and political strategy of resistance, and more so of liberation and freedom, inspired by Gandhi's successes against the British. This peaceful approach, while interrupted by occasional outbreaks of partisan violence by Africans against other Africans, or against the brutal apartheid police and security forces, was generally pragmatic, for the simple reason of the Africans' lesser access to weapons, and because of the divide-and-conquer tactics employed by the apartheid regime. South African liberation relied on protest marches, boycotts, sit-ins, appeals to international human rights institutions, and calls for economic sanctions. The regime's random shooting and wanton killing of protesting adults and schoolchildren, for example at Sharpeville in 1960, galvanized the forces of liberation and especially emboldened urban-educated youth to leave their schools for the streets, while drawing world attention and outrage. The parallels with the American civil rights movement—peaceful resistance, even under fire, taking note of Gandhi—are not coincidental.[10]

That said, after the Sharpeville Massacre, the ANC abandoned its tactics of nonviolent resistance. Whether subsequent resort to violence and sabotage during the 1970s and 1980s led directly to the unbanning of the ANC and the release of Nelson Mandela—or did so more directly than the nonviolent economic boycotts and sanctions imposed by the international community, supported openly by Martin Luther King, Jr.—is open to dispute.[11]

Demography was a potent additional factor in the final peaceful South African transition from apartheid. It could be more or less assumed that democracy, while multiracial, would be directed by an African majority toward remedying past injustices. Africans could be hopeful and peaceful and patient, but would they be forgiving? Or, would apartheid be answered by some form of retribution? If affirmative action was the price paid by whites for a peaceful democratic transition, amnesty was the price paid by Africans.[12]

The 1993 Interim Constitution of the Republic of South Africa established the Truth and Reconciliation Commission (commonly known as the

TRC) under its Promotion of National Unity and Reconciliation Act. The TRC's goals included clarification of the causes and extent of human rights violations, the suffering of victims, and the motives of perpetrators, so that a collective memory of the period could be constructed from a shared public record. Additionally, the TRC was to aid in the granting of amnesty to persons—most often whites, but also some Africans—who acknowledged their collusion to the public, and, importantly, to the victims. That Africans and other blacks also came under scrutiny indicates the TRC's commitment to illuminating the full horrors of apartheid, including violations not directed against the oppressors but against others under oppression (e.g., the "necklacing" of suspected informers, who were encased in rubber tires that were then set aflame). The TRC was also charged with hearing victims' claims, discovering the fate of missing victims, restoring the dignity of those who died without the opportunity to speak on their own behalf, and recommending reparations and compensation.

Over its six years, the TRC encountered deep skepticism from across the racial spectrum. Some argued that its revelations were incomplete, that testimony was rife with omissions, that whites were insufficiently remorseful and accepting of their responsibilities for apartheid, and that amnesty was granted for crimes that international courts would have punished rather than forgiven.[13] On the latter point, the South African Constitutional Court ruled that the National Unity and Reconciliation Act was fully constitutional, implying that the work of the TRC, begun in 1995, fell within the protection of South African law. Notwithstanding its legality, the TRC's process of reconciliation may not yet have concluded fully, and analysts who have studied the deracialization and unification of South Africans over the past decade still detect residues of an apartheid mentality. That residue must certainly color the future of affirmative action.

South Africa inscribed its commitment to resolving racial exploitation, injustice, and exclusion in its Constitution and Bill of Rights. Those founding documents created both the mission and the tools by which it could be achieved, including affirmative action. In the decade following peaceful liberation and transition to a democratic government, an African majority party, the ANC, twice assumed the mantle of government. A process of racial reconciliation was set in motion. What is unclear is whether these extraordinary ongoing processes will lead, ultimately, to deracialization in South Africa—to a moment when Africans, whites, coloreds, and Asians are South African first, without reactive reference to their racialized history, or retreat to group-based interests. Will they achieve the goals of racial and gender equity—that is, the realization of substantive equity—inscribed in their Constitution? There are reasons for doubt, just as there are reasons to doubt that Americans will soon fulfill the vision of equal access and opportunity put forth in the Thirteenth, Fourteenth, and Fifteenth Amendments to their Constitution.

Neither Country Is Blind to Race in Everyday Life of the Twenty-first Century

Notwithstanding those amendments to the U.S. Constitution or the civil rights and antidiscrimination legislation of the 1960s and 1970s, some would argue that America is reracializing, albeit in subtle and new ways.[14] One could say that a "Jim Crow mentality" still plagues America. This is apparent in the now historic policies of the New Deal, which were intended to lift Americans out of the Great Depression and the sacrifices of the war by expanding access to stable unionized jobs (Wagner Act); to housing and higher education (GI Bill); and to a secure old age with a safety net for the frail young (Social Security Act). None of the legislation was explicitly written to exclude black Americans. And overall blacks did thrive. A black middle class emerged. But the legislation was implemented in ways that primarily if not exclusively benefited whites by catering to Jim Crow Democrats and allowing implementation on a state-by-state, rather than a national, basis. All boats did rise; but white boats rose much higher. Racial inequality increased cumulatively across these various programs.[15]

Present-day America is not race-neutral let alone nonracial, as Nancy Cantor and Jo Thomas point out in their chapter, despite the widespread belief that legal guarantees of equal protection and opportunity guarantee race-blind justice. In fact, the realities of racial inequality appear to reflect entrenched racial bias, sometimes private and informal and other times structural and public. The heart of "American apartheid," to cite the title of another important book on the subject, is its racially segregated housing, which leads to "separate neighborhoods, separate schools, separate churches, separate stores, separate social networks, and separate jobs."[16] The failure to guarantee fully open housing—for example, race-neutral access to all listed homes for rent or sale; race-neutral access to housing loans at fair and fully comparable rates of interest—lead to a spiral of disadvantaging outcomes associated with the hypersegregation of African Americans (e.g., unemployment, poverty, single parenthood, crime-ridden neighborhoods, poor schools) and to supposed confirmation of the negative stereotypes that underlie housing market biases in the first place: "discrimination with a smile," as the sociologist Douglas Massey terms it. And while America elected its first biracial president in 2008, the campaign leading up to that election was marred by racialized innuendo and widely reported hesitations to vote for candidate Obama precisely because he was black.

Bruce Western describes in his chapter how the explosion of laws in the

1970s and 1980s aimed at stemming illicit drug dealing have contributed to the further deepening of racial inequality by imprisoning African American males en masse. Western's work powerfully describes how the American penal system shifted from a focus on rehabilitation to one emphasizing incapacitation, deterrence, and punishment. More acts were criminalized; sentences were lengthened; paroles became more difficult, and the nation embarked on a large-scale prison-building program. These changes came on the heels not only of the civil rights era, but of high unemployment among low-skilled men, civil unrest in urban cores, and white flight from the cities—phenomena that were again treated as confirmations of negative racial stereotypes. Some 30 years into the new carceral regime, Western found that as many as seven million men, or about 6 percent of adult males, fell under jurisdiction of the penal system.

Western's research has documented enormous racial inequalities in imprisonment. Black men are eight times more likely to be incarcerated for any crime than whites. More than 12 percent of black men ages 25 to 29 were behind bars as of 2004. And among African American males born in the late 1960s—that is, just after the civil rights era—30 percent of high school graduates (that is, men with no college education) had served time in prison by their mid-30s. A staggering 60 percent of high school dropouts had prison records. But imprisonment involves more than incarceration: It means greater difficulty in finding a job after release and, in some cases, even the loss of full citizenship; it means the disruption of family ties and marriages, often forever. By 2000, Western found that over one million black children, or 9 percent of those under 18, had a father who was incarcerated. In half these cases the father had been living with the child when he was arrested.

Deepened racialization is also tied to the threads of nativist sentiment that run though contemporary America. Such animus is largely focused on Hispanic Americans (or, to use the broader term, Latinos), who ironically were native to the former Mexican lands incorporated into the United States. Unfortunately, these legal ethnic Americans have been transformed in the eyes of too many into illegal immigrant invaders, who, in the words of Harvard's Samuel Huntington, one of the best-known proponents of this controversial view, threaten the "Anglo-Protestant values that built the American Dream" by splitting the nation into "two cultures and two languages . . . forming their own political and linguistic enclaves . . . from Los Angeles to Miami."[17]

America in the twenty-first century may not be the most racialized nation, but it surely is not race-blind. The United States now has the highest rates of incarceration and racial residential segregation in the world. America is also the most economically unequal among all OECD (Organisation

for Economic Co-operation and Development) countries.[18] In every respect, then, race and ethnicity matter: not just because of slavery or Jim
Crow or of waves of immigration, but because Americans simply are not
blind to race in their behavior.

Neither are South Africans. Survey research over time casts doubt upon
the success of the TRC's efforts to build interracial reconciliation and mutual trust.[19] Africans rarely interact with whites, even at work; Africans say
they cannot understand whites, and both Coloureds and Asians say they fail
to understand the customs and ways of Africans. Indeed, although they
have historically been categorized as non-African blacks, Coloureds and
Asians express considerable antipathy toward affirmative action, which
they view as benefiting Africans over their groups. Levels of trust among
racial groups—for example, over their truthfulness, their propensity to
commit crimes, levels of discomfort in their company—indicate lingering
psychological barriers to reconciliation. Africans seem to be the most socially isolated race, with a majority having no white friends at all.
Coloureds, Asians, and Whites enjoy more interracial ties socially and at
work. Africans also express the highest levels of interracial distrust and of
antigroup sentiments, especially toward Afrikaners and other groups associated with apartheid.

Racial group identities are strong and personally important. Still, a plurality growing toward a strong majority in each racial group also ascribes
importance to being a South African—a national identity that is not inconsistent with simultaneous self-identification as a Zulu, Xhosa, Afrikaner, or
white. What is striking is that such strongly held group identities are fully
consistent with strongly felt national identities, suggesting the close association many South Africans make between the political fate of their racial
group and the ensuing fate of the nation.[20] Racial groups remain a strong
basis for political solidarity and action.

As Neville Alexander points out in his contribution to this volume, the
racialized rhetoric and political strategies of the ANC and its leadership are
contributing to the rise of racial group politics in contemporary South
Africa.[21] The ANC's poverty-reduction programs—for example, building
new schools and clinics in areas like the Eastern Cape, where the ANC was
politically vulnerable in 1999—were aimed at undoing the harms of
apartheid and represented politically as "racial redress." In his chapter,
André du Toit offers critical skepticism, alleging that in the country's second postapartheid presidential election, the ANC used political patronage,
control over appointments in the state and parastatal sectors, and opportunities for legitimate and illegitimate business to retain its senior African
leadership to stem defections to rival and mixed-race parties.[22] Unsurprisingly, political animosities and perceived political threats are strongly felt

along racial lines. The four racial groupings of apartheid survive. Political tolerance—for example, a willingness to refrain from stifling dissenting views, especially of a rival minority—is not well ingrained in South African politicians and their supporters. These features are apparently fully consistent with a South Africans' fulsome endorsement of multiracialism as an ideal. Race neutrality and racial harmony as valued goals do not necessarily preclude racialized politics, an unresolved contradiction in both South Africa and America.[23]

Racial reconciliation remains a complicated work-in-progress in South Africa, as in America. In both nations, efforts to achieve this rapprochement shape emotions and debates about the rationale for, and beneficiaries of, affirmative action. So long as reconciliation is incomplete, race will remain an important part of politics and everyday life, even if only tacitly. But race takes on an even greater importance when it grows beyond a matter of sentiment and antipathy to take on economic significance. In both South Africa and the United States, race and economics are intertwined. And that single fact makes race-blind or race-neutral policy all the more elusive.

Each Country Is Deeply Divided by Economics as Well as Race

By almost any conventional standard of comparison, income inequality in the United States is exceptional. True, per capita income is 25 to 35 percent above that of other OECD countries, but the incomes of America's poorest one-third fall below the incomes of the bottom third of Europeans. At about 14 percent, poverty is more pervasive in the United States than in most industrialized countries, where it averages about 9 percent.[24] Adjusted for the relative purchasing powers of currencies, workers in the bottom 10 percent of OECD countries earn about 44 percent more than the bottom 10 percent of Americans. If we also consider the comparative benefits of state-subsidized child and health care, the disparities favoring European workers become even greater. In short, despite providing one of the highest per capita income levels in the world, the American economy generates economic inequality more typical of a developing country and only slightly less egregious than that in South Africa. In fact, since South Africa redistributes a far greater fraction of pretax incomes through taxation, transfers, and subsidies than America does, the posttax dispersions of income in the two societies are even closer.[25]

Inequality continues to grow into the twenty-first century. Many of the winners and losers in the half century since the civil rights era and the Great Society are utterly familiar, but others are new. In his 1964 Economic Report, President Lyndon Johnson declared an "attack" on poverty to lift the "forgotten fifth" of the nation above the poverty line. His policies anticipated that the economic growth that had benefited all Americans in the quarter century after World War II would continue, assuming continued federal economic stimulation. In reality, the general prosperity of that era—real earnings and family incomes rose for most, although one in five Americans were left below the official poverty line—did not last a decade beyond his presidency. The 1970s brought oil price shocks, a deep recession, and a fundamental restructuring of America's market-driven economy. That restructuring—involving the advent of new labor-saving technologies; the globalization of markets, and ensuing declines in inflation-adjusted wages, as well as in employee health and pension benefits; declines in union membership and contract coverage; and a reduced demand for low-skill labor—marked the end of America's post–World War II economic boom. The new decade ushered in a period of "divided fortunes" and "diminished prospects," during which the rich became much richer, and the poor much poorer and less likely to bounce back. Income inequality was greater going into the twenty-first century than it had been at the end of World War II. Poverty rates stood about where they were in the early 1970s. It was a period in which the federal government fought no wars against poverty. To the contrary, it lost interest in the topic, except for its efforts to "reform" the social welfare system by tightening up eligibility and benefits.[26]

The winners of the last quarter century include the college educated and high-skill workers. In 2005, college graduates earned 1.74 times more than high school graduates, up from 1.4 in 1979. But the increasing premium paid for college education by no means accounts fully for the far larger, accelerated income gains accruing to the very wealthy, including, since the economic boom of the 1990s, highly paid chief executive officers and the owners of assets yielding dividends from the equity and real estate markets.[27] By 2005, the richest top 1 percent of Americans—those with annual incomes in excess of $1.1 million—enjoyed 21.8 percent of the country's total income.[28] The winners group also included women, who joined the full-time labor force in record numbers after the mid-twentieth century, even while earning less than comparably skilled men. By the end of the century, however, they were completing university and postgraduate degrees at higher rates than men, although earnings disparities in the range of 25 percent remained, a fact discussed by Abigail Stewart and Danielle LaVaque-Manty in their contribution to this volume.[29]

Black Americans could also be counted among the winners, although the narrative of divided fortunes and diminished prospects holds as true within this minority as for the nation as a whole. The period of general prosperity after World War II, the qualified successes of the GI Bill, the civil rights legislation of the 1960s—especially federally mandated school desegregation, equal employment opportunities, and affirmative action—all helped boost African Americans' economic fortunes into the 1970s. Black working-class families could pass along their assets and contribute to the educational capital and intergenerational mobility of their offspring in unprecedented ways.[30] A black middle class consolidated; some of its members left their old neighborhoods to move into (mainly segregated) suburbs. A small vibrant economic and cultural African American elite assumed leadership positions in business, politics, the media, and the arts. Yet, at the same time, other black men and women remained chronically under- or unemployed, contributing to the growth of a restive urban "underclass." As jobs for low-skilled labor disappeared or relocated in the late 1970s and early 1980s, as the urban youth who were left behind became discouraged and dropped out of schools, as diminished neighborhoods became more violent and impoverished, as more young men disappeared from the streets into the penal system, the growing economic polarization of America was mirrored within the African American community.

Compared to whites, however, African Americans experienced less, or a less visible, separation of economic fortunes, at least statistically. Perhaps that illustrates the poverty of statistics, but the ratio of rich to poor grew larger and faster among whites than among blacks or Hispanics during this period. This difference is largely due to the fact that the number of rich white people (with incomes above seven times the poverty level for their family size) increased so much more rapidly than the numbers of poor whites fell, relative to other racial or ethnic groups. By 1999, for example, there were 3.5 times as many rich whites as poor ones; among Hispanics and African Americans, the rich were only 1.5 as numerous. Clearly, rich whites benefited more from prosperity than did their minority counterparts. And following the booming 1990s, poverty rates for African Americans and Hispanics remained about three times the rate for non-Hispanic whites.[31]

The new losers, meanwhile, were the recent immigrants—principally Latinos lacking the educational and linguistic skills to enter the labor market. These new immigrants generally lagged behind African Americans in their economic gains, and have higher poverty rates and lower family incomes. Still, their children's educational attainments are improving despite the handicaps of the parental generation and the children's own linguistic challenges in school.

Looking toward the next 25 years, some analysts are pessimistic that these large racial and ethnic disparities will be erased or even much diminished without another transformation of public policy, supported by a period of global economic prosperity. For example, Sheldon Danziger and Peter Gottschalk conclude that "if African Americans' median family income adjusted for family size were to grow by 34 percent over the next 20 years (the same rate as it grew over the last 20 years), then it would increase by 2019 to 3.3 times the poverty line—similar to the 1979 level of white non-Hispanics."[32] This calculation is important when thinking about the need for affirmative action in higher education, at about that point into the future.

In South Africa, trends in inequality since the fall of apartheid appear remarkably similar to America's over the last half century, and especially during its most recent decade. The categories of winners and losers, too, bear a remarkable resemblance. This pattern of similarities—admitting clear differences, as well—is an important justification for discussing the comparative future of affirmative action in higher education.

In a 1998 speech before Parliament, South African president Thabo Mbeki referred to "two nations" and "two economies." He called attention to lingering and profound economic inequalities among the races: specifically, that most of the poor and clearly the poorest of the poor were African and that the income gap between Africans and Whites remained huge.[33] This assessment would hold true throughout much of the first decade of ANC rule, but it was far from the whole picture. In fact, the Mbeki government's macroeconomic policies were creating new winners and losers in South Africa after 2001, although inequality continued its climb.[34]

In its first years, the ANC government adopted fiscal and trade policies that more or less conformed to the so-called Washington Consensus: that is, policies geared toward stimulating growth and freeing exports and international trade; attracting stable foreign investment; and controlling inflation and domestic debt. While the ANC also addressed some of the most glaring and massive depredations of apartheid, the economic winners in the initial postapartheid period were wealthy capitalists, largely but not exclusively white, along with a conspicuous minority of Africans with the skills and connections to profit from the government's affirmative action strategies—most visible in public employment, as well as from business profits in key private sectors. Overall economic inequality in South Africa—some of the starkest in the world—was undiminished in this first period and may actually have increased at its end. Clearly the biggest losers were the poor and the growing ranks of unemployed, the vast and disproportionate majority of whom were African, accompanied by somewhat more modest numbers of Coloureds.[35]

The second period, after 2001–2, marked a shift in economic policy away from the Washington Consensus. While promoting growth, it also reflected a shift in political strategy, namely, a more intense focus on domestic welfare and the role of government spending to achieve it: in housing and living conditions; job creation, especially in the public sector; expansion of social grants for child support (especially into rural areas); and pensions geared for the elderly. By 2006 the overall economy grew at 5 to 6 percent (if only for three or four quarters but well above the barely 1 to 2 percent characteristic of the first period), consumer spending increased, and the stock market showed greater robustness than those of developed economies in the northern hemisphere. However, the numbers of Africans and the young who sought work, or would do so, still outstripped the pace of job creation, and unemployment was at least 27 percent, and perhaps as high as 40 percent. As Haroon Bhorat demonstrates later in this book, efforts to fill new jobs in the growing segments of the economy remain thwarted by an increasing shortage of skilled labor, especially among those with high-quality advanced degrees. Poverty—which touches more than a third of South African households—may or may not have increased since 2001, depending on which data one consults and how one allows for the massive infusion of social grants and public works projects to the poorest townships. South African poverty remains linked to widespread and entrenched unemployment, even unemployability, and the poorest of the poor and Africans are the least likely to find work, followed distantly by Coloureds, Asians, and then Whites. The burdens of increased welfare spending and public-sector make-work programs constrain economic growth. Under these conditions, and under prevailing policies, it is difficult to foresee South Africa growing its way out of its hyperinequality to overcome the dire legacies of apartheid and HIV/AIDS.[36]

The winners, especially in this second period, have also been African. The fact that one finds a few Africans among South Africa's richest people, while they also make up the great majority of its poorest, bespeaks the new inequality. Racial difference, once the single most prominent factor, is now complicated if not supplanted by the effects of economic class and by its correlates, including educational qualifications for participation in a globalized marketplace. By the close of South Africa's first decade as a multiracial democracy, each racial group had become more internally unequal, especially Africans, in effect confirming President Mbeki's diagnosis of "two nations" or "two economies," but in terms of economic class rather than of race, as he had inferred. Overall economic inequality in the new South Africa has come to reflect the vastly different economic fortunes of employable winners and unemployable or underemployed losers in the new South African economy, as reflected in ANC macroeconomic policies and perhaps in racialized politics. Importantly, economic inequality within racial groups, notably among Africans, now exceeds economic differences among the races.[37]

Does race no longer matter? Of course it does, as is clear from poverty and unemployment statistics, as well as from the grim prevalence of HIV/AIDS. True, the relative shares of total national income flowing to

Africans and other blacks grew after apartheid. Blacks gained at the expense of whites, whose share fell, but from a very high median-income level. Yet in the second economic period—around 2001—whites' income share rose again, in large part because the richest whites' incomes increased relative to Africans'.[38] The richest whites—who gained more than anyone else from profits and dividends on capital—apparently retain their privileged place within the new South African economy. This is despite striking gains by well-educated Africans and other blacks toward the goals of a multiracial middle class, and a more diverse economic elite, a realm that had heretofore been the exclusive domain of whites.[39]

Race also matters to government efforts to ensure equity, and private responses to these efforts in the workforce and higher education. Expansion of employment in the public sector has favored Africans and many other blacks. Blacks have also enjoyed increased access to higher education, as several contributors to this volume point out, but preparation for matriculation and educational success in high-quality postsecondary universities remains a challenge. For an economy in need of high-skill employees, the growing unemployment among postsecondary graduates is surprising. This vexing pattern affects Africans more than other groups and is associated with the much lower postgraduation employment rates of Africans and others who pursued technical and nonuniversity degrees. Whereas the demand for well-educated, high-skill workers not only ensures employment for blacks (and especially Africans) who graduate from universities, but also drives up their wages relative to white graduates. The premium paid to university degree recipients over other workers of any race (e.g., graduates from the vocational schools formerly known as technikons) bespeaks employers' preference for high skill levels, as suggested by Bhorat in this volume.

These labor market responses reflect South Africa's two-tiered system of higher education, as described by Jansen in a subsequent chapter. Despite efforts at reform, the tiers are a legacy of apartheid and perhaps the unintended result of postapartheid policies of mass education, institutional consolidation, and targeted financing. One tier consists of a few formerly white and academically selective universities that are deracializing by enrolling more economically advantaged and academically prepared blacks. The lower and much larger tier of diverse institutions, including historically black universities and former technikons, enrolls variously prepared students and a plurality of matriculated blacks. The result, intentional or not, adds to divided futures and diminished prospects for Africans and other blacks according to their families' economic fortunes. It slows deracialization far short of equity.

The result is that the pursuit of equity is squarely on the table for South

Africa's higher-education system. The questions of who gets in and gets through, and therefore benefits, have measurable economic consequences. Who gets in and graduates under the policies of equity matters not only to individuals and their families, but also to the nation, inasmuch as it reflects on the strength of the country's constitutional commitment to principled equity and transformational justice. Since the stakes are high—for both individuals and polities—the tools South Africans use to move from a history of inequity to a future of equity must be just and wise. Universities and other institutions that use affirmative action to choose which citizens to educate or employ must come under scrutiny. For South Africa, like the United States, the main issues are equity and excellence: are they compatible or competing goals?

"Twins" Preparing the Future of Diverse Democracies

∾

As "twins born in different times," America and South Africa each must resolve the challenges of equity and excellence, especially in their institutions of higher education but more fundamentally as a challenge to any democracy endowed with diverse peoples. Their responses will be profoundly important to the next generation of young women and men of all racial and ethnic ancestries, and from all estates. It is important to their families, whose dreams and sacrifices for their children will be realized or dashed. And it is vital that all nations nourish not only the innovativeness beneath their prosperity but also the collective morale and mutual commitment sustaining a democracy. The burden, therefore, on institutions of higher education to be just and wise in resolving the challenges of equity and excellence is great. Fortunately, the "twins" can benefit from each other's experiences, as an opportunity for reflection and learning.

Fortunately, too, the twins' contemporary experiences are remarkably similar if not identical, given their different chronologies. The chapters that follow capture the voices of these twins. The reader will encounter monologues of self-understanding or self-reflection stimulated by engagement with the other. Conclusions emerge, but, just as often, questions remain: surely more refined and nuanced for the exchange, but begging to be analyzed and debated further. Profoundly important values that link private lives and public outcomes are not amenable to a once-and-for-all solution. Still, some kind of working resolution is imperative, and to achieve it the dialogue must be broadened to incorporate the reader as an active participant in a community of mutual reflection, learning, conversation, and, ultimately, informed action.

With those ends in mind, to which perspectives, questions, dilemmas, and possible resolutions should the ear be attuned? The introduction to each part of this book identifies specific issues of common concern. But the following are a few of the truly overarching challenges, which will surely warrant revisitation and reformulation over the next quarter century:

- Are equity and excellence competitive or complementary values in a diverse democracy? If a university seeks to adjust its admissions on the principle of equity—reflecting academic handicaps resulting from racial, economic, or gender inequality, for example—does it inevitably sacrifice its pursuit of academic excellence? Or alternatively, does pursuing both goals simultaneously—even if it means sacrificing one for the other, or some sacrifice to each—open the possibility of achieving a better outcome for both students and society? Recent critical commentaries on race-sensitive admissions under the banner of equity in South Africa echo long-standing doubts about the compatibility of affirmative action with equal opportunity and merit in America.[40] However, research on the pedagogical and later-life benefits of diversified student experience and diversified faculties and student bodies concludes otherwise. How should social science research and pragmatic cost-benefit analysis weigh in the balance with legal arguments and philosophical logic, shaping future public acceptance and judicial decision-making about affirmative action?
- Is it possible to pursue policies and practices aimed at equity or diversity—specifically, affirmative action—without perpetuating the premise that socially constructed categories such as Africans, Asians, Indians, Hispanics, Blacks, and Whites are categorically unequal, or essentially different? Do such policies perpetuate discriminatory stereotypes and implicate government in reifying race through racialized policymaking? On the other hand, if historic practices like apartheid or Jim Crow, and contemporary discrimination in housing and home loans, or in hiring and promotion, are based on ancestry and race—on the behavioral reality that we are not blind to skin color—then how can governments and public institutions ignore race? Must they not face it squarely as a real, if socially constructed "fact"? And yet, how might it be possible to "de-essentialize" categorical thinking? For example, if, as Patricia Gurin and coauthors ask later in this volume, racial and gender "diversity of experience and outlook on life" are pedagogical and educational assets within the university classroom, then what are the critical "experiences" or "life outlooks" that generate these benefits? And how are they tied to categories such as "black," "working class," or "female"?
- How should governments and public institutions of higher education

respond to growing economic and ethnic diversity within historic racial groups, when addressing the goals of equity and excellence? Latino and Asian immigration and Hispanic fertility are diversifying America and redefining the idea of minority status in America: soon, it will be whites of European ancestry who are the minority. Economic bipolarization also affects historic minorities in America, principally African Americans, and single parenthood and the penal system increasingly divide the fates of black men from black women. Economic diversification within race, notably among South African blacks and African Americans, paralleled by the rising educational and career employment aspirations of black women—and the enduring educational challenges faced by low-income whites in America, complicates the burden on higher education in both nations to be inclusive, to prepare cohorts of new leaders who reflect the changing composition of wider society, and to do so at high levels of excellence. Will these new burdens compromise universities' ability to function equitably by focusing them on the more academically prepared—and the more economically advantaged—among these new constituencies? If compromises are necessary, who will take up the burden of equity for those who are left behind? Will separate and unequal—a system of inferior education that extends from kindergarten into higher education—be reinvented, perhaps extended, by default?

- If affirmative action is a tool with broad (in South Africa) or narrow (in America) constitutional protection, is it possible to conceive a moment when it will no longer be required to achieve equity? Perhaps so, and arguably the ongoing use of racial and ethnic categories in the exercise of public policy should be strictly scrutinized, as the U.S. Supreme Court has counseled. However, projections by social scientists and educators cast doubt that racial groups will enjoy equal opportunity anytime soon, let alone proportionately equal educational and economic outcomes.[41] The burdens of history, augmented by such by-products as residential segregation, poverty, unemployment, poor schooling, underperforming economies, imprisonment, and "discrimination with a smile," will not be easily unshouldered.

But suppose aggressive enforcement of antidiscrimination laws and public reinvestment in human capital were to produce the conditions for achieving equity. Should higher education no longer practice affirmative action? Would that not be the moment when universities must become race neutral, as a way of assuming moral and educational leadership, toward a future that is truly blind to race and ethnicity as consequential realities? Perhaps so, if affirmative action is defined in the narrow sense by which

America practices it as an accommodation to racial discrimination. But perhaps not, as it is deployed in South Africa, where it is an emancipatory process leading toward a new social vision, as Njabulo Ndebele, asserts in his foreword. For example, if affirmative action is the fulcrum on which the goals of excellence and equity are balanced, and if America and South Africa continue along paths of economic and cultural diversification, then might it not be both necessary and desirable to act affirmatively indefinitely? How? By actively preparing potential applicants, selecting and admitting them, revising curriculum, promoting the graduation of a diverse student body, hiring faculty accordingly, and otherwise shaping our future leadership with an eye fixed upon the nation's ever-changing needs.

Acting affirmatively in this sense means acting with justice and foresight when fulfilling the mission of higher education. What is that mission? To create a learning and living community—even helping primary and secondary schools to "grow our own timber" from which this community will be constructed. To prepare and shape the future, exercising our precious academic freedom to educate and to lead, under the constraints of public accountability. To anticipate society's vibrant diversity by preparing minds and imaginations for future leadership at home and abroad and refining an eagerness and ability to embrace the evolving differences among humankind as a pleasure in their own right and an invaluable resource for our mutual survival. If that is affirmative action, then when would one wish universities to stop practicing it?

NOTES

1. See the chapter by Sandra Day O'Connor and Stewart J. Schwab ("Affirmative Action in Higher Education over the Next Twenty-five Years: A Need for Study and Action") in Part I of this volume; also Patricia Gurin, Jeffrey S. Lehman, and Earl Lewis, *Defending Diversity: Affirmative Action at the University of Michigan* (Ann Arbor: University of Michigan Press, 2004).

2. Postgenomic biology, the new genetics following the sequencing of the human genome, reopens the question of the relationship of race to genetics, especially in the practice of modern individually tailored medical care. The genetic distinction of race from ethnicity and of one ethno-racial category from another is at best probabilistic—based on statistical probabilities of gene occurrence and expression with highly overlapping distributions. They are not discretely bounded categories with nonoverlapping genetic profiles, for example. For an account of how this modern understanding of race and genetics is vastly different from the racial "science" of earlier historical periods see N. A. El-Haj, "The Genetic Reinscription of Race," *Annual Review of Anthropology* 4 (2007): 283–300.

3. M. J. Anderson and S. E. Fienberg, *Who Counts? The Politics of Census-Taking in Contemporary America* (New York: Russell Sage, 1999).

4. In generally accepted usage of racial terminology in South Africa today, "African" is a person whose first or family language is or was one of the Bantu language family,

such as isiZulu or isiXhosa. "Indian" is a person descended from indentured laborers brought to South Africa in the nineteenth century, or those classified as Indian under apartheid. "Coloured," while popularly seen as a person of mixed black and white descent, has little coherence as a category other than that conferred by apartheid classification. The term "Black" is sometimes used synonymously with "African" and at other times for any person or families who suffered political discrimination under apartheid (and who are therefore the intended beneficiaries, through redress, in the current Constitution and legislation). "White" designates those who benefited from apartheid legislation although biologically many of those classified White, and all Afrikaans families who can trace their lineage back before 1750, are of mixed genetic descent. Because the continuing use of race categories remains controversial, the editors of this volume have not attempted to standardize or define terminology in the chapters that follow, respecting individual author's rights of position and conscience.

5. G. M. Fredrickson, *White Supremacy: A Comparative Study in American and South African History* (Oxford: Oxford University Press, 1981).

6. S. Lieberson and M. C. Waters, *From Many Strands: Ethnic and Racial Groups in Contemporary America* (New York: Russell Sage, 1988).

7. J. Seekings and N. Nattrass, *Class, Race, and Inequality in South Africa* (New Haven: Yale University Press, 2005).

8. The phrase "apartheid mentality" is owed to J. L. Gibson, *Overcoming Apartheid: Can Truth Reconcile a Divided Nation?* (New York: Russell Sage, 2004). For an interpretation based on the infancy of democracy in practice in South Africa, see R. Mattes and M. Bratton, "Learning about Democracy in Africa: Performance, Awareness, and Experience," *American Journal of Political Science* 51 (2007): 192–217. Neville Alexander, in "The Struggle for National Liberation and the Attainment of Human Rights in South Africa," in Part I of this volume, offers a related interpretation but ties it more directly to the ANC's governing tactics that perpetuate, in his view, the legacy of the historic racial categories.

9. I. Katznelson, *When Affirmative Action Was White: An Untold History of Racial Inequality in Twentieth-Century America* (New York: Norton, 2006).

10. Before returning to India as the Mahatma, Gandhi himself lived in Natal, where he observed the British oppression of indentured Indian servants and other blacks. In his speeches following Sharpeville and in praise of the awarding of the Nobel Peace Prize to Chief Lutuli, president of the ANC, Martin Luther King, Jr., drew the civil rights movement's attention to the ANC's tactics of mass nonviolence, arrest, and imprisonment. The links between the American movement and Pan-Africanism are well documented, even if they are often misrepresented, as noted in G. M. Fredrickson, *Black Liberation: A Comparative History of Black Ideologies in the United States and South Africa* (Oxford: Oxford University Press, 1995).

11. Ibid.

12. A. M. Omar, foreword to *Confronting Past Injustices: Approaches to Amnesty, Punishment, Reparation, and Restitution in South Africa and Germany*, ed. M. R. Rwelamira and G. Werle (Durban: Butterworths, 1996); Gibson, *Overcoming Apartheid*.

13. Gibson, *Overcoming Apartheid*.

14. Gibson, *Overcoming Apartheid*; D. S. Massey, *Categorically Unequal: The American Stratification System* (New York: Russell Sage, 2007). See also Nancy Cantor and Jo Thomas, "Affirmative Action and Higher Education in the United States and South Africa," in Part I of this volume.

15. Katznelson, in *When Affirmative Action Was White*, explains how the resegregation of housing and schools and the enormous disparities in capital wealth of the 1960s

trace back to the unintended consequences of the New Deal, when, as he puts it in the title of his book, affirmative action was white.

16. D. S. Massey and N. A. Denton, *American Apartheid: Segregation and the Making of the Underclass* (Cambridge: Harvard University Press, 1993).

17. Views attributed to Huntington in Massey, *Categorically Unequal.*

18. Massey, *Categorically Unequal.* Also see R. B. Freeman, *America Works: Critical Thoughts on the Exceptional U.S. Labor Market* (New York: Russell Sage, 2007).

19. Gibson, *Overcoming Apartheid;* and J. L. Gibson, "The Legacy of Apartheid: Racial Differences in the Legitimacy of Democratic Institutions and Processes in the New South Africa," *Comparative Political Studies* 36, no. 7 (2003): 772–800.

20. Gibson, "Legacy of Apartheid." For converging interpretations based on different studies, see M. Bratton, R. Mattes, and E. Gyimah-Boadi, *Public Opinion, Democracy, and Market Reform in Africa* (Cambridge: Cambridge University Press, 2005); and Mattes and Bratton, "Learning about Democracy."

21. Seekings and Nattrass, *Class, Race, and Inequality,* 371–73, come to a similar conclusion.

22. While Seekings and Nattrass, *Class, Race, and Inequality,* arrive at a similar critical view, a more favorable analysis of ANC strategies and accomplishments appears in A. Hirsch, *Season of Hope: Economic Reform under Mandela and Mbeki* (Scottsville, South Africa: University of KwaZulu-Natal Press, 2005).

23. See Mattes and Bratton, "Learning about Democracy," for an interpretation of this conclusion about South Africa, based on political opinion surveys across several African nations and democratic governments of varying histories.

24. S. Danziger and P. Gottschalk, "Diverging Fortunes: Trends in Poverty and Inequality," in *The American People, Census 2000,* ed. R. Farley and J. Haaga (New York: Russell Sage, 2005), 1–27. For more extensive details of OECD countries, based on a different definition of poverty, see T. Smeeding, "Poor People in Rich Nations: The United States in Comparative Perspective," *Journal of Economic Perspectives* 20, no. 1 (2006): 69–90.

25. Freeman, *America Works;* J. Seekings, N. Nattras, and M. Liebbrandt, "Inequality in Post-Apartheid South Africa: Trends in the Distribution of Income and their Social and Political Implications," Report for the Centre for Development and Enterprise, Johannesburg (2003).

26. Danziger and Gottschalk, "Diverging Fortunes," offer this assessment to characterize the meaning of "divided fortunes" and "diminished prospects," their terminology.

27. Freeman, *America Works,* 48–52.

28. F. Levy and P. Temin, "Inequality and Institutions in 20th Century America," unpublished, Department of Urban Studies and Planning and Department of Economics, Massachusetts Institute of Technology (2007).

29. Ibid.

30. D. L. Featherman and R. M. Hauser, *Opportunity and Change* (New York: Academic Press, 1978).

31. Danziger and Gottschalk, "Diverging Fortunes."

32. Ibid.

33. Seekings and Nattrass, *Class, Race, and Inequality.*

34. *The Economist,* April 2006.

35. Seekings and Nattrass, *Class, Race, and Inequality.*

36. H. Bhorat and R. Kanbur, "Poverty and Well-Being in Post-apartheid South Africa: An Overview of Data, Outcomes, and Policy," Paper 05/101, Development Policy Research Unit, University of Cape Town (2005); and M. Leibbrandt, L. Poswell, N.

Pranushka, M. Welch, and I. Woolard, "Measuring Recent Changes in South African Inequality and Poverty Using 1996 and 2001 Census Data," Working Paper 05/94, Development Policy Research Unit, University of Cape Town (2005); also Haroon Bhorat, "Higher Education and the Labor Market in Postapartheid South Africa," in Part II of this volume. While statistics on prevalence and incidence of HIV/AIDS in South Africa are disputed, no one disagrees that estimated rates are among the highest in the world and reflect widespread infection among Africans and among the poor. Public health policy of the Mbeki government drew international criticism for questioning the scientific basis for treating HIV/AIDS via antiretrovirals; see N. Nattrass, *Mortal Combat: AIDS Denialism and the Struggle for Antiretrovirals in South Africa* (Scottsville, South Africa: University of KwaZulu-Natal Press 2007).

37. Seekings and Nattrass, *Class, Race, and Inequality.*

38. Leibbrandt et al., "Measuring Recent Changes."

39. Seekings and Nattrass, *Class, Race, and Inequality.*

40. For example, D. Benatar, "Affirmative Action: Not the Way to Tackle Injustice," *Cape Times,* April 12, 2007. For parallel, principled opposition to affirmative action in the United States, see Ward Connerly, as cited in M. E. Dyson, *Debating Race* (New York: Basic Books, 2007). However, André du Toit, "Social Justice and Postapartheid Higher Education in South Africa," in Part I of this volume, offers a very different interpretation growing out of South Africa.

41. Danziger and Gottschalk, "Diverging Fortunes"; see, in this volume, Michael S. McPherson and Matthew A. Smith, "Racial Disparities and the Next Twenty-five Years: The Continued Need for Affirmative Action," in Part IV, and Martin Hall, "Nothing Is Different, but Everything's Changed," one of the book's "Conclusions."

PART I ∿ Historical and Legal Context

Introduction to Part I, *Marvin Krislov*

Part I of this book frames the historic and legal contexts in which "affirmative action" policies arose in the United States and South Africa. The six distinguished authors (or sets of authors) show the extent to which affirmative action policies have evolved and the extent to which they have been limited by the constitutional framework of their respective countries. Among other questions, the authors help us understand why affirmative action, and not more radical policies, has emerged. They also challenge us to think about whether legal constraints have rendered such policies less than fully effective, and whether in fact affirmative action policies should be restructured.

Neville Alexander and David Garrow set affirmative action in the context of the respective black liberation struggles in the two countries. The contexts differ—in particular, the difference between a minority struggle and a majority struggle, yet in both countries the level of violence and armed struggle never reached the point of all-out civil war. As Alexander describes, South African regime change and the end of apartheid marked a compromise between the dominant Afrikaner population and African nationalists. He asks us to ponder whether the moderate form of social reform, as expressed in affirmative action policies, will survive the tensions of middle-class aspirations of all races and the demand for equality.

David Garrow looks at the origins of American affirmative action, setting it in the context of the civil rights movement but finding the creation in the hands of American bureaucrats following up on President Kennedy's and President Johnson's executive orders. He shows how the 1972 Office for Civil Rights decision applying Title VII of the Civil Rights Act's antidiscrimination provisions to colleges and universities expanded the reach of affirmative action. In his discussion of Supreme Court cases and the political challenges, he articulates a vision of individualized consideration that squares with the American brand of affirmative action.

How do the legal constraints define and shape the particular forms of affirmative action in the two countries? Judith February surveys the historic background and current reality of affirmative action in South African higher education. She analyzes the challenge to the University of Cape Town policies, and notes arguments familiar from the American context—reverse discrimination, climate of entitlement, benefits for the black middle class, the need for a sunset clause. However, she contends that in South Africa, race and group identity continue to have relevance as means to the end of a "nonracial society." Moreover, February shows how the modern South African Constitution aimed at substantive, not simply procedural or formal, equality. This framing ensures that affirmative action is integral to social transformation. In South African jurisprudence, the crucial question is whether the discrimination is "fair" or not, including whether it remedies previous discrimination against a racial group.

By contrast, the United States Supreme Court has traveled a distance from the notion of benign discrimination. As Justice O'Connor and Stewart Schwab explicate, the critical question for race-sensitive policies in higher education or elsewhere is whether the categorization survives strict scrutiny—that is, serves a compelling interest and is "narrowly tailored." This method of parsing the governmental action, under the equal protection clause of the Fourteenth Amendment of the U.S. Constitution, focuses more on the individualized implications of such policies. By recognizing the value of student body diversity, Justice O'Connor in her majority opinion in *Grutter v. Bollinger* allowed individualized consideration of race and ethnicity under certain guidelines. As she and Schwab make clear, race-blind admissions schemes have not provided student body diversity in those states that have legislatively banned affirmative action in higher education. Since it is her statement about the next 25 years that gives this volume its name, her prognostication attracts our attention. The authors sound a cautionary note and encourage further study and experimentation.

We cannot predict the direction of future courts in South Africa and the United States, but the O'Connor and Schwab chapter shows the far narrower construction under the current American Supreme Court of affirmative action policies. As the final group of chapters in this part shows, claims of social justice and any "moral imperative" are similar in both countries—at least by their advocates. André du Toit argues that, despite concerted efforts by the ANC (African National Congress) government, the apartheid legacy lingers. While the number of Black students enrolled in higher education has increased, the differentiation between the formerly elite White institutions and the Historically Disadvantaged Institutions has increased dramatically. Moreover, the Black participation rate in higher education has increased only nominally (from 9 percent to 12 percent), while White participation has remained roughly equal (60 percent). Du Toit concludes that affirmative action policies have failed to produce the change foreseen by the notions of redress and equity because secondary schools have not created a large increase in qualified Black applicants. Affirmative action, then, has not resulted in equal social justice.

Nancy Cantor and her colleague, Jo Thomas, emphasize many of the common threads running through the American and South African experiences. They note the importance of affirmative action programs in promoting diversity and student body engagement. Pointing to continued segregation, they argue that integration at lower levels of schooling is essential. Moreover, they believe that recognizing group membership as part of cultural identity improves education and understanding among students.

At least among academics and intellectuals, the notion of color blindness continues to be contested in American politics and law. As André du Toit and Judith February suggest, the debate at UCT may foreshadow greater debate in South African society about the time line for redress. For du Toit, the time may be now to rethink the relative tameness of affirmative action policies (perhaps observing the American experience). For Cantor and Thomas, while other policies should be pursued, affirmative action is necessary to maintain diversity and preserve opportunity in American higher education, at least in the near future.

These six perspectives thus shape our understanding of these two countries, illuminate the political and legal choices made in the United States, and may shed light on those choices facing South Africa and the United States going forward.

Affirmative Action and the
U.S. Black Freedom Struggle

༺

David J. Garrow

Affirmative action was an unexpected, but also inevitable, by-product of the U.S. black freedom struggle of the 1960s. It was unexpected by the activists, presidents, and legislators who shaped federal government policy between 1961 and 1965. But it also was an inevitable result of the fair employment policies that those actors had fervently sought. Once the major focus of their efforts—Title VII of the Civil Rights Act of 1964—became law, the absence of any clear consensus on the definition of racial discrimination guaranteed that the implementation of federal antidiscrimination policies would gradually give the word *affirmative* a substantive import far beyond what its earliest uses had suggested.

The most thorough histories of affirmative action trace its roots to the efforts of Interior secretary Harold L. Ickes and his aides in the 1930s to insure that Public Works Administration contractors hired some percentage of black employees in areas that had an "appreciable Negro population."[1] According to the late Hugh Davis Graham, the actual phrase *affirmative action* first appeared in a nonracial context in the National Labor Relations Act of 1935 (also known as the Wagner Act) and was only used with regard to race 10 years later, in New York state's 1945 Law Against Discrimination.[2]

Many summary accounts, however, understandably date the birth of affirmative action to March 6, 1961, when President John F. Kennedy issued Executive Order 10925. The 4,500-word order created the President's Committee on Equal Employment Opportunity, and directed the committee to "consider and recommend additional affirmative steps which should be taken by executive departments and agencies to realize more fully the national policy of nondiscrimination" in government employment. It also mandated that all federal contracts henceforth include a provision binding each contractor to "take affirmative action to ensure that applicants are employed, and that employees are treated during employment, without regard to their race, creed, color, or national origin."[3]

Hobart Taylor, Jr., a young black attorney from Texas whom Vice President Lyndon B. Johnson recruited to help draft the order, recalled in a 1969 oral history interview, "I was searching for something that would give a sense of positiveness to performance under that Executive Order, and I was torn between the words 'positive action' and the words 'affirmative action.'" He chose *affirmative* "because was it was alliterative," he explained.[4]

Historians of affirmative action have rightly highlighted how modest a meaning those words carried at the time of Kennedy's order. Hugh Davis Graham, noting that the phrase appeared only once and "rather casually" in the lengthy order, observed that the term was ambiguous right from its inception.[5] On one hand, it represented what Graham labeled "classic nondiscrimination," in that "affirmative action was required to ensure that citizens were treated *without regard* to race, color, or creed." But the order also, in his eyes, seemed to expect more proactive recruitment strategies from employers and special training for minorities.[6]

Like Graham, Terry Anderson, in his comprehensive history of the policy, recognized that Kennedy's 1961 order seemed to do nothing more than insist on racially neutral hiring.[7] A second Kennedy mandate, Executive Order 11114 of June 22, 1963, made it a matter of federal policy "to encourage by affirmative action the elimination of discrimination" in all federally funded activities, while a third decree, Executive Order 11246, issued by President Lyndon B. Johnson on September 24, 1965, again invoked Kennedy's (or Hobart Taylor's) "affirmative action" phrase.[8]

Although Johnson's 1965 order would define affirmative action for years to come, it was his signature into law 14 months earlier of the landmark Civil Rights Act of 1964 and its Title VII that enacted the antidiscrimination commands embedded in Kennedy's executive orders into law, expanded their reach to all employers with 25 or more employees, and created the Equal Employment Opportunities Commission as a new executive branch enforcement agency. Yet Section 703(j) of Title VII also mandated that "nothing contained in this title shall be interpreted to require any employer . . . to grant preferential treatment to any individual or to any group" on account of "race, color, religion, sex, or national origin." Thus the new law prohibited discrimination, but also appeared to bar any government-ordered preferential action toward any group that had been subject to discrimination.

But the most important indicator of how federal antidiscrimination policy would be implemented in the middle and late 1960s came not from any statute or executive order, but from President Johnson's commencement address at Howard University in Washington, DC, on June 4, 1965. "We seek not just freedom but opportunity," Johnson intoned in his characteristic drawl, toward the halfway point of his address. "We seek not just legal equity but human ability, not just equality as a right and a theory, but equality as a fact and equality as a result." This would become the most quoted passage of Johnson's Howard address, and one of the most quoted remarks he ever made. But further into his oration he added, in words that qualified, if not undercut, his first invocation of "opportunity," that "equal opportunity is essential, but not enough, not enough." Black Americans, Johnson continued, had to move "beyond opportunity to achievement."[9]

The confusion over what "opportunity," "equality" and "affirmative action" might mean, or require, was brought home even more starkly by Edward C. Sylvester, Jr., the first director of the Johnson administration's newly created Office of Federal Contract Compliance. Speaking at an early 1967 conference, Sylvester frankly acknowledged, "There is no fixed and firm definition of affirmative action. I would say that in a general way, affirmative action is anything that you have to do to get results. But this does not necessarily include preferential treatment. The key word here is 'results.'"[10]

Sylvester was echoing President Johnson's word-choice, but it is crucial for twenty-first-century readers to appreciate just how obscure and muddled the conception of affirmative action as a civil rights policy actually was. Historian Thomas Sugrue rightly notes that "between 1963 and 1969, affirmative action moved from obscurity to become the single most important federal policy for dealing with employment discrimination."[11] Indeed, it was only at the very close of the Johnson years, and in the earliest months of the new, ostensibly conservative Republican Nixon administration, that the implications of Johnson's and Sylvester's formulations became manifest.

This slow emergence of federal policy took place at a great distance from the heralded protest activism of the era. Dr. Martin Luther King, Jr., observed in early 1964, "Some kind of compensatory crash program" was needed "to bring the standards of the Negro up and bring him into the mainstream of life." King previously had called publicly for "some concrete, practical preferential program," "a crash program of special treatment," but, following the advice of one of his top advisors, Clarence B. Jones, King began to qualify his public statements, explaining that the programs he was calling for were in no way racially exclusive.[12] "Any 'Negro Bill of Rights' based upon the concept of compensatory treatment as a result of the years of cultural and economic deprivation resulting from racial discrimination," King wrote, "must give greater emphasis to the alleviation of economic and cultural backwardness on the part of the so-called 'poor white.' It is my opinion that many white workers whose economic condition is not too far removed from that of his black brother, will find it difficult to accept a 'Negro Bill of Rights', which seeks to give special consideration to the Negro in the context of unemployment, joblessness, etc."[13]

But the simple truth of the matter is that federal antidiscrimination policy developed and evolved inside a handful of government office buildings in downtown Washington, DC, and not in the streets of Birmingham or

Chicago, or within the movement's own councils. The lack of real interaction between movement leaders and activists, on one hand, and relevant executive branch officials like Edward Sylvester, on the other, may be surprising. But the absence of any substantive policy input from the movement to government officials was simply one more inevitable result of the nonstop challenges and demands movement leaders like King were racing to confront.

The reader may be disappointed to discover that federal antidiscrimination policies were much more the handiwork of little-remembered officials like Ed Sylvester than of marquee names like Martin Luther King. But this fact underscores the extent to which meaningful political change is often the result of efforts by a variety of historical actors, heralded and unheralded. As Roger Wilkins, a knowledgeable student of the movement and a staffer in the Johnson administration, observed at the time of Ed Sylvester's death, "part of what we did was carry out the legislation that the civil rights movement had started."[14] Sometimes, as with affirmative action, that modest phrase "carry out" signified a sometimes dramatic degree of initiative and innovation.

The most important turning point in the history of federal antidiscrimination policy came in 1968–69, with the decisive battle over the so-called Philadelphia Plan. Federal regional administrators intent upon integrating several virtually all-white building trade unions in the city crafted the initial approach in late 1967. "Although affirmative action is criticized as ambiguous," the lead official wrote, "the very lack of specific detail and rigid guideline requirements permits the utmost in creativity, ingenuity, and imagination." The goal, he explained, was to "achieve equal opportunity results": three familiar words now conjoined.[15]

In practice, as Terry Anderson recounts, the Philadelphia Plan required that contractors' bids "must have the result of producing minority group representation in all trades and in all phases" of any federally funded construction project. This provision gave a more tangible meaning to affirmative action, and certainly advanced the "result" that President Johnson had called for in his 1965 speech at Howard. But, as Anderson observes, a result-oriented approach designed to increase minority hires was incongruous with the original intent of Title VII, which required race-blind employment.[16]

Opposition from the General Accounting Office and the comptroller general stymied any actual implementation of the Philadelphia Plan during the waning months of the Johnson administration. The decision thus passed to Johnson's successor, Richard M. Nixon, and more particularly to Nixon's new secretary of labor, George P. Shultz, who strongly endorsed the policy.[17] After several months of highly incongruous legislative tussling in which utterly unlikely alliances had most liberal Democrats lining up alongside organized labor in opposition to the Philadelphia Plan, and most congressional Republicans siding with their president in support of the plan, which Shultz and his top aides energetically championed, the program won an unexpected vote of confidence from both houses of Congress in December 1969.

The evolution toward an executive branch focus on results may have been inevitable during the Kennedy and Johnson years, but nothing could have been more politically unexpected than a conservative Republican administration championing the most aggressive pursuit of results yet. Once again, the story of how this came to pass is a densely complicated, inside-Washington piece of policy history with strikingly few connections whatsoever to the most publicized aspects of the black freedom struggle.

The upshot of Nixon's position was that, in Terry Anderson's words, "the Philadelphia Plan eclipsed Title VII and became the official policy of the U.S. government."[18] Two significant policy events in relatively quick succession expanded the effect of this decisive shift.

The first was the U.S. Supreme Court's 1971 ruling in the case of *Griggs v. Duke Power Co.* Before Title VII, Duke Power had explicitly limited the job prospects of its black employees. Once the 1964 law was enacted, however, the company added new education and testing requirements for any employee seeking to transfer to a better job. Those preconditions effectively held back black applicants, who had endured segregated schools, and when their challenge to the new prerequisites reached the Supreme Court, the justices unanimously agreed with their position.

Title VII, the Court observed, "does not command that any person be hired simply because he was formerly the subject of discrimination, or because he is a member of a minority group. Discriminatory preference for any group, minority or majority, is precisely and only what Congress has proscribed." Instead, the opinion continued, "What is required by Congress is the removal of artificial, arbitrary, and unnecessary barriers to employment when the barriers operate invidiously to discriminate on the basis of racial or other impermissible classification."

"Tests or criteria for employment or promotion may not provide equality of opportunity," the Court observed, and Title VII requires that "the posture and condition of the job-seeker be taken into account." In other words, the law "proscribes not only overt discrimination but also practices that are fair in form, but discriminatory in operation. The touchstone is business necessity. If an employment practice which operates to exclude Negroes cannot be shown to be related to job performance, the practice is prohibited."

Griggs was a judicial endorsement of the enforcement policies that had evolved within the executive branch agencies. According to Terry Anderson, the case "defined affirmative action for the next two decades," making fair employment "more a group than an individual right": a development that could be seen as wholly in keeping with Johnson's explicit demand for results back in 1965.[19]

The second major policy event that followed the Philadelphia Plan's acceptance was the wholesale extension to the educational arena of antidiscrimination policies that had originally been developed for the industrial workforce. Given that the nationwide debate about affirmative action would in later years become so intensely focused on hiring and admissions policies in higher education, it is utterly amazing how little attention scholars have paid to the 1972 decision by the federal Office for Civil Rights (OCR) to expand its equal employment enforcement efforts to U.S. colleges and universities holding federal contracts.

The earliest and most influential efforts to extend enforcement to higher education came in response to reports from women's groups about widespread sex discrimination in faculty hiring.[20] Public controversy over the incipient federal expansion burgeoned in late 1971 and early 1972, and in the spring of 1972 Health, Education, and Welfare secretary Elliot L. Richardson, whose department oversaw the OCR, publicly upbraided unhappy academics by reminding them that universities, as federal contractors and employers, "incur the obligations of other contractors and other employers."[21]

Richardson told reporters that "the primary responsibility for finding methods to increase the numbers of women and minorities must come from the universities themselves," but just as his department was preparing to issue a formal mandate, Congress passed and President Nixon signed into law the Equal Employment Opportunity Act of 1972, which amended Title VII to make all colleges and universities—not just those holding government contracts—subject to federal antidiscrimination policies.[22]

Initial press coverage of the new statute was spotty, but within a few weeks word quickly spread about the significantly increased scope of enforcement it portended.[23] The OCR was moving forward irrespective of the statutory change, and on October 1, 1972, OCR director J. Stanley Pottinger formally issued the office's Higher Education Guidelines.

"The premise of the affirmative action concept," Pottinger explained, "is that unless positive action is undertaken to overcome the effects of systemic institutional forms of discrimination, a benign neutrality in employment practices will tend to perpetuate the 'status quo ante' indefinitely." Then, echoing clearly and directly the Supreme Court's language in *Griggs*, the director stated that "the affirmative action concept does not require that a university employ or promote any persons who are unqualified. The concept does require, however, that any standards or criteria which have had the effect of excluding women and minorities be eliminated, unless the contractor can demonstrate that such criteria are conditions of successful performance in the particular position involved."[24]

That mandate brought federal antidiscrimination enforcement into the world of higher education with dramatic effect. Some leading universities had already initiated race-conscious admissions policies with the acknowledged goal of increasing the number of racial-minority students. But the first legal ruling disallowing those policies was quickly handed down by a Washington state trial court in the fall of 1971. Oddly, that case, *DeFunis v. Odegaard,* was brought by a rejected law school applicant seeking preferential treatment for in-state, as opposed to out-of-state, applicants. The trial court ordered his admission after uncovering racially disparate admissions standards, but by the time the case reached the U.S. Supreme Court the student was on the verge of graduation, thus allowing the justices to dismiss the case as moot.

Dissenting from that judgment, liberal icon William O. Douglas wrote that admissions decisions must be made "on the basis of individual attributes, rather than according a preference solely on the basis of race." Each applicant, Douglas said, "had a constitutional right to have his application considered on its individual merits in a racially neutral manner."

But "racially neutral" did not mean simply color blind. Instead, Douglas explained, distinct treatment based on race or a similar attribute could pass legal muster if "the reason for the separate treatment of minorities as a class is to make more certain that racial factors do not militate against an applicant or on his behalf." Douglas was envisioning how to counterbalance factors such as standardized tests, which might disadvantage entire groups of applicants, and instead evaluate each applicant's individual merits, including racial and ethnic identity, without according such identities any systematic advantage.

The issue of preferential admissions was again brought before the Court four years later, in *Regents of the University of California v. Bakke.* Speaking for a closely divided Court, Justice Lewis F. Powell, Jr., found that the admissions program at the Medical School of the University of California at Davis had indeed imposed an unconstitutional racial quota. At the same time, however, Powell stated that admissions officers could properly consider applicants' racial identities pursuant to universities' First Amendment right to select student bodies that possess "genuine diversity." That compelling interest, Powell explained, "is not an interest in simple ethnic diversity, in which a specified percentage of the student body is in effect guaranteed to be members of selected ethnic groups." Instead, true diversity "encompasses a far broader array of qualifications and characteristics of which racial or ethnic origin is but a single though important element."

In admissions decisions, Powell wrote, race or ethnic background could be counted as a "plus" for individual applicants, "without the factor of race being decisive." Policies had to be "flexible enough to consider all pertinent elements of diversity," and "on the same footing." So long as "race or ethnic background is simply one element—to be weighed fairly against other elements—in the selection process," he explained, affirmative action admissions could pass constitutional muster.

Justice Harry A. Blackmun, one of the four colleagues who voted with Powell to authorize race-conscious admissions policies, nonetheless confessed, "I yield to no one in my earnest hope that the time will come when an 'affirmative action' program is unnecessary and is, in truth, only a relic of the past. I would hope that we could reach this stage within a decade at the most." He quickly added that the history of school desegregation suggested "that that hope is a slim one," but that "At some time, however, beyond any period of what some would claim is only transitional inequality, the United States must and will reach a stage of maturity where action along this line is no longer necessary. Then persons will be regarded as persons, and discrimination of the type we address today will be an ugly feature of history that is instructive but that is behind us."

Powell's one-justice, but nonetheless definitive opinion seemed to resolve the debate over affirmative action in university admissions. But soon after *Bakke* was decided, it became clear that some Americans were unwilling to accept at face value Powell's statement that race could only serve as "simply one element" in a multifaceted evaluation of student diversity, "without . . . being decisive."

Paul J. Mishkin, the senior author of the University of California's brief in the case, observed in 1983 that "the experience following the *Bakke* decision was that the vast range of race-conscious programs of special admission to universities continued in full force and effect." Mishkin felt that this continuation was wholly in keeping with the underlying meaning of Powell's opinion. He praised the justice's decision as "a wise and politic resolution" and a "masterful stroke of diplomacy," but he also asserted that Powell's position could not be "supported by articulated principle."[25]

That was because, in Mishkin's view, Powell's "academic diversity justification once accepted could, and should, sustain all forms of special admissions programs designed to achieve that objective," including the very one that the *Bakke* ruling had held unconstitutional. In other words, all Powell's opinion had articulated was "a matter of form over substance," and in no way really precluded admissions officers from continuing to admit minority students in whatever numbers they might choose. Using Powell's "plus," programs considering "the size of the plus will set that size in terms of the number of minority students likely to be produced at the level set."[26]

Mishkin passingly acknowledged that Powell's opinion "tended to equate race with other variables," but he otherwise did not address Powell's effort to describe "genuine diversity" as encompassing a host of nonracial elements "on the same footing." Instead, Mishkin opined that "wise and effective government may at times require indirection and less-than-full-candor," so as to "avoid such visibility in its operations."[27]

If Mishkin's was a forced and indeed troubling interpretation of Powell's opinion, it was seemingly validated a decade later, when John C. Jeffries, Jr., a former Powell clerk, propounded that same reading in his authorized biography of the justice. Baldly asserting that "diversity was not the ultimate objective but merely a convenient way to broach a compromise," Jeffries contended that Powell had been guilty of "pure sophistry" in concluding that there was any meaningful difference between the admissions process he condemned and those he embraced. The multifaceted approach Powell described and approved, Jeffries claimed, was, in reality, no different than the program he voided, except for the absence of "fixed numbers." Powell's decision, Jeffries said, "simply penalized candor": "You can do whatever you like in preferring racial minorities, so long as you do not say so."[28]

A decade later, Jeffries implicitly abandoned this position when he admitted the need "to curtail or eliminate racial 'plus' factors as soon as possible."[29] But, in the interim, other influential voices adopted his and Mishkin's claims. Commenting on this development in 1996, legal scholars Akhil Reed Amar and Neal Kumar Kaytal tellingly observed, "At some point, when a racial plus looms so much larger than other diversity factors, an admissions scheme would, it seems, violate the letter and spirit of *Bakke*."[30] Their acute criticism was echoed by others, who noted how readings of *Bakke* that ignored key aspects of Powell's analysis allowed their exponents to advance "racial preferences that were plainly inconsistent with the very language in Justice Powell's opinion," and thus "defied the Court *sub silentio*."[31]

The realization that Powell's standard had so often been implemented— or not implemented—in such a dishonest and disobedient manner did not, however, end all efforts to extend Mishkin's interpretation. Indeed, writing in 2007, Yale law professor Robert Post and a younger colleague reviled "the eccentric and slippery logic of Powell's distinction between constitutional and unconstitutional affirmative action programs." Powell had only propounded a "largely fictional system of 'individualized consideration,'" Post claimed, which "would produce virtually the same 'net operative results' as the explicit 'set-aside' plan" *Bakke* had struck down.[32]

But Post's efforts, like Mishkin's before him, were ultimately futile. Terry Anderson terms the years from 1969 to 1980 "the zenith of affirmative action," for soon after *Bakke* the winds began to change.[33] In 1980, the Supreme Court in *Fullilove v. Klutznick* narrowly upheld Congress's power to include a 10 percent set-aside provision for minority business enterprises in the Public Works Act of 1977, perhaps the high-water mark of the post-Johnson quest for race-conscious "results."

But, as Anderson notes, public support for affirmative action was always very tenuous. The administrations of Ronald Reagan and then George H. W. Bush brought a major shift in executive-branch attitudes. By the end of the 1980s, the Supreme Court, too, had changed direction, essentially reversing *Griggs v. Duke Power Co.* in a case known as *Wards Cove Packing Co. v. Atonio*. Congressional passage of the Civil Rights Act of 1991 momentarily suggested the legislature's indirect endorsement of affirmative action, but the act's purposeful vagueness hamstrung its influence.[34]

In short, the failure to clearly define and delimit the meaning of affirmative action during the Kennedy, Johnson, and Nixon years left the policy highly vulnerable to both judicial intervention and changing political tides. The stage was thus set for Ward Connerly's 1995 embrace of the California Civil Rights Initiative, an anti-affirmative action measure proposed by two conservative white state academics. A black member of the University of California Board of Regents, Connerly was able to successfully push the regents to end admissions preferences, even before the statewide popular vote on what came to be called Proposition 209 in November 1996.

Connerly believed that a key problem was a serious misreading of Powell's opinion in *Bakke*. "We are relying on race and ethnicity not as one of many factors but as a dominant factor to the exclusion of all others," he complained. Proposition 209 was designed to amend the state constitution by prohibiting public institutions from giving preferential treatment on the basis of race, sex or ethnicity. On November 5, 1996, California voters approved it by a margin of better than 54 to 46 percent. Looking back at that vote almost a decade later, Terry Anderson termed the outcome "the demise of affirmative action."[35]

The impact of Proposition 209 on the number of black and Latino students at California's top public universities was immediate and drastic. Within one year the percentage of undergraduates at the University of California at Berkeley who were black, Latino, or Native American dropped from 23 percent to 10 percent. Black admissions at the Berkeley and UCLA law schools declined by more than 80 percent, and Latino admissions by half.[36]

California's change would soon spread. Just two years later, in November 1998, voters in Washington, another generally liberal West Coast state, approved Initiative 200, a statutory ban on affirmative action modeled on Proposition 209, with more than 58 percent of the vote. Then, in late 1999, Florida governor Jeb Bush announced his intent to eliminate race-based admissions at all state public universities. His One Florida Initiative was approved and implemented early in 2000.

It turned out, however, that the California, Washington, and Florida prohibitions had merely set the scene for the Supreme Court's landmark reconsideration of Lewis Powell's *Bakke* opinion, when challenges to the undergraduate *(Gratz v. Bollinger)* and law school admissions *(Grutter v. Bollinger)* programs at the University of Michigan reached the High Court in 2002. Notwithstanding the many derisive attacks in the interim, 25 years after Powell articulated the fundamental distinction between race-determinative and race-conscious admissions practices, the Supreme Court unanimously embraced his standard, while disagreeing about its particular applications.

In a decision that did not surprise most careful observers, the Court struck down Michigan's undergraduate admissions policy because of the 20-point bonus that the program automatically awarded to every black, Hispanic, or Native American applicant.[37] But in the second, more closely contested case, challenging admissions practices at Michigan's law school, Justice Sandra Day O'Connor led a five-justice majority in upholding the program pursuant to Powell's 1978 standard. "Today we endorse Justice Powell's view that student body diversity is a compelling state interest that can justify the use of race in university admissions," O'Connor wrote. "Outright racial balancing," she emphasized, "is patently unconstitutional." Instead, "truly individualized consideration demands that race be used in a flexible, non-mechanical way." "When using race as a 'plus' factor in university admissions," O'Connor explained, "a university's admissions program must remain flexible enough to ensure that each applicant is evaluated as an individual and not in a way that makes an applicant's race or ethnicity the defining feature of his or her application. The importance of this individualized consideration in the context of a race-conscious admissions program is paramount."

O'Connor's standard was as strong and stark a vindication of Powell's meaning as could be imagined. In the case at hand, she said, Michigan Law School's admissions program "seriously weighs many other diversity factors besides race that can make a real and dispositive difference for nonminority applicants as well. By this flexible approach, the Law School sufficiently takes into account, in practice as well as in theory, a wide variety of characteristics besides race and ethnicity that contribute to a diverse student body."

Michigan Law School, O'Connor said, "considers race as one factor among many," echoing how Powell had identified the crucial distinction a quarter century earlier. But the O'Connor majority went on to emphasize another point, one reminiscent of Harry Blackmun's anguished comments in *Bakke*. "Race conscious policies must be limited in time," O'Connor declared. "This requirement reflects that racial classifications, however compelling their goals, are potentially so dangerous that they may be employed no more broadly than the interest demands. Enshrining a permanent justification for racial preferences would offend this fundamental equal protection principle. We see no reason to exempt race-conscious admissions programs from the requirement that all governmental use of race must have a logical end point. The Law School, too, concedes that all 'race-conscious programs must have reasonable durational limits.'"

The majority opinion closed by making that sunset point most explicit. "It has been 25 years since Justice Powell first approved the use of race to further an interest in student body diversity," O'Connor observed. "Since that time, the number of minority applicants with high grades and test scores has indeed increased. We expect that 25 years from now, the use of racial preferences will no longer be necessary to further the interest approved today."

The majority opinions in *Gratz* and *Grutter* may have utterly vindicated Lewis Powell's clear yet nuanced opinion in *Bakke*, but affirmative action opponents like Ward Connerly were far from satisfied with Sandra Day O'Connor's signal that the clock was inexorably ticking down. Connerly promised to mount a campaign for a statewide popular vote in Michigan just like those he previously had won in California and Washington. When Proposition 2 came before the state's voters in November 2006, it won approval by an almost landslide margin, with more than 58 percent of the vote.

The University of Michigan administration unwisely responded to the popular vote by declaring they would use every legal avenue at their disposal to avoid implementation of the measure, but a storm of editorial censure soon forced them to recant.[38] The question now before Michigan's public universities is whether to respond honestly and forthrightly to Proposition 2, or whether, like Mishkin after *Bakke*, to choose evasion, dissembling, and deceit.

Dissenting in *Gratz*, Justice Ruth Bader Ginsburg stated that "fully disclosed" racially decisive admissions policies were certainly "preferable to achieving similar numbers through winks, nods, and disguises."[39] Cynical readers of Ginsburg's dissent, or perhaps readers with long experience in U.S. academia, might think that Ginsburg expected university leaders to choose artifice and mendacity over good-faith implementation of legal standards with which they might personally disagree. This is not a new question to students of the black freedom struggle in America, but it was more commonly asked about the segregationist South after *Brown*, not top-flight national universities at the advent of the twenty-first century.

Some news reports have suggested that Michigan's public universities have chosen the path of disobedience and dissembling by continuing to favor students who attest that they have overcome prejudice and discrimination, or who come from the largely black city of Detroit.[40] Some students of U.S. constitutional history might see this as an ironic reversal of *Milliken v. Bradley;* others might instead ponder its relationship to *Gomillion v. Lightfoot.*

The liberal constitutional commentator Michael Dorf already has warned that "one could well imagine a court saying that an admissions essay question that asks applicants to identify discrimination or prejudice they have overcome is merely a disguised affirmative action program." Indeed, Dorf says, all evasive policies "may be vulnerable to the charge that they are merely covert forms of race-based affirmative action, and thus invalid on that basis."[41]

In the not-so-long run, such tactics are indeed destined to fail. Meanwhile, Ward Connerly and his allies are moving forward with further ballot initiatives in additional states, and their prospects for victory are bright. But the writing is on the wall, and some of it has been there a very long time. From Martin Luther King, Jr., in the 1960s through William O. Douglas, Lewis Powell, and Harry Blackmun in the 1970s, to Sandra Day O'Connor and her fellow members of the majority in *Grutter,* the call for truly individualized consideration of persons who have suffered social or economic disadvantage has been profoundly consistent. The sad truth may be that American universities refuse to hear that call, not on account of any reparative principle or belief, but simply because of the administrative costs and inconveniences of modifying their admissions policies.

Yet the path forward is clear. "Any selection process that does in fact consider the entire individual will be time-consuming, labor-intensive, and expensive," observed an impressive report issued in the wake of *Grutter* and *Gratz* by Educational Testing Service.[42] "Institutions that shy away from an admissions regime whose components reflect the seriousness of the task reveal a very great deal about the true nature of their commitment," the report most warned. If, instead, "we are honest about our objectives, and those goals involve considered decisions reflecting a desire to assemble a truly diverse student body, we must also be willing to pay the costs associated with them."[43] That conclusion does honor not only to the rulings of Lewis Powell and Sandra Day O'Connor, but also to the sacrifices and efforts of all the Martin Luther Kings and Ed Sylvesters, both famous and forgotten.

NOTES

A more fully annotated version of this chapter appears as "The Evolution of Affirmative Action and the Necessity of Truly Individualized Admissions Decisions," *Journal of College and University Law* 34 (2007): 1–19.

1. Terry H. Anderson, *The Pursuit of Fairness: A History of Affirmative Action* (New York: Oxford University Press, 2004), pp. 12, 46.

2. Hugh Davis Graham, *The Civil Rights Era: Origins and Development of National Policy* (New York: Oxford University Press, 1990), p. 33. Ch. 18, [1945] N.Y. Laws 457.

3. Executive Order 10925 (accessible at www.eeoc.gov/abouteeoc/35th/thelaw/eo-10925.html).

4. Hobart Taylor, Jr., Oral History Interview with Stephen Goodell, January 6, 1969, pp. 12–13, Lyndon Baines Johnson Library, Austin, TX.

5. Graham, *The Civil Rights Era*, p. 28.

6. Graham, *The Civil Rights Era*, p. 42.

7. Anderson, *The Pursuit of Fairness*, p. 61.

8. Executive Order 11114, 28 Federal Register 6485–88 (25 June 1963) (accessible at www.presidency.ucsb.edu/ws/index.php?pid=59053). Executive Order 11246, 30 Federal Register 12319–25 (28 September 1965) (accessible at www.eeoc.gov/abouteeoc/35th/thelaw/eo-11246.html.

9. Lyndon B. Johnson, "To Fulfill These Rights," 4 June 1965 (accessible at www.lbjlib.utexas.edu/johnson/archives.hom/speeches.hom/650604.asp).

10. *Report of the 1967 Plans for Progress Fifth National Conference*, 23–24 January 1967, pp. 73–74, as quoted in Anderson, *The Pursuit of Fairness*, p. 103.

11. Thomas J. Sugrue, "The Tangled Roots of Affirmative Action," *American Behavioral Scientist* 41 (April 1998): 886–97, at 895.

12. David J. Garrow, *Bearing the Cross: Martin Luther King, Jr., and the Southern Christian Leadership Conference* (New York: William Morrow, 1986), pp. 310–11, 680n20.

13. Martin Luther King, Jr., to Hermine Popper, 3 February 1964, Hermine Popper Papers, Box 17, Schlesinger Library, Radcliffe College, Cambridge, MA.

14. Matt Schudel, "Labor, Hill Official Edward Sylvester Dies," *Washington Post*, 18 February 2005, p. B6.

15. Warren P. Phelan, "Memorandum to Philadelphia Federal Executive Board," 27 October 1967, as quoted in Graham, *The Civil Rights Era*, p. 290.

16. Anderson, *The Pursuit of Fairness*, p. 105, 108.

17. See "U.S. Plans Formula To Get Contractors To Hire Minorities," *New York Times*, 28 June 1969, p. 61, and Paul Delaney, "Shultz Defends Minority Hiring," *New York Times*, 7 August 1969, p. 23.

18. Anderson, *The Pursuit of Fairness*, p. 124.

19. Anderson, *The Pursuit of Fairness*, p. 129.

20. See Linda Greenhouse, "Columbia Accused of Bias on Women," *New York Times*, 11 January 1970, p. 55, Harold Orlans, "Affirmative Action in Higher Education," *Annals of the American Academy of Political and Social Science* 523 (September 1992): 144–58, at 150, John D. Skrentny, *The Minority Rights Revolution* (Cambridge: Harvard University Press, 2002), pp. 242–49, Anderson, *The Pursuit of Fairness*, pp. 142–45.

21. On the controversy over expansion see, e.g., Paul Seabury, "HEW and the Universities," *Commentary*, February 1972, pp. 28–44. On Richardson's message to universities and colleges, see Elliot L. Richardson, "To the Editor of Commentary," *Commentary*, May 1972, p. 10. A similar letter from OCR's assistant director for public affairs stated that "in order to overcome the discrimination of the past, we have no alternative at this point in time but to use the race factor as a means of restoring equal opportunity." Robert E. Smith, "To the Editor of Commentary," *Commentary*, May 1972, pp. 10–11, at 11.

22. Joyce Heard, "Richardson: Women and the Ivory Tower," *The Harvard Crimson*, 24 April 1972 (accessible at www.thecrimson.com/article.aspx?ref=495266).

23. "Job Unit Widens Women's Rights," *New York Times*, 31 March 1972, pp. 1, 17,

"College Group to Tell Members of New Hiring-Bias Regulations," *New York Times,* 9 April 1972, p. 44.

24. Department of Health, Education, and Welfare, Office for Civil Rights, "Nondiscrimination Under Federal Contracts—Higher Education Guidelines," 37 Federal Register 24686–96 (18 November 1972). See also J. Stanley Pottinger, "The Drive Toward Equality," *Change* 4 (October 1972): 24, 26–29, Seth A. Goldberg, "A Proposal for Reconciling Affirmative Action with Nondiscrimination Under the Contractor Antidiscrimination Program," *Stanford Law Review* 30 (April 1978): 803–33, at 811–21, Skrentny, *The Minority Rights Revolution,* pp. 249–51.

25. Paul J. Mishkin, "The Uses of Ambivalence: Reflections on the Supreme Court and the Constitutionality of Affirmative Action," *University of Pennsylvania Law Review* 131 (March 1983): 907–31, at 922, 929, 930.

26. Mishkin, "The Uses of Ambivalence," p. 929n78, 926.

27. Mishkin, "The Uses of Ambivalence," pp. 924, 928.

28. John C. Jeffries, Jr., *Justice Lewis F. Powell, Jr.* (New York: Charles Scribner's Sons, 1994), pp. 500, 484.

29. John C. Jeffries, Jr., "Bakke Revisited," 2003 *Supreme Court Review* 1–25, at 20.

30. Akhil Reed Amar and Neal Kumar Kaytal, "Bakke's Fate," *UCLA Law Review* 43 (August 1996): 1745–80, at 1777n142.

31. Alan J. Meese, "Bakke Betrayed," *Law and Contemporary Problems* 63 (Winter–Spring 2000): 479–506, at 482.

32. Robert C. Post and Neil S. Siegel, "Theorizing the Law/Politics Distinction: Neutral Principles, Affirmative Action, and the Enduring Legacy of Paul Mishkin," *California Law Review* 95 (2007): 1473–1513, at 1495, 1493. "Net operative results" was a phrase Mishkin himself had deployed in "The Uses of Ambivalence," p. 928.

33. Anderson, *The Pursuit of Fairness,* p. 157.

34. Anderson, *The Pursuit of Fairness,* pp. 160, 203–4, 213, Note, "The Civil Rights Act of 1991: The Business Necessity Standard," *Harvard Law Review* 106 (February 1993): 896–913, John David Skrentny, *The Ironies of Affirmative Action* (Chicago: University of Chicago Press, 1996), p. 227.

35. Anderson, *The Pursuit of Fairness,* p. 256.

36. Anderson, *The Pursuit of Fairness,* p. 258.

37. See e.g. Jeffries, "Bakke Revisited," p. 14n55 (terming the outcome "clearly foreseeable"). See also, in an earlier context, David J. Garrow, "The Path to Diversity? Different Differences," *New York Times,* 2 September 2001, p. IV-4.

38. See, e.g., Tamar Lewin, "Michigan Rejects Affirmative Action, and Backers Sue," *New York Times,* 9 November 2006, p. P1, Steve Chapman, "University of Michigan vs. the People," *Chicago Tribune,* 23 November 2006, Dave Gershman, "U-M Files for Delay on Prop 2," *Ann Arbor News,* 12 December 2006, Tamar Lewin, "University to Comply With Ruling," *New York Times,* 11 January 2007, p. A27, and [Editorial], "A New Diversity at Michigan," *Chicago Tribune,* 14 January 2007.

39. 539 U.S. at 305.

40. See, e.g., Tamar Lewin, "Colleges Regroup After Voters Ban Race Preferences," *New York Times,* 26 January 2007, p. A1.

41. Michael C. Dorf, "Universities Adjust to State Affirmative Action Bans," Findlaw, 29 January 2007 (accessible at http://writ.news.findlaw.com/dorf/20070129.html).

42. Mark R. Killenbeck, *Affirmative Action and Diversity: The Beginning of the End? Or the End of the Beginning?* (Princeton, NJ: Educational Testing Service, 2004), pp. 25–26.

43. Killenbeck, *Affirmative Action and Diversity,* p. 26.

The Struggle for National Liberation and the Attainment of Human Rights in South Africa

༄

Neville Alexander

Conquest, Resistance, and Liberation

༄

In South Africa, the period of primary resistance can be said to stretch more than 400 years, from that fateful day in the first week of February 1488 when the first Khoe herder threw the first stone at Bartolomeu Diaz and his Portuguese buccaneers as they arrived in the *Bahia dos Vaqueiros* (probably Mossel Bay) until the killing of Chief Bambatha in April 1906. It was in April 1652, however, that the colonizing process and the penetration of capital begun to take shape, leading over a period of some 250 years to a contradictory and uneven process of resistance, accommodation, and collaboration among the indigenous people across the subcontinent. By the end of the seventeenth century, for example, when the children of the first slaves and the conquered Khoe clans were well on the way to becoming enforced subjects of the Dutch colony, virtually all of the indigenous people beyond the Hex River mountains were still living in independent, if fragile, sovereign political communities. Many of them continued to do so until the second half of the nineteenth century, when, as the result of the discovery of diamonds, gold, and other minerals, they were rapidly subjugated and dispossessed. The patriarchal racial-caste system of the precapitalist period provided the raw materials from which the subsequent system of racial capitalism was fashioned.

By the time the Union of South Africa came into being in 1910, the negotiated settlement between the British government and the defeated Boer generals created or, in some respects reinforced, the template upon which the political dynamics of the next century would be shaped. In brief, the sociopolitical system of segregation and its successor, apartheid, was based on the blueprint provided in the Report of the South African Native Affairs Commission of 1903–5, which met under the chairmanship of Sir Godfrey Lagden. (Ironically, most of the ideas associated with apartheid the notorious Afrikaner ideologues of the racist system actually derived from this "British" document.) The commission's most decisive recommendations

included the creation of a macro-apartheid scheme of territorial segregation, by which blacks in the rural hinterland would be ghettoized in "native
reserves" controlled by hereditary and government-appointed chiefs, and
into urban locations (later townships), "influx" into which would be regulated through a system of Pass Laws. It was proposed that white members of
Parliament represent those black people who fulfilled certain literacy and
property requirements.[1] The report led to the creation of hundreds of segregation and apartheid laws over more than 60 years—measures that were
notoriously justified in terms of social-Darwinist and other so-called scientific forms of racism, including Nazism.

Bluebeard's Castle and the Shattered Dream

∽

The struggle for national liberation—that is, the political and cultural, as
well as the organizational, response of the oppressed black majority to
white supremacism—was shaped by the acceptance among the so-called
mission elite and other incipient middle-class groupings among the oppressed that it was not only necessary, but possible, to achieve freedom and
equality within the emerging system. The Christian message and the politics of liberal philanthropy were etched very deeply into the consciousness
of the movement's prospective political leadership. In my past work I have
detailed how the caste consciousness of this leadership gave rise to the notion of four "national groups," three of which—Africans, Coloureds, and
Indians—in the words of the African National Congress Youth League,
were "oppressed," and three of which—Whites, Coloureds, and Indians—
were "minorities."[2] Each leadership cadre struggled to elevate the status and
prospects of "its" community, although, on occasion, they would form what
passed for alliances against particularly onerous measures. This happened,
for instance, when the Act of Union was being discussed in London
(1908–9) and again, much later, during the Defiance campaign of 1952–53.

The delusion that British fair play and liberal-democratic principles
would eventually permit the oppressed to "go inside"—to quote a phrase
from a 1983 speech by David Curry, then deputy-leader of the (Coloured)
Labour Party, explaining his party's decision to participate in P. W. Botha's
racist tricameral "parliament"—proved tenacious among the middle-class
opposition leadership. It can only be compared with Derek Bell's use of
Bartok's tragic allegory of Bluebeard's Castle in his analysis of American
civil rights activists. In retrospect, South African apologists for gradualism
and pacifism argued that their approach bore fruit, even if it did take the
best part of a century. Such a proposition overlooks important details, how-

ever, including the fact that the authors of this strategy had clearly hoped to obtain immediate relief. Indeed, it would be no exaggeration to maintain that until the beginning of the 1970s, the curve of South Africa's achievements in human rights sloped downward. Previous so-called accomplishments, such as the limited racial franchise of the 1910 constitution, and the limited access to university education and to apprenticeships for certain categories of non-Europeans, were systematically dismantled through repeal of the relevant legislation by the apartheid regime.

It is also a fact that, with episodic exceptions, the movement for national liberation accepted the international legality, if not the legitimacy, of the South African state. The key to the synchronization of these two spheres was attainment of the franchise for all adult male (and later female) South Africans. The territorial integrity of the South African state, as defined in 1910, was never seriously questioned by any faction within the movement, although in the early 1930s the Communist Party of South Africa briefly floated the idea of a Federation of Independent Soviet Socialist Republics based on linguistic-ethnic criteria. If truth be told, it is doubtful whether even the collaborationist Bantustan leaders of the 1970s and 1980s seriously believed in the "independence" that had been thrust upon them and "their" peoples.

Noncollaboration and Nonviolence

ᦾ

Until 1960, when the massacre of Sharpeville removed the blinders from the eyes of the entire prodemocracy political leadership, nonviolent approaches to the attainment of reforms and improvements were the stock-in-trade of the movement for national liberation, ranging from abject petitioning of the relevant authorities by respectful delegations of prominent black people, to militant boycotts of racially defined government institutions. In spite of profound philosophical and strategic differences within the movement, a range of nonviolent methods including street protests, passive resistance and defiance campaigns, strikes, boycotts, petitions, mass meetings, conferences, and memoranda were tried, in many different contexts and for many different purposes: some excessively opportunistic, others hopelessly rigid and self-defeating. But, before 1960, there was seldom any serious talk about armed revolution or insurrection, even though there was much rhetoric on the left about overthrowing the state. Even those like the members of the Non-European Unity Movement who accused the leaders of the Congress Movement of being "pacifist" and "compromisist" tended to believe that, one fine day, a general strike would bring down the racist regime.

Political Programs

✺

The fact of the matter is that while tactics may have differed, after 1949 the strategic differences between and among the different tendencies of the liberation movement (African nationalist, socialist, communist, and Pan-Africanist) were hardly significant. The overwhelming might of the apartheid state simply limited the options available to the forces of liberation.

In South Africa, as elsewhere, the Russian Revolution and, after 1945, the Cold War left their enduring imprint on the movement as a whole. The entire spectrum, from the liberal-democratic center to the extreme-socialist Left, was represented in this political landscape. (The political influence of the traditionalist Right on the popular movement was negligible after 1945. The penetration of capital into the subcontinent had weakened its social and political force, although its cultural and symbolical significance would endure, much like that of the British royal family.) Though there were numerous variants within each of these political milieus, it is possible to generalize.

Essentially, all these movements accepted the basic legacy of the rights of man, which had become an integral component of political discourse in all the colonies of Europe, especially after 1945. However, the socialist Left and the Communist Party of South Africa considered these demands for equality and liberty to be minimum demands, rather than the end of the struggle. They believed that socioeconomic rights were either unarticulated in bourgeois democratic programs, or were hobbled by the democrats' explicit acceptance of the right to private property in the means of production. In other words, the socialists and Communists felt that the bourgeois democratic approach fundamentally precluded any effort at redistribution. Between the non-Communist Left and the Communist Party of South Africa (CPSA, later known as the SACP) there was, generally speaking, a deep disagreement about whether the struggle for civil and political rights implied a segmentation of the national liberation struggle into two stages, in the first of which the minimum program would be realized, and in the second of which the struggle for socialist democracy would be conducted in a relatively peaceful manner. For some tendencies within the non-Communist Left (organizations such as the Non-European Unity Movement, for example), the right to the land was "the alpha and omega "of the struggle. Because rural and migrant workers would be unable to exercise their right to buy land on the morrow of the bourgeois democratic revolution, the revolution would remain incomplete. This tragic contradiction pushed the bourgeois democratic revolution over into socialist revolution.

Real historical developments have since rendered most of these debates irrelevant. However, besides the fact that this dispute over the land question demonstrates an acute awareness of the difference between substantive notions of democracy and mere procedural or minimalist understandings of the concept, the opposing viewpoints were clearly informed by the global divide between radical and liberal notions of social transformation.[3] More important, however, is the fact that all these discussions presumed that democratic rule would necessarily be black majority rule. Of course, the more conservative tendencies took it for granted that this transition would be a secular process, the tempo of which would be dictated by the speed with which the white man would jettison his racist beliefs and practices.

Thus, beginning with the CPSA's seminal discussions about the Black Republic in the late 1920s, it was assumed as a matter of course that (in the male chauvinist discourse of the time) the goal of the struggle was "one man, one vote." Group rights hardly featured as a point of discussion, except for a period during the mid-1950s, around the time when the Freedom Charter was being debated in the Congress Movement. Even point number 2 of the charter—"all national groups shall have equal rights"—was generally interpreted to refer to the right of individuals to live out their social and cultural preferences within the social category with which they identified. The main justification for this position, besides the hegemony of individualist liberalism, was undoubtedly the fear of playing into the hands of apartheid strategists and ideologues. Indeed, it can be said that one of the major challenges facing the postapartheid dispensation has been the creative resolution of this tension between the historically evolved ethnic and racial consciousness of the population, and their intuitive aversion to group affiliations because of the ways in which such categories were abused by the white supremacist regime. The promotion of national unity, national identity, and social cohesion will, with due regard to the contradictory and often conflicting nature of these goals, ultimately depend on how this fundamental tension is resolved.

The major premise of most of the programmatic documents of the South African struggle, no matter how inarticulate, is that a democratic South Africa would inevitably be framed in terms of a nonracial ethos: as a system in which ideas and practices based on the concept of race, whether viewed through the discredited lens of biology or through the more realistic lens of sociology, would wither away in the face of a demographically real black majority that had been brutally oppressed through precisely these notions of race. It is, therefore, pertinent to note that it was the Congress Movement, whose multiracial ideology accepted the social reality of the four "races," which became the heir to the apartheid regime, rather than any of the other tendencies that had explicitly emphasized their nonracial orientation. These ideological dilemmas and ambivalences manifested themselves most powerfully during the 1970s and the 1980s, when the Black Consciousness Movement set out to create a unifying paradigm for the liberation movement as a whole: one that was to be based on the paramount interests and independence of the black man, but which promised to inaugurate a nonracial era after the demise of apartheid. The mobilizations of the 1980s under the banner of the National Forum and, much more prominently and enduringly, under that of the United Democratic Front, appeared to decisively shift the focus toward the nonracial wing of the movement; but it was clear to perceptive analysts and commentators that that focus could easily be changed, depending on the balance of political forces. At the time of writing, there is no doubt at all that it has indeed shifted back toward the multiracial pole. The fact that South Africans in the post-apartheid era continue to contest the relationship between an unavoidable national identity and their various subnational identities clearly demonstrates the tenacious hold of history on the consciousness of the masses. The most optimistic conclusion to draw from this ongoing contestation is that it is continuing—that no "end of South African history" is in sight.

The Historic Compromise and Affirmative Action

∾

In South Africa, affirmative action is a direct consequence of the fact that the apartheid regime was not overthrown by military means.[4] In a nutshell, regime change was accomplished through a historic compromise between Afrikaner and African nationalist leaders. To be accepted, such a compromise had to demonstrate visible and immediate benefits for the majority of the people. Since the profound social and economic inequalities of the apartheid era did not disappear the morning after the settlement was signed, the real beneficiaries of the deal have been the bourgeoisie and the rising black and established white middle and professional classes.

For South Africa's owners of capital, the agreement has opened the door to an inflow of foreign direct investment, multinational mergers and joint ventures, and investment in and trade with the rest of the world (especially the rest of Africa), free of the sanctions that helped choke the apartheid regime to death.[5] The consistent growth of the economy in favor of capital accumulation incontestably testifies to this conclusion. For the black middle class, the new dispensation is a dream come true—albeit much in the manner of Bell's version of the Bluebeard allegory. On the one hand, the demand for skilled labor that necessarily accompanies all this economic growth creates apparently limitless opportunities for the lucky ones who manage to escape from the desolation of the rural areas and urban shacklands. These are, clearly, the real beneficiaries of an affirmative action strategy based on race (and gender and disability, be it noted), because they alone have qualifications comparable to those of their white counterparts, who, ironically, are the progeny of people who directly benefited from the prowhite affirmative action strategies of the segregationist and apartheid regimes. On the other hand, these same black middle strata have not accumulated the same economic and (in the Eurocentric universe in which they compete) cultural assets as their white counterparts, and are, therefore, always skating on very thin ice.

The potentially devastating consequences of this scenario are now being realized in the first years of the new millennium. Defensive racist attitudes of entitlement and professional incompetence, which breed inferiority complexes and resentment toward any hints of excellence; elitist attitudes and aspirations; glamorous lifestyles amidst the devastation of the townships and former homelands; rent-to-own fantasy worlds that crumble into dust within a few months; the blight of corruption, fraud, and outright theft, as well as a tendency toward denialism with respect to anything that points to the nightmarish quality of the "dream": these features, among many others, are voiding the advantages of democracy and freedom that have fallen into the lap of this class. They are every bit as common among the white middle classes, of course, since white men and women are also living and working in an integrated economy where the pressure is always in the direction of seizing the main chance. There is no doubt, however, that the likelihood and frequency of these features is much higher among upwardly mobile black people than among whites.[6] It is in this context that institutions of higher education have to grapple with the dilemmas and contradictions of affirmative action, as currently understood and applied in South Africa.

NOTES

1. R. Davenport and C. Saunders, *South Africa: A Modern History* (London: Macmillan; New York: St. Martin's Press, 2000).

2. N. Alexander (No Sizwe), *One Azania, One Nation: The National Question in South Africa* (London: Zed Press, 1979), and N. Alexander, "Approaches to the National Question in South Africa," *Transformation* 1, no. 1 (1986): 63–95.

3. N. Alexander, "Capitalism and Democracy in South Africa," in *The Limits of Capitalist Reform in South Africa*, ed. A. Nash (Cape Town: University of the Western Cape, 1993).

4. For my particular view on the process and the implications of the transition in South Africa, see N. Alexander, *An Ordinary Country: Issues in the Transition from Apartheid to Democracy* (Pietermaritzburg: University of Natal Press, 2002).

5. Elsewhere I have pointed out that for historical reasons, this class consists almost exclusively of people labeled "white" and, except in the unlikely event of some radical social transformation, will remain so for the foreseeable future. N. Alexander, "Brown v. Board of Education: A South African Perspective," in *With More Deliberate Speed:*

Achieving Equity and Excellence in Education—Realizing the Full Potential of Brown v. Board of Education, ed. A. Ball (Malden, MA: Blackwell, 2006).

6. I have tried to discuss some of the alternatives to this apparently unstoppable development in an as yet unpublished paper. N. Alexander, "South Africa Today: The Moral Responsibility of the Intellectuals," lecture delivered at the Tenth Anniversary celebration of the Foundation for Human Rights, in Pretoria, South Africa, November 29, 2006.

Affirmative Action in Higher Education over the Next Twenty-five Years

A Need for Study and Action

ᑢ

Sandra Day O'Connor and Stewart J. Schwab

Affirmative action in higher education remains controversial and vexing. Few people argue that consideration of race in college or law-school applications would be the best policy in an ideal world. In that world, skin color would be treated like eye color (or perhaps like one's religion, whose differences the ideal world would tolerate and celebrate but not rank invidiously). In today's America, however, race still matters in painful ways.

No one knows for sure how best to move toward that ideal world. As with many contested legal or policy propositions, the arguments in the affirmative action debate tend toward absolutes. One position asserts that a university should never consider race in admissions decisions, no matter how grave the problem it seeks to remedy. Another counters that all race-conscious efforts—be they goals, quotas, or something else—are permissible in the name of diversity, regardless of whether they intensify the very racial antagonism they seek to remedy. Whatever the attractiveness of these absolutes, the Supreme Court has never adopted them, and we do not advocate for them here.

The tension between the competing absolute positions was apparent in the 1978 case of *Regents of the University of California v. Bakke.* In the 1970s, the University of California at Davis Medical School employed an affirmative action policy in which 84 of the 100 available spots for incoming students were filled through a standard admissions process focusing on grades and standardized test scores. The 16 remaining spots, however, were filled through a separate process designed to increase the low numbers of racial minorities being admitted under the standard process. These 16 slots were in effect reserved for racial minorities, and cut-off scores for these places were lower than for students admitted under the standard criteria. A 32-year-old NASA engineer named Allan Bakke contested Davis's admissions program, asserting that it operated as an impermissible quota system.

The breakdown of the Court's votes in *Bakke* revealed the polarized positions at issue. Four justices thought that the program should be invalidated simply because it used race to allocate slots. Another four justices thought with equal fervor that Davis's admissions program should pass constitutional muster because, by their lights, the plan had no stigmatizing intent or effect. Writing only for himself, Justice Powell attempted to carve out some middle ground and, in the process, explain to all eight of his colleagues why they were wrong—or, as Justice Powell himself might have put the point, to demonstrate why those eight colleagues were *somewhat* correct. His opinion (which became the controlling opinion in the case) showed how university admissions officials could constitutionally use race in a tempered but not single-minded way. The opinion succeeded admirably, allowing universities to experiment with affirmative action while counseling them against becoming too comfortable in doing so.

One difficult issue that Justice Powell's opinion confronted was the level of applicable scrutiny. The university contended (and four justices agreed) that because its program sought to include rather than exclude racial minorities, the Court should apply a diminished standard of review, rather than the usual "strict scrutiny" otherwise applicable to racial classifications. Justice Powell rejected this contention, however, asserting that strict scrutiny applied even to supposedly benign racial classifications. Drawing on the Court's precedent in *Hirabayashi* and *Korematsu* (which applied strict scrutiny but nevertheless upheld the constitutionality of the government's curfew and exclusion during World War II of Japanese-Americans from large military zones in California), Justice Powell wrote: "Racial and ethnic distinctions of any sort are inherently suspect and thus call for the most exacting judicial examination."

Nevertheless, Justice Powell did not believe that strict scrutiny doomed all university efforts to foster racial diversity. In analyzing the Davis program, he found that it was impermissibly race conscious because it set aside a certain number of places for racial minorities, establishing what was in effect a spoils system. According to Justice Powell, this approach unfairly insulated the 16 spots from competition: "Fairness in individual competition for opportunities, especially those provided by the State, is a widely cherished American ethic," he wrote. Looking beyond the specifics of the Davis program, however, Justice Powell reasoned that some admissions programs that took race into account in composing the entering class, like the one at Harvard, could survive constitutional scrutiny. Such programs were permissible, according to Justice Powell, because "race or ethnic background may be deemed a 'plus' in a particular applicant's file, yet it does not insulate the individual from comparison with all other candidates for the available seats. The file of a particular black applicant may be examined for his potential contribution to diversity without the factor of race being decisive when compared, for example, with that of an applicant identified as an Italian-American if the latter is thought to exhibit qualities more likely to promote beneficial educational pluralism." And Justice Powell was careful to note that racial diversity was but one type of diversity that universities could pursue: "[E]thnic diversity . . . is only one element in a range of factors a university may properly consider in attaining the goal of a heterogeneous student body."

Justice Powell rejected absolute positions because he thought they were ill-suited to addressing the complex and competing concerns swirling around affirmative action in higher education. He rejected the color-blind absolute because he was wary of the educational resegregation that would have likely occurred in the absence of race-conscious admission programs. And he rejected the benign racial classification absolute, in turn, because he did not want to abandon the goal of transitioning, however deliberately, toward a color-blind society. Instead, Justice Powell confronted the world as he saw it, without extinguishing the promise of the world that he hoped we would all one day see.

Perhaps predictably, commentators attacked Justice Powell's decision from a wide variety of vantage points. In a 1979 article in the *Washington University Law Quarterly* titled "The Disease as Cure," then-professor Antonin Scalia (now a Supreme Court justice) wrote that "Justice Powell's opinion . . . strikes me as an excellent compromise between two committees of the American Bar Association on some insignificant legislative proposal. But it is thoroughly unconvincing as an honest, hard-minded, reasoned analysis of an important provision of the Constitution."[1] Not to be outdone, then-professor Guido Calabresi (now a judge on the U.S. Court of Appeals for the Second Circuit) published a piece entitled "Bakke as Pseudo-Tragedy" in the *Catholic University Law Review* that same year, in which he declared: "It may be that Justice Powell is right. But the dangers of using subterfuges are sufficiently great and the temptation to rely on them unnecessarily so substantial, that any uncandid solution should be suspect. For that reason I remain unconvinced, and continue to regard the opinion in *Bakke* as more tragic than the underlying choices."[2] Despite the initial criticism, Justice Powell's approach has endured.

Justice Powell's opinion helped shape the views of many on affirmative action in higher education, admittedly including the authors of this article, one of whom wrote the majority opinion in *Grutter v. Bollinger*. In considering the University of Michigan Law School's affirmative action program, the majority opinion stated: "[T]oday we endorse Justice Powell's view that student body diversity is a compelling state interest that can justify the use of race in university admissions." Following Justice Powell's lead, the majority applied strict scrutiny in reviewing both the Michigan law school's program in *Grutter* and the university's undergraduate program in *Gratz*. In *Grutter*, the Court acknowledged the importance of context, contending that "[n]ot every decision influenced by race is equally objectionable, and strict scrutiny is designed to provide a framework for carefully examining the importance and the sincerity of the reasons advanced by the governmental decisionmaker for the use of race in that particular context."

Applying strict scrutiny, the Court reached different conclusions in assessing the two University of Michigan programs. The Court invalidated the undergraduate admissions program at issue in *Gratz* because out of 100 points needed to gain admission it rigidly assigned a 20-point bonus to applicants from racially underrepresented backgrounds. This program, the Court reasoned, defied the individualized assessment that was the hallmark of the permissible race-conscious admissions programs that Justice Powell validated in *Bakke*.

When the Court examined the law school's admissions program, in contrast, it rejected calls demanding a totally race-blind admissions process. Instead, the Court concluded that educational institutions should be permitted to consider race because prohibiting them from doing so might intensify the nation's racial problems, rather than eliminate them. The Court was guided to this conclusion in part by an amicus brief filed by retired military leaders, who contended that without affirmative action they would have a nearly all-white officer corps commanding an overwhelmingly minority group of enlisted soldiers. The military leaders suggested that such a stark racial disparity could damage the military's morale. The Court also heard from many corporations who urged that some minimal forms of race consciousness be permitted because today's workforce must be prepared to work with colleagues and customers from a wide variety of backgrounds. Acknowledging that law schools often act as paths to power and leadership, the majority declared that "[e]ffective participation by members of all racial and ethnic groups in the civic life of our Nation is essential if the dream of one Nation, indivisible, is to be realized. In order to cultivate a set of leaders with legitimacy in the eyes of the citizenry, it is necessary that the path to leadership be visibly open to talented individuals of every race and ethnicity."

While the Court in *Grutter* validated the University of Michigan's law school program, it also echoed Justice Powell in stressing that affirmative action should be a temporary bandage, rather than a permanent cure. "Enshrining a permanent justification for racial preferences would offend this fundamental equal protection principle," the Court wrote. The *Grutter* majority further suggested that these programs must eventually fade away. "It has been 25 years since Justice Powell first approved the use of race to further an interest in student body diversity in the context of public higher education," the Court noted. "Since that time, the number of minority applicants with high grades and test scores has indeed improved. We expect 25 years from now, the use of racial preferences will no longer be necessary to further the interest approved today." That 25-year expectation is, of course, far from binding on any justices who may be responsible for entertaining a challenge to an affirmative action program in 2028. Those justices will be charged—as Lewis Powell was in *Bakke* in 1978, and as the Court was in *Grutter* in 2003—with applying abstract constitutional principles to concrete educational endeavors.

Educators should not take this 25-year expectation, however, as a grace period to postpone consideration of affirmative action for another generation. Thought, study, and action are needed now.

Three modest points merit attention in this context. To restate our most basic point: our society does not want to be in the same quandary 20 years from now (over five having already gone by since the 2003 *Grutter* decision) that it currently faces in affirmative action in higher education. Freeing ourselves from this quandary will require many types of action, but perhaps most essentially it will require continued research, debate, and innovation by academics, policymakers, and the public at large. Educators should use the next 20 years to evaluate their admissions dilemma, rather than carry on business as usual. Indeed, the deference society shows to higher-education leaders in formulating policy obligates them to use their talents and resources continually to assess themselves. These 20 years should be sufficient time to gather data and experiment with alternatives to directly considering race to promote student-body diversity and excellence.

Voters in several states have already mandated that educators not wait 20 years. In 1996, California voters passed Proposition 209, which required that the state's public universities abandon race-based affirmative action. The state of Washington passed a similar measure in 1998. Public universities in Florida and Texas have also eliminated affirmative action. In 2006, Michigan voters passed Proposal 2, designed to end "preferential treatment" in university admissions based on race, gender, ethnicity, and national origin. Similar ballot initiatives are under way in other states. Like it or not, change is upon us. One benefit of cultivating various approaches to affirmative action is the opportunity to assess whether effective alternatives exist to considering race in achieving educational quality and diversity.

Our second point is that higher education cannot resolve the admissions dilemma on its own, because higher education is powerless to alter the basic profile of its applicant pool. Unless major changes are made in our K–12 education system, higher education 20 years from now will face the same conflict between educational talent and diversity that it faces today. But K–12 is not the only culprit. African Americans face a myriad of challenges that powerfully alter the profile of applications to higher education, including an extraordinarily high imprisonment rate among black males and a culture that often discourages academic success.

Our third point is a plea for more social-science information on the benefits of diversity itself. When the time comes to reassess the constitutionality of considering race in higher-education admissions, we will need social scientists to clearly demonstrate the educational benefits of diverse student bodies, and to better understand the links between role models in one generation and the aspirations and achievements of succeeding generations.

The K–12 Problem

⤳

Admissions officers working to achieve a racially diverse student body are currently faced with the stark realization that the academic qualifications of black applicants to selective colleges and law schools are substantially weaker than those of white applicants. This disparity forces a conflict between efforts to select the most academically able students and parallel efforts to create a diverse class. Universities can either set aside their interest in academic quality, or ignore the goal of racial diversity, or try to balance the two goals as best they can. But unless our K–12 system narrows this gap, higher education will face the same quality-versus-diversity dilemma in 20 years that it faces today.

Attendance and achievement data on the American K–12 system reveal troubling racial disparities. Blacks are more likely than whites to have poor attendance records in school and to drop out of high school.[3] Blacks consistently score lower than other ethnic groups in reading, mathematics, and science, and the performance discrepancies between white and black students have not significantly improved since the mid-1980s.[4] Some evidence indicates that the black-white gap, particularly in mathematics, increases in junior high and remains constant in high school,[5] suggesting that the transition to adolescence poses a particular academic challenge for blacks. Black students are less likely than whites to take advanced academic classes in high school, and are far less likely to take advanced-placement tests.[6]

The trends are not uniformly bleak. Black students have substantially narrowed the gap with whites since the 1970s in their mathematics and reading scores on the SAT and National Assessment of Educational Progress (NAEP) examinations.[7] The black-white difference in high school/ GED completion rates has also narrowed substantially in roughly the same period.[8] Programs for very young children, such as the Head Start prekindergarten program, may be particularly effective in increasing the

relative achievement of blacks. Put more pessimistically, differences in outcomes at age three are similar to those among adolescents, suggesting that
efforts to reduce test-score gaps must start in preschool.[9]

A key question is whether K–12 administrators may themselves explicitly
consider race in making school assignments or other policies. School assignments are critical because more than two-thirds of black students are
enrolled in schools with predominantly minority student bodies.[10] The
Supreme Court recently addressed this issue in *Parents Involved in Community Schools v. Seattle School District No. 1*, 127 S. Ct. 2738 (2007). As always,
the facts of the particular case are critical. But we found persuasive Justice
Kennedy's perspective that the simple "postulate that '[t]he way to stop discrimination on the basis of race is to stop discriminating on the basis of
race' . . . is not sufficient," and that "[f]ifty years of experience since Brown
v. Board of Education . . . should teach us that the problem before us defies
so easy a solution" (id. at 2791). A mandate that school officials ignore the
racial makeup of our schools ignores the complexity of the situation.

Cascades and the Prison Problem

∾

The racial disparities familiar to college admissions officers do not arise just
from primary schools, however. Other factors contribute to the racial gap.
While all children face challenges in becoming high academic achievers,
black children confront more of these challenges. Motivated children can
overcome poor primary education, but it is harder to do so if one is poor,
has unstable family support, lives in a dangerous neighborhood, or is
threatened with prison.[11] The cumulative challenges create a devastating
cascade for many black children, greatly impeding their academic progress.

Let us comment briefly on the prison issue. The number of black males
in prison is staggering. In 2004, almost 13 percent of black males age 25 to 29
were in prison or jail, compared to only 1.7 percent of whites.[12] One-third of
black men can expect to be imprisoned sometime in their life, compared to
6 percent of white men.[13] Perhaps most appalling is the statistic that more
black men graduate from prison than college.[14] Imprisonment harms not
only the individual, but also family members and others in their social network, raising the economic, social and psychological hurdles to success.[15]
Moreover, the relative imprisonment rates for black versus white men are
considerably higher than those of black versus white women.[16] This illustrates that there is considerably more to the racial-gap problem than K–12
education, important as that may be, since girls and boys generally attend
the same schools.

A final point we observe here is the multifaceted racial and ethnic tapestry of contemporary America, compared to a generation ago. In 1970, most policymakers could focus solely on black/white comparisons, because blacks and non-Hispanic whites made up 98.6 percent of the U.S. population.[17] Today, a higher percentage of the U.S. population is Hispanic or Latino (14.5 percent) than African American (12.1 percent), while Asian-Americans comprise another 4.3 percent of the population.[18] Many of these racial shifts have come from changes in immigration policy, including the major alterations to the quota system of the 1965 Hart-Cellar Act.[19] Policymakers should not lump all racial and ethnic minorities together, and of special concern is the specter that African Americans remain on the low rungs of academic and economic achievement as other ethnicities surge ahead.

Understanding the causes of the racial differences we have sketched, and figuring out policy responses, remains a huge task for our nation's scholars and policymakers. But unless substantial progress is made, higher education will continue to face the dilemma of choosing between educational achievement and diversity.

The Value of Diversity in Higher Education

∾

Many benefits flow from having a racially diverse student body in colleges and graduate and professional schools. This is an article of faith for many, but further social science research is needed in order to refine our appreciation of diversity's value and to enable us to balance the value of diversity against the cost of achieving diversity through race-conscious programs.

It is widely understood that diversity enriches the college experience both in and out of the classroom. The claim is not so much that members of one race necessarily offer a distinctive viewpoint that others would find worth hearing. Rather, it is that, given our diverse society, all students will benefit from learning how to interact with and understand individuals of different races. Very often, the invaluable lesson is that we are more similar than different.

Another benefit of educational diversity comes from the value of role models. If children can identify with prominent persons in our society, they may be inspired to surmount hurdles and achieve similar positions. We collectively hope that a young person will take as role models persons in socially acceptable positions, like doctors and lawyers, rather than drug dealers or others in undesirable positions of influence. Assuming that children most emulate persons from their own race, then members of all races need to obtain the necessary college, graduate, and professional degrees to be effective role models. Today, they cannot do so in substantial numbers unless admissions officers consider race as a factor. Racial diversity in leadership positions can also increase productivity in the workplace. The amicus briefs filed by retired military officers and by various corporations in *Grutter* garnered significant attention, and were cited by the Court, for making this argument.

A third benefit of educational diversity comes from the diversity it creates in our political process. College graduates participate more frequently and effectively in our democratic institutions than do less-educated citizens. For example, over 70 percent of blacks with at least a bachelor's degree voted in the November 2000 elections, while only 42 percent of those failing to complete high school cast a ballot.[20] Promotion of racial diversity among college students, then, should promote diversity in our institutions of democracy.

We hesitate to cite scholarly work to back our speculations in this part. Certainly useful studies have already been conducted on the benefits from diverse student bodies, but in our view more needs to be done. "Diversity studies" are fraught with political implications, and many fear that the results of any particular study will be manipulated. But the response to this fear should be a call for more studies by scholars of all stripes, rather than a reluctance to examine seriously for fear the answers will be used to distort rather than inform policy.

The various hypothesized benefits of diversity have different long-run implications, and social science will have to evaluate the hypotheses in various ways. To examine the educational benefits of a diverse student body in higher education, for example, researchers will need to discern how the relative degree of school integration helps or harms the educational achievements of black, white, Hispanic, and Asian students. Does variance along this dimension lead to measurable differences in classroom discussions on subjects like immigration, abortion, ecological diversity, or capital punishment? Do students become more or less tolerant of members of other racial groups, as they are exposed to classmates from those groups?

Any social-science consensus that could be reached on these questions would help educational policymakers, even if the resulting prescriptions vary. For example, if the educational achievement of both black and white students seems to be harmed by the classroom integration of students with varying academic qualifications, surely that would give proponents of continued affirmative action some pause. What if classroom discussions are found to be less robust in integrated settings, as students are chilled from saying what they really think about policies affecting other racial groups who might be present? Perhaps most disturbing for affirmative action would be studies suggesting that integrated student bodies make students less, rather than more tolerant. The importance of the topic should not prevent us from asking questions whose answers might disappoint us. We applaud here the hard-minded work by political scientist Robert Putnam, who reports that ethnically diverse neighborhoods tend to have less trust and cooperation, thus reducing in the short run a society's social solidarity and social capital.[21]

The benefits of role models are also potentially measurable, although we have a harder time envisioning precise studies. One question is whether children in K–12 achieve more if they personally identify with a lawyer, doctor, or politician. Is the identification stronger with persons of the same racial or ethnic group? Or does affirmative action backfire as a means to foster role models, by fueling cynicism that positions are obtained by status rather than achievement—a cynicism that would inhibit, rather than promote, achievement in the next generation? Can we find others methods to document the productivity gains provoked by racial diversity in corporate leadership?

Current Experience in Race-Blind Admissions
∾

Public universities in at least five states are now mandated to ignore race in their admissions decisions. Their experience bears continued watching, especially as more states may soon follow suit. This chapter is not the place to document all that is happening, but a few observations may be helpful.

California has had the longest experience with race-blind admissions, and that experience suggests the effect on minority enrollments is dramatic. In 1995, the Board of Regents of the University of California System banned consideration of "race, religion, sex, color, ethnicity, or national origin" in admissions via Special Resolution SP-1, and in employment via Special Resolution SP-2. One year later, a successful ballot initiative, Proposition 209, expanded these prohibitions to all public entities in California. Minority enrollments soon plunged. In 1995, the eight-campus California system enrolled 945 African American freshmen. A decade later, in 2005, the system had only 909 African American freshmen, despite a 37 percent increase in the overall size of the freshman classes and a series of ameliorative efforts designed to continue recruiting minorities. The absolute number of Chicano and Latino freshmen increased from 3,432 to 4,652, but declined as a percentage of the student body, and substantially declined as a percentage of overall applications.[22]

The flagship campuses at UCLA and Berkeley saw the largest drops in African American enrollment. These elite campuses have the most stringent admissions standards, and affirmative action had consequently played a larger role in enrolling African Americans prior to Proposition 209. UCLA counted only 96 African American freshmen in fall 2006, down from 211 in fall 1997. Berkeley dropped from 258 African American freshmen to 140 in 2006. In a recent speech, UC president emeritus Richard Atkinson reported that "African American men, in particular, are virtually disappearing from our campuses," and that nearly half of the 83 African American men that UCLA and Berkeley admitted in 2004 entered on athletic scholarships.[23] In contrast to Latino enrollments, the percentage of African Americans at Berkeley and UCLA has not rebounded over the decade since Proposition 209.[24] The UC system's San Diego and Santa Barbara campuses also saw declines in African American enrollment during this period, albeit less dramatic ones than at Berkeley and UCLA, while the number and percentage of African Americans actually increased at the Davis, Santa Clara, Irvine, and Riverside campuses.

The admissions experience of Chicanos and Latinos at the University of California since Proposition 209 differs significantly from that of African Americans, a good illustration that minority groups in this country have distinct histories and experiences that should not be mindlessly lumped together. After Proposition 209, both Berkeley and UCLA experienced a sudden drop in Chicano and Latino freshmen. Berkeley went from 487 Chicano and Latino freshmen in 1997 to 264 in 1998, a decline of 46 percent. UCLA enrollment dropped from 600 to 451 during the same period, a 25 percent decline. But over the next decade, the absolute numbers of Chicano and Latino students gradually increased at both Berkeley and UCLA, so that by 2006 there were more Chicano/Latino freshmen enrolled (509 at Berkeley and 659 at UCLA) in absolute numbers than there had been a decade earlier. As a percentage of all students, however, Chicano/Latino enrollment in fall 2006 remained below the fall 1997 percentage at both campuses.[25]

The absolute decline in African American students and percentage decline in Chicano/Latino students at Berkeley and UCLA occurred despite considerable efforts by the University of California system to remain inclusive after Proposition 209. President Emeritus Atkinson recently outlined their indirect strategies. Outreach campaigns, which previously directly targeted candidates by race and ethnicity, now focus on low-performing high schools, which disproportionately include African Americans and Latinos. Admissions officers began to emphasize achievement tests over aptitude tests, and looked more closely at the obstacles applicants had overcome to succeed academically. The UC system also expanded transfer programs from community colleges.

Universities in other states with race-blind admissions have also emphasized outreach and related programs in an attempt to maintain racial and ethnic diversity. Richard McCormick, then-president of the University of Washington, helpfully categorized these efforts in a 2000 speech to the

American Association of Colleges and Universities as short term, medium term, and long term.[26] In November 1998, voters in his state passed Initiative 200, which banned the use of race or ethnicity in college admissions. The University of Washington saw a 32 percent drop in underrepresented minority freshmen the following year. As a short-term response, the University rethought the "personal factors" in its admissions criteria, and began to more highly value evidence of leadership, overcoming personal adversity, and cultural awareness, among other factors. Admissions staff also increased their recruiting efforts in areas of Washington and the west with large minority populations.

Pipeline efforts are the medium-term response. The University works with K–12 schools to identify and mentor talented minority students, raising their ambitions, counseling them to take college preparatory classes, and explaining the value of higher education. Methods can include tutorials by current college students, visits to campus, summer programs, and science contests. The goal is to increase the number of academically talented minorities who apply to college.

The long-term issues, as President McCormick framed them, involve overall K–12 school reform and changing dysfunctional cultures that perpetuate academic underachievement. As President McCormick observed, "For too many black youngsters, doing well in school is stigmatized as 'acting white.'" While universities can help these efforts by increasing our understanding of the issues and making policy prescriptions, the problems are society-wide.

Percentage plans for admissions are the most publicized feature of the new race-blind admissions policies. Texas was the first to implement a percentage plan, in 1997, in response to the *Hopwood* decision of the Court of Appeals for the Fifth Circuit, which declared that any race-conscious admissions policy violated the federal Constitution's equal protection clause. By statute, the top 10 percent of graduating students in any public or private high school in Texas are now guaranteed admission to the Texas public university of their choice, regardless of SAT scores or other factors. Because many Texas high schools have heavy minority enrollments, the 10 percent plan fosters some racial diversity without directly considering race. In 2000, Florida implemented a "Talented Twenty" plan as part of Governor Jeb Bush's One Florida executive decree, which forbade the university system from considering race in admissions. The Talented Twenty plan guarantees admission for the top 20 percent of every public high school in the state into one of the University of Florida campuses. In 2001, the University of California system implemented its 4 percent Eligibility in Local Context plan, which guarantees admission into the UC system for all students graduating in the top 4 percent of their high-school class.

The percentage plans vary in important details beyond the 4, or 10, or 20 percent cutoffs.[27] Florida limits its plan to public-school students, while the Texas and California plans include private schools. Florida and California only guarantee admission to a school in the system, while Texas guarantees admissions into the campus of the student's choice, including the more selective programs at the University of Texas–Austin and Texas A&M. Coursework requirements vary, as do such important details as how and by whom GPAs are calculated.

The effectiveness of these plans in increasing minority enrollment is debatable. The most competitive campuses see the least benefit. As we noted above, California's 4 percent plan does not offer direct access to UCLA or Berkeley, and those two campuses have seen no increases in African American enrollment over the last decade, and only limited absolute increases in Chicano/Latino enrollment. The Texas 10 percent plan does guarantee admission into the University of Texas–Austin to those who desire it, and over 70 percent of UT students are now admitted from the plan. African American undergraduate enrollment at UT rose above the 1996 pre-*Hopwood* levels for the first time in 2005 and 2006, after a 14 percent decline between 1996 and the low in 1999.[28] Some critics suggest that those campuses would have admitted most of the same students even without the plan, and that targeted recruiting and financial aid is more important than the percentage plan itself.[29] Furthermore, the effectiveness of percentage plans in promoting diversity depends entirely on segregated high schools, and so will not work in many states. Washington state, for example, did not consider a percentage plan because very few of its high schools were predominately minority.[30]

Michigan's Proposal 2, passed in November 2006, is the most recent state initiative mandating race-blind admissions in public universities. Responses are already under way. Wayne State University Law School, located in Detroit, has made a notable effort to comply with the law while still pushing for racial diversity. Wayne State admissions officers will now consider a variety of factors beyond grades and LSAT scores, including whether an applicant has overcome socioeconomic disadvantage, whether the applicant is bilingual, whether the applicant is a first-generation college graduate, and whether the applicant is a resident of (predominantly black) Detroit. In addition, law-school applicants will be invited to describe their experiences overcoming discrimination. Despite the new admissions plan, Wayne State administrators fear that their law school's 17 percent minority enrollment will drop considerably as it complies with Proposal 2's requirements.

Other Michigan universities are also responding. Shortly after Michigan voters passed the state constitutional amendment, University of Michigan president Mary Sue Coleman convened a task force to explore available options, seeking to avoid a sharp decline in minority enrollment. In its final report the task force suggested that the University should increase its outreach to minority communities and distribute proposed financial-aid packages to admitted students more quickly. But the task force was far from optimistic that these strategies would do much to sustain racial diversity among incoming students, at least in the near future. Surveying the experiences of states that had adopted measures similar to Proposal 2, the task force noted that those states "have experienced setbacks in demographic representation and discouraging dynamics in their campus interactions." The report further noted that given "the political similarities between the recent changes to the Michigan State Constitution and the situations faced in these states, there is little to suggest that our initial experiences will be any different."

The state initiatives do not purport to limit how private universities may determine which students gain admission. Rather, private schools would seem to be limited in their admissions schemes only by federal law, which to date closely tracks the Constitution. As interpreted by the United States Supreme Court in *Bakke* and now *Grutter,* the Constitution still permits nuanced consideration of race in admissions decisions. The result, oddly, could be that private universities can directly seek racial diversity while elite public universities are forbidden from doing so. As University of Michigan Law School dean Evan Caminker recently told the *New York Times,* "You'd think public universities are charged with special responsibility for ensuring access, but it could come to be exactly the opposite, if there are a lot of state initiatives."

Concluding Thoughts

∽

Our society needs citizens who participate in our democratic institutions and who are productive, broad-minded, and tolerant. A college education, and increasingly a graduate or professional degree, is the most reliable path for developing such citizens, as well as the most reliable path to individual success and fulfillment. This path must be practically available to individuals of every race. For now, affirmative action remains an important strategy for many universities in enabling individuals of all races to walk this path to success. With hard work, study, and experiment over the next 20 years, we will be in a position to assess whether affirmative action remains necessary to our efforts, or whether society can move on to the next step in our quest for a just society.

NOTES

1. Antonin Scalia, "The Disease as Cure," *Washington University Law Quarterly* (1979): 147, 148.

2. Guido Calabresi, "*Bakke* as Pseudo-Tragedy," *Catholic University Law Review* 28 (1979): 427–44.

3. See U.S. Department of Education, National Center for Education Statistics, Institute of Education Sciences, *Status and Trends in the Education of Blacks*, NCES 2003-034 42 (September 2003).

4. Ibid. at 48–53; U.S. Department of Education, National Center for Education Statistics, Office of Educational Research and Improvement, *Educational Achievement and Black-White Inequality*, NCES 2001-061 32–42 (July 2001).

5. U.S. Department of Education, *Black-White Inequality*, 32–42.

6. U.S. Department of Education, *Status and Trends*, 56–61

7. U.S. Department of Education, *Black-White Inequality*, 6–7.

8. Ibid., 4–5.

9. G. Farkas, "How Educational Inequality Develops," in *The Colors of Poverty: Why Racial and Ethnic Disparities Exist*, ed. A. Chih Lin and D. R. Harris (New York: Russell Sage, 2008).

10. U.S. Department of Education, *Status and Trends*, 28.

11. For example, two-thirds of children born to black mothers are in single-parent homes, a 31 percent increase from 1970, compared to 29.4 percent of children of white mothers (up from 5.5 percent in 1970). National Center for Health Statistics. *Health, United States, 2005* (Washington, DC: U.S. Government Printing Office, 2005).

12. U.S. Department of Justice, Bureau of Justice Statistics, Office of Justice Programs, *Prison and Jail Inmates at Midyear 2004*, NCJ 208801 11 (April 2005).

13. T. Bonczar, *Prevalence of Imprisonment in the U.S. Population, 1974–2001*, U.S. Department of Justice, Office of Justice Programs, Bureau of Justice Statistics Special Report NCJ 197976 (August 2003).

14. See B. Western, "Retrenching Civil Rights: Mass Imprisonment in America," in this volume (reporting that "recent birth cohorts of black men are more likely to have prison records [22.4 percent] than military records [17.4 percent] or bachelor's degrees [12.5 percent]").

15. D. Wheelock and C. Uggen, "Race, Poverty and Punishment: The Impact of Criminal Sanctions on Racial, Ethnic, and Socioeconomic Inequality," in Chih Lin and Harris, *The Colors of Poverty*.

16. U.S. Department of Justice, *Prison and Jail Inmates at Midyear 2004* (showing the number of inmates in state or federal prison or local jails per 100,000 residents to be 4,919 for black men, 717 for white men, 359 for black women, and 81 for white women).

17. Bureau of the Census, "Table 1. United States—Race and Hispanic Origin: 1790 to 1990," http://www.census.gov/population/documentation/twps0056/tab01.pdf, 2002 (visited on May 16, 2007).

18. Bureau of the Census, *American Community Survey Data Profile Highlights*, available at http://factfinder.census.gov/servlet/ACSSAFFFacts?_submenuId=factsheet_1&_sse=on, 2005 (visited on May 16, 2007).

19. Chih Lin, A. and D. Harris, "Why is American Poverty Still Colored in the 21st Century?" in Chih Lin and Harris, *The Colors of Poverty*.

20. Ibid., 125.

21. R. D. Putnam, "E Pluribus Unum: Diversity and Community in the Twenty-first Century, The 2006 Johan Skytte Prize Lecture," *Scandinavian Political Studies* 30 (2007): 137.

22. University of California, *Application, Admissions, and Enrollment of California*

Resident Freshmen for Fall 1995 through 2005, available at http://www.ucop.edu/news/factsheets/Flowfrc_9505.pdf (last visited March 21, 2007).

23. R. C. Atkinson and P. A. Pelfrey, "Opportunity in a Democratic Society: A National Agenda," paper presented at the conference Futuring Diversity: Creating a National Agenda, Ann Arbor, MI, May 18, 2005.

24. Over the decade beginning fall 1997, the percentage of all freshmen who were African American at Berkeley was 7.3 percent, 2.7 percent, 3.1 percent, 3.7 percent, 3.4 percent, 3.5 percent, 3.9 percent, 3.1 percent, 3.2 percent, and 3.3 percent, a steady trend at best. The comparable numbers at UCLA were 5.4 percent, 3.1 percent, 3.7 percent, 3.5 percent, 3.0 percent, 3.7 percent, 2.8 percent, 3.1 percent, 2.6 percent, 2.0 percent, which looks like a downward trend.

25. University of California, *Distribution of Statement of Intent to Register (SIRs) for Admitted Freshmen, Fall 1997 through 2006,* table 2, available at http://www.ucop.edu/new/factsheets/2006/froshsirs_table2.pdf (last visited March 21, 2007).

26. R. L. McCormick, "Advancing Diversity in a Post-Affirmative Action State: Implications for the Future," speech to the Association of American Colleges and Universities, Washington, DC, January 20, 2000, available at http://www.washington.edu/president/articles/AACU.html (last visited March 25, 2007).

27. See generally C. L. Horn and S. M. Flores, *Percent Plans in College Admissions: A Comparative Analysis of Three States' Experiences* (Cambridge: Civil Rights Project at Harvard University, 2003).

28. University of Texas at Austin Office of Institutional Research, 2005–6 and 2006–7 Statistical Handbooks, table S4A, "Fall Enrollment by Level and Ethnicity," available at http://www.utexas.edu/academic/oir/statistical_handbook/05-06/pdf/0506students.pdf (last visited January 23, 2000).

29. M. Tienda, K. Leicht, T. Sullivan, M. Maltese, and K. Lloyd, *Closing the Gap? Admissions and Enrollments at the Texas Public Flagships before and after Affirmative Action* (Princeton, NJ: Texas Top 10% Project, 2003).

30. McCormick, "Advancing Diversity."

From Redress to Empowerment

The New South African Constitution and Its Implementation

∽

Judith February

One of the fundamental characteristics of democracy is that it provides the institutional framework to process and address competing interests. Early in its transition to democracy, South Africa faced the challenge of establishing institutions through which its divided communities could realize their own interests. It was naturally an uncertain process, as if the creation of a new democracy required the assimilation of this uncertainty into its very institutional core.[1] This dilemma has shaped debates around affirmative action: how can one confront the problem of inequality, while simultaneously reassuring those who benefited under the previous regime that corrective measures would not amount to retribution? It was under such conditions that the South African concept of affirmative action developed, legislatively and philosophically.

The African National Congress (ANC) formally put the notion of affirmative action on the table as part of the negotiated settlement of the mid-1990s.[2] The two options before the drafters of the Constitution were quite clear. The first was to simply repeal all apartheid laws, adopt a new Constitution, and incorporate a Bill of Rights. A new Constitution based on the liberal notion of equality would not, however, have automatically improved the social order or created substantive equality. Indeed, an unqualified liberal Constitution could have served as a barrier to the redress of past injustices, as while its intentions would certainly have been noble, its implementation would have been a perhaps insurmountable challenge. The second option was to correct the injustices of the past by seizing and redistributing any wealth that had been accrued under apartheid. Although this might have wiped the slate clean, it could also have brought about the collapse of political negotiations, with the potential for an ensuing civil war, capital flight, and international isolation. The liberation movement prioritized the cautious negotiation of an affirmative action strategy that would correct the imbalances of the past over time, ensuring that race and gender would not continue to determine access to opportunities, but acknowledging that the process would have to be a judicious one.

According to Nelson Mandela, the question for the ANC was not about the need for affirmative action policies, but "how to apply affirmative action in a way that is resolute, fair and just to all concerned." He went on:

> Affirmative action must be rooted in principles of justice and equity. Affirmative action is a principal means of dealing in as just and realistic a manner as possible with the progressive eradication of the guilt created by the past discrimination. It must be seen as an alternative . . . to waiting for centuries for the market on its own to eliminate the massive inequalities left by apartheid.[3]

Regardless of one's views on the apartheid system's role in creating and entrenching systemic inequality, employment statistics argue in favor of affirmative action policies. From 1995 to 2002, a period during which many affirmative action policies were already in place, the number of people employed in South Africa rose from 9,557,185 to 11,157,818.[4] The proportion of black top managers increased from 12 percent to 13 percent between 2000 and 2001, and of senior managers from 15 percent to 16 percent. Skilled professionals and middle managers grew only by a marginal 0.2 percent. Black ownership in public companies increased from 3.9 percent in 1997 to 9.4 percent in 2002, and the number of Previously Disadvantaged Individuals (PDIs) identified as directors of public companies grew from 14 (1.2 percent) in 1992 to 438 (13 percent) in 2002.

The data on professional, associated professional, and technical employment shows that blacks comprised 61.4 percent of the individuals in these categories in 2001, up from 57.6 percent in 1996. In March 2006 the unemployment rate was 30.7 percent among black Africans, 18.9 percent for coloreds, 11.2 percent for Indians/Asians, and 4.7 percent for white youth. Thirty-six percent of African women were jobless, compared to only 6 percent of white women.[5] The number of women in top management increased 1 percent in 2000, to 13 percent overall, while women increased the share of top management positions from 1.7 percent to 17.7 percent.

These statistics make it clear that the employment (and skilled employment) rates for those groups disadvantaged under apartheid have risen since the implementation of affirmative action; but it is equally clear that vast inequalities remain to be overcome. While these statistics do not conclusively justify affirmative action, the high levels of continuing inequality (despite the progress of the last several years), and the lack of access to economic opportunity (especially for black Africans) at the very least, point to the continuing need for corrective measures. Essentially, the problem that affirmative action has made some progress in rectifying remains, and thus the need for such policy remains as well. Of course, it is possible to make the argument that the fact that inequalities remain means that affirmative action is not working, but that neglects the very statistics cited above, which show marked improvement in levels of employment equity.

In South Africa, as in the United States, disagreements over affirmative action projects often take the form of legal dispute, even though they are more properly a policy matter. This is often due to the fact that affirmative action policies are legislated—unlike economic policies, which are implemented without first being adopted into laws. As such, we should begin any study of affirmative action in higher education by looking at the legal provisions surrounding its implementation, since these form the basis for future legal challenges and defenses.

Legal Context
ᕁ

The central goals of the South African Constitution and Bill of Rights are to transform society and ensure both formal and substantive equality. Like the U.S. Constitution, the South African document includes an equal protection clause (although the American version was actually added years after the original drafting, as an amendment). Section 9(1) of the South African Constitution declares that "everyone is equal before the law and has the right to equal protection of the law," providing so-called blind equality and prohibiting discrimination on any of the listed grounds, including race, gender, sex, pregnancy, ethnicity, and color. Section 9(2) goes on to state that the definition of equality includes "the full and equal enjoyment of all rights and freedoms. To promote the achievement of equality, legislative and other measures designed to protect or advance persons, or categories of persons, disadvantaged by unfair discrimination may be taken." This "equality clause" authorizes action to correct previous injustices. To quote the sociologist Kanya Adam, affirmative action is therefore understood in South Africa as a "remedial strategy that seeks to address the legal historical exclusion of a majority."[6]

Education is the portfolio with the greatest budgetary expenditure in South Africa. Overall enrollment at schools has increased by 15 percent since 1992, and literacy and matriculation pass rates have also generally increased.

The President's 2006 Macro-Social report included a number of important findings on education:

- A decline of 14.4 percent in the percentage with no schooling and an increase of 11.9 percent with some primary education in the age group 0–19 years

- A decline in the proportion of Africans with no primary education from 28 percent to 13 percent, and an increase in the number of those with some primary education from 42 percent to 55 percent
- An increase in the percentage of population with Grade 12 completion or higher from 2.39 percent to 3.08 percent[7]

These numbers document an important positive trend in access to basic education. But access to higher education is still bedeviled by persistent constraints on economic and social mobility. The Higher Education Act of 1997 was adopted to deal with exactly this issue: Section 37 of the act states that all South African universities are required to develop and comply with "appropriate measures for the redress of past inequalities," but "may not unfairly discriminate in any way." The operative word is, of course, "unfairly." This apparently simple word has become a touchstone for much of the debate over the act, since it implies that there might be such a thing as "fair discrimination." As Albie Sachs, a justice on the South African Constitutional Court, has suggested, affirmative action policies are not inherently unconstitutional, "not because they are exempt, but because they are not unfair."[8] The language of "fair discrimination" is controversial, and in fact, completely absent from the American debate on affirmative action. It is essential, though, to understanding that South African affirmative action is a unique breed, in that it acknowledges the inherent discrimination in the system, but insists that this type of discrimination is both justified and necessary.

In the United States, by comparison, the legal legitimacy of affirmative action rests entirely on the Fourteenth Amendment and the Civil Rights Act of 1964, a fact that in various ways both complicates and simplifies the matter. Because of the dearth of concrete language on which one can build a solid conception of affirmative action, debates about the larger legal concept have more readily taken hold in the United States. Whereas in South Africa, as is usually the case in circumstances where policies are designed to address past wrongs, the disputes focus less on legal provisions than their implementation and effects. Despite the fact most South Africans seem to share a commitment to building an egalitarian society, as envisaged in the Constitution, they are engaged in heated debates over the effects of specific affirmative action policies on their society, rather than on the philosophical merits of affirmative action as a general concept. These debates have been replicated within the higher-education sector—always a microcosm of society's tensions and imbalances. Before attending to these popular debates, however, we need to understand the judiciary's interpretation of affirmative action legislation.

Judicial Interpretations of the Legal Context

ᴖ

In its attempt to correct past injustices through legislation, South Africa has drawn much from the American experience. But there are a number of important differences between the two countries' policies. First, American affirmative action is designed to assist a racial minority, whereas in South Africa, the policy is meant to aid the majority. Further, while affirmative action in South Africa has the support of a majority of citizens, in the United States it continues to be perceived as dependent on the paternal conscience of the majority. These differences in the interaction between the minority and the majority may seem insignificant at first, but they are particularly evident in the judicial interpretations of legislative and constitutional manifestations of affirmative action.

The important thing to note about the U.S. Supreme Court's *Bakke* and *Grutter* decisions is the hesitancy of the American judicial system (as well as the legislative branch) to formalize affirmative action. The Court's rejection of concrete, definable quotas as unconstitutional can be read as an assertion about the abstract and informal nature of affirmative action, and hence as a demonstration of the key difference between American and South African philosophies of the practice. In the United States, affirmative action was an almost accidental outgrowth of the civil rights movement—one that was not even considered until the 1960s, almost 200 years after the original drafting of the Constitution. In South Africa, of course, debates over affirmative action were a core element of the constitutional drafting process. The difference here is that in South Africa, affirmative action was seen as a necessary component of government structure and policy, essential enough to be stated specifically and explicitly in the language of the Constitution. In the United States, this was clearly not the case; not only is affirmative action an addendum, it is an informal one, with no official or explicit language to define it or integrate it into the basis of the democracy. If anything, it is carefully hidden from view: most affirmative action policies are formulated on an institution-by-institution basis, and are not standardized nor legislated (with the exception of the requirement that no quotas be used). In the United States, affirmative action is a clandestine affair, while in South Africa, it is widely acknowledged and applauded, which is clear in the legal language used to define it in both countries.

Perhaps even more significant is the "vested interest" argument used in both U.S. cases. The odd suggestion that universities cannot always justify their use of affirmative action to equalize opportunity and access across racial lines, but can most certainly justify those same policies in terms of an interest in student-body diversity, is essential to understanding the American concept of affirmative action. Affirmative action can be seen in the

American context, then, as not about the collective good of a previously oppressed racial group, but about the good of the individual educational institution. The importance of individual versus group rights will be addressed at greater length later in the discussion.

The story has been quite different in South Africa. Because such policies are relatively new in South Africa, particularly in regard to higher-education admissions, there is a comparative dearth of legal precedent. That said, there have been a number of significant cases that shed light on the country's judicial approach to the issue.

One of the earliest legal challenges to affirmative action came in the 1995 case of *Motala and Another v. University of Natal.* The parents of an Indian matriculant, Motala, filed a court petition challenging the University of Natal Medical School's decision to reject their daughter's application. It was submitted that Motala's matriculation results—through which applications to the school were assessed—were such that she should have been admitted. Motala further argued that some African students with lower grades than hers had been admitted, and that the university admission policy therefore discriminated unfairly on the basis of race.

The university argued that its admission policy took into account the poor standard of education available to African students under apartheid, which failed to adequately prepare them to meet the stringent criteria for university admission, particularly in specialized fields like medicine. The university's admission policy, argued its dean of health sciences, endeavored to overcome this difficulty by means of an affirmative action program. The university argued that its program took into consideration the "educational disadvantages to which certain students have been subjected and is directed at determining the true potential of each aspirant student." Furthermore, the university conceded, "matriculation results of accepted African applicants will in almost all cases be lower than those of other applicants who are not accepted."

The Court considered two questions in this case. The first was whether or not the university's policy violated the right to equality and equal protection of the law, and, if so, whether such a violation was reasonable and justifiable in an open democratic society. The second was whether an African applicant should be granted preference over an Indian applicant, since both groups could be categorized as historically disadvantaged. In other words, the case did not necessarily challenge affirmative action programs per se, but rather the distinction between Africans and Indians within that framework. The judge held that "while there is no doubt whatsoever that the Indian group was decidedly disadvantaged by the apartheid system, the evidence before me establishes clearly that the degree of disadvantage to which African pupils were subjected under the four-tier system of education was significantly greater than that suffered by the Indian counterparts."

The coherence and constitutionality of affirmative action policy also came under scrutiny in *Rugnath v. University of Cape Town*. The facts in this case were similar to those in the *Motala* case. The Indian applicant sought to challenge the admissions policy in the University of Cape Town (UCT) school of medicine, once again contending that the decision not to admit constituted unfair racial discrimination. It was submitted that the applicant's academic record was "superior to other Indian, African, colored and white students who had been admitted into the program." The applicant stated further that UCT's admission policy, if it constituted a policy at all, was "vague, unreasonable and irrational." In its response, UCT explained that its admission policy "gave effect to the statutory requirement that appropriate measures for the redress of past inequalities be provided," taking into consideration "that the conditions prevailing at schools for African and colored students are worse than those at other schools." Therefore, it was argued, the university's admission committee "attempts to provide an appropriate racial and gender diversity."

While the applicants and respondents agreed that the policy was prima facie discriminatory, the respondents argued that such discrimination was "reasonable, justifiable and necessary to redress the past inequalities."[9] The court dismissed the application, holding that Section 37(4) of the Higher Education Act allotted to the university the power to formulate its own admissions standards and requirements, as long as, in so doing, it dealt with the need to redress past inequalities, with the concepts of fairness and nondiscrimination in mind. It further insisted that the court "would be slow to interfere with the proper exercise of that power."[10]

The *Motala* and *Rugnath* decisions raised several issues. First of all, in South Africa "disadvantaged" was increasingly becoming not-synonymous with "black." This raised the question of whether race should be a determinant, or indeed the chief determinant, of student access to affirmative action. If these policies were intended to redress past inequalities, should their application be dependent on the extent of past inequalities suffered by the individual in question? Because of the intricate relationship between race and class in South Africa, race-based affirmative action acts as a proxy for socioeconomic disadvantage. Has class therefore become the new determinant for access? And, if so, is a race-based system of affirmative action inadequate to redressing inequality of access? Is it even fair? This same question has been raised in the American context, as well, and raises a much deeper issue: what, in fact, determines access? In both countries, it appears that race is still an important component, but perhaps not the only one.

Significantly, despite the conflict over the standards for affirmative action candidates, the general concept of affirmative action is not generally under attack in South Africa. In many legal cases, the applicant is not contesting the idea of formal affirmative action, but access to the benefits of those policies. Access to opportunity is the issue, and the language of "interest in diversity" and "interest of the university" that is so familiar in the American tradition is completely absent. While South African affirmative action is based on human rights principles, American policies are based on civil rights, which are more locally or nationally based than universally guaranteed.[11] The defense for affirmative action in the United States is somehow weaker and more tentative as a result.

Legacy and Statistical Transformation

∾

Affirmative action has led to sharp debates because it involves, or is perceived to involve, different groups of people competing for the same opportunities. While there may be general agreement on the broader principles of equality and justice, it has proven more challenging to produce consensus on the best way to realize these principles, or even acknowledgment that specific efforts are in fact required to pursue them.

One thing that most South Africans do accept is the existence of a legacy of inadequate and unequal education, produced by the previous system of legally segregated higher education. The Bantu Education Act of 1953 segregated universities and other schools both by race and, within the black population, by "tribe." It also closed down many nonpublic or religious schools in order to ensure the government's monopoly on black education, which it intentionally geared toward careers in trade or labor. As a result, by 1993 nearly 70 percent of white adult South Africans were enrolled in institutions of higher education, compared to 12 percent of blacks from the same age group.[12]

The collapse of apartheid has produced a measurable change in the proportion of black male enrollment in institutions of higher education. The proportion of women has also increased, from 42 percent in 1990 to 53 percent in 2000. The proportion of black students enrolled in South African universities increased from 32 percent in 1990 to 60 percent in 2000, while in the technikons it rose from 32 percent to 72 percent over the same period. By 2000, African students were the majority both in the universities (60 percent) and in technikons (72 percent). At some institutions, the composition of the student population changed even more dramatically. The balance of the student body at Nelson Mandela Metropolitan University changed from 62 percent white in 1995 to 87 percent black in 1999.[13] In the United States, too, participation by minorities and women in employment, education, business, and government contracts has been on the rise. Enrollment of black college students rose from 7.8 percent in 1970 to 11.3 percent in 1990. And according to the U.S. Bureau of Labor Statistics, between 1982 and 1995 the percentage of female managers and professionals increased from 40.5 percent to 48.0 percent; blacks from 5.5 percent to 7.5 percent; and Hispanics from 5.2 percent to 7.6 percent.

Serious discrepancies remain, however, in specialized fields such as mathematics, science, and engineering. Because these areas of study are generally only open to a few, their demographics often mirror the extent of access to opportunities, both social and economic, in society more generally. These are the areas where resistance has arisen as institutions of higher learning have attempted, through affirmative-action admission policies, to equalize access.

Breeding a Culture of Entitlement? Entitlement for Whom?

⁓

One of the major arguments against the use of affirmative action in education (as well as employment) is that it creates a culture of entitlement. Critiquing what he considers ill-conceived and poorly implemented affirmative action policies, the political scientist, physicist, and columnist Sipho Seepe has written that "the new black elite is spared the rigors of development. To demand excellence is regarded as blaming the victim and to deny the helplessness imposed by the heritage of oppression."[14] In essence, Seepe and his fellow critics of affirmative action argue that the beneficiaries of affirmative action are given a free pass, and are not forced to work as hard for their achievements, or to reach the same levels as their counterparts.

Seepe further argues that, because affirmative action policies impose a victim-versus-oppressor paradigm, affirmative action tends to crush the competitive instinct required to survive in the academic or professional world. He claims that such policies produce a new black generation lacking the competitive spirit and self-confidence necessary to compete academically, and thereby harm the very groups they are supposed to benefit.

Even proponents of affirmative action admit that "empowering the disempowered inevitably requires one sector of society to curtail its own advantage."[15] This difference in framing is important: while affirmative action's opponents describe the policy as disadvantaging the advantaged, its supporters speak of the advantaged merely curtailing their disproportionate advantage. The frame favored by the opponents only makes sense if someone is being deprived of something owed to them, not if an unfair advantage is being eliminated. While Seepe describes affirmative action as completing the cycle of entitlement, others believe that it completes the cycle of disadvantage by refusing to acknowledge that the disadvantaged are also entitled to the same educational opportunities as the rest of the population.

Racism of Another Kind / Reverse Discrimination
∾

The idea that affirmative action constitutes reverse racism in South Africa raises several interesting points about the idea of merit and the definition of advantage itself. Those who favor compensatory justice and advocate the correction of historical disadvantage claim that protective discrimination is a prerequisite for equality. Historically disadvantaged communities consider affirmative action policies necessary to bring about parity of knowledge and skill. Most importantly, though, the arguments in favor of affirmative action in South African higher education are centered on equality of access, the implication being that this equalizing of opportunity opens the doors to economic and professional access in turn.

But those who are overlooked in admissions and employment, or feel that they have been, argue that there is no room for such protectionism in the postapartheid society. This debate is muddled by struggles to reconcile the liberal notion of individual merit with the notion of group or community rights. The assumption here is that merit is not an independent variable, but rather a function of various other enabling factors. The question thus arises: how can one speak in terms of individual merit when one community has access to facilities and resources and another does not? South African communities' unequal access makes it difficult to judge applicants against one another, or against a single standard. The myth that merit is a quality independent of individual opportunity and access, and that it can therefore be evaluated separately from the two, is a cornerstone of many anti-affirmative action arguments. At the same time, of course, admissions processes become completely unfeasible in the absence of objective criteria.

The debate over whether affirmative action nurtures merit or breeds incompetence is often reduced to anecdotal observation. One common suggestion is that large-scale affirmative action policies have made local South African governments inefficient. But the validity of this example depends on perception: some would say this inefficiency is largely due to a dearth of skills and training, while other might suggest that the labor and capacity is there, but that affirmative action prevents its full utilization.

Nor is implementation ever free from politics, either. In the recent controversy over the University of Cape Town's affirmative action admission policies, Tony Leon—then leader of the Democratic Alliance, the country's main opposition party—questioned whether middle- and upper-middle-class black students were reaping the benefits of the policies instead of the poor and disadvantaged. The UCT registrar Hugh Amoore responded that past educational adversity was measured at the level of racial groups, rather than individuals.

This opposition of individual against group rights has clearly taken a different turn in the United States, where the courts and legislatures have been far more hesitant to create specific groups that could benefit from affirmative action. As mentioned earlier, the Supreme Court's invalidation of quota systems speaks to this culture of individual rather than group disadvantage, whereas the UCT decision clearly negated the individual merit argument in South African affirmative action.

It is possible to see this difference as indicative of the divergent treatment of race more generally in the two countries. The American reluctance to formalize racial categories and groups is emblematic of the country's prevailing philosophy of color blindness. Many Americans seem to believe that the race problem can be solved by eliminating the category from public discourse altogether; while in South Africa racial pride, consciousness, and affirmation are far more popular steps toward the ultimate goal of a nonracial society. Rather than ignoring race, South Africa has more typically confronted it, undoing its legacy of discriminatory use by temporarily institutionalizing racial categories in the framework of reconciliation and reparations.

The Sunset Clause

Critics of affirmative action, confronted with the claim that affirmative action is a necessary stepping stone on the path to a nonracial society, are increasingly calling for a sunset clause. This is very much in line with the premise that affirmative action is only a means to an end. But how and when will we know that affirmative action is no longer necessary?

Recently, the Tuks Afrikaanse Studente, a national Afrikaans student interest organization, asserted that the existing affirmative action policies should be amended to apply only to those individuals born before 1994. The group's formal submission to the Parliamentary Committee on Labour reasoned that those who had grown up with equal opportunities in the postapartheid era did not have a right to preferential treatment. Even though this argument negates the idea of historical injustice and path-dependent development, it has been supported by such organizations as the Federation of Unions of South Africa. The National Union of Metalworkers of South Africa (NUMSA), however, asserted that a black child born in a squatter camp in 2006 still does not enjoy the same privileges and opportunities as a white child. As long as there are black children who are disadvantaged because of their race, argued NUMSA, affirmative action will be necessary. Whether or not this is too reductive is subject to debate: what is evident, though, is that many South Africans believe race-based disadvantage still exists, and requires redress.

Calls for a sunset clause got a further boost when, in the 1996 case *George v. Liberty Life Association of South Africa,* the bench called for a similar qualification. The court focused on personal circumstances, noting that the plaintiff, George, was historically disadvantaged in his access to education. The decision held that affirmative action could not become a permanent feature of South African life; it could be countenanced only long enough to ensure that designated groups could compete on equal footing. Unlike the Supreme Court in *Grutter,* however, the South African court refrained from establishing a time when it should become possible to abandon the policy.

Paradoxically, the idea of a time horizon should actually be less important in the American context, of course, because the vested interest argument has no expiration date. Unless universities' interest in creating a beneficially diverse academic community somehow lessens with time, then there is no need to impose a deadline on affirmative action efforts to ensure campus diversity. It is only when affirmative action is seen exclusively as an equalizer of opportunity, as in South Africa, that the issue of an end date becomes relevant. This difference, too, is symptomatic of the vast separation between the American and South African interpretations of affirmative action.

The debate over affirmative action in South Africa is taking place in a context of extensive inequality, limited access, and few opportunities. The country has relatively few institutions of higher learning, creating a heightened competition for admission. Affirmative action is important in creating an environment where access to opportunity is not solely determined by one's race or gender, but it is not a monolith policy, and can take different forms, according to circumstance. Although South Africa and the United States use the same term and profess the same goals, affirmative action in these two countries continues to evolve quite differently.

NOTES

1. G. O'Donnell, P. Schmitter, and L. Whitehead, *Transitions from Authoritarian Rule* (London: Johns Hopkins University Press, 1986).

2. Albie Sachs, *Affirmative Action and the New Constitution* (ANC Dept. of Information and Publicity, 1995).

3. Nelson Mandela, ANC Constitutional Committee's Conference on Affirmative Action, 1991.

4. J. Seekings and N. Nattras, *Class, Race, and Inequalities in South Africa* (New Haven: Yale University Press, 2005).

5. Labour Force Survey, *Statistics South Africa,* March 2006.

6. Kanya Adam, "The Politics of Redress: South African Style Affirmative Action," *Journal of Modern African Studies* 35 (1997): 231–49.

7. Ibid.

8. Albie Sachs, "The Constitutional Principles Underpinning Black Economic Empowerment," in *Visions of Black Economic Empowerment,* ed. Xolela Mangcu, Gill Marcus, Khehla Shubane, and Adrian Hadland (Auckland Park, SA: Jacania Media, 2007), 9–17.

9. *Rugnath* at 5 par. 8.

10. *Rugnath* at 8 par. 11.

11. Akil Kokayi Khlfani, *The Hidden Debate: The Truth Revealed about the Battle over Affirmative Action in South Africa and the United States* (New York: Routledge, 2006).

12. Katherine C. Naff and Frederik Uys, "Representative Bureaucracy in South Africa: Success or Failure," paper presented to the annual meeting of the Midwest Political Science Association, April 7–10, 2005, Chicago.

13. Nico Cloete, "Equity and Development in Post-Apartheid South African Higher Education," in *South African Higher Education,* ed. Nico Cloete, Pundy Pillay, Saleem Badat, and Teboho Moja (Cape Town: James Currey, Oxford, and David Philip, 2004).

14. Sipho Seepe, "Can Affirmative Action Be Rescued? I Think Not," *Sunday Times,* February 6, 2005.

15. Sachs, "Constitutional Principles," 10.

Social Justice and Postapartheid Higher Education in South Africa

ᕲ

André du Toit

More than a decade after the 1994 launch of South Africa's postapartheid democracy, public debates remain much concerned with the role of "affirmative action" and "employment equity" policies in higher learning. David Benatar's 2007 inaugural lecture as professor of philosophy at the University of Cape Town, in which he questioned the logic and morality of current affirmative action policies, provoked a wide-ranging debate, not just in South African university circles but also in the correspondence columns and opinion pages of local newspapers.[1] These debates may look familiar to American eyes. However, the shared terminology of "affirmative action" may be misleading if taken at face value. It has long been recognized that, even if the wrongs of racial discrimination are universal, the politics of redress are contextual: the exclusion of minorities in the American context differs significantly from the exclusion of the majority in South Africa, and the logic of affirmative action therefore must also operate in different ways. Individual and institutional concerns about affirmative action are only elements in a complex set of problems, in which the general principles of equity and redress interact with those of efficiency, development, and differentiation. What this means is that a systemic perspective and longer historical view are required.

As a matter of social justice, the restructuring of South African higher education cannot be considered only at the level of policy discourse, official objectives, and planning; one must be as concerned with actual equity outcomes (including unintended or unanticipated reactions) as with matters of principle. The political and ideological functions of redress and affirmative action need to be understood within the historical context of transition from apartheid to postapartheid. They also need to be viewed within the structural context of the South African "distributional regime."[2] As we will see, it is in the tensions between principled policy objectives and their unintended outcomes that the issues of social justice are most sharply posed. While postapartheid South Africa clearly wishes to make a dramatic symbolic break through the transformation of higher education, the continuities and systemic limitations inherited from the apartheid regime may still prove the more serious challenge.

Manifest Transformation?

～

On the face of it, the South African transition brought about a dramatic shift, from the systemic injustices and inequities of apartheid-era education, to a restructured higher-education system informed by the principles of equity and redress. Forty years after the introduction of so-called Bantu education by the Bantu Education Act in 1953, followed by Prime Minister Verwoerd's closing of the "open universities" through the Extension of University Education Act in 1959, the National Commission on Higher Education (NCHE) Report of 1996 announced a new and different epoch in higher education. The apartheid ordering of higher education had been epitomized in Verwoerd's infamous statement that the education of black South Africans should be structured so as to avoid "showing him the green pastures of European society in which he is not allowed to graze."[3] In this respect, apartheid education was part and parcel of what Jeremy Seekings and Nicoli Nattrass have termed the inequitable "distributional regime" of general social and economic policy in apartheid South Africa: "First, no other capitalist state (in either the North or the South) sought to structure income inequalities as systematically and brutally as did SA under apartheid. . . . Second, and unsurprisingly, inequality in the distribution of income was extreme in SA throughout the apartheid period. At the end of that era . . . South Africa recorded one of the highest levels of income inequality in the world."[4] Postapartheid higher-educational planners were forced to confront the profound legacies of apartheid inequality by the 1990s—inequalities that were insistently rehearsed in official and academic publications alike.[5]

The new dispensation for higher education sought a manifest break from the apartheid order, on both symbolic and principled grounds. While desegregation of the historically white universities had already been initiated, the new Constitution required the inclusion of all institutions of higher education within a single national system, explicitly based on the principles of equity and democratic transformation. The consequences were dramatic, especially for access and composition of the student body. The unprecedented mobility for black students within the national system of higher education, coupled with the introduction of a national student bursary scheme, brought about a massive increase in black student enrollments and a revolution in the general student profile. Head count student enrollments more than doubled in the course of a decade, while the racial and gender composition of the system also changed dramatically. To cite the recent survey by Ian Bunting and Nico Cloete: "In 1986, White students had a 60% share and African students a 27% share of total higher education enrollments. By 1994 . . . the White student share of enrollments had fallen to 38% and the African student enrollment had risen to 50%. In 2005, the African share of the total enrollment was 62% and that of White students 25%."[6] In short, while there were about equal numbers of white and African students in higher education in 1994, by 1999 there were almost twice as many African students as whites.[7] This is a remarkable achievement by any standard. Nico Cloete and Jaamiah Galant claim that it may have been the greatest change in racial and gender composition of a student body anywhere in the world during the same period.[8] In this sense, at least, South Africa's reorientation of its higher-education system made manifest progress toward its stated objectives.

However, on closer analysis the apartheid legacies in higher education proved to be more insidious and ambivalent than expected, while the attempted restructuring also had unintended, and even counterintuitive consequences. These consequences go beyond such modest reforms as the equity changes effected by the Department of Labour's requirement that all institutions submit staff equity plans.[9] Nor is it just that this was a so-called skewed revolution, in which African students tended to complete fewer years of higher education, to enroll in technikons rather than top universities, and to be underrepresented in the more professional courses, such as engineering and accountancy.[10] These might still be considered delayed aftereffects of apartheid and Bantu education, which would be corrected as new cohorts of postapartheid students moved through the system. That was indeed what the NCHE had anticipated: in its 1996 report it projected that enrollment in higher education could be virtually doubled over the decade from 1995 to 2005.[11] However, the actual trends turned out to be very different: the major surge in higher-education enrollments had actually taken place during the last decade of apartheid. From 1986 to 1994 there had been an annual enrollment growth rate of more than 7 percent, but then, quite unexpectedly, this leveled off sharply between 1995 and 1999 with an average annual increase of less than 1 percent for these years. Indeed, as Bunting and Cloete point out, "the numbers of students enrolled in the public higher education system in 1999 and 2000 were in fact lower than the total in 1996, the year in which the NCHE report was published."[12] These two sets of problems are no doubt interrelated; the unintended consequences of the postapartheid restructuring of higher education are likely to have more than a little to do with the mistaken assumptions and projections on which public debate and official planning at the time had been based.

But access to higher education is not just a matter of enrollment numbers. An even more problematic feature of postapartheid higher education is that of overall participation rates, that is, the trends in comparative enrollment shares for the various population groups.[13] The basic inequities of the apartheid legacy are highlighted by the fact that, in 1995, when overall participation rates in higher education stood at 14 percent, with those for Africans at 9 percent, the rate for Whites was no less than 61 percent. In terms of its ambitious "massification" proposals the NCHE in 1996 proposed as target an increase of overall participation rates to 30 percent by 2005.[14] But overall participation actually only increased to 16 percent by 2005, with participation rates for Africans improving to only 12 percent, while participation rates for Whites remained virtually unchanged at 60 percent.[15] The much-touted increase in raw numbers of African students, from 287,000 in 1995 to almost 450,000 by 2005, looks more problematic when viewed from this perspective. Indeed, Bunting and Cloete have concluded that "the inequality in participation rates has remained similar to the apartheid era.... Africans have access to higher education comparable to some third world countries, while access for whites to universities is similar to that of most first world countries."[16]

The major institutional trends during that first decade after apartheid were similarly unexpected. Emerging out of apartheid, South African higher education was divided between the formerly White or "Historically Advantaged Institutions" (HAIs) and the formerly Black or "Historically Disadvantaged Institutions" (HDIs). In the new democratic context, with an ANC government and with the higher-education system opened to a massive influx of Black students, it was widely assumed that such institutional disparities would be redressed. Between 1995 and 2000 student enrollments were indeed significantly redistributed between the two categories, but with rather unexpected results. Bunting and Cloete provide the overall picture:

> Black student enrollments ... increased by 79,000 (or 22%) in 1999 compared to 1995, and white student enrollments fell by 50,000 or 23% over this period. The historically white institutions took nearly 80% of the increased enrollment of black students. ... Institutions which had previously been designated as "for Whites only" were able to move into what was, in effect, a new higher education market. Some were able to recruit large numbers of students who before 1995 had not been permitted to enroll at "White institutions" ... while the system's overall enrollments of African and Coloured students increased, enrollments at the historically black institutions fell. The lack of growth in student numbers, the changing notion of access and the competition amongst public institutions ...

led to an increased differentiation in the system, with the historically black institutions faring the worst.[17]

In other words, actual trends have contradicted the state's commitment to equity as a basic principle of higher education. Thus, Bunting found that by 2001 the higher-education system had actually become more differentiated and unequal than it was in 1994, while Cloete concluded that the equity objective had not been met, with restructuring instead producing a more elite system.[18] In large part this was a matter of a shift from a crudely racialized system in which basic inequities had coincided with racial differences, to a more complex and increasingly class-based system, in which inequities were increasingly being reproduced *within* racial categories. As such, the higher-education problem was part and parcel of a more general challenge for social justice advocates in postapartheid South Africa.[19] The transformation of higher education, like much else in the new South Africa, turns out to be more complex and problematic, especially from a social-justice perspective, than one might have expected at first glance. Instead of a simple contrast between apartheid inequities and postapartheid transformation, South Africans have encountered more complex continuities and even exacerbations of inequality. In order to better appreciate these distortions and limitations, we first have to understand them in relation to the apartheid project and its legacy.

Revisiting Verwoerd and Bantu Education

⤳

In retrospect, it is clear that the introduction of Bantu education and the attempted closing of the "open universities," iniquitous as these racist interventions of the 1950s undoubtedly were, also began a substantive extension of public secondary and higher education to South Africa's African majority. By the onset of apartheid, a century-long legacy of mission education for Africans had developed into a network of state-aided mission schools and teacher-training institutions serving about 1.2 million pupils. Effectively, though, this system was operating only at the level of primary education: only 35,000 Blacks out of a total of some 10 million were receiving any form of secondary education in 1956, with only about 2,300 at the universities. And of these, Africans constituted a further minority: excluding students at the nonresidential University of South Africa (UNISA), only 572 Africans were enrolled in higher education in 1956, of which 101 were at the two "open universities," the Universities of Cape Town and Witswatersrand. Just over a thousand Africans possessed a university degree at the time, with another 200 or so graduating annually.[20] This was the backdrop for the introduction of Bantu education in the 1950s, and the racially segregated universities, long denigrated as "Bush Colleges," in the 1960s.

On a quantitative level, Bantu education succeeded in providing basic schooling.[21] According to Seekings and Nattrass:

> This expansion occurred in two distinct periods. First, from the mid-1950s onwards there was a massive increase in the provision of primary schooling for African children. The effect of this was to raise adult literacy rates among urban African people from 21 percent in 1946 to 60 percent by the mid-1960s. Second, from 1972 onward there was a massive expansion of secondary schooling in urban areas. Secondary school enrollments rates among African children rose from a mere 4 percent in 1960 to 16 percent in 1970 and 35 percent in 1980. By 1980, secondary education had been transformed from "the prerogative of the elite" into "a mass phenomenon."[22]

Notwithstanding our abhorrence for apartheid's racist premises and distorted ends, these developments surely cast a different light on the overall trajectory of African education in South Africa. On the one hand, we must understand Bantu education in relation to what preceded it. As historian Cynthia Kros explains, "Our abhorrence of Bantu Education should not blind us to the deep flaws and basic inadequacies of its predecessor. . . . Effective critiques of Bantu Education need not romanticize what had passed for 'Native' education—a sprawling and inchoate system . . . in the decades prior to the 1950s."[23] On the other hand, we must more closely examine the nature and function of Bantu education itself. In his account of the major revisionist research project, *The History of Education under Apartheid*, Peter Kallaway posed a number of unsettling questions, including that of the historical significance of Prime Minister Verwoerd's supposed founding statement:

> How far did the blueprints match the reality in the schools? . . . To put it bluntly—did Verwoerd's much cited statements about the goals of Bantu Education actually represent policy on the ground in the 1960s? . . . Most simply, there is a real need to engage with the taken for granted assumptions about apartheid education and Bantu Education—and critically engage with the works and statements of Eiselen [the anthropologist W. M. Eiselen, who became the first Permanent Secretary for Native Affairs under the apartheid regime] and Verwoerd or the policy statements of the ICNO [the Institute for Christian National Education]—rather than reading them simply as examples of outmoded racist ideology.[24]

Critical interrogation suggests that Verwoerd's notorious statement merely articulated the mainstream assumptions behind official approaches to African education characteristic of the preapartheid period. But his words should by no means be taken as a reliable guide to the aims and function of the new Bantu education system introduced by Eiselen's ministry. While overtly enacting an ideology of exclusion and separation, the system of Bantu education also was the state's first acknowledgment of a responsibility for educating the majority of Africans. In that sense, as both Cynthia Kros and Brahm Fleisch have argued, Bantu education was actually a modernizing project of rational planning and social engineering. As an exercise in social engineering it was not, Kros notes, all that different from mass education programs in other countries.[25]

In some ways the revisionist discovery of Bantu education's modern character merely confirms a familiar interpretation, advanced by Heribert Adam in his *Modernizing Racial Domination* of 1971, that analogies with the racist ideologies of fascism and national-socialism misconstrued the main thrust of the apartheid project. But it also requires that we reassess the relationship between the legacy of apartheid education and its postapartheid transformation.

Of particular relevance for our concern with social justice is the surprising fact that the basic distributional regime of the apartheid-era South African state does not quite accord with the prevailing perceptions of its discriminatory, oppressive and exploitative nature. In a series of papers, political sociologist Jeremy Seekings has argued that the early 1940s saw the introduction of relatively progressive social and tax policies—amounting to the beginnings of a redistributive welfare system that extended to the African majority a variety of welfare provisions that were already available to poor and working-class whites.[26] Though apartheid did not fully follow through on these wartime reforms, it retained enough key provisions, in the view of Seekings and his coauthor, Nicoli Nattrass, to characterize what in historical and comparative perspective was a surprisingly generous distributional regime:

> Compared to other developing countries, South Africa has long had— and continues to have—a very high level of redistribution by means of the government budget. This entails a progressive and efficient tax system, an exceptionally generous system of public welfare provision (based on non-contributory old-age pensions), and pro-poor spending on public health services and public education. If inequality is measured after taxation, and cash transfers, and the benefits in kind of public services, then SA ceases to be at the top end of the international inequality league.[27]

For all its inequalities, apartheid education, too, had its redistributional side. According to Seekings and Nattrass, the 1953 introduction of Bantu education meant that "the expansion of state spending on schools for African children was tied once more to the level of African taxation; the grant from general revenue was kept at a constant R13 million, and inflation eroded the real value of this figure."[28] But this statutory limitation on expenditure was abandoned in 1972, leading to a rapid increase in spending on African education—a 600 percent rise between the mid-1970s and early 1990s—accompanied by a similarly rapid narrowing of the interracial spending gap. Seekings and Nattrass note that this rise was partly the result of increasing enrollments, but that there was nonetheless a threefold increase in real spending per pupil.[29] All of this was paralleled by a marked expansion of higher-education opportunities for African students, even if within the racist confines of the apartheid system. In 1960 there were fewer than 800 African students at university, excluding UNISA. By 1983 this number had soared to roughly 20,000, with a further 12,700 enrolled in UNISA. It was on this basis that, as we have seen, the most dramatic increase in the access of African students to higher education actually took place *prior to* the end of apartheid in 1994. But it would be quite wrong to take this as an achievement of apartheid education. To the contrary, it was a striking testimony to the final collapse of the apartheid project in higher education. In effect, the state had lost the political will to enforce exclusionary access to racially designated institutions, allowing the "open universities" to use the permit system as a loophole to evade its strict ideological objectives: "Each of the racially divided institutions was permitted to admit and to enroll as many students as it saw fit from its designated race group," Bunting and Cloete explained. "No enrollment targets were set by the various government departments. . . . Access to higher education became, by the late 1980s, a process determined by institutions themselves, and in particular by those which were prepared to play the 'permit game' in pursuit of equity of access."[30] Seen in this context, the post-1994 restructuring was also the state's attempt to reestablish its hold on higher education.

The Dynamics of Restructuring Postapartheid Education

❧

Restructuring proceeded through a series of distinct phases. In retrospect, analysts have identified four markedly different periods, each with its own characteristics and dynamics: (1) the collapse of apartheid (1986–94), (2) the period of symbolic policy (1995–2000), (3) state intervention and resumed enrollment growth (2000–2004) and (4) the current post-2004 period of enrollment capping and differentiated policy interaction.[31] This sequence indicates that the restructuring process did not proceed smoothly from the initial formulation of policy principles and objectives through implementation and development. Instead, planners soon found themselves overtaken by the unintended consequences of various institutional-sector initiatives, as well as by the unexpected post-1995 plateau in enrollment growth.[32] These unexpected developments, occurring as they did simultaneously with changes in the government's macroeconomic and social policies from the RDP to GEAR,[33] prompted the emergence of three types of social-justice issues: those related to *equity of access* (tied up with the controversial massification of higher education); issues of individual and institutional *redress* (connected to the crisis of the Historically Disadvantaged Institutions, or HDIs); and the more specific controversies over affirmative action and employment equity policies.

We have already discussed Phase 1, the collapse of apartheid. Phase 2—represented by the work of the National Commission on Higher Education (NCHE), followed by a series of government Green and White Papers and resulting in the Higher Education Act of 1998—effectively operated at the level of symbolic policy and signaled a break with the past and the beginning of a new direction.[34] Bunting and Cloete have termed this the "first reform framework": governance during this period was based on democratic principles, including equity, democracy, and redress. "The policy change was driven," they go on, "by a strong social demand for democracy and equity, not for efficiency, quality or skills."[35] This process of policy formulation and legislative enactment inevitably took considerable time. In practice, it was beset by delays, with the National Plan for Higher Education (NPHE) only appearing in 2001, and key mechanisms such as the introduction of a new government funding formula (to replace the apartheid-era South African Post-Secondary Education, or SAPSE, formula) postponed for several more years.

This did not mean, however, that there were no significant changes in higher education during the so-called implementation vacuum.[36] On the contrary, these were years of substantial changes and radical realignments in the institutional landscape. But the changes were effected on the ground, by actors from different sectors of the newly unified higher-education system, and not via uniform policy. It proved especially consequential that distinct adaptive strategies were adopted during this period by the various institutional sectors. Analysts have identified and characterized these as

1. The *wait for redress but aspire for equality* strategy adopted by all of the historically black universities;
2. The *continue with business-as-usual* strategy of the historically black and some of the historically white technikons;

3. The *expand student enrollments and ensure financial sustainability* strategy of the historically white Afrikaans universities and some of the historically white technikons;

4. The *do current business in better ways* strategy of the historically white English universities.[37]

The implementation delay proved especially disastrous for the HDIs, which had staked their strategy on the expectations of redress, while, counterintuitively, the Afrikaans HAIs emerged from the first few years of the postapartheid dispensation with significant increases in black student enrollments and financial resources. In the case of the former, symbolic government policy had generated unrealistic expectations about redress, while at the same time these institutions were suddenly having to deal with intensified market competition, as black students voted with their feet. Between 1995 and 1999 the HDIs lost 28,000 students from their rolls, or 25 percent of their total enrollment, to the HAIs. Several HDIs were pushed to the brink.[38]

With the adoption of the National Plan for Higher Education in 2001, and, more particularly, with the introduction of the institutional merger process, through which the total number of higher-education institutions was reduced from 36 to 21, the state initiated a new, more centrally directed phase in the restructuring of higher education, though one in which it also had to accommodate assertions of institutional autonomy. This new phase was marked by muted but definite shifts in policy. In Phase 3, which spanned the period from 2000 to 2004, or during what Bunting and Cloete terms the "second reform framework," the basic commitments shifted from equity and redress to efficiency and responsiveness, with efficiency defined primarily in terms of student throughputs.[39] This shift is described by Aslam Fataar as follows:

> The discourse shifted rapidly from a strong equality-driven focus to an alignment with the government's macro development and growth path. . . . By the late 1990s the growth and human resources discourse had trumped discourses of equality and redress in the higher education policy field. . . . Equity and redress, prominent in the pre-1997 policy moment, were secondary to the more primary task of making higher education more responsive to the labor market with its attendant requirements for knowledge workers and innovation.[40]

As we have seen, this phase was also marked by the resumption of growth in student enrollments, though the government has since indicated that enrollments may be capped. In this current "third reform framework," with the merging process completed and the new funding formula in place, central policy is being reoriented toward differentiated steering, allowing for consultation and specified institutional contracts.[41]

Equity in Access as an Issue of Social Justice

∿

The initial achievements of the postapartheid restructuring in South African higher education can be seen in an overall increase in enrollments, and above all in the dramatic increase in the number of African students. That African students became an overall majority in South African higher education by 1995 was a major demonstration of their improved access to an arena from which they had historically been excluded. But it did not yet constitute equity in access, by any means. That fact becomes clear once we look beyond headcount numbers to participation rates. As we have seen, only 9 percent of African students were participating in 1995, and that number had only improved to 12 percent by 2005—compared to White participation rates holding steady at 60 percent. What this means is that the South African system of higher education has maintained its elite character, effectively structured along racial lines. But the basic problem is not so much the racial differentiation as such; rather, it is the fact that the African majority is not gaining adequate access. As Bunting and Cloete observe, "the problem is that within a relatively small elite system, almost all the students can be African, and the participation rate will still be under 20%."[42]

In principle, this issue was addressed at the outset of the restructuring process, through proposals for the massification of the system. In its 1996 report, the NCHE identified increased participation, or massification, as one of three main pillars in the transformation process. Indeed, the NCHE's central proposal was that massification would provide the vehicle for equitable transformation.[43] However, while the NCHE's other main proposals were received with general acclaim, its central massification proposal was not accepted by the minister of education. Instead, the Department of Education concluded that massification was not affordable, and in a 1997 White Paper argued for "a planned expansion of higher education."[44] This was the subject of much debate at the time, especially since the NCHE's massification proposal was certainly in line with the general optimistic thrust to "open the doors of higher learning." On top of the remarkable surge in student enrollments that had already taken place over the previous decade, the NCHE's projections that an overall participation rate of 30 percent and a participation rate of 20 percent for African students could be achieved by 2005 might well have appeared feasible. In retrospect, these projections look very different. As we have seen, contrary to all expectations the overall increases in student enrollments leveled off during the period

1995–2000, and the actual headcount numbers and participation rates by 2005 were much closer to the 1995 baselines than to the NCHE's projections. So, in "realistic" terms, one could say that the DoE's rejection of the NCHE massification proposal was vindicated, and in the latest phase of post-2005 policy objectives the state is instead increasingly committing itself to definite enrollment caps.

From a social justice perspective, the state's 1997 rejection of massification is so fateful that the question must be raised whether this was a case of realism, or simply of self-fulfilling prophecy. Consider the counterfactual question: what would have been the implications and consequences if the state had accepted the NCHE's massification proposals at the time? How different might the overall enrollment figures and relevant participation rates have looked, by 2005? To ask this question is not merely to speculate about the road not taken within the higher-education system itself. Higher education is also dependent on external inputs, including public education funding, and higher education in particular, as well as throughput from the secondary education system, which supplies the candidates for institutions of higher education.

First, as far as public funding is concerned, one can make the crude generalization that while the share of South Africa's overall expenditure on education as a fraction of its national budget compares well with international norms, its spending on higher education in particular falls below those standards.[45] Anything like the massification of higher education projected by the NCHE would have required both a relative increase in overall education spending—at the expense of budget items like health, social welfare, and defense—as well as a substantial increase in expenditures on higher education in particular (that is, if a drastic deterioration of resources and standards was to be avoided). It was probably on such financial grounds that the DoE at the time rejected the NCHE's massification proposals. As such, the validity of its decision remains subject to dispute.

But second, even if the funding could have been found, there loomed the further question of whether South Africa's secondary education system could produce a sufficient number of matriculants qualified for admission to higher education, in order to make a massified higher-education system feasible. In 1996, when the new postapartheid program known as Curriculum 2005 was only just being put into place, the NCHE could anticipate that the movement of the first cohorts of the postapartheid generation through the restructured primary and secondary education system would strengthen the higher-education applicant pool. It was in this context that the NCHE could conceive of the prospects for a massified system of higher education by 2005. Today, however, the picture looks entirely different. John Kane-Berman, the director of the South African Institute of Race Relations, has grimly summarized the secondary schooling system's wholesale failure to produce anything like an improved applicant pool:

> Of more than 1-million pupils who were in grade 10 in 2004, only a third passed matric at the end of [2006], and only 8% passed matric well enough to qualify for university. . . . There were fewer university-entrance matric passes among all races [in 2006] (85,830) than in 1994 (88,497). Africans account for most of these matriculants. Their results have shown virtually no improvement in the past 12 years. In 1994, altogether 392,434 Africans wrote their senior certificate exams, of whom 51,016 (13%) obtained university-entrance passes. At the end of [2006] 442,800 Africans wrote senior certificate exams, of whom 51,180 (11.6%) obtained university-entrance passes. These last set of figures tell us that the number of Africans obtaining university-entrance matric certificates was not much higher after 13 years of democratic rule than after 40 years of Bantu Education. The lack of progress is all the more alarming if one remembers that discriminatory funding no longer applies. Previously, African pupils received very much less public funding than pupils of other races. At one stage, in the early 1970s, average per capita spending on white pupils was 18 times the figure for African pupils. . . . Today there is no longer any racial discrimination in how the state allocates resources to education.[46]

The fact of the matter is that, more than a decade into our postapartheid democracy, the secondary schooling system evidently produces only a small elite core prepared for effective entry into higher education. The racial composition of that core may be significantly different from what it had been under apartheid, but its order of magnitude remains much the same. It would be very instructive to know to what extent this group of potential university entrants has changed in terms of its class, institutional, and regional background. Theoretically it is, of course, possible that the 85,830 South Africans who achieved university-entrance matric passes in 2006 (including 51,180 Africans) came from different schools, regions, and social sectors than the 88,497 (including 51,016 Africans) who achieved the same passes in 1994. But closer analysis is much more likely to show that they come from much the same set of largely urban-based schools, although these schools are now also serving the new Black middle class, a world away from the rural and township schools in which the vast majority of African children are being taught.

The reality is that an identifiable set of secondary schools constitutes a stable but small (deracialized) elite system. And it is this set of schools on which higher education effectively depends, for the entrants to its own small (deracialized) elite system. As long as that relationship continues, the prospects for equity of access to higher education seem remote. There is, of course, the alternative of proceeding with the massification of higher education, even if the secondary system fails to supply an expanded applicant pool. This may be what Bunting and Cloete had in mind when they concluded their discussion of the Department of Education's 1997 rejection of massification by observing that "it could be argued that government succeeded, by these means, in preventing a fairly common phenomenon in Africa. This is the phenomenon of elite systems not massifying but becoming overloaded by uncontrolled increases in numbers of students, leading to a serious deterioration in quality."[47] On that scenario such deterioration would also pose social justice problems, but a different set of problems than those related to the current lack of equity in access.

The Principle and Politics of Redress
as an Issue of Social Justice

∾

As we have seen, equity and redress featured prominently in South Africa's postapartheid restructuring of higher education. This principled stand was integral to the first, symbolic policy phase, which was focused on breaking with and then redressing the inequalities inherited from apartheid-era education. In due course, the generalized commitment to equity and redress had to be unpacked in more specific terms, and applied in different contexts. According to Bunting and Cloete's helpful analysis,

> the notion of equity was used in at least three ways during the period of policy formation: (a) equity as redress, (b) equity as equality, and (c) equity as distributive fairness. In the first sense of redress, equity requires special benefits to be awarded to those harmed by the apartheid system. In the second sense of equality, equity requires all social benefits to be distributed equally across a society. In the third sense of distributive fairness, equity requires that all be given equal opportunities of gaining access to societal benefits, but does not require equal distribution of these benefits.[48]

The salience of "equity as redress" was not only hotly contested during restructuring, but was interpreted in particular ways that reveal much about the institutional politics of the period.

The issue of redress was sharpened during the preparation of the Department of Education's 1997 White Paper in response to the NCHE report and proposals. According to Aslam Fataar, the first version of the draft White Paper conspicuously departed from a focus on equity as redress: "It differed fundamentally from the NCHE report and the Green Paper by focusing primarily on the role of higher education in national development and by stressing fiscal and managerial efficiency, while neglecting the equality goals of the previous documents. The draft was written by a World Bank expert who had the remit of aligning higher-education policy with the recently accepted GEAR macro-economic policy (the ANC's Growth, Employment, and Redistribution program). The draft omitted critical recommendations for overcoming and going beyond the legacy of apartheid, and failed to provide clarity about how transformation was to take place."[49] This draft White Paper provoked intense opposition and lobbying especially from representatives of the HDIs, but also within the parliamentary portfolio committee on education, and the ANC's parliamentary education study group. The draft was reworked with their input, and the emphasis on equity and redress restored in the final White Paper on Higher Education. But now the stress was decidedly on *institutional* redress, evidently with the HDIs very much in mind. The White Paper itself still distinguished, Bunting and Cloete emphasize, "between institutional and individual redress; between benefits which would go to institutions damaged by the effects of apartheid and benefits which would go to individuals harmed by the effects of apartheid." The concern over institutional redress for the HDIs had been moved to the top of the restructuring agenda, with momentous but, again, unintended consequences for those very institutions.[50]

As we have seen, these strategies were adopted during the "implementation vacuum" of 1995–2000 in the light of what was at the time viewed as the promise (or threat) of institutional redress. The historically black universities effectively relied on the perceived promise of institutional redress to resolve the legacies of discrimination and exclusion. Unlike the Afrikaans-medium universities, the HDIs did not perceive the official commitment to redress as a threat, which might have motivated them to engage in new entrepreneurial strategies. Conversely, they tended to rely on the state in anticipation of redress to remedy their weak institutional bases. But the expected funding was not forthcoming. The state failed to increase the amount earmarked for redress between 1995 and 1997. Annual allocations of 28 million rand, 60 million rand, and 30 million rand were made to universities and technikons between 1998 and 2001 for redress purposes, but these were of a different order entirely.[51] In short, the adaptive strategy of "waiting for redress" proved little short of disastrous. With their weak institutional bases, the HDIs found themselves exposed to the pressures of a more competitive academic marketplace, fueling a further spiral of institutional decline, if not literal collapse. The Council on Higher Education (CHE) had to report that in three cases (the universities of Fort Hare, the North, and Transkei) "governance had collapsed altogether, prompting the Minister to request a report in each case by an independent assessor, and followed by the appointment of an administrator to fulfill the governance functions of disbanded councils."[52]

The debate over institutional redress to the HDIs was, of course, complicated. Historically these institutions, with the partial exception of Fort Hare, had been launched as creatures of apartheid. In the course of the 1970s and 1980s, sustained student resistance on these campuses played a major part in the history of the internal antiapartheid struggle, to the extent that by the 1990s the former "Bush Colleges" had been transformed into "Historically Disadvantaged Institutions," which could claim and expect redress. But while there can be no doubt that the individuals and communities associated with these universities had indeed been victims of apartheid injustices, their institutional position and function was ambiguous, to say the least. In the apartheid-era state funding scheme, for example, these universities did not fall under the general SAPSE funding formula that applied to white universities and could benefit in various ways from direct state support. Ironically, then, their postapartheid inclusion into a unified national higher-education system brought an end to their relative benefits and protections. In effect it meant that, from 1995 onward, the historically black universities were also brought on to the general SAPSE formula, and so were exposed to the quasi-market principles on which this formula operated. As a consequence, the level of state funding for these universities declined in both absolute and relative terms.[53] It was in this context that the historically black universities attempted to claim that the state's general commitment to redress should take the specific form of institutional redress to them, as Historically Disadvantaged Institutions. The outcome of this campaign has been well summarized by Aslam Fataar:

> While there was a lack of clarity over its form, whether it should be block grants or earmarked funding, the expectation of redress had caused many HDIs to attach the resolution of their institutional crises to receiving extra government funding. Institutional redress policy was however dropped after a small amount of R27 million was paid out in 1998. . . . The policy was sidelined in the context of a strong efficiency agenda that had come to dominate government policy. . . . By 1998 the policy discourse around the HDIs had swung from that of them being "redress-deserving" to "crisis ridden" and as highly inefficient in terms of their student output and responsiveness.[54]

In the event, the plight of the historically black universities was, after 2001, addressed neither under the banner of institutional redress, nor by turning them into scaled-down "bedrock institutions," but through institutional mergers.

What did this outcome signify for the basic commitment to equity and redress? The government's backing away from institutional redress to the HDIs did not necessarily amount to a rejection of the principle as such. According to Fataar, it could instead be interpreted as a shift from institutional to individual redress: "The unexpected continuation of the Apartheid-based SAPSE funding formula after 1994, which was founded on student numbers, had the effect of shifting the redress focus away from Historically Disadvantaged Institutions to mobile individual black students. These students were now in a position to leave the Historically Disadvantaged Institutions for Historically Advantaged Institutions."[55] This is also how the CHE Task Team conceptualized the issue of redress in its "Size and Shape" report: "Social redress and institutional redress are connected, but the former is not reducible to the latter. . . . The categories of 'historically advantaged' and 'historically disadvantaged' as applied to institutions are becoming less useful for social policy purposes."[56]

In effect, this signaled two related shifts in official discourse and policy orientation: on the one hand, it meant that redress was to be achieved in individual rather than institutional terms; that is, individual black students could use their new mobility to gain access to formerly white universities. On the other hand, it also indicated that backward-looking equity-as-redress was being assimilated to forward-looking equity-in-development. In this sense, the change was in line with more general shifts from a national concern for "dealing with the past" and the individual and collective reparations associated with the Truth and Reconciliation Commission, to the developmental state discourse of the ANC government under President Thabo Mbeki. When President Mbeki finally responded to the TRC's long-delayed proposals for reparation in his parliamentary debate at the beginning of 2002, he articulated his unease with the very idea of any kind of redress unless this was embedded in a more forward-looking language of development.[57] Perhaps not coincidentally, a very similar debate over redress in higher-education restructuring had been playing out in recent years.

Postapartheid Affirmative Action and Employment Equity in Historical Context

∽

In the foregoing discussion, I have tried to contextualize the ideas of affirmative action and employment equity in ways that might enable us to see them as problems of social justice more generally. In conclusion, I would like to make some claims about what the relevance of a social justice perspective on these issues in the particular context of postapartheid higher education might be.

The most controversial aspect of affirmative action and employment equity policies is the way these policies rely on race-based categories of the apartheid era to undo the legacies of apartheid injustice and inequality. While the intentions and objectives are quite the opposite, the fact remains that the policy instruments being employed are identical. In order to ensure that university student admission policies and staff appointments will be more equitable and to undo the iniquitous legacies of apartheid education, individuals need to be classified as "White," "African," "Coloured," and "Asian." It must be noted that, while the new South African Constitution provides a basis for redress in general and affirmative action in particular, it does *not* require that these efforts be conceived in terms of race-based categories. Indeed, that would have gone strongly against the grain of the historical and political tradition of "nonracialism" that so strongly informed the making of our new Constitution.

What, then, is the relevance of my account of the postapartheid restructuring of higher education for current affirmative action and employment equity policies? In the first place, it is necessary to reflect on the fact that, though the postapartheid higher-education system has been significantly deracialized, especially with regard to the composition of the overall student body, it has not been able to achieve anything like general equity of access. For the time being, postapartheid higher education remains a small, if now deracialized, elite system. This means that any affirmative action and employment equity policies can only be implemented *within* this small elite system, and thus do not and cannot affect the majority, who are unable to gain access to this system in the first place. Moreover, the throughput from the secondary school system into the higher-education system is of vital importance. If the core group of school-leavers with the equivalent of university-entrance matric passes, which effectively constitutes the pool from which higher education can draw, had significantly expanded along the lines anticipated by the NCHE in 1996, then that would have created an entirely different context for affirmative action in current admission policies. Quite simply, if the 50,000 Africans with university-entrance matric passes in 1994 had doubled or even trebled by 2006, then that would have enabled a significant massification of higher education—and significantly decreased the need for affirmative action admissions in the first place. (In the longer run it would also have established conditions under which staff employment equity was both possible and necessary.) But the reality is that there was no such expansion of the university applicant pool, and that the number of Africans with university-entrance matric passes has remained of the same order of some 50,000 annually. This must raise serious questions about the significance and function of affirmative action admission policies *in these circumstances.* If the small elite pool of Africans with university-entrance matric passes is not expanding but remaining stable, then fiddling with admission procedures or ratcheting up admission targets is unlikely to produce demographic representativeness. To the extent that such affirmative action measures are to be effective, their impact must of necessity be confined within the small, deracialized elite system of higher education. That means that the beneficiaries of these "affirmative action" measures will also decreasingly be individuals who themselves have been relatively disadvantaged: the black students in the first cohorts of entrants to postapartheid higher education were likely to have been first-generation university students, on their way into the new black middle class. But by now entrants are more likely to be the products of an elite secondary schooling system, the children of black middle-class parents, and, in an increasing number of cases, second-generation university students. If so, then affirmative action admission policies and employment equity staffing policies will increasingly reproduce the established black elite, rather than benefiting historically disadvantaged individuals or groups. Indeed, it could be argued that in these circumstances affirmative action policies couched in apartheid-derived racial categories now provide an ideological justification for privileging established black elite groups, at the expense of the African majority.

This holds true insofar as affirmative action and employment equity policies are defined in terms of some general notion of redress. As we have seen, equity-as-redress was a core objective at the outset of the postapartheid restructuring, but became increasingly controversial when it was interpreted to mean either institutional redress (to the HDIs) or individual redress (in the case of black students who used their newfound mobility to gain access to HAIs). In the case of the first cohorts of such black students who made this move in the course of the 1990s, it was likely to have been a recognizable form of individual redress. But this became less likely as the postapartheid system of higher education became more firmly elitist by the end of the first decade of democracy. *In these circumstances,* one must raise serious questions about the redress value of affirmative action and employment equity policies. In recent years, these policies have increasingly been justified in terms of the need, not so much to secure redress for previously disadvantaged individuals, but to achieve demographic representivity (where demography is conceived in apartheid-derived racial categories). In other words, though a particular individual has not been personally disadvantaged, he or she may still qualify as a beneficiary of affirmative action by virtue of being a member of a historically disadvantaged demographic group. This is a peculiar, *representative* interpretation of race-based redress, far removed from the original use of the term to describe individual or communal redress. However, this race-based "representative" meaning is perfectly couched to serve the interests of an established black elite that enjoys insider access to the higher-education system, in the midst of the large majority of Africans who have no such equity of access.

In sum, the legacies of apartheid inequality are proving more resilient than might at first sight appear to be the case. As we have seen, in its historical context and comparative terms apartheid itself involved a not entirely ungenerous distributional regime of basic social policies, while Bantu education, despite its manifest inequalities and injustices, also laid the foundations for the expansion of African education at the primary, secondary, and, eventually, even tertiary levels. The iniquity of apartheid education was not just a question of the absolute or comparative levels of inequality, but above all of its race-based objectives and justifications. In many ways, the postapartheid restructuring of higher education was able to build on the material achievements of the apartheid-era expansion of African education. When access to a unified system of higher education was enabled during the 1990s, a substantial number of African students were already in a position to make use of this opportunity. The deracialization of the higher-education system that had begun during the final years of the apartheid era was consolidated, and could have provided a launching stage for greater equity in access to higher education in the new democratic South Africa. That equity of access has not yet come about, primarily, it would seem, due to the secondary system's failure to produce a sufficient pool of qualified candidates. In the context of this failure to ensure equity of access to higher education for the African majority, the insistence on couching affirmative action and employment equity policies within what is in effect a small elite system of higher education in apartheid-derived racial terms must be considered increasingly problematic from a social justice perspective.

NOTES

1. Martin Hall, "The Case for Equity," *UCT Monday Paper,* April 23–May 6, 2007.

2. Jeremy Seekings and Niccoli Nattrass, *Class, Race, and Inequality in South Africa* (New Haven: Yale University Press, 2005).

3. Dan O'Meara, *Forty Lost Years: The Apartheid State and the Politics of the National Party* (Randburg, South Africa: Ravan Press; Athens: Ohio University Press, 1996), 71–72.

4. Seekings and Nattrass, *Class, Race, and Inequality,* 2–3. "Explicit racial discrimination affected earnings and income directly and blatantly. Black people and white people with the same qualifications were paid different wages for performing the same job, especially in the public sector. . . . Prospects for promotion also depended on race. . . . More important, state policies affected inequality by limiting the opportunities open to the black majority of the population. People were dispossessed of or denied access to property simply because of their racial classification. Business opportunities were curtailed. Discriminatory expenditure on education meant that black people entered the labour

market with big disadvantages. The 'colour bar' prevented them from getting better-paid jobs, even if they had appropriate skills and experience."

5. Ian Bunting, *A Legacy of Inequality: Higher Education in South Africa* (Rondebosch, South Africa: UCT Press, 1994); NCHE Discussion Document, *A Framework for Transformation*, April 1996, 9–25; *NCHE Report*, 1997, 28–50; Department of Education *Green Paper*, 10–13, 1997; and Council on Higher Education, *South African Higher Education in the First Decade of Democracy*, 2004, 59–61.

6. Ian Bunting and Nico Cloete, "Project on Governing Access to Higher Education. County Report: South Africa," mimeo (Cape Town: Centre for Higher Education Transformation, 2007), 5.

7. David Cooper and George Subotzky, *The Skewed Revolution: Trends in South African Higher Education, 1988–1998* (Cape Town: Education Policy Unit, University of the Western Cape, 2001); Nico Cloete and Jan Bunting, *Higher Education Transformation: Assessing Performance in South Africa* (Pretoria: Centre for Higher Education Transformation, 2000), 18–19.

8. Nico Cloete and Jaamiah Galant, *Capacity Building for the Next Generation of Academics*, review report for the Carnegie Corporation Project to Train and Retain the Next Generation of Academics (Cape Town: Centre for Higher Education Transformation, 2005); and see likewise Bunting and Cloete, *Project on Governing Access*, 30. "It could be argued that nowhere in the world, during the decade 1995 to 2005, has there been a bigger equity change than that which occurred in South Africa."

9. Cloete and Galant, *Capacity Building*, 13. See also Council on Higher Education, *South African Higher Education*, 72–77, 85–90.

10. Cooper and Subotzky, *The Skewed Revolution*. See also Cloete and Bunting, *Higher Education Transformation*, 18–19.

11. NCHE, *A Framework for Transformation*, 94.

12. Bunting and Cloete, *Project on Governing Access*, 19.

13. Bunting and Cloete, *Project on Governing Access; NCHE Report*. Participation rates are calculated by dividing head count enrollment totals for the given years by the closest applicable census data on those in the 20-to 24-year category.

14. *NCHE Report*, 100.

15. Bunting and Cloete, *Project on Governing Access*, 6.

16. Ibid., 31.

17. Ibid., 16, 18.

18. Ian Bunting, "Funding," in *Transformation in Higher Education: Global Pressures and Local Realities in South Africa*, ed. Nico Cloete, Peter Maasen, Richard Fehnel, Teboho Moja, Trish Gibbon, and Helene Perold (Cape Town: Juta, 2002), 179; Nico Cloete, "New South African Realities," in *Transformation in Higher Education*, 422.

19. Seekings and Nattrass, *Class, Race, and Inequality*.

20. E. G. Malherbe, "Higher Education of Non-Europeans in South Africa," *South African Outlook*, 6, no. 1 (1956): 101.

21. Jonathan Hyslop, "Social Conflicts over African Education in South Africa from the 1940s to 1976," Ph.D. diss., University of the Witwatersrand, 1990; Jonathan Hyslop, *The Classroom Struggle: Policy and Resistance in South Africa, 1940–1990* (Pietermaritzburg: University of KwaZulu-Natal Press, 1999).

22. Seekings and Nattrass, *Class, Race, and Inequality*, 105; and Philip Bonner and Lauren Segal, *Soweto: A History* (Cape Town: Maskew Miller Longman, 1998), 61; J. Hyslop, *The Classroom Struggle*, 1999, 151; and P. Pillay, "The Development and Underdevelopment of Education in South Africa," in *Education: From Poverty to Liberty*, ed. Bill Nasson and John Samuel (Cape Town: David Philip, 1990), 34; and Colin Bundy, "Street

Sociology and Pavement Politics: Some Aspects of Student/Youth Consciousness during the 1985 Schools Crisis in Greater Cape Town," *Journal of Southern African Studies* 13 (1987): 312.

23. Cynthia Kros, "W.W.M. Eiselen: Architect of Apartheid Education," in *The History of Education under Apartheid, 1948–1994: The Doors of Learning and Culture Shall Be Opened*, ed. Peter Kallaway (Cape Town: P. Lang, 2002), 54.

24. Peter Kallaway, "Understanding Apartheid Education: Putting History to Work in Relation to Critical Policy Development," University of the Western Cape, 2000, 10.

25. Cynthia Kros, "Economic, Political and Intellectual Origins of Bantu Education, 1926–1951," PhD diss., University of the Witwatersrand, 1996; and Brahm Fleisch, "State Formation and the Origins of Bantu Education," in Kallaway, *History of Education under Apartheid*.

26. Jeremy Seekings, "The Origins of Social Citizenship in South Africa," *South African Journal of Philosophy* (2000): 386–404.

27. Seekings and Nattrass, *Class, Race, and Inequality*, 4.

28. Ibid., 134.

29. Ibid., 150.

30. Bunting and Cloete, *Project on Governing Access*, 9.

31. Ibid., 5ff. Previously, in 2002, Cloete offered this summary overview: "The post-1994 period can be summarised as having started with a huge participatory policy effort within a context of optimism for both the expansion of the system and redress for past inequities. This was followed by an 'implementation vacuum' in relation to the new policies, a shift after 1997 to efficiency, and finally a reassessment of priorities and a more interventionist approach by government in 2001" (*Transformation in Higher Education*, 105). For a similar periodization of four distinct "historical moments," though characterized somewhat differently, see Andre Kraak, "Policy Ambiguity and Slippage: Higher Education under the New State," *Human Sciences Research Council* (2001): 4; and see also CHE, *South African Higher Education*.

32. The term "institutional-sector initiatives" here encompasses the range of initiatives embraced by various groupings of higher-education institutions, without central government planning.

33. Kraak, "Policy Ambiguity and Slippage."

34. Nico Cloete and Peter Maassen, "The Limits of Policy," in *Transformation in Higher Education: Global Pressures and Local Realities in South Africa*, ed. Nico Cloete et al. (Sunnyside, Pretoria, South Africa: Centre for Higher Education Transformation; Lansdowne, Cape Town, South Africa: Juta and Company, 2002), 449.

35. Bunting and Cloete, *Project on Governing Access*, 27.

36. CHE, *South African Higher Education*.

37. Bunting and Cloete, *Project on Governing Access*, 15. The typology was originally introduced by Ian Bunting, "Students," in *Transformation in Higher Education*, 175ff., and developed in somewhat different terms by Nico Cloete and Richard Fehnel, "The Emergent Landscape," in Cloete et al., *Transformation in Higher Education*.

38. Bunting and Cloete, *Project on Governing Access*, 14, 28.

39. Ibid., 28–29.

40. Aslam Fataar, "Higher Education Policy Discourse in South Africa: A Struggle for Alignment with Macro Development Policy," *South African Journal of Higher Education* 17, no. 2 (2003): 31–39; see also Kraak, "Policy Ambiguity and Slippage."

41. Bunting and Cloete, *Project on Governing Access*, 11, 29.

42. Ibid., 31.

43. NCHE, *A Framework for Transformation*, 94–100.

44. CHE, *South African Higher Education,* 26.

45. Gert Steyn and Pierre de Villiers, *The Impact of Changing Funding Sources on Higher Education Institutions in South Africa* (Pretoria: Council on Higher Education, 2006), 14–16, 87–92, 162ff.

46. John Kane-Berman, *Business Day,* June 21, 2007. "Matric" is the highest secondary-level qualification, comparable to the British Sixth Form or the American twelfth grade. Not all matriculants qualify for university admission, which is traditionally known as "matriculation exemption." It should be noted that while matriculation exemption has been the traditional university entrance requirement, increasing numbers of students with so-called matriculation endorsements have also been admitted to higher-education institutions. Moreover, the traditional matriculation exemption requirement itself is due to be phased out, so that universities will in future have to rely on setting their own admission tests. Significant as these developments may be, they do not alter the dismal realities described by Kane-Berman.

47. Bunting and Cloete, *Project on Governing Access,* 30.

48. Ibid., 13.

49. Fataar, "Higher Education Policy Discourse."

50. Bunting and Cloete, *Project on Governing Access,* 14.

51. Steyn and de Villiers, *Impact of Changing Funding,* 43. See also Kraak, "Policy Ambiguity and Slippage," 20; Cloete and Bunting, *Higher Education Transformation,* 64.

52. CHE, *South African Higher Education,* 178.

53. Ian Bunting, "Funding," in Cloete et al., *Transformation in Higher Education,* 137.

54. Fataar, "Higher Education Policy Discourse," 9.

55. Ibid.

56. CHE, *Towards a New Higher Education Landscape,* report of the Size and Shape of Higher Education Task Team, 2001, 13–14.

57. Thabo Mbeki, speech in the parliamentary debate on the tabling of the TRC's reparation proposals, February 2002, reprinted in E. Doxtader and P. Salazar, *Reconciliation in South Africa: The Fundamental Documents* (Cape Town: Institute for Justice and Reconciliation, 2007), 459–67.

Affirmative Action and Higher Education in the United States and South Africa

❧

Nancy Cantor and Jo Thomas

As we think about higher education's special role in divided societies, we should not overlook the process through which the government of South Africa, in the decade following the collapse of apartheid, sought to heal these divisions in ways that are still bitterly contested in the United States, more than 200 years after the founding of our nation and a century after the Civil War.

The South African Bill of Rights explicitly endorses affirmative action, recognizing that many of the country's citizens are not yet in a position to enjoy equality in any phase of their lives. The South African Constitution also assigns reconciliation a vital role in the establishment of a new and more just society. In the United States, on the other hand, the Constitution protects the rights of individual citizens from abridgement by government, and thus equal protection—a right as much social as individual—has historically been largely ignored, and is now deeply disputed.[1]

The two countries' divergent philosophies regarding social justice and government's role in guaranteeing equality are reflected in their individual laws, and arise from their unique historical experiences.

Individual Protections, Group Advancement

❧

The roots of the American approach to human rights, equality, and liberty are embedded in our colonial experience of British tyranny and oppression. Although Britain's unwritten constitution granted its citizens deep and complex "customary rights," these were often denied to the colonists.[2] Accordingly, the first ten amendments to the Constitution were framed to protect these individual rights from infringement by government.

The Thirteenth Amendment was intended to erase all badges and incidents of slavery but fell short of this goal. Congress passed the Civil Rights Act of 1866 and the Freedmen's Bureau Acts to protect former slaves from efforts by states to abridge their individual rights as citizens, then drafted the Fourteenth Amendment to make those statutes constitutional.[3] The

Fourteenth Amendment decrees that no state may deny any person equal protection under the law or deprive any person of life, liberty, or property without due process of law.

But the nation abandoned Reconstruction after the election of 1876, and the Supreme Court dictated a much narrower reading of the Fourteenth Amendment in 1883, when it held that the first and second sections of the Civil Rights Act of 1875 were unconstitutional. "Government has nothing to do with social, as distinguished from technically legal, rights of individuals," wrote Justice Harlan. "No government ever has brought, or ever can bring, its people into social intercourse against their wishes. Whether one person will permit or maintain social relations with another is a matter with which government has no concern."

Eventually, even the notion of group rights fell under suspicion. As the majority in *Hunter v. Erickson* remarked almost a century later, in 1969: "Because the core of the Fourteenth Amendment is the prevention of meaningful and unjustified distinctions based on race, all racial classifications are 'constitutionally suspect,' and subject to the 'most rigid scrutiny.' They 'bear a far heavier burden of justification' than other classifications."

In the most recent cases in which the Supreme Court has addressed the connection between race and educational opportunity—in the Seattle and Louisville public schools—sixty historians of civil rights and the Reconstruction era objected to the Court's interpretation in *Hunter v. Erickson,* asserting that "there is simply no evidence from the Reconstruction period to suggest that those who framed and ratified the Fourteenth Amendment ever meant for it to limit voluntary, race-conscious integrative measures like those adopted in Seattle and Louisville. Indeed, the relevant historical record points powerfully in the opposite direction."[4] The Congress of the time clearly understood that the denial of educational opportunities to blacks was a by-product of slavery. Its desire, as expressed in the Fifteenth Amendment, also passed during Reconstruction, was to "bring people of all races together in the nation's political institutions, including the jury box and the town square."[5]

Nelson Mandela's postapartheid South African government could ignore neither race nor categories. It was starting fresh after centuries of oppression that ultimately categorized the population into racial groups kept separate by law and force. The apartheid government made race a central feature of every aspect of life, from the workplace to the ballot box, and the bedroom to the schoolroom. In framing their Bill of Rights in the aftermath of apartheid, South Africans felt the urgent need to advance whole groups toward equality. The South African Constitution not only guarantees all individual citizens "the full and equal enjoyment of all rights and freedoms," but also asserts that, to achieve equality, "legislative and other measures designed to protect or advance persons, or categories of persons, disadvantaged by unfair discrimination may be taken."[6] In other words, the Constitution recognizes that groups—categories of persons—as well as individuals had been disadvantaged, and explicitly provides for affirmative action as a remedy.

Unlike the United States after Reconstruction, when revenge and the Ku Klux Klan played increasingly important roles and southern states passed Jim Crow laws to resegregate blacks and whites, the South Africans recognized the importance of reconciliation to both nation-building and policy-making.[7] In his inaugural speech, President Nelson Mandela said, "We place our vision of a new constitutional order for South Africa on the table not as conquerors, prescribing to the conquered. We speak as fellow citizens to heal the wounds of the past with the intent of constructing a new order based on justice for all."[8] The new Constitution recognized not just individual rights, but the legitimacy of groups and categories, and the relationships between those groups. The reconciliation sought by the South Africans was based on restorative—rather than retributive—justice. More than a tool for personal defense, the law is seen as a protector of common interests.[9] In South Africa, reconciliation has meant demystifying the past and rebuilding relationships in the present. As the country drafted legislation to empower its black majority, the Truth and Reconciliation Commission simultaneously sought to expose and redress the terrible wrongs of the past.

Shared Difficulties

❧

Regardless of this history of differences, the goals of social justice and racial equality have so far eluded both South Africa and the United States. As South African minister of labor Membathisi Mdladlana noted in September 2006, "although some employers may have made huge strides in implementing employment equity, the overall picture remains bleak. If we continue at this pace we would most probably reach equitable workplaces only in forty to fifty years from now."[10] He went on, "I am tired of hearing that there is an insufficient pool of suitably qualified people from the designated groups, particularly people with disabilities. The question employers should be asking themselves is what are they doing to ensure that there are a sufficient number of suitably qualified people from the designated groups, especially when employers have enabling legislation such as the Skills Development Act. We must all remember that barriers to employment and the work environment, in most cases, were not there—we put them there! We therefore carry the responsibility to remove them."[11]

New laws and procedures in South Africa have been critical, but not sufficient. The Centre for the Study and Violence and Reconciliation, a South African NGO (nongovernmental organization), has called for improvement in the lived experiences of ordinary people for a broader commitment to social justice that includes social, cultural, and economic rights and the redress of historical inequities.[12] Looking back over the first 10 years of democracy, others have also remarked on their society's failure to achieve the level of reconciliation necessary to repair the fabric of social relationships. Damage is still evident at every level, from the intimate circle of family life to the more public relationship between citizens and state. A 2004 article in the *SA Reconciliation Barometer* observed: "Beyond the handful of black South Africans who can today afford to share in a shopping mall culture of corporatist reconciliation, relations between the races have not fundamentally transformed over the past ten years—with just half (46 percent) of South Africans reporting that they never socialize across racial boundaries and a further quarter (23 percent) stating that they do so only rarely."[13]

This story is not all that different from the American experience since the 1960s, when millions of white American families fled the nation's cities for the suburbs, abandoning urban neighborhoods to desolation and decay. Some cities have recovered, but many—dealt a double blow by the exodus of manufacturing—have not. And recovery has in any case not been synonymous with racial reconciliation. In fact, in the 1990s, resegregation accelerated. As a result, more than 50 years after the *Brown* decision ended de jure segregation in the South, only 14 percent of white students in the United States attend multiracial schools, while almost 40 percent of black and Latino students find themselves in schools with 90 to 100 percent minority populations.[14] Drawing on class segregation and income concentration data from the period 1950–2000, sociologists Douglas S. Massey and Mary J. Fischer of the University of Pennsylvania concluded that the increasing concentrations of affluence in safe neighborhoods, where the rich interact only with each other, "while the poor remain stuck in poor areas," creates the risk of "a divided society that runs counter to the egalitarian ideology of the United States and its historical commitment to equality."[15]

Studies have documented the dire academic and social consequences of the racial and socioeconomic resegregation of America's public school system, where inner-city teachers and principals with inadequate financial resources and facilities are forced to cut costs and improve test scores at the same time.[16] "What kind of childhood, it may be asked, are we designing for these children, who already have so little opportunity to play in safety in their neighborhoods?" the journalist Jonathan Kozol asked, after visiting the stinking, bullet-pocked stairways in which children made up little games. "Pediatricians and psychiatrists may be disturbed to hear of schools where recess is truncated or abolished in the desperation to carve out a bit more time for drilling children for exams; but from the point of view of businesslike efficiency—'time management' and 'maximizing productivity'—it may seem to make no sense to squander time on something that has no apparent benefit beyond the fact that it may be enjoyable and healthy."[17]

Societies such as ours, the philosopher Jonathan Sacks has observed, have become procedural and managerial and have shoved moral considerations to the margin. Sacks calls for recovering an older tradition "that spoke of human solidarity, of justice and compassion, and of the non-negotiable dignity of individual lives."[18] Segregation works against compassion, dignity, and human solidarity because different groups are invisible to each other except through the media, where our culture of consumerism and celebrity heaps adulation on the rich and famous, including some people of color. On the whole, however, people who are poor, black, or brown have been portrayed as criminals or undesirables, while our fixation with sensational crime news has frightened every neighborhood and promoted the punitive transformation of our nation's criminal code. The War on Drugs, which was launched at the end of the Reagan administration, created long mandatory sentences, tripled the African American prison population, and has made an appalling impact on African American communities, damaging the most intimate family relationships and creating a deep crisis of legitimacy for a legal system that, in the eyes of black America, constitutes "a real threat to the promise of equality before the law."[19]

Middle-class South African families, citing their own fear of crime, have also begun retreating behind high walls and private security, withdrawing from public space and "pre-empting the possibility of relationship-building." These added walls and fences are viewed by many as the new face of exclusion, dividing the haves and have-nots, and fueling resentment and a sense of injustice on one side of the wall, "a sustained sense of entitlement and privilege on the other."[20] In the United States, we also live with these walls. Visible and invisible, they exist in a myriad of practices that deny rights, hope, and opportunity to citizens of color.

In South Africa, the initially widespread and uncritical acceptance of "the reconciled rainbow nation" created in its own disequilibrium. "Each incident of racial violence is accompanied by a renewed sense of surprise, as though there is a genuine belief that in 1994 the country merely stepped across a threshold into unity and solidarity," the *Reconciliation Barometer* reported.[21] We have seen that same sense of surprise and anger in the United States among those who cannot understand why institutions of higher education can't seem to get past affirmative action. As Justice Harry Blackmun wrote in the *Bakke* case, "In order to get beyond racism, we must first take account of race. There is no other way."[22]

Many disagree, objecting to any acknowledgment of race, no matter how well intentioned. In denying that diversity has any impact on the educational experience, the Fifth Circuit Court of Appeals in *Hopwood v University of Texas* declared: "The use of race, in and of itself, to choose students simply achieves a student body that looks different. Such a criterion is no more rational on its own terms than would be choices based upon the physical size or blood type of applicants."[23] Such reasoning denies not only the lessons of history, but the realities of the present. As Victor Bolden, David Goldberg, and Dennis Parker have pointed out, "No compromise was required over blood type; no civil war was fought and no Southern Manifesto signed over physical size."[24]

Nonetheless, the American longing for color blindness is as strong as the South African disappointment over the shortcomings of reconciliation. The key difference is that the South African government, elected democratically in 1994, took positive steps toward reconciliation and passed legislation to rebuild its society. For our part, too many of us in the United States seem to believe we can simply declare structural violence—racial segregation, discrimination, and disadvantage—out of existence. We act surprised at the suggestion that anything else must be done. But something must be done, and quickly.

Changing Visions of Diversity and Education

⤳

At the same time the population of the United States is becoming more heterogeneous, the national will to support diversity in higher education is weakening. Two trends in popular culture are responsible for this paradox: one historical; the second contemporary. Each tends to obscure the need to incubate a shared sense of social responsibility, rebuild our communities, and educate a diverse workforce.

The historical hindrance arises from our common conceptions of democracy. Americans, and especially members of the white majority, traditionally have not treated difference as being compatible with unity. As psychologist Patricia Gurin—a fellow contributor to this volume—and her coauthors wrote in 2002, popular understandings of democracy and citizenship usually include such individual acts as voting for a political candidate or participating in some variation of a town meeting with individuals of similar backgrounds. "Both of these conceptions privilege individuals and similarities rather than groups and differences," they noted.[25] This conception has become more problematic as our society has grown more complex. People do identify themselves as members of groups now, especially when they are excluded on that basis. The civil rights movement inspired other disadvantaged groups, including women, indigenous peoples, the elderly, the disabled, the LGBT (lesbian, gay, bisexual, and transgender/transsexual) community, and immigrants. Group membership is still often defined in the breach. It is telling in this regard that the leaders of such groups have often been dismissed as "agitators" or "advocates," terms that marginalize, rather than include.

The second, contemporary roadblock for American higher education has been the inexorable shift toward viewing college admissions as a zero-sum competition, in which applicants vie for precious opportunities in the knowledge economy. Instead of focusing on the public benefits of higher education, we fight over access to its private gains, with the result that applicants are constantly on the lookout for supposedly unfair advantages gained by their competitors. Such suspicions fueled California's 1996 passage of Proposition 209, to cite a relevant example.

Skepticism about the value of "preferences" in improving education or pursuing social justice has now reached the top of the American court system. During oral arguments in the Seattle and Louisville cases, in which white parents opposed the assignment of students to public schools by race in order to achieve integration, Chief Justice Roberts said the purpose of equal protection under law is "to ensure that people are treated as individuals rather than based on the color of their skin"—thus standing the Fourteenth Amendment on its head by invoking it against the very minorities it was created to protect.

In California after Proposition 209, in Texas after *Hopwood,* and in Florida after it adopted a plan similar to the one in Texas, public schools, colleges, and universities have quickly resegregated, resulting in a fully predictable range of distortions and injustices.[26] California, which educates one child in every eight in the United States, has become a national leader in the educational isolation of both blacks and Latinos. The racial disparities in high school graduation rates are massive, and stem largely from the disproportionate concentration of black and Latino children in racially segregated and inferior schools.[27]

As the analysts William G. Bowen, Martin A. Kurzweil, and Eugene M. Tobin observe, "It is historically indefensible and morally wrong to think of race as 'just another' dimension of disadvantage—or, in the language of much of the debate over affirmative action, as 'just another' dimension of diversity."[28] As Ronald Dworkin has put it, "the worst of the stereotypes, suspicions, fears, and hatreds that still poison America are color-coded."[29] The ongoing damage of racial stereotypes crosses all economic boundaries. If we refuse to speak of race, we reinforce the status quo—racial segregation, disadvantage, and stereotypes that damage the heart and the mind—and work against the best interests of our young people, and our nation's future.

Building the Case for Diversity, a Compelling Interest

∾

Twenty-four years after *Brown*, Justice Lewis Powell wrote in *Bakke* that "It is not too much to say that the 'nation's future depends upon leaders trained through wide exposure' to the ideas and mores of students as diverse as this Nation of many peoples." In selecting students who would contribute the most to the "robust exchange of ideas," Powell wrote, the University of California was seeking "a goal that is of paramount importance in the fulfillment of its mission." This idea was reaffirmed in *Grutter v. Bollinger*. Its importance, as Linda Greenhouse observed in the *New York Times,* was that "Justice Powell's solitary view that there was a 'compelling state interest' in racial diversity, a position that had appeared undermined by the court's subsequent equal protection rulings in other contexts and that some lower federal courts had boldly repudiated, has now been endorsed by five justices and placed on a stronger footing than ever before."[30] The majority opinion in *Gratz v. Bollinger* also affirmed the compelling interest of diversity in higher education and the appropriateness of narrowly tailored race-conscious admissions procedures, even as they objected to the specific point system used at the time for undergraduate admissions at the University of Michigan.

In *Brown, Bakke,* and now *Grutter* and *Gratz,* intelligence and excellence are seen from a fundamentally *social* perspective, in which education and achievement are understood as shared activities whose quality depends in large part on the mix of people and ideas, not only in affirmative access but also in affirmative integration. This mix is neither a fixed proportion nor a quota, as lawyers for the American Educational Research Association and the American Association for Higher Education argued in support of the University of Michigan in *Grutter*. It is a "critical mass," a flexible concept that focuses on "the need for students to feel safe and comfortable" and serves as a counter to "the lack of safety or comfort felt when one finds oneself a 'solo' or 'minority of one.'"[31] A critical mass implies "enough students to overcome the silencing effect of being isolated in the classroom by ethnicity/race/gender. Enough students to provide safety for expressing views."[32] A study of University of Michigan Law School alumni, in fact, led its authors to observe that the small numbers of Latino students during the 1970s added tremendous burdens of tokenism and isolation to their classroom experiences. Specifically, it made them reluctant to speak out because they feared putting at risk the reputations of all minority students.[33] In addition, as Patricia Gurin stated in her expert report to the Supreme Court in this case, a critical mass is a group large enough to represent varied views and outlooks within an underrepresented group, with enough variety to dispel stereotypes that all students within the group have identical views and perspectives. A critical mass is essential if there is to be a free and vibrant exchange of ideas. Even if critical mass is not a concept defined by a particular number or percentage, it is easy to recognize when various groups are represented by as much diversity within the groups as between them—that is, when *difference* is widely distributed, not just a matter of black and white.

Integrated environments can reduce stereotypes and enhance empathy. A recent meta-analysis of over 500 studies that collectively involved 250,000 participants confirmed that greater contact between different groups is, in fact, associated with lower levels of prejudice among them.[34] Preliminary results from the Multiversity Intergroup Dialogue Project directed by Patricia Gurin, and involving 10 institutions across the nation, show powerful impacts on the students involved, majority and minority alike, when they talk across differences. Participants in these dialogue groups said afterward that they think harder about how their lives are affected by their own race and ethnicity. They are also better able to perceive the structural factors underlying racial, ethnic, and gender inequality. In addition, the participants in dialogue groups showed a far greater increase in empathy than students in a matched-control group who expressed similar interests in joining the dialogue courses but were not selected to participate by a random-assignment procedure.[35] The experience of intergroup dialogues simultaneously strengthened the social or group identities of participants *and* their intergroup relationships and commitments.

We should remember the example of *Brown* and the words of *Bakke:* there is a compelling national interest in diversity, and there are compelling moral and social issues of justice and human rights. Although affirmative action has provided a vital point of access to higher education—and we must support it—we must also develop new ways to include the broad sectors of our population in the pursuit of equity and excellence. As the South African experience has shown us, it is best to have more than one way, and procedures alone are not enough. The reconstruction of coalitions will be absolutely critical to this effort. We must reconvene supporters from industry, academia, labor, politics, and the military who were so instrumental in persuading the Court in *Grutter,* as well as foundations, NGOs, citizen action groups, the media, and members of professional fields from architecture to health care. This coalition should work together to turn public attention back onto the value of higher education, and the enormous potential benefits of diversity in that arena.

Affirmative action should be seen not only as a procedure, but also as a state of mind and an institutional and public commitment, essential to integration and our ability to tap the individual opportunities and collective societal benefits that flow from it. So how do we go about this task?

Engaging Race

∾

As William Bowen and his coauthors wrote in *Equity and Excellence,* "Americans have an endless appetite for the 'painless alternative,' but all of the work that has gone into examining various approaches to achieving diversity persuades us all over again that the most straightforward way of proceeding—by explicitly taking race into account as one factor among others—is the most sensitive and efficient. There is much to be said for avoiding charades and not dissembling."[36]

After the *Hopwood* decision in Texas and Proposition 209 in California, attempts were made in both states to achieve integration without regard to race. Texas established a new system that promised all students who ranked in the top 10 percent of their high school classes would automatically be admitted to any state college or university. With segregated high schools, this would—in the short term—give access to a proportionate number of talented students of all races. But this proxy for race has had unintended consequences. Although the proportions of Hispanic and black students at the flagship University of Texas at Austin remain roughly the same as before *Hopwood,* the proportion of the student body who came from the top 10 percent of their high school class has jumped from 41 percent to 71 percent, reducing the flexibility of admissions officers to admit students with high achievements in other areas, such as class presidents, science-fair winners, high scorers on the SATs, or artists. It also means that top students—black, Hispanic, or white—who attend the best high schools may not make the 10 percent cut because the numbers of academic achievers in their high schools are very high.[37]

Since the passage of Proposition 209, the Berkeley campus of the University of California has made strenuous efforts to reach out to disadvantaged students. In 2006, more than one-fourth of the university's 23,000 undergraduates were the first in their families to attend college, and nearly one-third came from families earning $35,000 a year or less. In fact, in 2006 Berkeley enrolled more low-income students eligible for federal Pell grants than did all of the Ivy League schools combined.[38] And yet, as 19 former chancellors of the University of California noted in their amicus brief during the Seattle and Louisville cases, "UC's enrollment has not kept pace with the state's changing diversity." In the academic year 2005–6, 8 percent of students in California public high schools were black and 43 percent were Latino, but only 3 percent of University of California undergraduates were black and 14 percent were Latino. The chancellors told the Supreme Court that "given the state ban on race-conscious affirmative action, this underrepresentation of black and Latino students fundamentally reflects the unequal quality of K–12 education afforded to our grandchildren."[39]

No one denies that it is essential to create access or promote economic mobility. Indeed, a number of universities, including Syracuse (where one of the authors of this piece is currently president), are mounting large fundraising campaigns for exactly this purpose. In the past, colleges and universities have had to open their doors to new categories of students—women, GIs returning from World War II, those in need of financial aid, the disabled. Relatively few Americans cried foul, even though making room for these new constituencies intensified the overall competition for admission. It is unfortunately true, as the University of California has found, that class is not a sufficient proxy for race. Instead, a properly broad view of affirmative action would acknowledge that some categories—race and ethnicity first among them—have histories that are not easily erased by upward economic mobility. American society is still deeply segregated, and this refutes, in part, a growing body of criticism that is coming, not from the right, but from the left. These critics ask: Who really benefits from new policies on diversity? Members of minority communities, the argument goes, have no choice but to interact with people from different backgrounds. Unless they're very strictly cloistered, they live diversity every day. Only the white majority has the luxury of not dealing with people of different origins than itself, and therefore whites stand to benefit most from diversity on campus.

This line of thinking is fatally flawed not only by its premise, that members of minority communities live diversity every day in our deeply segregated society, but also by its inference that diversity ultimately works against justice. While access to educational opportunity (and the upward mobility it brings in our society) is a necessary condition for social justice, in and of itself, it is not sufficient. Members of minority communities must be assured that they can actually take advantage of the education and the opportunities to which they are given access. Diversity must be leveraged to create new and democratic communities that welcome minorities as individuals and as members of groups with diverse identities. Members of the white majority will also find that experience with diversity will promote their own commitment to social justice. In such a setting, the entire community is positioned to discern the structural reasons for inequality and discrimination, and members of the minority community can describe it without internalizing it.

Like South Africa, America must recognize as a society the need to act in the spirit of the Thirteenth, Fourteenth, and Fifteenth Amendments. We must acknowledge that all citizens, regardless of their ethnicity or skin color, are entitled to the benefits of diverse schools, neighborhoods, and campuses. As Congress recognized when it passed these amendments, we cannot survive as a democracy if the right to fully participate in our society is not universally guaranteed. It has taken more than a century, through *Brown v. Board of Education,* the civil rights movement of the 1960s, urban riots, the Kerner Commission report, innumerable lawsuits, and strenuous efforts by hundreds of groups and thousands of individuals to bring this fact back to the attention of the American public. In *Grutter,* the Supreme Court acknowledged that "effective participation by members of all racial and ethnic groups in the civic life of our Nation is essential if the dream of one Nation, indivisible, is to be realized."[40]

What we must constantly ask ourselves, however, is what enables *effective participation?* The compelling interest of diversity in higher education is about much more than access. It is about leveraging that diversity to build relationships where they do not routinely exist today, to understand the structural inequalities that got us historically to where we are today as a quite divided society, and, most importantly, to reveal our common interests in overcoming those divisions in order for our democracy to thrive. The Court also declared: "Ensuring that public institutions are open and available to all segments of American society, including people of all races and ethnicities, represents a paramount government objective." Higher education, public and private, has a critical role in this effort, nurturing thoughtful citizenship and promoting democracy among our students and our communities. It is time for a collective, "we" perspective to overtake the zero-sum, "I," stance on either of the many sides of our many national divisions.

Engaging Integration and Creating Diversity

∾

The practical pursuit of integration and diversity entails moving from questions of access and recruitment—issues of structural diversity—to questions about how to foster the intergroup and personal exchanges that make for the best learning, inside and outside the classroom. It takes hard work to overcome boundaries that have been widened by the erosion of years of separation. As the psychologist Claude Steele observed during his expert testimony in *Grutter* and *Gratz,* stereotypes are so threatening and so pervasive that we must strategically design "wise" learning environments to overcome them.[41] We must create environments where people can live and work harmoniously, communicating across the lines of race. This effort demands flexibility and the courage to confront discomfort, mistrust, fear, and even conflict.

Eighty years ago, Leo Sharfman, chair of the Department of Economics at the University of Michigan, described to a men's club a vision of diversity that has yet to be fulfilled: "One cannot sanction the desire for unity which seeks the complete fusion of individuals, racial strains, religious sections, social classes, national groups, or geographical areas—the elimination of their differences and the standardization of their character," he said. "Under such circumstances, life would be impoverished; self-expression would be restrained; curiosity would be stifled; spontaneous experimentation would cease; the irrepressible yearning for progress would be repressed, conditions of status would displace the onward march of mind and hand and heart; the creative spark whereby men are moved to strive ever forward and upward would be dimmed if not extinguished; drab monotony would prevail. True unity is a matter of inward spirit rather than outward manifestation. It involves respect for differences rather than their elimination."[42]

Many deliberate choices will be required, encouraged by a learning environment that places a premium on reconciliation, trust, and the ability to see past superficial differences. The interweaving of diversity and academic excellence is a project just as difficult and just as important as the project of creating affirmative access, and it is absolutely necessary for changing the intellectual and social climate for university students and their communities. At the same time, we must focus on integration in our schools and residential neighborhoods, working to knock down the walls of separation. Attention must be paid to financial equity among K–12 public schools across communities, but as *Brown* told us more than half a century ago, separate is not equal.

We must create ways to build everyday social and intellectual interactions and exchanges between students in these schools, to create friendships that will expand beyond the schoolyard into neighborhoods and homes. The literature on school desegregation is very clear on the benefits of achieving real integration—real contact and interaction—at the earliest age possible. Equity and integration are not alternatives. Both are critical to affording real opportunity and to ensuring a productive society.

The question of how long it will take to achieve enough equity and integration to make procedural affirmative action unnecessary is truly impossible to answer. Justice O'Connor suggested 25 years, or roughly one generation. We would like to believe this, but we consider it unrealistic, as residential divisions—and the accompanying disparities in education, housing, employment, perceptions of safety, and incarceration—have hardened substantially in subsequent years. And even if we could dispense with affirmative action, we could never stop taking groups seriously. While differences may initially pose obstacles to intergroup trust, persistence produces great benefits through multicultural and multiethnic interaction. The most important work, the hardest work, lies ahead.

Here, again, we can draw inspiration and hope from Nelson Mandela, whose humanity and strength even in the isolation of his jail cell inspired a broad social movement that brought down the mighty, entrenched, and unjust structure of apartheid, and laid the foundation for a new nation committed to social justice and democracy.

NOTES

1. *Parents Involved in Community Schools v. Seattle School District No. 1, et al.,* and *Crystal D. Meredith, Custodial Parent and Next Friend of Joshua Ryan McDonald v Jefferson County Board of Education, et. al,* Supreme Court of the United States, 05-908 and 05-915.

2. D. H. Fischer, "Whig Images of Particular Liberties: Visions of an 'American Bill of Rights' before 1776," in *Liberty and Freedom* (New York: Oxford University Press, 2005), 107–12.

3. Brief of Historians as *Amici Curiae* in Support of the Respondents, *Seattle School District No. 1* and *Jefferson County Board of Education,* U.S. Supreme Court, 05-908 and 05-915 (2005).

4. Ibid.

5. Regarding Congress's views on educational opportunities, see the concurring opinion of Justice Thomas in *Zelman v. Simmons-Harris,* 536 U.S. 639, 676 (2002), cited in *Amici* brief in note 3. On the Fifteenth Amendment, see C. Vann Woodward, "The Political Legacy of Reconstruction," *Journal of Negro Education* 26 (1957): 231, 234–35 (also cited in *Amici* brief in note 3).

6. Republic of South Africa, Constitution, Act 108 of 1996, Chapter 2, Section 9 (1) and (2).

7. D. C. Landsberg and S. Mackay, "South Africa 1994–2004," in *Reflections on Democracy and Human Rights: A Decade of the South African Constitution (Act 108 of 1996)* (Johannesburg: South African Human Rights Commission, 2006), 1.

8. Nelson Mandela, "Address to the People of Cape Town, Grand Parade, on the Occasion of His Inauguration as State President," delivered in Cape Town, on May 9, 1994, accessed on February 2, 2007, at http://anc.org.za/ancdocs/history/mandela/1994/inaugct.html.

9. A. Dissel, "Giving a Face to Crime: Report on the Second Phase of the Restorative Justice Initiative Victim Offender Conference Project," *Report of the Restorative Justice Initiative,* April 2003, retrieved January 4, 2007, from http://www.csvr.org.za/papers/papdis11.htm.

10. Membathisi Mdladlana, speech given at the launch of the Sixth Commission for Employment Equity Annual Report, September 11, 2006, accessed November 30, 2006, at http://www.labour.gov.za/media/speeches.jsp?speechdisplay_id=10821.

11. Ibid.

12. Centre for the Study of Violence and Reconciliation, "Evolution of Our Vision and Mission," retrieved January 4, 2007, from http://www.csvr.org.za/aims.htm.

13. N. Valji, B. Harris, and G. Simpson, "Crime, Security and Fear of the Other," *SA Reconciliation Barometer* 2, no. 1, retrieved January 4, 2007, from http://www.csvr.org.za/articles/artvhgs.htm.

14. E. Frankenberg, C. Lee, and G. Orfield, *A Multiracial Society with Segregated Schools: Are We Losing the Dream?* (Cambridge, MA: Civil Rights Project, 2003), 29.

15. D. S. Massey and M. J. Fischer, "The Geography of Inequality in the United States, 1950–2000," in *Brookings-Wharton Papers on Urban Affairs: 2003,* ed. W. G. Gale and J. Rothenberg Pack (Washington, DC: Brookings Institution Press, 2003), accessed De-

cember 6, 2006, at http://www.brookings.edu/press/books/brookingswhartonpaperson urbanaffairs2003.htm.

16. The NAACP Legal Defense and Educational Fund, the Civil Rights Project of Harvard University, and the Center for the Study of Race and Law at the University of Virginia School of Law, *Looking to the Future: Voluntary K–12 School Integration; A Manual for Parents, Educators, and Advocates* (New York: NAACP Legal Defense Fund, 2005), 10. See also D. S., Massey, C. Z. Charles, G. F. Lundy, and M. J. Fischer, *The Source of the River: The Social Origins of Freshmen at America's Selective Colleges and Universities* (Princeton: Princeton University Press, 2003).

17. J. Kozol, *The Shame of the Nation: The Restoration of Apartheid Schooling in America* (New York: Crown, 2005), 120–21.

18. J. Sacks, *The Dignity of Difference: How to Avoid the Clash of Civilizations* (New York: Continuum, 2002).

19. On the impact on families, see W. J. Wilson, *The Truly Disadvantaged: The Inner City, the Underclass, and Public Policy* (Chicago: University of Chicago Press, 1987), and S. D. Lane, R. H. Keefe, R. A. Rubinstein, B. A. Levandowski, M. Freedman, A. Rosenthal, D. A. Cibula, and M. Czerwinski, "Marriage Promotion and Missing Men: African American Women in a Demographic Double Blind," *Medical Anthropology Quarterly* 18, no. 4 (2004): 405–28. On the crisis of legitimacy, see L. D. Bobo and V. Thompson, "Unfair by Design: The War on Drugs, Race, and the Legitimacy of the Criminal Justice System," *Social Research* 73, no. 2 (Summer 2006): 2.

20. Valji, Harris, and Simpson, "Crime, Security and Fear."

21. Ibid.

22. Justice Harry Blackmun, concurring in part and dissenting in part, in *Regents of University of California v. Bakke,* 438 U.S. 265, 407 (1978).

23. *Hopwood* (1996, 950), cited by P. Gurin, E. L. Dey, S. Hurtado, and G. Gurin, "Diversity in Higher Education: Theory and Impact on Educational Outcomes," *Harvard Educational Review* 72, no. 3 (Fall 2002): 331.

24. Cited by Gurin et al., "Diversity in Higher Education," 332.

25. Ibid., 340.

26. For additional details see J. Rogers, V. Terriquez, S. Valladares, and J. Oaks, *California Educational Opportunity Report: Roadblocks to College* (Los Angeles: UC/ACCORD and UCLA IDEA, March 2006); S. Loeb, L. Darling-Hammond, and J. Luczak, "How Teaching Conditions Predict Teaching Turnover in California Schools," *Peabody Journal of Education* 80, no. 3 (2005): 44–70; K. M. Borman, T. McNulte Eitle, D. Michael, D. J. Eitle, R. Lee, L. Johnson, D. Cobb-Roberts, S. Dorn, and B. Schircliffe, "Accountability in a Postdesegregation Era: The Continuing Significance of Racial Desegregation in Florida's Schools," *American Educational Research Journal* 41, no. 3 (Fall 2004): 605–31; and J. Berger, "Adjusting a Formula Devised for Diversity," *New York Times,* December 13, 2006, late edition, B7.

27. On California's racial disparities, see the *Amicus* brief by 19 former chancellors of the University of California in support of respondents in *Parents Involved in Community Schools.* On demographic concentrations, see G. Orfield and C. Lee, *Racial Transformation and the Changing Nature of Segregation* (Cambridge: Civil Rights Project at Harvard University, 2006), 26, cited by the chancellors in their *Amicus* brief.

28. W. G. Bowen, M. A. Kurzweil, and E. M. Tobin, *Equity and Excellence in American Higher Education* (Charlottesville: University of Virginia Press, 2005), 141.

29. R. Dworkin, "Affirming Affirmative Action," *New York Review of Books,* October 22, 1998, 91–102, quote on pp. 99–100, cited in Bowen, Kurzweil, and Tobin, *Equity and Excellence,* 141.

30. L. Greenhouse, "The Supreme Court: Affirmative Action: Justices Back Affirmative Action by 5 to 4, but Wider Vote Bans a Racial Point System," *New York Times*, June 24, 2003, A1, cited in Bowen, Kurzweil and Tobin, *Equity and Excellence*, 148.

31. R. H. Gudeman, "Faculty Experience with Diversity: A Case Study of Macalester College," in *Diversity Challenged: Evidence on the Impact of Affirmative Action*, ed. G. Orfield and M. Kurlander (Cambridge: Harvard Publishing Group, 2001), 251, 267–68 .

32. Ibid., at 268.

33. D. L. Chambers, R. O. Lempert, and T. K. Adams, "Michigan's Minority Graduates in Practice: The River Runs through Law School," *Law and Social Inquiry* 25 (2000): 395.

34. T. Pettigrew and L. Tropp, "A Meta-analytic Test of Intergroup Contact Theory," *Journal of Personality and Social Psychology* 90 (2006): 751–83, cited in *Amicus* brief of 19 former chancellors of the University of California in the Seattle and Louisville cases.

35. Preliminary information supplied in private correspondence with Professor Gretchen E. Lopez, director of the Syracuse University project for the 10-institution Multiversity Intergroup Dialogue Project.

36. Bowen, Kurzweil, and Tobin, *Equity and Excellence*, 151.

37. Berger, "Adjusting a Formula."

38. *Amicus* brief of 19 former chancellors of the University of California, 19.

39. Ibid.

40. *Grutter, et al., v. Bollinger, et al.,* 539 U.S. at 331, cited in Bowen, Kurzweil, and Tobin, *Equity and Excellence*, 150.

41. Expert report of Claude M. Steele, in *Gratz, et al., v. Bollinger, et al.,* No. 97-75321 in the U.S. District Court for the Eastern District of Michigan, and *Grutter, et. al., v. Bollinger, et al.,* No. 97-75928 in the U.S. District Court for the Eastern District of Michigan.

42. L. Sharfman, speech delivered to Men's Club, Temple Beth El, November 15, 1927, cited in Patricia Gurin, Jeffrey S. Lehman, and Earl Lewis, with Eric L. Dey, Gerald Gurin, and Sylvia Hurtado, *Defending Diversity: Affirmative Action at the University of Michigan* (Ann Arbor: University of Michigan Press, 2004), 2.

PART II ∼ Higher Education in the World

Labor Markets and Social Mobility

Introduction to Part II, *David L. Featherman*

Higher education, both in South Africa and the United States, creates both private and public goods, as I noted in the introduction to this volume. Among them are equipping graduates with the knowledge and skills for competitive employment in higher-paying jobs—a private good—and opening visible channels of social mobility across generations that inspire hope for the future throughout a society—a public good. Three chapters in this section plumb the significance of affirmative action in the context of higher education's dual relationships to the labor market and to social mobility.

In the new South Africa, education of blacks would seem a key ingredient in its successful transformation and in pervasive social mobility. Yet Jonathan Jansen argues that South Africa's education system is highly dysfunctional. Despite massive infusion of financial aid for the college-bound, aggressive efforts to increase enrollments especially in the former nonwhite institutions, and the governmental priority of increasing enrollment of black students in underrepresented fields, higher education is failing its mission. The causes lie in underprepared high school graduates and within the institutions that would educate them: lax admission standards in some universities, insufficient sustainable financial aid for the neediest, and the misalignment of college curriculum and pedagogy with the multicultural backgrounds and learning styles of matriculating students. If the young democracy is to be served by social mobility for majority blacks, Jansen argues, what is broken needs to be fixed. What threatens to persist is a two-tiered system, with the better-prepared (and comparatively affluent) black students recruited into formerly white, urban, and well-resourced universities, while most others enter underfunded, rural, and predominantly black universities and other postsecondary institutions.

This two-tiered educational system adds perversely to the economic inequality mounting among black South Africans if not also to the rising importance of economic disparities in the country as a whole. Haroon Bhorat, examining the most recent decade of evidence about the economic value of education, documents a severe and growing mismatch between the jobs being created in the new South African economy and the knowledge and skills developed by the contemporary educational system, especially by nonuniversity higher education (e.g., the former technikons, now called technical universities). The result is a paradox: high and rising unemployment of skilled labor in a market of high demand for skilled labor, coupled with a declining wage advantage for workers with postsecondary certification when compared to those without it. Notably, those with university degrees do more readily find employment and premium wages. Bhorat explains the paradox as a failure of the educational system, especially nonuniversity higher education, to supply the skills required in the new economy. And he shows that the cost of this paradox is borne most heavily by Africans. On the one hand, black university graduates are in very high demand and in short supply, and garner premium wages (even when compared to their white peers). On the other hand, Africans gaining certification and diplomas for technical and other high-level skills but not from universities are increasingly falling behind, in wage levels and in employment opportunities. The root of the paradox is failing postsecondary institutions— contemporary ones—that should be stepping stones for economic success and social mobility, after apartheid.

Bruce Western ends this section on a discordant note. America elected its first black president, Barack Obama, in November 2008, capping decades of apparent racial progress and social mobility for well-educated men and women of all races. But according to Western, America also embarked upon a course of rapid mass imprisonment in the last two decades of the twentieth century. Working-age males, often recent school dropouts, unemployed, predominantly African American and, to a lesser degree, Latino, entered the prison system in rising numbers and rates far in excess of their white, more educated counterparts. Indeed, the black-white difference in these rates became far greater than racial differences in unemployment, nonmarital childbearing, infant mortality, or wealth. In effect, mass imprisonment of black men masks what otherwise might be even greater numbers of unemployed or not employed workers, even wider disparities in poverty by race, for example, had men not been institutionalized. But once released, former prisoners suffer cumulative economic disadvantages from stigmatization, low levels of on-the-job experience or productivity, and few networks of regularly working peers providing leads to opportunities in more stable jobs. Western argues that the period of mass and differential incarceration of black men coincided with the disappearance of low-skill, low-wage jobs in cities; it also was coupled with a rise in political conservatism and racial reactivity in the post-civil rights era that led to an abridgment of equal protection for those accused of crimes. While Western does not state this inference, the retrenchment of civil rights through mass and disparate incarceration could be viewed as a counterforce to affirmative action. If affirmative action on the part of higher education increases the public good by extending the benefits of social mobility, then Western's analysis might suggest that the public good is diminished to the degree that the foundation of mass incarceration of black men rests upon retrenched civil rights. Taking this point of view for argument's sake, one might say that affirmative action provides some remedy for a contemporary inequity in the penal system.

Moving on Up? The Politics, Problems, and Prospects of Universities as Gateways for Social Mobility in South Africa

∽

Jonathan D. Jansen

Black South Africans have continued to highly prize university education in the postapartheid era. Understanding this well, the new political leadership briefly introduced the vocabulary of massification into the higher-education lexicon. But massification did not happen, in large part because the country's schools failed to deliver sufficient numbers of graduates who could qualify for university entrance, and then succeed once they gained access to these institutions. The period from 1997 to 2003 saw a constant decline in the number of high school students writing the Grade 12 end-of-school examination. It is in light of this fact that we can best understand the limits of higher education as a gateway for social mobility, more than a dozen years after the legal demise of apartheid.

South Africa's chronically dysfunctional school system is the key obstacle to black citizens' social mobility. Less than 50 percent of those who start in Grade 1 complete all 12 years of schooling; about a third of those who write the high-stakes Grade 12 examination fail; of the remainder, only 16 percent achieve marks high enough to gain university entrance. In the so-called gateway subjects, mathematics and physical science, less than 5 percent of students pass math on the advanced level, less than 6 percent in physical science. Worse still, when disaggregated by race, the passing grades are largely accounted for by white minority students and the small percentage of mainly middle-class black students who can now attend desegregated, former white public schools.[1] In short, the pool of high school graduates qualifying for university entrance is small and weak, leaving most black students falling short at a critical juncture where all-important life chances are sorted and allocated.

What, in this limiting context, is the role of the South African university in the social mobility of its graduates? There are what one might call pull-in and push-out factors working against each other in determining social mobility. On the pull-in side, there are three main factors that enable greater numbers of high-school graduates to access higher education and thereby increase their chances of social mobility.

The first is the massive increase in financial aid available to students with financial need and academic promise. The new government has committed itself to a policy in which virtually no student who meets these two basic criteria is turned away. Whereas, under apartheid, black students desiring a university education were channeled into the public service sector (teaching, nursing, police, etc.) through a limited number of state bursaries—the equivalent of scholarships, which may or may not require repayment after graduation—the new National Student Financial Aid Scheme, alongside a range of institutional and private-sector bursaries and loans, offers a broad choice of disciplines to ever-increasing numbers of students who would otherwise not be in a position to continue their studies.

The second factor is the desperate need to increase enrollments as a matter of institutional survival, especially for the weaker two-thirds of universities in South Africa, most of which are black and rural. Since state funding is based in part on enrollment rates, the institutions are intensely competing for the small pool of university-qualifying students. Compounding this problem is the fact that the end of university segregation meant that high-achieving middle-class black students could now more easily enter former white institutions, which themselves sought to increase their student diversity as proof of their transformation. As a result, the black universities increasingly found themselves able to attract only those students who passed poorly, and in most cases without the university-entrance pass, otherwise known as the matriculation exemption. In response, university senates (the campus assemblies responsible for setting academic policy) often broadened their institutions' discretion to admit students without exemption. The strategy of widening access to ensure institutional survival created serious problems for black universities, and resulted in some institutions literally registering poor and academically weak students off the streets.

The third pull-in factor is the political demand to increase access for black students at both the undergraduate and graduate levels, especially in underrepresented fields like science, technology, and engineering. There is tremendous pressure on institutions—especially the former white institutions—to be seen as responsive to this call from government. The 2001 National Plan for Higher Education set out strategies to increase access, and a series of more recent government programs (including the Accelerated Shared Growth Initiative of South Africa, or ASGISA; and the Joint Initiative on Priority Skills Acquisition, or JIPSA), backed by special funding, are drawing institutional attention to the need to increase the number of minority (especially black) graduates in these fields. By now South Africa has built up a long tradition of academic support programs of various kinds, which help promising but poorly prepared black students succeed in university life. In sum, there is no shortage of political pressure on universities to draw more and more black students into critical fields of study.

In a perfect world, this combination of government pressure, institutional need, and financial support would create ideal conditions for increased access and social mobility among black students. But there are several powerful push-out factors that undermine access to higher education, preventing students from making their way through university and into productive careers.

The first of these push-out factors is the weak preparation of high school graduates for higher education, resulting in very high dropout rates, especially among black students. After the initial triumph of gaining access to the educational system, these students find themselves struggling with academic failure and its consequences, whether institutional exclusion or individual dropping-out. Either way, the personal and social costs are very high. South Africa's dropout rate is in part a function of the careless admission policies, mentioned earlier, in which institutions readily admit weak students without university entrance passes, only to fail them during the course of their studies. The chasm dividing high school and university education is generally quite wide in South Africa; it is impassable for students who barely pass their end-of-school examinations.[2]

The second push-out factor is the extraordinary high cost of tertiary education, so that even when finances are available for needy students, the monetary assistance may not be sufficient to cover the tuition, accommodation, and living expenses of a black student from a rural area, for example, who may require full funding. The marginal difference between available state support and the actual amount of funding students require increases the hardship for poor students. To make matters worse, students who struggle to meet the minimum academic requirements for initial funding and fail to meet the threshold for continued state support (that is, who are unable to pass more than 50 percent of their courses) must struggle with both academic and financial problems. The opportunity costs are especially high for black students who forego income to complete a four or five-year degree, a considerable burden on their families, who may have to delay income while a sibling is in training. As the pressure mounts, such students are often coerced into leaving the university system.

The third push-out factor is the inability of institutions to accommodate students from a range of nontraditional backgrounds. This is especially common among the former white universities. Black students find that they have to cope with the unfamiliar demands of academic English, and in the former Afrikaans universities also encounter situations in which Afrikaans is still the dominant language—an experience that most of them find profoundly alienating.[3] All of the former white universities have made mistaken assumptions about entry-level social and instrumental skills of their black students, many of whom in actuality are the first-generation university entrants in their families. These institutions routinely assume that their students come from a reading culture, can navigate a well-stocked university library, have had access to computers and the Internet, and possess basic studying and writing skills, family mentors with university degrees, and supplementary sources of income. In short, South Africa's problem is not simply a matter of poorly prepared students; it is also a matter of poorly adapting universities.

It is worth noting that the social mobility of black South Africans enjoyed one of its most powerful surges when hundreds of master's and doctoral students were literally removed from the country during the apartheid years and transferred with full scholarships to universities in the United States under the Educational Opportunities Program and the leadership of then-bishop Desmond Tutu, in partnership with the New York–based Institute for International Education. The most prominent persons in virtually every sector of South Africa society today—higher education, government, the private sector—are mainly graduates of this program. And as the education scholar Vijay Reddy has shown, almost every one of them ascribes his or her success to being lifted out of the damning institutional cultures that dominated all apartheid universities in South Africa, black and white.[4]

Taken together, the pull-in factors explain the dramatic changes in the ratio of white to black South Africans now enjoying access to higher education compared to 15 years ago, whereas the push-out factors explain the highly inefficient system of higher education that is taking a huge individual, institutional, and social toll on this young democracy.

The problems of social mobility are compounded when one moves beyond broad trends to examine them in the context of individual academic disciplines. Black students are heavily underrepresented in fields in which science and mathematics are firm entrance requirements: for example, information technology, engineering, the natural sciences, and medicine offer black students relatively few opportunities for social mobility. Again, this reflects onto a school system where very few black students take mathematics and science at all, and even fewer take these subjects on the level required for access to university-level training.

Medicine represents a special challenge, because the places are few enough and the competition fierce enough to powerfully concentrate the politics of race, and the consequences for social mobility. University administrators in the former white institutions are clearly conscious of the reasons, political, social, and economic, to train a more diverse class of doctors, and have broadened the criteria for admission beyond high school academic performance. White students and their parents have cried foul, showing reporters certificates of distinctions in six or more school subjects, and claiming that they were excluded by virtue of race. Given the relative historical advantage enjoyed by Indian students over their African counterparts, the same justifications are sometimes used to admit African students over their Indian counterparts. Such selection is also commonly justified by a demographic argument: whites and Indians are a small minority in relation to the country's more than 80 percent African population, and very few graduates from those minority groups (especially whites) will choose to practice medicine in rural black communities, if they stay in South Africa at all. These are difficult choices for institutions, where the precision of empirical criteria meets the wisdom of political judgment. Few get the balance right.

Teacher training is another important challenge. During the apartheid years, black South Africans' opportunities for social mobility were restricted to civil-service occupations like teaching, nursing, and policing. As a consequence, there was an overproduction of black trainees in these fields. After the end of apartheid, teaching was no longer seen as a vehicle for social mobility and advancement. Black students who graduated with university-entrance qualifications enrolled instead in high-income, high-status fields like economics and accounting. As a result, most new teachers are now white and women, and serious teacher shortages are predicted especially for the country's black schools. Here, the problem is the direct opposite of what it is in medicine: students of all backgrounds are recruited, and bursaries are readily available for any student wanting to pursue a teaching career.

Universities have responded to critical shortages in fields like science and engineering with a variety of programs, include bridging (preuniversity entrance programs to strengthen skills in basic science and math), support (additional tuition support alongside the mainstream courses), and extended programs (in which students are given an additional year to complete their studies). Millions of dollars are spent on such compensatory programs every year, and it is clear that where selection, design, and delivery are managed carefully, individual students can successfully make their way through the higher-education system. It is unclear, though, whether such investment adequately compensates for 12 years of poor schooling among black students as a group.

One point of real concern to the South African government is the question of where its graduates go after they've enjoyed the privileges of access and success in the country's national higher-education system. There is growing evidence of a debilitating brain drain, which is no longer restricted to white citizens.[5] Europe has become a major attraction for the socially mobile in fields like teaching and nursing and dentistry; in fact, the largest percentage of expatriate teachers from Commonwealth countries in the United Kingdom comes from South Africa. The more favorable salaries and conditions of service there are a major draw to skilled South African professionals, at considerable costs to the postapartheid taxpayer. The growing reach and impact of violent crime has also contributed to this out-migration. The implications for postapartheid national reconstruction are enormous. There is, however, little that can be done to reverse such trends, in a global economy where skilled people are free to mobilize their assets.

It cannot be argued that South African universities are selective gatekeepers in any significant sense; in fact, the argument could be made that they are hardly even efficient gatekeepers at all. External political pressure and internal institutional demand are powerful pull-in factors for almost any high school graduate desiring a university education. But, at the same time, the social, financial, and intellectual demands for academic progress exercise a powerful push-out effects on those otherwise desperate for postschool training.

There is one last phenomenon that should be taken into account in our thinking about the social mobility of black South African students: the growing evidence that, as former white high schools desegregate, they bring into their midst a racially mixed middle class of students who enjoy superior facilities, trained teachers, predictable timetables, and strong learning cultures.[6] These middle-class black students in turn choose to study at the former white universities, which are connected with the high schools from which these students graduated. What emerges is a two-tiered system, with an upper tier of well-resourced, urban, and former white universities that are racially integrated, and a lower tier of underresourced, mainly rural universities that remain black. As can be expected, the trajectories of social mobility in such a system are not determined simply by the fact that you studied, but by *where* you studied.

So what are the prospects for South African universities' role in advancing the social mobility of black high-school graduates? First, it should be clear that this problem cannot be overcome without fixing the school system. There are simply too few graduates graduating from the system with sufficient skills and grades to enter university. If this deficit persists, it will simply transfer pressure onto the country's universities to admit weaker students, in larger numbers.

Second, a national strategy to increase mobility will have to create more viable and credible alternatives to the university, as the perceived "one best system" for all high school graduates. A limited number of well-equipped technical colleges with high-quality staff, operationally linked to major industries, will help erode categorical prejudices toward such institutions.

Similarly, viable community colleges and other forms of postsecondary education must be established so that students have the choice of training in a number of institutional types, all of which deliver competent graduates who will be valued and embraced by the economy. There are some governmental efforts in this direction, such as the restructuring and recapitalization of technical colleges, but it is unclear whether these investments are sufficient to encourage a more even distribution of enrollments across the postsecondary ecology.

Third, universities must forego the idea that broadening access to promising but disadvantaged students means lowering quality. Both ideals can and must be attained. Doing so will require, however, that universities recognize the need to define success more broadly, accepting this as a challenge to their own institutional cultures, behaviors, and rules, rather than simply treating the issue as a matter of individual student pathology. Increasing the number of languages in which an education can be earned would be an important start. But this will mean more aggressive efforts to recruit more and more talented black academics and researchers—already a debilitating problem for virtually all of the former white universities. The dearth of highly qualified black academic staff is even more acute than the shortage of black students. The lack of academic role models contributes to feelings of isolation and alienation among black students, and even among young black academics.

Fourth, and finally, universities must begin to build powerful, sustainable partnerships with selected black high schools within their catchment areas. In a developing country like South Africa it is simply not enough to wait for the students to come knocking—and then to make damning judgments about who is fit enough to enter. Community service is, alongside teaching and research, a crucial element of every institution's mission, one that is best fulfilled by working with high school students to improve their science and math results; working alongside schoolteachers to deepen their subject-matter knowledge; guiding and counseling schoolchildren about the widest range of their future career opportunities; and helping schools to build strong and sustainable managerial cultures, in the often-unpredictable, if not chaotic, township school environments.

NOTES

1. M. Kahn, "Changing Science and Mathematics Achievement: Reflections on Policy and Planning," *Perspectives in Education* 19, no. 3 (2001): 169–74; M. Kahn, "For Whom the School Bell Tolls: Disparities in Performance in Senior Certificate Mathematics and Physical Science," *Perspectives in Education* 22, no. 1 (2005): 149–56.

2. J. Jansen, H. Sehlapelo, and R. Tabane, *How Students Negotiate Academic Cultures* (Pretoria: Council on Higher Education, 2007).

3. Ibid.

4. V. Reddy et al., *The Educational Opportunities Council: Life, Impact, and Prospects* (Johannesburg: Educational Opportunities Council, 2002).

5. Kahn, "For Whom the School Bell Tolls"; R. de Villiers and R. Degazon-Johnson, "The Political Economy of Teacher Migration," *Perspectives in Education* 25, no. 2 (June 2007): special issue.

6. S. Motala, "Education Resourcing in Post-apartheid South Africa: The Impact of Finance Equity Reforms in Public Schooling," *Perspectives in Education* 24, no. 2 (2006): 79–93.

Higher Education and the Labor Market in Postapartheid South Africa

Haroon Bhorat

South Africa's formal 1994 transition from White minority rule justifiably received international attention and acclaim. The country's first democratically elected party, the African National Congress (ANC), was voted into power in April of that year. Overshadowing the relatively peaceful transition, however, was the challenge of dealing with the economic vestiges of apartheid. Nowhere has this challenge been more apparent than in the country's labor markets, where it manifests itself in at least two interrelated ways: first, in one of the highest unemployment rates in the world (officially 26.7 percent, but rising still higher to 38.8 percent when discouraged workers are included); and second, in a rapid increase in demand for educated workers, the upshot of which has been an ongoing and severe skills shortage.[1] This particular form of labor market segmentation, in which an excess supply of unskilled labor coexists alongside a chronic shortage of skilled labor, hinges, of course, on the particular supply characteristics of individual workers. Thus, any student of the South African economy has to acknowledge the importance of higher education in training workers for the labor market.

That market has been defined and shaped by several key trends. First of all, the survey data indicate that aggregate employment increased from 9.5 million in 1995 to 12.3 million by September 2005. This translates into a growth in employment of 29 percent, or about 2.67 percent annually. Economic growth over the same period averaged 3.27 percent annually, suggesting that, for the given level of economic growth, the economy has been creating a fairly acceptable number of jobs.[2]

However, it is important to note that while South Africa did not experience jobless growth during this period, the country's employment growth was clearly insufficient to absorb the growth of the labor force. Although 2.8 million jobs were created, the labor force grew by just over twice this amount, adding about 6.3 million new entrants into the labor market. The consequence, naturally, has been a significant rise in unemployment: only 44 jobs were created for every 100 individuals who entered the labor market in search of employment during the first decade after the end of apartheid.

It is important, however, to look at employment shifts during this period in terms of years of schooling. Doing so allows us to gauge the extent to which those individuals with higher levels of skill, or human capital, are in fact being absorbed into long-term employment. Figure 1 illustrates the employment absorption rate (EAR)—the ratio between actual employment growth and the desired rate of growth—for the three categories of students who passed through the higher-education system between 1995 and 2005.[3] The leftmost bar includes data on individuals who completed their general education and training, or GET, and specifically those who passed Grade 11 in the South African system, or began but did not complete their qualification at a technikon. The next ("Matric") cohort refers to individuals who have passed the 12th grade. Individuals with some form of nonuniversity certification are included in the next two bars, noting that these qualifications can be attained with or without a matric. Finally university qualifications are captured by the "Degree" bar.

The figure illustrates what is now well known: that the South African schooling system does not sufficiently prepare individuals for the labor market. Hence, we find that during this decade half of all individuals with a matric or even a completed technical qualification who were searching for a job did not find one. Of even greater interest for readers of this book, however, is the further fact that the postschooling institutions—with the possible exception of universities—do not seem to be doing an adequate job in securing employment for their graduates, either. Hence, we find that over the 1995–2005 period, somewhere between 68 and 72 percent of all diploma and certificate holders with some secondary schooling were absorbed into employment. For those who never completed their secondary schooling or technical college certification the EAR measure stood at an even more worrisome 43 percent. Conversely, approximately 95 out of every 100 university graduates who were job-searching over this same period successfully found employment.

At first glance, these results suggest that educated and skilled individuals are not guaranteed employment in South Africa's domestic economy, despite the country's severe skills shortages.[4] Specifically, they point to the fact that the system of secondary and higher education may not be efficiently providing employers with the level and quality of worker they desire.

The Specter of Graduate Unemployment

❧

The EAR figure, while useful, also masks some important facts about joblessness among graduates of higher education.

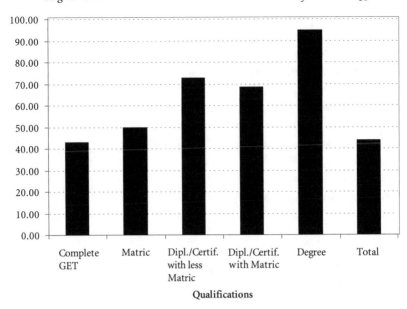

Fig. 1.   Employment absorption rates by education cohorts: 1995–2005. (Data from OHS 1995; LFS 2005, 2 [Statistics SA].)

Finer-grained unemployment statistics hence show that race remains an important determinant in the postapartheid labor market. African unemployment rates are higher than White unemployment rates, and, indeed, higher than the national averages, as well. For example, while the unemployment rate for degreed Whites stood at 2.3 percent in 2005, the figure was a full 7 percent for African individuals with comparable qualifications (see table 1). The same data also reveal that approximately 240,000 individuals with some form of postsecondary training were unemployed in 2005. While as an absolute figure this is low, particularly relative to overall national unemployment levels, the graduate unemployment rate, derived by summing three education cohorts, stands at 10.5 percent for the same year.

In addition, graduate unemployment rates have been the fastest-growing over the period under consideration, thanks to rapidly rising unemployment among workers with diplomas and certificates, who are a subset of the graduate category. Hence, we find that graduate unemployment grew by 51.2 percent over the 1995–2005 period, compared to a 26 percent increase in national unemployment overall. Unemployment among African graduates has increased faster than among Whites or any other racial group, so that what is referred to as a growing graduate unemployment problem is more accurately an *African* graduate unemployment problem.

Labor Market Mismatches and Outcomes

∾

As graduate joblessness grows, we also have to consider the fact that individuals are accumulating their degrees, certificates, or diplomas in different fields of study, and at institutions of differing levels of quality (perceived or actual).

The evidence provided in table 2 suggests that the vast majority of unemployed graduates—close to 70 percent—have studied in one of four fields, namely business, commerce, and management studies; physical, mathematical, computer, and life sciences; education training and development; and manufacturing, engineering, and technology. Graduates of non-degree-granting institutions of higher education dominate the unemployment figures. One could argue that the further education and training sector and the technikon system are the heart of the graduate unemployment problem. These institutions therefore are either not producing the types of graduates employers want, or are not producing graduates of satisfactory quality. The fact that, of the four fields of study that are so dominant in the unemploy-

TABLE 1. Unemployment Rates by Years of Schooling, 1995 and 2005

Category	Unemployed, 2005	Unemployment Rate		
		1995	2005	% Change
African				
Complete GET	2,990,488	42.42	50.81	19.79
Matric	1,756,727	42.07	48.98	16.41
Graduate	204,799	10.60	17.21	62.35
Dipl./Certif. with less than Matric	34,035	15.31	28.66	87.18
Dipl./Certif. with Matric	147,229	11.28	19.99	77.28
Degree	23,535	6.15	7.03	14.34
Total	6,903,309	37.77	44.80	18.61
White				
Complete GET	47,612	11.80	15.29	29.55
Matric	90,751	4.94	9.22	86.44
Graduate	21,587	2.50	2.58	3.20
Dipl./Certif. with less than Matric	366	3.06	0.62	−79.76
Dipl./Certif. with Matric	11,978	2.56	3.22	25.62
Degree	9,243	2.34	2.28	−2.43
Total	170,739	5.75	7.89	37.23
Total (All Racial Groups)				
Complete GET	3,386,308	35.81	47.37	32.29
Matric	2,034,309	27.03	37.77	39.77
Graduate	237,453	6.93	10.48	51.23
Dipl./Certif. with less than Matric	36,233	11.03	18.10	64.14
Dipl./Certif. with Matric	165,062	7.91	13.24	67.49
Degree	36,158	3.89	4.41	13.51
Total	7,799,557	30.82	38.80	25.91

Source: October Household Survey 1995; Labour Force Survey 2005, 2 (Statistics SA).

ment numbers, three are clearly areas of high employment demand, suggests that employers are not concerned only about field of study, but also quality.[5]

Ultimately, then, the national graduate unemployment problem in South Africa is characterized first by disproportionate joblessness among African graduates, and second by nonuniversity institutions of higher education supplying wrongly or poorly qualified graduates. The latter, however, should not be allowed to completely obscure the university system's own failure to produce reliably employable graduates, albeit a failure of considerably lesser degree.

While we cannot begin to do justice to the many dimensions of this severe institutional mismatch, the data do illustrate one important consequence. When we examine average wages for 2001 and 2005 (calculated in 2000 prices), by educational cohort, the ratio of mean wages for all workers to mean wages for workers with a postsecondary degree, the result provides a startling indicator of a severe mismatch in the labor market. Over this very short time period, while the real wages of all the relevant education cohorts increased, wages of individuals with degrees did so most rapidly, with the average wage of a degreed individual increasing 52 percent during a four-year period, from 8,417 rand to 12,788 rand per month. The increase for African workers, meanwhile, was more than three times higher, at roughly 185 percent.

To some extent these increases reflect a shortage of African graduates, as companies struggling to meet their employment equity targets and fulfill their goals for Broad-Based Black Economic Empowerment (the South African government's ambitious wealth-distribution plan) are forced to offer huge premia to attract these scarce individuals.

However, the disparity may also reflect a market for more highly edu-

TABLE 2. Graduate Unemployment by Field of Study, 2005

Field of Study/Education	Number	Share of Total	Share: Tertiary Degree
Communication Studies and Language	9,133	3.85	8.40
Education, Training, and Development	33,476	14.10	24.83
Manufacturing, Engineering, and Technology	25,851	10.89	6.20
Human and Social Studies	12,965	5.46	7.58
Law, Military Science, and Security	11,528	4.85	32.95
Health Sciences and Social Services	20,757	8.74	9.03
Agriculture and Nature Conservation	8,781	3.70	50.39
Culture and Arts	4,576	1.93	19.32
Business, Commerce, and Management Studies	62,633	26.38	10.01
Physical, Mathematical, Computer, and Life Sciences	40,819	17.19	17.74
Physical Planning and Construction	1,408	0.59	0.00
Other	5,526	2.32	0.00
Total	237,453	100.00	15.23

Source: Labour Force Survey 2005, 2 (Statistics SA).
Note: Column 2 does not sum to 100 percent because of rounding.

cated individuals that is too dependent on outputs from the university system. To put it differently, the results may reflect a poor and malfunctioning FET and technikon system, whose failures are forcing the country's employers to recruit more expensive university graduates instead. The latter represent a much smaller pool of appropriately trained and qualified individuals to draw from. The failure of the nonuniversity higher education system has, in technical terms, forced a leftward shift of the supply curve for skilled individuals, which has rapidly increased the price of their labor. The data on the expanding wage gap are evident in the last two columns of table 3. It is clear that the overall ratio of nonuniversity to university average wages has declined over this period. For example, an African FET (Further Education and Training) graduate in 2001 could have expected to earn between 51 and 57 percent of her counterpart with a degree; but, by 2005, her expectations were reduced to somewhere between 36 and 38 percent. Simply put, the evidence suggests that the value of a nondegree postsecondary education has declined dramatically over the last few years.

When we discuss the linkages between South Africa's higher-education system and its labor market, we have to recognize that this is a society characterized by what at first might seem like a statistical paradox: the coexistence of a severe labor shortage and high graduate unemployment rates. Normally, an economy short on labor should rapidly absorb skilled jobseekers. Instead, the data indicate that South Africans who get their training

TABLE 3. Mean Real Monthly Wages and the Relative Wage Gap by Education Cohorts, 2001 and 2005

Education Cohort	Monthly Real Wage (in rand)		Wage Gap (%)	
	2001	2005	2001	2005
Total				
Complete GET	1,705.29	1,551.24	20.26	12.13
Matric	3,084.57	2,933.62	36.65	22.94
Dipl./Certif. with less than Matric	4,254.50	4,634.86	50.55	36.24
Dipl./Certif. with Matric	4,778.15	4,892.86	56.77	38.26
Degree	8,417.11	12,788.88	100.00	100.00
Total	2,241.44	2,343.64	26.63	18.33
African				
Complete GET	1,249.08	1,122.51	21.77	6.86
Matric	2,020.94	1,971.75	35.22	12.05
Dipl./Certif. with less than Matric	3,197.90	3,370.79	55.73	20.60
Dipl./Certif. with Matric	3,710.16	4,071.36	64.66	24.88
Degree	5,738.32	16,364.30	100.00	100.00
Total	1,496.41	1,778.10	26.08	10.87

Source: Labour Force Survey, 2001, 2; Labour Force Survey 2005, 2 (Statistics SA).

outside of the degree-granting system are not at all assured of employment. Indeed, the data show that the unemployment rate among this group is rising faster than it is in other education cohorts. The problem lies overwhelmingly with South Africa's nonuniversity system of higher education, although universities are not absolved of all responsibility. Given the nature of the challenges in South Africa's domestic labor market, policymakers have to ensure that these institutions are producing high-quality graduates in areas of the economy where workers are in demand, and where, by implication, the probability of long-term employment is high.

NOTES

1. For an historical account of the evolution of skills shortage in the South African labor market, see H. Bhorat and J. Hodge, "Decomposing Shifts in Labor Demand in South Africa," *South African Journal of Economics* 67, no. 3 (1999): 155-68; H. Bhorat, "The Impact of Trade and Structural Changes on Sectoral Employment in South Africa," *Development Southern Africa*, special issue, September 17, 2000 (3), and L. Edwards, "Globalisation and the Skill Bias of Occupational Employment in South Africa," *South African Journal of Economics* 69, no. 1 (2001): 40–71.

2. Within the South African research and policy community, this is an extremely important deduction, given that there was a very widely held, and influential, view that the economy had experienced "jobless growth" in the post-1994 era. See H. Bhorat, "Labor Market Challenges in the Post-apartheid South Africa," *South African Journal of Economics* 72, no. 5 (2004): 940–77; H. Bhorat and M. Oosthuizen, "Employment Shifts and the 'Jobless Growth' Debate in South Africa," *Human Resource Development Review* (Pretoria: HSRC Press, 2008).

3. The desired or target employment growth rate is represented by a growth in employment that would provide jobs to every single work seeker over the stipulated time period. More formally, it is represented by

$$EAR_k = \frac{\dfrac{L_{k,t+1} - L_{k,t}}{L_{k,t}}}{\dfrac{EAP_{k,t+1} - EAP_{k,t}}{L_{k,t}}} = \frac{L_{k,t+1} - L_{k,t}}{EAP_{k,t+1} - EAP_{k,t}}$$

where EAP_k refers to the economically active population of group k, defined by any given covariate, and L_k is the number of employed group k individuals.

4. V. Chandra et al., "Constraints to Growth and Employment in South Africa," Report 1: Statistics from the Large Manufacturing Survey, World Bank Discussion Paper 14, Washington, DC, 2000.

5. Indeed, evidence from a recent survey of large South African companies, concentrating on the issue of graduate unemployment, indicates that employers experience constant problems with the quality of the graduates at all levels of the higher-education system—be it the FETs, technikons, or universities. K. Pauw, H. Bhorat, S. Goga, L. Ncube, and C.van der Westhuizen, "Graduate Unemployment in the Context of Skills Shortages, Education and Training: Findings from a Firm Survey," DPRU Working Paper No. 06/115, Development Policy Research Unit, University of Cape Town, 2006.

Retrenching Civil Rights

Mass Imprisonment in America

∾

Bruce Western

Citizenship rights for African Americans greatly expanded through the 1960s. The desegregation of public accommodations, the extension of voting rights, and prohibitions on discrimination in the housing and labor markets helped equalize the status of blacks and whites. This enlarged citizenship was further buttressed by the liberalization of college admissions and the hiring practices of large firms and government agencies. These measures helped erode the institutionalized dominance of whites over blacks, and raised hopes for racial equality.

Although the sixties saw the significant deinstitutionalization of racial segregation in America, the great legislative and public policy victories of the civil rights movement also set in motion a political reaction that vastly increased the institutionalization of African Americans in prisons and jails. Partly because of the erosion of white privilege, rising crime, and sometimes riotous social unrest, and partly because of concentrated urban poverty, criminal justice policy turned in a punitive direction through the 1970s and 1980s, creating a mass incarceration of young black men with little schooling. And this incarceration in turn helped cement the economic and social disadvantage of African Americans in poor urban communities during the post-civil rights era. This trend can be understood as a partial repudiation of the gains to citizenship produced by the civil rights movement, and a reinstitutionalization of American racial inequality through penal confinement.

The Politics and Economics of the Prison Boom

∾

The American prison boom of the late 1990s can be traced to a rightward shift in American politics and the collapse of urban labor markets for low-skilled men. Barry Goldwater's fated presidential run in 1964 was a pivotal episode in this story.[1] In accepting the Republican nomination, Goldwater warned that crime and disorder were threats to human freedom, and that freedom must be "balanced so that liberty lacking order will not become the license of the mob and of the jungle." The GOP campaign in the 1964 race linked the problem of street crime to civil rights protest and growing white unease about racial violence. Goldwater was roundly defeated by Lyndon Johnson in the general election, but his law-and-order message continued to resonate, particularly among southern whites and northern working-class voters of Irish, Italian, and German descent—constituencies that for this among other reasons, turned away from the Democratic Party in the 1970s.[2] Fears about crime were realized as rates of murder and other violence escalated in the decade following the 1964 election, while urban riots in Los Angeles, New York, Newark, Detroit, and dozens of other cities created a socially combustible mixture of disorder and racial politics.

Elevated crime rates and realigned race relations made some voters more receptive to the GOP's law-and-order themes during the post-civil rights period. Republican governors and state legislators were elected throughout the South and West, and placed themselves in the vanguard of movements for mandatory minimum sentences, sentence enhancements for repeat offenders, and expanded prison capacity.[3] Liberals joined conservatives in the 1970s to call for limits on judicial discretion in criminal sentencing, but progressive plans for more sparing use of incarceration were quickly overwhelmed by punitive sentiments. Quantitative analysis shows that incarceration rates grew fastest under Republican governors and state legislators in the 1980s and 1990s. While Republicans were quick to promote prison expansion and tough new criminal sentences, Democrats also came to support punitive policies.[4] One of the clearest signals of the Democratic shift was President Clinton's 1994 introduction of the Violent Crime Control and Law Enforcement Act. The bill earmarked $9.9 billion for prison construction and added life terms for third-time federal felons. By the 1990s, Democrats and Republicans alike were supporting sentencing policies and prison construction efforts that fueled the growth of the penal population.

While all of this was going on, urban deindustrialization was simultaneously undermining the labor market for unskilled young men. From 1969 to 1979, America's major cities recorded enormous declines in manufacturing and blue-collar employment. Employment rates dropped by 30 percent among black high-school dropouts in metropolitan areas, and by nearly 20 percent among black high-school graduates. The drop was only a third as large among noncollege whites of comparable age. Tellingly, after witnessing the emergence of antidiscrimination law and affirmative action, and increases in earnings and employment among African Americans through the mid-1970s, in 1992 the labor economists John Bound and Richard Freeman felt compelled to ask "what went wrong" with the promise of economic opportunity for young black men in the 1980s.[5]

The answer was, in part, the criminal justice system. Punitive criminal justice policy and the jobless ghetto together swelled the prison population. Prison admission rates climbed right alongside jobless rates among black men. Population turnover increased in poor urban neighborhoods, as young men churned through jail and prison. Arrest rates for drug crimes increased rapidly among blacks through the 1980s, and incarceration rates for drug crimes and public order offenses ballooned. Prison terms for serious violence also increased significantly. By the 1990s, individuals ensnared in the net of the criminal justice system were finding it increasingly difficult to work their way free, as mandatory sentences added more inmates to the prison population, and rising rates of parole revocation kept them there.

Skeptics may object that young black men filled the prisons in the 1980s and 1990s not because of unemployment, but because they were so heavily involved in crime. This objection misses the argument in two ways. First, even though young black men were disproportionately involved in street crime, there is little doubt they were punished more harshly in 2000 than they had been 30 years earlier. Second, inequalities in punishment are not fully explained by inequalities in crime. In some cases, laws are enforced more aggressively against the disadvantaged. For instance, studies have shown that blacks and whites use drugs at similar levels, but police focus on black drug users nonetheless produces racial disparities in drug possession arrests.[6] In other cases, real racial differences in crime rates influenced authorities' sense of the threat posed by blacks. The perception of blacks as threatening was sharpened by the black community's low social and economic status. Perceptions of black criminality—partly based on fact, partly inflated by white fears about socioeconomically disadvantaged African Americans—were woven into the routines and rules of criminal justice. In this way, the law enforcement and court systems magnified relatively small inequalities in crime into relatively large disparities in punishment.

The Scope of Mass Imprisonment

∾

By the year 2000, the U.S. incarceration rate was comparatively and historically large, but the scale remained small in absolute terms. Even at the height of the prison boom, less than 1 percent of the population was incarcerated. Can a penal system of this scale possibly have large effects?

The prison boom's main significance came in the social and economic disparities it created in incarceration rates. Large disparities typically reinforce lines of social disadvantage. Through the last two decades of the twentieth century, America's national incarceration rate grew from about one-fifth of 1 percent of the population to seven-tenths of 1 percent—more than

2.1 million inmates were in prison and jail by 2004. Because most inmates are males under age 50, the incarceration rate among working-age men is nearly three times the national average. Incarceration rates for minority men are even higher. By 2000, more than 3 percent of Hispanic men and almost 8 percent of African American men of working age were in prison or jail.

Black-white differences in incarceration rates are especially striking. In the general population, black men are eight times more likely to be incarcerated than whites—a discrepancy unmatched in statistics on unemployment (two to one), nonmarital childbearing (three to one), infant mortality (two to one) or wealth (one to five).[7]

Stratification by race and education produced extraordinary incarceration rates for young black male high school dropouts. Nearly a third were in prison or jail on a typical day in 2000, three times the rate just 20 years earlier. And this steep increase has also drawn a sharp line between the black underclass and the middle class: just 1 in 25 college-educated blacks were incarcerated in 2000. In relative terms, black dropouts were around four times more likely to be incarcerated than college-educated African Americans in 1980; 20 years later, they were more than eight times more likely to be behind bars.

Another way to appreciate this profound shift is by looking at how the risk of incarceration accumulates over an individual's life, calculating the likelihood that he will go to prison by age 25, 30, or 35. Instead of providing a snapshot of the broad social risk of incarceration, such life-course analyses, as they're known, try to capture a single, typical biography.

By 1999, a typical white dropout faced a one-in-nine chance that he would go to prison by their early thirties. This lifetime risk of imprisonment declines as we go up the educational ladder: white high-school graduates faced only a 3.6 percent likelihood of imprisonment by their early thirties that same year, while college-educated whites were largely spared from the prison boom altogether, with the typical college graduate's lifetime risk of imprisonment growing from just five- to seven-tenths of 1 percent between 1979 and 1999.

Although the risks of imprisonment are much higher for blacks, they are similarly stratified by education. Incredibly, a black male dropout born in the late 1960s had nearly a 60 percent chance of serving time by the end of the 1990s. The cumulative risks also increased among black high school graduates, so that a typical black graduate was saddled with a nearly one out of five chance that he would be in prison by his early thirties. Indeed, nearly a third of all blacks who had not attended college—or the bottom half of the educational distribution—had gone to prison by their midthirties in 1999, compared to one in eight just two decades earlier. As for whites, virtually all the increase in the risk of imprisonment among blacks fell on those with just a high school education or less.

This cumulative risk of imprisonment can also be compared to other experiences marking the transition to adulthood, including college graduation, military service, and marriage. Comparing imprisonment to these other life events suggests how the pathway through adulthood has been changed by the prison boom. Whites by their early thirties are more than twice as likely as blacks to hold a bachelor's degree. Blacks are about 50 percent more likely to have served in the military. However, black men in their early thirties are about seven times more likely than whites to have a prison record. Indeed, recent birth cohorts of black men are more likely to have prison records (22.4 percent) than military records (17.4 percent) or bachelor's degrees (12.5 percent). The share of the population with prison records is particularly striking among noncollege men. Noncollege black men in their early thirties in 1999 were more than twice as likely to be ex-felons than veterans. By 1999, imprisonment had become a common life event for black men, sharply distinguishing their pathway through adulthood from that of white men.

Legal scholar and sociologist David Garland coined the term *mass imprisonment* to refer to the high rate of incarceration in the contemporary United States. In Garland's definition, mass imprisonment has two characteristics. First, he writes, it "implies a rate of imprisonment that is markedly above the historical and comparative norm for societies of this type."[8] Certainly the American rate of incarceration by the late 1990s was far higher than that in western Europe, and without precedent in U.S. history. Second, Garland argues, the demographic concentration of imprisonment produces not the incarceration of individual offenders, but the "systematic imprisonment of whole groups of the population."[9]

The criteria are more slippery in this case: how high does the incarceration rate have to be before we can say that our society is imprisoning not the individual, but the group? The demography of incarceration help us answer this question. Not only did incarceration become common among young black men at the end of the 1990s, but its prevalence far exceeded that of other life events usually associated with passage to adulthood. More than college graduation or military service, for example, incarceration typified the biographies of African American men born since the late 1960s.

The Economic Effects of Imprisonment

∾

Serving time in prison increases economic inequality by reducing the earnings and employment prospects of the disadvantaged in three main ways.

First, it imposes a stigma that deters employers from hiring ex-offenders. Second, it blocks the accumulation of work experience and other human capital, and reduces productivity (and hence earnings). Third, spells of imprisonment may obstruct or undermine offenders' social connections to legitimate sources of employment.

My own studies of the economic effects of imprisonment have analyzed data from the National Longitudinal Survey of Youth, which interviewed a national sample of young men and women each year or so since 1979. The survey includes an annual residence item that identifies respondents interviewed in prison or jail. By 2002, about one in five of the black male NLSY respondents had recorded at least one survey interview in prison. Analysis shows that respondents who have been incarcerated have significantly lower wages, employment rates, and annual earnings than men who have never been incarcerated. Incarceration is generally estimated to reduce hourly wages by about 15 percent, but the effect is slightly smaller for African Americans (12.4 percent). Similarly, in terms of employment, formerly incarcerated black and Hispanic men were found to work approximately eight fewer weeks per year, or nearly 15 percent less than a similar group of nonoffenders. The effect is slightly smaller for white men, reducing employment by 9.7 percent, or about five weeks a year.

The negative effects of incarceration on hourly wages and annual employment combine to substantially reduce the annual earnings of ex-offenders. Men with prison records are estimated to earn about 30 to 40 percent less each year than similar men who have never been incarcerated. For example, a black 30-year-old high school dropout with no prison record will average nearly $9,000 a year—a paltry sum in this society in any case, but an expectation further reduced by incarceration to a mere $6,600. White men in the NLSY with the same characteristics and no prison record earn $14,400 each year, a number reduced by imprisonment to $9,200.

Incarceration not only reduces earnings and employment; it also relegates ex-prisoners to the secondary labor market, in which employment is insecure and wages are stagnant. This insecurity is reflected in figures on job tenure: black ex-prisoners in the NLSY are estimated to have spent about 14 weeks less in their current job than men who have never been incarcerated. As for wage growth, the wages of never-incarcerated men typically grow substantially in the 10 years from age 25 to 35. Average hourly wages for white men who are involved in crime but never go to prison grow during this stage of life from $11.18 to $13.81. White ex-prisoners, on the other hand, experience virtually no wage growth from their starting wage of $10.61 an hour at age 25. And wages for African American men are even lower than those for whites. A 25-year-old black man without a criminal record earns about the same wage as a white man with a criminal record—

around $10.60 an hour. By age 35, the black worker's wage increases by 15 percent, to an average of around $12.15 an hour, whereas the wages of black ex-prisoners grow only a third as fast—just 5 percent, from about $9.85 to $10.40.

Conclusion

ᕦ

African American history is often written as a political contest over citizenship and full membership in American society. The last chapter of this history, the civil rights movement, offered the promise of full African American citizenship. By 1968, a 25-year campaign to secure the legal equality of blacks had abolished segregation and discrimination in public accommodations and employment, and eliminated the largest impediments to black suffrage. Lawmakers and civil rights activists were hopeful that the main barriers to blacks' full participation in American social life had finally been removed. This cautious optimism was misplaced, however: as a result of the prison boom, the promise of full citizenship began to recede immediately after civil rights were proclaimed.

The contraction of citizenship produced by mass imprisonment did not affect all blacks equally. Men with little schooling bore the brunt of the impact. College-educated blacks, although more likely to go to prison than whites, overall escaped the rising incarceration rates of the 1980s and 1990s. The relationship between school dropout and imprisonment is complex, and causation runs in both directions. It is clear, however, for the 60 percent or more of young black male dropouts now marked with a prison record, social and economic disadvantage is more severe. In this way, mass imprisonment has institutionalized the marginality of poor blacks, setting them apart from white society and crystallizing social inequality within the African American community.

The social inequality produced by mass imprisonment is a creature of the post-civil rights era. Although racial animus certainly plays some part, everyday discrimination is not the main driver. Mass imprisonment was instead produced by a historic collision between the political forces of racial conservatism and the collapse of urban labor markets. It was this collision that massively increased the scale of criminal punishment. While civil rights established a legal equality between blacks and whites, they could not protect against the powers of economic dislocation and political reaction.

NOTES

1. K. Beckett, *Making Crime Pay: Law and Order in Contemporary American Politics* (New York: Oxford University Press, 1997); T. Gest, *Crime and Politics: Big Government's Erratic Campaign for Law and Order* (New York: Oxford University Press, 2001).

2. T. B. Edsall with M. D. Edsall, *Chain Reaction: The Impact of Race, Rights, and Taxes on American Politics* (New York: Norton, 1991).

3. B. Western, *Punishment and Inequality in America* (New York: Russell Sage, 2006); J. D. Davey, *The Politics of Prison Expansion: Winning Elections by Waging War on Crime* (Westport, CT: Praeger, 1998); D. Jacobs and J. T. Carmichael, "The Politics of Punishment across Time and Space: A Pooled Time-Series Analysis of Imprisonment Rates," *Social Forces* 80 (2001): 61–91.

4. On incarceration rates, see Western, *Punishment and Inequality,* chap. 3.

5. J. Bound and R. B. Freeman, "What Went Wrong? The Erosion of Relative Earnings and Employment among Young Black Men in the 1980s," *Quarterly Journal of Economics* 107 (1992): 201–32.

6. K. Beckett, K. Nyrop, L. Pfingst, and M. Bowen, "Drug Abuse, Drug Possession Arrests, and the Question of Race: Lessons from Seattle," manuscript, University of Washington, 2004; M. Tonry, *Malign Neglect* (New York: Oxford University Press, 1995), 104–16.

7. Western, *Punishment and Inequality.*

8. D. Garland, "Introduction: The Meaning of Mass Imprisonment," in *Mass Imprisonment: Social Causes and Consequences,* ed. D. Garland (Thousand Oaks, CA: Sage, 2001), 1.

9. Ibid., 2.

PART III ∾ The World in Higher Education

Admissions, Curriculum, and the Classroom

Introduction to Part III, *Martin Hall*

This section turns to issues that are specific to the "internal world" of higher-education institutions—issues such as admissions policies, the formal curriculum, and the affective influences on learning. How have issues of race and gender shaped the internal environments of universities in South Africa and the United States, and what are the similarities—and differences—between the two countries?

Admissions policies and processes are the front line in battles about affirmative action and equity. Marta Tienda and Teresa Sullivan take as their point of departure the 1997 Texas law that guarantees automatic admission to any public university to applicants who graduated in the top 10 percent of their high school senior class. They document both gains and challenges in the Texas admissions system and make comparisons with California and Florida, the other two states that use ranking in high school class as the major factor in making admissions decisions. Nan Yeld begins her chapter with a key difference between higher-education admissions in South Africa and in the United States: while affirmative action policies in the United States are restricted by the Constitution, and have been continually challenged as unconstitutional, in South Africa equity policies are required in order to address prior and continuing disadvantage. She highlights three significant challenges in achieving equitable higher-education admissions in South Africa: a generally poor schooling system, very large and continuing inequities in access to schooling, and the continuing effects of apartheid on educational performance.

Once admitted to higher education, students' experiences will be a critical factor in their academic success and the benefits they take away from their undergraduate years. Crain Soudien comes to these issues from the complex intersection of race and class in South Africa. Working from the testimony of black students, he notes that, while they experience persistent prejudice, race and racism are rarely to be seen as autonomous phenomena that can be isolated and addressed in themselves. Sylvia Hurtado looks at the issue from a different angle. Rather than exploring the experience of students "looking out" at the circumstances in which they find themselves, she reviews the growing evidence from the United States that racial and ethnic diversity is, in itself, of educational value. This perspective also informs the chapter by Patricia Gurin, Biren (Ratnesh) Nagda, and Akua Campanella, who look in detail at an intervention at the University of Michigan that addresses diversity through "intergroup dialogue" (IGD), a pedagogy that seeks to achieve a deeper understanding of the issues at stake. The Michigan example can be compared with a model of similar intent developed and applied at the University of Cape Town and described here by Martin Hall, Dorrian Aiken, and Nazeema Mohamed.

Soudien and Hurtado, as well as the two accounts of detailed interventions at the universities of Cape Town and Michigan, work from the assumption that university educators must work, for the most part, within the "received wisdom" of the established curriculum. Ian Scott, however, takes a more radical position, arguing that this curriculum must be restructured if excellence and diversity are not to be in opposition with one another. Building on the long and well-documented experience of academic development programs in South African universities, Scott argues that the "articulation gap" between high school and university stacks the cards against learners from disadvantaged backgrounds to such an extent that they will be fortunate if they graduate—an observation supported by South Africa's low completion rates in higher education. This concern is extended to the preparation of teachers by Jennifer Lewis and Deborah Loewenberg Ball. Their chapter focuses on K–12 teaching and the role that teachers have in shaping society. They ask how undergraduate education could contribute to a more equitable society by training those who will teach the next generation. Although their focus is on the United States, this concern is as relevant to South Africa, where it is widely recognized that the challenges of teacher education and provision lie at the heart of policy issues and continuing transformation.

The Promise and Peril of the
Texas Uniform Admission Law

∾

Marta Tienda and Teresa A. Sullivan

During the late 1990s, as the debate over affirmative action escalated, Texas moved into the national limelight. After the U.S. Court of Appeals for the Fifth Circuit found the use of race or ethnicity in college admissions unconstitutional in *Hopwood v. Texas,* the state embarked on a bold experiment.[1] In 1997, the Texas legislature passed HB 588, commonly termed the Top Ten Percent Law, which guaranteed automatic admission to *any* public university for applicants who graduated in the top 10 percent of their high school senior class. Legislators cited both general principles of equal access and empirical evidence that high school grades are strong predictors of college success, and hoped that the new approach would increase, or at least maintain, ethno-racial diversity at the state's selective public institutions.

The law, which went into effect in 1998, is deceptively simple. Seniors from every high school—large or small, public or private—are evaluated using a uniform measure of "merit." Heralded as a race-neutral alternative to affirmative action, the law complied with the judicial ban imposed by *Hopwood* because it did not propose the consideration of ascriptive attributes in admission decisions. Students must formally apply for admission and submit test scores from college-entrance exams, but their scores do not affect admission decisions, as long as the applicants qualify for the 10 percent guarantee. The opportunity remains open for two years after high school graduation, as long as the graduate does not enroll in any other postsecondary educational institution in the interim.

Although the Supreme Court's 2003 *Grutter* decision reaffirmed that a narrowly tailored consideration of race was permissible to achieve the educational benefits that are a consequence of a diverse student body, the Texas uniform admission law remains in force unless it is repealed by the Texas legislature.[2] (Actually, it will remain in force for a full year following its repeal, to allow schools and students to plan for a revised admission regime.) Initially endorsed by affirmative action opponents and supporters alike, the Texas Top Ten Percent Law has become as controversial as the use of race preferences itself. This is in part because the law merely shifted the terms of the debate from individuals to schools as the basis for exclusion. Such a shift is problematic in a state where social class drives competition for slots at the most selective postsecondary institutions, and where the number of such slots is sharply limited because of historical underinvestment in higher education, relative to the size of the college-eligible population.

Affirmative Action and Uniform Admissions

~

Since the middle of the twentieth century, the policy debate about access and equity in higher education has shifted from an emphasis on the desired ends, to a discussion of means that are acceptable to achieve those ends. Just 50 years ago, the debate revolved around *whether* integration was necessary for opportunity to be equal. The *Brown* decision settled that question legally, if not entirely practically. In a series of subsequent decisions, the Supreme Court reiterated and clarified its message that separate is inherently unequal, and that integration is a necessary, albeit insufficient condition for the leveling of the educational playing field.

In higher education, affirmative action addresses a need to broaden access to selective institutions by forging a compromise between the principles of democratic inclusion and the requirements of a merit-based system of rewards. Although seldom defined in prescriptive terms, affirmative action policies attempted to go beyond the simple prohibition against discrimination, by using race or ethnicity as one of many factors considered in college admissions. Not surprisingly, civil rights groups embraced affirmative action as a strategy for equalizing access to selective postsecondary educational institutions. Although affirmative action was ended by judicial action in Texas and by popular vote in California, the results were the same in both states: a precipitous drop in the number of minority applicants and admits.[3]

That race-sensitive admissions policies have been challenged at the polls and in the courts attests to the lack of consensus about which strategies are acceptable for equalizing educational opportunity. The controversy is not likely to subside soon, for at least three reasons: first, the demand for slots at selective institutions is rising; second, well-funded opposition groups have organized to orchestrate strategic attacks; and third, the college-age and national populations are becoming more diverse because of immigration from new source countries and because of differential fertility.

Opponents of affirmative action have proposed three alternatives to using race and ethnicity in college admissions—"pure" academic achievement, social class, and percentage plans—each with different implications for increasing campus diversity. At one extreme, proponents of narrowly defined measures of academic achievement favor the consideration of standardized test scores, high school grades, and completion of advanced-placement courses as allowable criteria to identify meritorious students. The naive presumption is that ignoring race and ethnicity in favor of an exclusive focus on measured academic achievement results in color-blind admissions.

Although high school grades are strong predictors of college success, pervasive grade inflation, exemplified in the prevalence of grade point averages over 4 on a four-point scale, weakens the attractiveness of this indicator unless it is standardized across high schools, as class-ranking distributions do. Class ranking serves as a forcing function to identify the highest achievers, even in a Lake Wobegone–type school whose children are all above average. Standardized test scores are also sometimes touted as a way to compare students from many different high schools. When used as the primary measure of academic merit, however, these scores are problematic for a number of reasons. First, although often misinterpreted as measures of intrinsic ability, in fact test scores largely measure developed ability. Second, as studies have shown, compared with grades, standardized test scores are far less reliable predictors of college success.[4] Third, in part because of the ability and propensity of middle- and high-income white students to pay for costly test-taking programs and individual coaching, social class has become an important correlate of high test scores.[5] Consequently, this public screening tool has been subverted to a private good by virtue of ability to pay. Fourth, whether by design or default, over time admissions committees have placed greater weight on standardized scores, thereby increasing the apparent "bonus" associated with minority group status. As a result, black and Hispanic students' lower average scores on standardized tests, compared with white students, provide the main rationale for opposing affirmative action; yet this result is partly predetermined by the changing weights these two achievement indicators are given in admissions decisions.[6]

Because minority students are more likely to hail from the lower rungs of the socioeconomic scale, the use of class preferences has been proposed as an alternative to race-sensitive policies, in the effort to diversify campuses.[7] In practice, however, although such an approach may diversify a campus's class profile, it is unlikely to significantly alter its racial or ethnic diversity. Instead, such programs may privilege high-achieving students from low-income white families. In Texas, low-income blacks and Hispanics are poorer, on average, than low-income whites and are more likely to attend underperforming schools than equally situated white students.[8] Researcher William Bowen and his associates claim that minority enrollments at 19 selective colleges would drop by half if class preferences replaced race preferences.[9]

The third alternative—guaranteeing admission to any high school student who graduates at or above a predetermined threshold in the class rank distribution—is a relatively recent development. Percentage plans are a variant of the academic merit criteria, except that they standardize diverse grading policies and grade inflation. They have so far not been subject to the same scrutiny, in part because of their recency relative to race- and class-sensitive programs.

Percentage Plans and College Admissions: Solution or Problem?

In a research project dating back to 1999, we have sought to evaluate the consequences of the Texas law, the most controversial of the percentage plans.[10] Ultimately, the controversy hinges on assumptions about high schools. Supporters of affirmative action found the plan controversial because, they claimed, the plan relied on the continued segregation of Texas high schools to achieve college diversity. Those who opposed affirmative action on the grounds of "merit" also opposed equating achievement in low-quality high schools with achievement in the most elite preparatory academies. The Texas Top Ten Percent Law also disregards altogether test scores for rank-eligible applicants, challenging their value as indicators of college success.

The Texas program is particularly important because the state has witnessed unprecedented demographic diversification in recent years; because its college-eligible population is projected to grow well into the future, even after that of other states slows; because the state fares poorly on various educational indicators, compared with other states of comparable wealth; and because the state has historically underinvested in its public postsecondary educational system.[11] California and Florida, the other two states that implemented percentage plans in the late 1990s, have also experienced rapid growth and diversification of their college-eligible populations; consequently, it is possible to appraise the relative costs and benefits of the plans in these three states. A brief overview of higher-education demographics helps illustrate our claim that the "college squeeze" is partly responsible for growing angst about race-sensitive admissions in higher education.

Demography of Higher Education

That both Texas and California have been declared "majority minority" states by the U.S. Census Bureau implies an ample supply of minority students to diversify college campuses. Owing to their younger age structure, the result of immigration and higher fertility rates, black and Hispanic minorities comprise a higher share of the school-age population than they do of the population age 25 and over. The consequences of racial and ethnic differences in fertility are evident in the changing composition of high school graduates, as shown in table 1.

Notwithstanding that Texas has one of the lowest high school graduation rates in the nation, the state's rapid demographic growth, combined with appreciable diversification, has increased the share of graduates from minority groups.[12] Between 1994 and 2004, the number of high school graduates increased 50 percent. Despite a low overall rate of high school completion, Hispanic high school graduates nonetheless increased numerically by 78 percent during this period, raising their share of the total annual graduate pool from 29 percent in 1994 to 35 percent by 2004. Because the number of white graduates rose only 29 percent during this same period, their share of diploma recipients fell from 56 percent to less than half. Meanwhile, the shares of black and Asian graduates inched up by a percentage point each, implying growth at a rate well above the statewide average.

Figure 1 shows projected and actual percentages changes in the numbers of high school graduates for the country as a whole and for four populous, high-immigration states. New York was projected to experience a decline but actually experienced a small percentage increase. California and Florida also experienced a bulge in their number of high school graduates during the 1990s, although a less dramatic one than Texas. According to the Western Interstate Commission for Higher Education (WICHE), the number of public high school graduates grew only 19 percent nationally between 1994 and 2004, compared with 30 percent in California and 25 percent in Florida.[13] These estimates are conservative because the numbers for 2003 and 2004 were projected from 2002 data. In Texas, for example, actual increases exceeded projections by 3 and 5 percent, respectively.

The numbers of students graduating from Texas and Florida public high schools are projected to grow well in excess of the national average during

TABLE 1. Composition of Public High School Graduates: Texas, 1994–2004 (%)

	1994	2004	Numerical Increase (%)
Hispanic	29	35	78
White	56	48	29
African American	12	13	65
Asian and Other	3	4	81
Total graduates (in thousands)	163	244	50

Source: Texas Education Agency, *Texas Public School Statistics, Pocket Edition,* 1994–95 and 2004–6, http://ritter.tea.state.tx.us/perfreport/pocked/2005/pocked0405 .pdf.

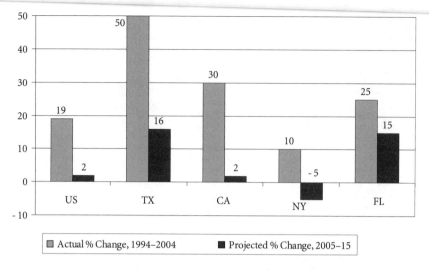

Fig. 1.   Actual and projected change in public high school graduates, 1994–2015: United States and Selected States. (Data from Western Interstate Commission for Higher Education, *Knocking at the College Door: Projections of High School Graduates by State, Income, and Race/Ethnicity* [Boulder: Western Interstate Commission for Higher Education, December 2003]. Figure was computed from tables in Appendix A.)

the next decade, even as other states witness modest growth or declines in their college-eligible cohorts (national growth is estimated at a meager 2 percent over the same period). WICHE projections indicate that California's high school graduates will grow a modest 2 percent between 2005 and 2015.

These changes bear directly on future college enrollment trends. Figure 2 shows that college enrollment in Texas rose faster than the national average between 1994 and 2004—the period bracketing implementation of the percentage plan. The expansion of postsecondary opportunities, particularly at four-year institutions, did not keep pace with demographic trends, however: enrollment in the state's postsecondary institutions rose 27 percent, including both two- and four-year institutions—a rate well below the 50 percent increase in the number of high school graduates during that period.[14] Of course, not all high school graduates pursue postsecondary education, but the number seeking to do so has increased as the labor market premiums for higher education continue to rise.

Texas differs from many other states and the nation as a whole in another important respect—namely, the changing composition of its postsecondary education system. At the national level, enrollment at both two- and four-year institutions grew by 19–20 percent, but figure 2 shows this

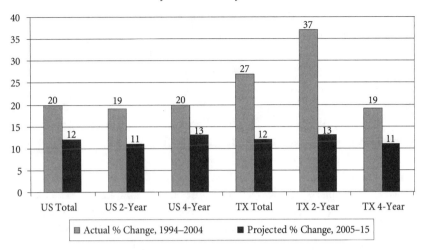

Fig. 2. Growth of overall college enrollment, 1994–2004, and projected, 2005–2015, United States versus Texas. (Data from Texas Higher Education Coordinating Board.)

was not the case in Texas. Instead, two-year institutions recorded a 37 percent increase in enrollment, and the total enrollment at two-year institutions surpassed that of four-year public institutions in 1995, a few months before the *Hopwood* decision.[15] Enrollment at Texas private colleges and universities has risen very slowly, and while these institutions were bound by the *Hopwood* decision until its repeal by *Grutter*, they were never bound by the provisions of the Top Ten Percent Law, which only applied to public institutions.

Taken together, the rapid growth of the college-age population, coupled with the comparatively slow expansion of four-year institutions, created a college squeeze that manifested itself in intensified competition for access to the most selective four-year public institutions. It is not entirely surprising that support for affirmative action would wane as a result of this squeeze, because many students who are denied admission to their preferred institution presume that race preferences are responsible for the admission crunch. Because of the increased competition, many white applicants would inevitably be denied admission to their preferred institution, and affirmative action provided a face-saving excuse for their rejection. Affirmative action was widely discussed and controversial, while the demographic pressures were more subtle and rarely noticed. The impact of the Texas college squeeze was intensified by the state's rapid demographic diversification and the growth in contenders for slots at the selective institutions.

Percentage Plans: One Size Does Not Fit All

ᴄᴡ

The percentage plans currently used in Texas, California, and Florida share one basic feature: namely, they guarantee admission to students who graduate above a specified ranking threshold for their senior class. The thresholds used vary widely, from a very generous 20 percent in Florida to only 4 percent in California. The plans also differ in several other highly consequential respects: specifically, in students' ability to choose a campus, the students' obligation to complete a specified curriculum, and the methods for calculating class rank.

The California percentage plan is more complex than that of either Texas or Florida. To ration access to the highly competitive University of California system, which includes the prestigious Berkeley and UCLA flagship campuses, California crafted a two-tier system that includes both a statewide rank and a local high school rank. All seniors are rated using a multicriterion index based on various indicators of academic achievement, including standardized test scores, grades, and class rank. (Since 2004 many highly qualified applicants based on the multicriterion index have been denied admission to the UC system campuses because there were insufficient slots to accommodate them.) Significantly, California's automatic admission guarantee kicks in only if the top 4 percent of students from a particular high school were not ranked highly enough on the statewide index to guarantee admission to the UC system. Not only is this a very stringent threshold, but as a strategy to boost campus diversity the California 4 percent plan mainly involves students from low-performing schools with large minority populations. Another important distinction is that the admission criteria were devised and implemented by the UC system, not mandated by statute.

The Texas plan differs from both Florida and California in how campus assignments are made. Texas, unlike Florida and California, allows rank-eligible students to select any public campus in the state, including the flagship campuses at the University of Texas–Austin and Texas A&M University in College Station. This means that Texas, unlike Florida and California, lacks an efficient mechanism for regulating the allocation of students among its various campuses to maintain system-wide balance in cohort size and composition.

Second, unlike California, which requires a specified high school curriculum for eligibility to the UC system, the Texas plan initially did not require students to complete a recommended college preparatory curriculum. This fueled criticisms that the law enabled students to game the system by avoiding rigorous courses to boost their grade point averages and, thus, class rank. Worse, critics alleged, the absence of a recommended curriculum allowed many students who were ill prepared for college work to qualify for the admission guarantee. To strengthen accountability, in 2001 the Texas legislature passed a law requiring that, beginning in 2004, all high school graduates complete the recommended or advanced curriculum in order to qualify for the admission guarantee. Whether this change altered application or admission outcomes is not yet known because the first cohort impacted by the new requirement graduated in 2008, so its effect will not be evident until they begin to apply for college in 2008.

The lack of a uniform curriculum is related to a third difference among the percentage plans: namely, whether individual high schools, secondary school districts, or a centralized university system office should calculate the high school class rank distributions. This is important because many schools do not offer honors or advanced courses; because high schools that do offer such courses weigh them differently when calculating grade point average; and because the lack of uniform weighting and ranking criteria opens myriad opportunities for both students and administrators to manipulate the system. For example, in a high school located outside of Austin, administrators were concerned about students' growing tendency to avoid taking math courses during their senior year to protect their class ranking. In an effort to encourage seniors to complete their fourth year of math, school officials promised that senior-year math grades would not be used in computing class rank.[16]

California has the most rigorous procedure among the three states for computing class rank. Participating schools must submit students' transcripts, from which UC administrators determine the top 4 percent of the pool, based on students' grade point averages for UC-approved coursework that they completed in the tenth and eleventh grades. This system provides consistency across secondary-school campuses, while also adhering to the curriculum requirements, but it led to complaints of unfair treatment of public schools in low-income areas where advanced or honors courses were unavailable.

Not only does the Texas plan provide the greatest flexibility of the three in the calculation of class rank, but the period during which rank can be established is broader: either at the end of 11th grade, the middle of 12th grade, or at graduation, whichever is most recent to the submission of the student's application. Moreover, the Texas admission guarantee remains in effect for up to two years after high school graduation or until rank-eligible students enroll in a postsecondary institution, whichever comes first. This means that top 10 percent graduates who elected to defer enrollment to a public four-year campus would relinquish their automatic admission if, for example, they enrolled in a community college for a refresher course.

Uniform Admissions in Texas and Beyond: Promise and Peril

～

If the uniform admission plan is appealing as a meritocratic entitlement, it nevertheless imposes considerable opportunity costs. Well before the *Grutter* and *Gratz* decisions, the Texas uniform admission law was being heralded as a successful race-neutral alternative to affirmative action. Among its benefits, supporters emphasized that the law increased geographic diversity by qualifying students from high schools that seldom sent students to the flagship campuses, and that it helped restore ethno-racial diversity after the judicial ban on the use of race preferences.

By guaranteeing admission to a fixed percentage of top-ranked graduates at all high schools, the number of high school campuses represented in both the flagships' admission cohorts and their freshman classes rose steadily. According to the UT Admissions Office, for example, 795 different Texas high schools were represented in the 1996 admission cohort, compared with 943 high schools in 2004—an increase of nearly 19 percent.[17] Although the number of schools represented among enrolled students was lower—616 in 1996, versus 815 in 2004—because not all admitted students enroll, both trends indicate that the law equalized access to the public flagships. This is a highly appropriate result for a publicly funded state institution. Nonetheless, students who attended high schools with established traditions of sending large numbers to the public flagships retained an enrollment advantage because, conditional on admission as either top 10 percent graduates or general admits, they were more likely to enroll.[18] Economics is a major explanation for this outcome, and has important implications for further expansion of college access in Texas.

The Top Ten Percent Law has also been credited with restoring ethno-racial diversity at these same flagship campuses. Again taking the UT-Austin campus as an example, we find clear evidence of campus diversification in the applicant pool, the admit pool, and the freshmen enrollment cohort. In 1996, 63 percent of all first-time freshmen admits were white; but by 2005 this share had plummeted to 55 percent.[19] International students account for another 2 to 3 percent of admitted applicants, and blacks, Hispanics, Native Americans, and Asians constitute the remainder.

Of special interest are the admission trends among black and Hispanic students. Under affirmative action, blacks comprised 4 percent of the admission pool, but this share dropped to 3 percent in the immediate aftermath of the *Hopwood* decision. They now make up 5 percent of first-time freshmen admits. Likewise, Hispanic students sustained a modest drop in representation in 1997 and 1998; however, they now represent 18 percent of admitted students, a full 3 percentage points above the 1996 average. Still, this gain is less than the growth in their share of high school graduates overall, as seen in table 1. Meanwhile, Asian Americans turn out to be by far the biggest beneficiaries of the Top Ten Percent Law, making up 17 percent of all admitted freshmen in 2005, up from 14 percent in 1996, and this even though their overall share of high school graduates is a meager 4 percent.

Whether these admission and enrollment trends are due to the uniform admission law or to statewide demographic diversification is unclear, but there is indisputable evidence that diversity of the flagship campuses has rebounded. (Because of its location outside a metropolitan area, Texas A&M has had a more difficult time restoring campus diversity, even with the admission guarantee. However, an aggressive outreach campaign has begun to yield increases in the numbers of Hispanic and black freshmen.) This rebound is driven by changes in the applicant pool. Although black and Hispanic students remain underrepresented and Asian students overrepresented relative to their respective shares of high school graduates, the trends indicate that these gaps are closing. Between 1996 and 2004, the total number of applications to the University of Texas at Austin rose 38 percent, from over 17,000 to nearly 24,000 applicants. Consequently, the admission rate plummeted from 66 to 51 percent. Thus, even though the number of white applicants rose 18 percent between 1996 and 2005, their admission probability fell from 61 to 52 percent. Applications from underrepresented minority students, particularly Hispanics, increased even more, with the Hispanic share of the applicant pool rising from 14 percent in 1996 to 19 percent by 2005.

Demography was not the only driver of campus diversification, however. The Top Ten Percent Law's contribution to campus diversification can be seen by comparing the representation of minorities among rank-qualified enrollees. In 2005, for example, blacks comprised 6 percent of all first-time freshmen from Texas high schools who qualified for the automatic admission guarantee, but made up only 4 percent of their race counterparts who did not graduate in the top decile of their class. Similarly, 22 percent of the Top Ten Percent enrollees were Hispanic in 2005, but among enrollees who did not qualify for the automatic admission guarantee, only 13 percent were Hispanic.[20]

Finally, the Texas admissions experiment has shown that emphasizing class rank in the definition of academic merit while ignoring test scores for the highest-achieving students actually does qualify a broader cross-section of students for college admission. Even more importantly, the uniform admission law has demonstrated that standardized test scores, which are the primary criterion used by opponents of affirmative action to justify exclusion of blacks and Hispanics, are not indispensable metrics for establishing academic merit and measuring a student's potential for postsecondary study. Consistent with a large body of research showing that grades are better predictors of college success than standardized test scores, UT freshmen admitted under the Top Ten Percent provision achieve higher grades during their freshmen year and have higher persistence rates than their lower-ranked counterparts who scored 200–300 points higher on the SAT.[21] This finding is worthy of note by the postsecondary institutions that have been placing greater weight on test scores as an indicator of academic merit.[22]

Admission officers have wisely understood that a guarantee of admission does not automatically lead to enrollment. As we have said before, economics are also a powerful factor in enrollment decisions. Motivated by this realization, both of Texas's public flagships developed tuition scholarship programs targeted to rank-eligible graduates of resource-poor high schools with weak traditions of college attendance. *Hopwood*'s implication was that scholarships could not be based on minority group membership, but the Court's decision explicitly permitted consideration of geographic distribution, such as high school location. The fact that the eligible high schools tend to have large minority student bodies has helped the uniform admission law diversify the flagship campuses, while strengthening institutional ties between the universities and selected resource-poor secondary schools.[23] Although the numbers of scholarship recipients from any given high school are not large, over time the state's Longhorn and Century Scholarship programs have improved these schools' college orientation, while also increasing the number of students from these high schools who actually enroll at the flagships.[24]

Figure 3 depicts the college destinations of Texas high school seniors from the class of 2002 who enrolled in college the year after graduation. The graduates are categorized by type of high school and type of postsecondary institution. Using data published by the Texas Education Agency, we developed a typology of Texas high schools based on income level of the student population and the relative strength of a school's college-going traditions.[25]

The five strata include

1. feeder high schools, the 28 high schools that in 2000 supplied between one-fifth and one-quarter of the freshmen at the two public flagships;
2. affluent high schools, with average college enrollment rates;
3. typical high schools, which are not either resource-poor or affluent;
4. resource-poor schools with average college-going traditions; and
5. Longhorn/Century schools, which are low-income schools (70 in the Longhorn program and 58 in the Century) with low college-going traditions, but whose top-ranked students are eligible for fellowships to UT-Austin or Texas A&M.

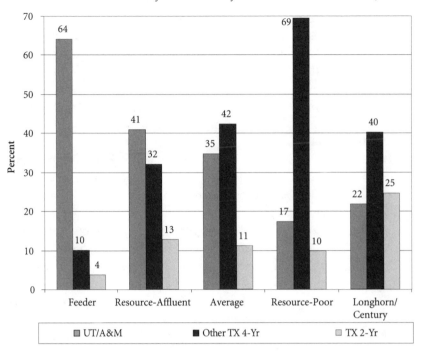

Fig. 3.   College destinations of top 10 percent graduates by type of high school attended (as percent of enrolled). (Data from THEOP, Senior Wave 1 and 2 Data.)

The number of students from any particular high school who qualify for the admission guarantee depends on size, of course, but so too does the likelihood that qualified students eventually enrolled in college. Many high school graduates—even those who excel academically—do not go to college.

Overall, the numbers are promising: more than 90 percent of all Texas seniors who graduated in the top 10 percent of their high school classes in 2002 were enrolled in college the following fall. But this share varied from 97 percent of the top-tenth graduates of affluent schools, to 80 percent of those from Longhorn/Century schools. Even among those who do enroll, there are large differences in college choice. As figure 3 shows, only 35 percent of top decile graduates from typical Texas high schools enrolled at UT-Austin or Texas A&M, compared with 41 percent of the graduates from resource-affluent schools, and nearly two-thirds of those from the 28 feeder schools (the percentages do not add up to 100 because enrollment at private schools or public schools outside Texas is not shown). Seen from another angle, nearly one-quarter of top-tenth graduates from the Longhorn/Century schools enroll in community colleges, compared with only 4 percent of comparably ranked students from the major feeder high schools. Thus, despite complaints that the Top Ten Percent Law privileges students from underperforming schools, graduates from the major feeder schools, and, to a lesser extent, from resource-affluent schools, were significantly more likely to enroll at one of the public flagships than graduates from the typical Texas high school.[26]

The success of the school-targeted scholarship programs for top-tenth graduates is evident in the higher enrollment of graduates from the Longhorn/Century high schools, compared with typical resource-poor high schools: 22 percent to 17 percent. The numbers involved are not large, but sufficient to improve the likelihood of enrollment among top-performing students. Sociologist Thurston Domina reports that each scholarship program averages 225–50 scholarships per year, which should render their impacts relatively similar.[27] Overall, these results suggest that by itself, the Top Ten Percent Law may be a necessary condition for broadening college access, but is insufficient without financial aid to qualifying students.

Although it has been successful in broadening access to competitive four-year public institutions, the Texas law also has numerous drawbacks. Some derive from the law's considerable flexibility, while others are a by-product of the intensifying "college squeeze." Some critics complain that high-performing students from low-performing schools are being privileged over lower-ranked students from more competitive schools in their access to the flagships. Others allege that the law fostered a brain drain to neighboring states, by crowding out talented students who rank in the second decile of their class at the most competitive high schools,.

Both allegations are empirically unsubstantiated, but they reflect growing frustration among parents and students from affluent school districts who are denied admission to their preferred four-year institution.[28] The math is rather straightforward, in that the slow expansion of the four-year postsecondary system relative to the growth of applicants implies that more students will be denied admission to their top choice institution (in fact, the state's private institutions have also have experienced significant growth in their applicant pool, attesting to the increasing demographic squeeze in college admissions).

The major pitfalls of the Texas law have to do with carrying capacity, a tendency to build on (rather than undo) the legacy of segregation, and the reliance on a single criterion to establish merit. We are not able, in the space allotted, to discuss other pitfalls of lesser consequence, including incentives to game the system by choosing an easier course of study; manipulating weights in the calculation of class rank; and transferring from a more-competitive to less-competitive school in order to increase the likelihood of qualifying for the admission guarantee.

Physical infrastructure—in particular, classroom and lab space—and faculty resources constrain the size of any school's student body. The most popular short-term response to this constraint is to adjust enrollment targets by tightening or loosening admissions policies, but campus expansion is a viable medium-term solution. The two flagship campuses have employed both strategies. With the share of top-tenth applicants to UT-Austin rising significantly, in 2000 UT president Larry Faulkner temporarily increased the size of the undergraduate class. This enabled the school to continue meeting other aspects of its institutional mission through selective admissions. The increase eventually proved untenable: institutional carrying capacity was exceeded, and the number of applicants admitted was subsequently reduced. All of the reduction, of course, was borne by applicants who were not in the top 10 percent, irrespective of their academic qualifications, which only fueled criticism of the law. In contrast, Texas A&M University has been expanding both the size of its undergraduate body (by 500 students per year between 2002 and 2007) and its faculty, which was increased by a bold 447 new hires.[29] Coupled with a vigorous outreach initiative, A&M has been successfully restoring campus diversity along many dimensions.

While the distribution of its denied applications shifted to include growing numbers of students from competitive high schools, the University of Texas campus has become saturated with automatically admitted students, crippling the institution's ability to shape its freshman class. In 1996, 42 percent of first-time freshman admits ranked in the top decile of their high school class. A temporary increase in the size of the freshman class in 2000 and 2001 kept the share of automatic admits at 47 and 51 percent, respectively. But by 2005 nearly three in four admitted students had qualified for admissions under the Top Ten Percent provision, reflecting (as seen in fig. 4) an average annual growth in top-tenth applicants of about 9 percent. Although Texas A&M has also witnessed an increase in the share of applicants who qualify under the guarantee, only about half of those students are automatically admitted, leaving admission officers some latitude to shape the freshman class.

Using the 9 percent growth rate to project the composition of future admission cohorts, figure 4 reveals that by 2009 the UT-Austin campus will have exceeded its carrying capacity. Moreover, its ability to shape its freshman class will be virtually nonexistent within a year. One solution would be to index the admission threshold to the carrying capacity of the state's higher-education system and the changing demand for college based on the population of high school graduates. Surprisingly, the architects of the law

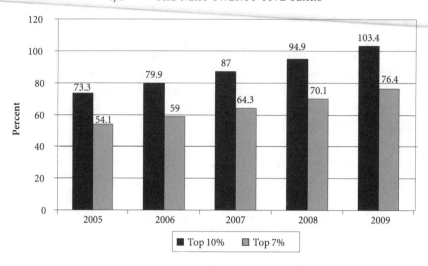

Fig, 4.   Actual and projected top 10 percent and top 7 percent admits: UT-Austin, 2005–2009. (Note: Projections for UT-Austin Based on Ethnic Distribution of 2005 HB588 Admits as of March 28, 2006.)

did not do so. Nor did they think to cap the number of applicants automatically admitted, in order to avoid saturating campuses with students admitted solely on the basis of class rank. For example, lowering the class rank threshold for the admission guarantee from 10 percent to 7 percent would reduce the share of automatic admits from 95 to 70 percent in 2008, and from 103 to 76 percent in 2009. Unfortunately, the law as written has greatly diminished public universities' discretion to consider the many elements of their mission. The 2007 session of the Texas legislature considered and rejected a proposed campus cap on the fraction of the freshman class admitted through the Top Ten Percent Law.

Furthermore, and despite claims that the law is race-neutral, the success of any percentage plan designed to restore diversity to selective institutions is heavily dependent on segregation. Minority students primarily benefit from the top-tenth rule if they attend a segregated school. Minority students who attend integrated schools experience a significantly lower chance than their white classmates of graduating in the top decile of their class. Moreover, white students who attend "majority minority" high schools (e.g., 60–80 percent nonwhite) are more likely to qualify for the admission guarantee than their counterparts.[30] In large measure, this reflects social class differences that are also related to college-going behavior, which the law does not address. Not surprisingly, rank-eligible black and Hispanic students are less likely than similarly qualified white and Asian students to enroll in college.[31] In the short run, then, the law works only in a relatively segregated system; but in the long run, of course, that segregation serves neither the interests of high school students nor the public institutions that recruit them under the uniform admission law.

Finally, by relying exclusively on a single criterion to adjudicate college applications, the uniform admission law blunts the broad-ranging diversity that can only be achieved by thorough review of a student's full dossier. To be sure, the large freshman cohorts at the Texas public flagships provide some guarantee of diversity even on a simple statistical level. But the law has not only proven to be a less efficient tool than affirmative action to increase campus diversity, it has also reified class boundaries because large numbers of admitted students do not enroll for economic reasons. In his last State of the University address, for example, former Texas A&M president (now secretary of defense) Robert Gates admitted that "Texas A&M remains a 'middle class university' with about 40 percent of incoming freshmen having incomes of $80,000 or less."[32]

Uncertain Future

∽

Texas legislators have made several attempts to amend the uniform admissions law, but their efforts—ranging from strengthening the curriculum eligibility requirements to imposing uniform criteria for calculating class rank to outright repeal—have failed to win majority support. Notably, the Top Ten Percent Law is backed by Democrats from minority districts and Republicans representing rural white districts, who argue that the law gives students from their areas access to the public flagships that they would not otherwise enjoy. Unless the law is modified or repealed, however, the growing saturation of the UT-Austin campus with automatically admitted students will eliminate the last modicum of its ability to fulfill its institutional mandates. This threat appears to be less imminent for Texas A&M, whose capital fund-raising campaign has enabled it to expand both the size of its undergraduate class and the faculty. Given the likelihood of continued increases in the size of future high school graduation cohorts, this situation may change at other campuses as well, as it has already been doing at the state's selective private institutions.

Because Texas responded to the judicial repeal in *Hopwood* with legislative action, any attempt to redress the law's unintended consequences will require yet another legislative solution. In the long run, efforts to bring Texas's other public institutions up to the same academic level as the two flagships would expand the carrying capacity of the state's postsecondary system as a whole. In the short run, the admission guarantee could be modified by adopting the provisions of the California or Florida approaches, including those that preclude students from selecting a campus at will or that use system-wide criteria to establish admission eligibility. Alternatively, the law could cap the number of students that can be automatically admitted in a given year (e.g., to 50 percent). The allotted slots could then be used to promote the positive features of the law: namely, by ensuring that the number of feeder schools continues to expand. At a minimum, though, the percentage plan must somehow be more directly linked to the system's carrying capacity.

The Top Ten Percent Law might or might not be successful in diversifying the college freshman class at public universities in other states. As the Texas case shows, diversification is most likely to result when there is an expanding base of high school graduates, especially minority graduates; when there are many highly segregated high schools; when the set of selective public institutions is relatively small; and when financial aid is used to reinforce the opportunity for admission. Whether the law should be viewed as a success depends partly upon whether one views the glass as half-full or half-empty. There are, however, several lessons that could be put into use in nearly every state.

First, expanding the number of high schools represented in the student body does represent a type of diversity, but one that could be achieved with geographic set-asides instead of a percentage plan. In places with both residential segregation and geographic attendance zones, such set-asides could result in greater minority representation.

Second, less affluent students will continue to need financial aid, and minority students are disproportionately included in this number. But the majority of the needy will be the majority of the population—usually white students. Geographic targeting can increase the probability that minority applicants will receive the aid, compared with relying solely upon the determination of individual need.

Third, where a state has only one recognized flagship school—or in the case of a large state, only a couple of flagships—provisions that allow students to select their institution will result in saturation of the most highly ranked institution. The impact on other four-year public universities may well be negligible, unless the demand for college outstrips the supply of slots. Percentage plans may accelerate the out-migration of young high school graduates from some parts of the state, or they may even work to the disadvantage of smaller institutions. Legislators concerned about regional institutions, or simply about increasing access for the most talented students, may want to ponder the effects of percentage plans on local communities.

Fourth, the percentage plans function, in effect, as the opposite of the idealized admission process set out in *Grutter*. Rather than considering many factors, such as leadership, different talents, and so on, the admissions office is constrained to consider only one criterion: rank in class. In the long run, this selection regime may undermine other aspects of campus diversity. Talented musicians and dancers, students who are extremely gifted in one subject (such as mathematics), and students with demonstrated but unmeasured accomplishments may eventually be squeezed out from flagship campuses.

Fifth, a percentage plan creates a new entitlement. This entitlement may be hard to rescind, even when a state experiences financial constraints. Especially in a state with a growing population, percentage plans imply additional costs to colleges.

NOTES

1. *Hopwood v. Texas,* 78 F.3d 932(5th Cir.), cert. denied, 518 U.S. 1033 (1996).

2. Following the *Grutter* decision, the University of Texas Board of Regents passed a resolution permitting schools in the Texas system to consider race and ethnicity in admissions that are not automatic. Texas A&M University decided not to consider race and ethnicity in admissions.

3. M. C. Long and M. Tienda, "Winners and Losers: Changes in Texas University Admissions Post-*Hopwood*," paper presented at the symposium "Equal Opportunity in Higher Education: The Past and Future of Proposition 209," Berkeley, CA, October 2006.

4. W. G. Bowen and D. Bok, *The Shape of the River* (Princeton: Princeton University Press, 1998); J. M. Rothstein, "College Performance Predictions and the SAT," *Journal of Econometrics* 121, nos. 1–2 (2004): 297–317.

5. P. M. McDonough, "Buying and Selling Higher Education: The Social Construction of the College Applicant," *Journal of Higher Education* 65, no. 4 (1994): 427–46.

6. S. Alon and M. Tienda, "Diversity, Opportunity and the Shifting Meritocracy in Higher Education," *American Sociological Review* 72, no. 4 (2007): 487–511.

7. W. G. Bowen, M. A. Kurzweil, and E. M. Tobin, *Equity and Excellence in American Higher Education* (Charlottesville: University of Virginia Press, 2005).

8. M. Tienda and S. Niu, "Capitalizing on Segregation, Pretending Neutrality: College Admissions and the Texas Top 10% Law," *American Law and Economics Review* 8 (2006): 312–46.

9. Bowen, Kurzweil and Tobin, *Equity and Excellence.*

10. Texas Higher Education Opportunity Project (THEOP), http://theop.prince ton.edu. This Web site includes information on the design of this study.

11. M. Tienda, "Harnessing Diversity in Higher Education: Lessons from Texas," in *Ford Policy Forum, 2006: Exploring the Economics of Higher Education,* ed. M. Devlin (Washington, DC: National Association of College and University Business Officers and the Forum for the Future of Higher Education, 2006), 7–14 .

12. Senator E. Shapleigh, *Texas on the Brink: How Texas Ranks among the 50 States,* 2nd ed. (El Paso County, Texas, 2005).

13. WICHE, *Knocking at the College Door: Projections of High School Graduates by State, Income, and Race/Ethnicity* (Boulder, CO: Western Interstate Commission for Higher Education, December 2003).

14. Texas Higher Education Coordinating Board (THECB), "Report on Academic Performance of Texas Public Universities" (Austin, 1998).

15. THECB, "Participation and Success Forecast, 2005–2015: Texas Institutions of Higher Education" (Austin, February 25, 2005).

16. Personal communication, Michelle Guzmán, July 2005, THEOP data training institute.

17. University of Texas at Austin Office of Admissions, "The Number of Texas High Schools Represented in the Entering Freshman Classes of the University of Texas at Austin, 1996–2004" (2005) accessed at www.utexas.edu/student/admissions/research/FeederSchool_1996-2004.pdf.

18. M. Tienda and S. X. Niu, "Flagships, Feeders, and the Texas Top 10% Law: A Test of the "Brain Drain" Hypothesis," *Journal of Higher Education* 76, no. 4 (2006): 712–39.

19. These figures refer to first-time freshmen admitted for the summer and fall semesters combined. UT Office of Admissions, "The Number of Texas High Schools Represented in the Entering Freshman Classes of the University of Texas at Austin, 1996–2004," May 5, 2005.

20. University of Texas at Austin Office of Admissions, "Implementation and Results of the Texas Automatic Admissions Law (HB588) at the University of Texas at Austin: Demographic Analysis of Entering Freshmen, Fall 2005" (Austin, 2005), accessed at www.utexas.edu/student/admissions/research/HB588-Report8.pdf.

21. On grades versus standardized tests, see Bowen and Bok, *Shape of the River,* and Rothstein, "College Performance Predictions"; on persistence rates, see L. R. Faulkner, "Top 10 Percent Helps Students," *San Antonio Express-News,* October 25, 2000, 5B; and L. R. Faulkner, "Class Rank Predicts Student Success," *USA Today,* April 5, 2002, 11A.

22. Alon and Tienda, "Diversity, Opportunity."

23. Tienda and Niu, "Capitalizing on Segregation."

24. T. Domina, "Higher Education Policy as Secondary School Reform: Texas Public High Schools after Hopwood," presented at the 2006 Summer Institute of the Texas Higher Education Opportunity Project.

25. Tienda and Niu, "Flagships, Feeders."

26. Tienda and Niu, "Capitalizing on Segregation"; and M. Tienda and S. X. Niu, "Texas' Top 10 Percent Plan: The Truth behind the Numbers," *Chronicle of Higher Education,* January 23, 2004, B10.

27. Domina, "Higher Education Policy."

28. Tienda and Niu, "Flagships, Feeders"; and "Texas' Top 10 Percent Plan."

29. Texas A&M News Archives, "Gates' State-Of-University Address Broad Based," September 8, 2006, accessed at http://newsarchives.tamu.edu/stories/06/091106news-3.html.

30. Tienda and Niu, "Capitalizing on Segregation."

31. S. X. Niu, T. A. Sullivan, and M. Tienda, "Minority Talent Loss and the Texas Top 10% Law," *Social Science Quarterly* 89, no. 4 (2008): 831–45.

32. Texas A&M News Archives, 2006.

Admissions Policies and Challenges

∽

Nan Yeld

In stark contrast to the situation in the United States, higher education in South Africa is governed by both constitutional and statutory requirements for redress. South African law not only allows, but actively *requires,* certain types of preferential treatment toward people from previously disadvantaged groups. The South African Constitution, in its Bill of Rights, stipulates that "Equality includes the full and equal enjoyment of all rights and freedoms. To promote the achievement of equality, legislative and other measures designed to protect or advance persons, or categories of persons, disadvantaged by unfair discrimination, may be taken." Building on this, the preamble to the country's Higher Education Act states that one of the act's aims is to "redress past discrimination and ensure representivity and equal access," thereby requiring that each public institution of higher education make provision in its admissions policy for the redress of past inequality. As is discussed in some detail in what follows, continuing disparities in educational provision on the grounds of race and class, and the overall poor quality of K–12 schooling in South Africa, mean that some quite pronounced form of affirmative action is not only desirable, but essential.

South Africa's history of apartheid has made its citizens acutely aware of discriminatory practices, and much debate has focused, as a result, on higher-education admissions policy. As is the case elsewhere, higher education in South Africa is a key component in status mobility, and as such is a crucial tool in the normalization of South African society.

It seems uncontroversial that public educational institutions should aim to constitute their student bodies in such a way as broadly to reflect the general population. Beyond that aim, however, they also need to ensure that only the most talented students are admitted—that is, those with the most likely chance of success. In essence, the admissions challenge in South Africa is exacerbated by three related but distinct factors: a generally very poor school system, massive inequities within that system, and the pervasive and lingering effects of apartheid on educational performance. Each of these three factors poses significant challenges for admissions.

The Schooling System and Overall Quality Issues

∾

South African schooling ends at Grade 12, when all students write the national senior certificate examination. The educational progress of the cohort dubbed by the media "Madiba's children, " after the clan name of former president Mandela, illustrates a dismal situation. This is the cohort that entered school in 1995, immediately after the advent of democracy in 1994.

Of the 1,666,980 students who entered Grade 1 in 1995, 66 percent dropped out before reaching Grade 12. While only 21.1 percent passed the senior certificate examination, it is important to note that barely 5 percent of the cohort, or 85,830 students, obtained a senior certificate with endorsement, the statutory requirement for entry to degree study. This makes the national quest for a 20 percent participation rate in higher education seem very like a distant hope, and highlights a somewhat counterintuitive phenomenon in South African higher education—that even within the tiny elite eligible to enter higher education, the majority of students are underprepared for degree study. (In "Who Is 'Getting Through' in South Africa? Graduate Output and the Reconstruction of the Formal Curriculum," in Part III of this volume, Ian Scott reports on the very high failure and dropout statistics of this supposed elite group.)

Performance in mathematics, a key "gateway" subject in higher education, as pointed out by Jonathan Jansen in his contribution to this volume ("Moving on Up? The Politics, Problems, and Prospects of Universities as Gateways for Social Mobility in South Africa," in Part II), confirms this troubling state of affairs. Mathematics is generally offered in two forms: Mathematics Higher Grade and Mathematics Standard Grade. Only the higher grade is normally acceptable for numerate disciplines such as science and engineering. In 2006, of the 317,642 students who wrote their exams in either grade of mathematics, just over half passed; of the 46,945 students who wrote mathematics on the higher grade, however, only 25,217 passed.

The numerous initiatives aimed at addressing this situation have so far not produced promising results: indeed, the numbers of students passing mathematics and science on the higher grade actually dropped in 2006.[1] In the 2007 examination, figures just released show a reduced matriculation endorsement rate of 15.1 percent compared to 16.3 percent in 2006, a virtually static number of passes in Mathematics Higher Grade, and a decrease in the number of Physical Science HG passes from 29,781 to 28,122.

South Africa's very poor levels of educational achievement have been well documented. Indeed, the country fares badly even in comparison with poorer countries with similar medium-of-instruction challenges (i.e., where the majority of students are schooled in a language other than their native tongue). In 2003, for example, South Africa came last of the 50 participating countries in the TIMSS (Trends in International Mathematics and Science Studies) tests, which included five other African countries: Botswana, Egypt, Ghana, Morocco, and Tunisia.

The impact of these low levels of achievement on higher-education admissions is evident in a study of the entry-level performance in mathematics and academic literacy of 5,780 students at seven South African higher-education institutions (both advantaged and disadvantaged). The study concluded that "even the most selective institutions are admitting a significant number of students whose levels of performance are alarmingly low," and, more generally, that the data "give a chilling picture of the very low levels of preparedness of incoming students to South African higher education institutions."[2]

One of the explanations for this sad state of affairs is the pressure for improved results on the senior certificate exam: the only point in the K–12 educational process where external examinations are set, and a certificate is issued. The previous minister of education, Dr. Kader Asmal, presided over a situation in which the annual pass rate accelerated astonishingly. Despite empirical evidence of "grade inflation" and steadily increasing public disquiet, it was not until 2004 that Umalusi,[3] the government's quality assurance agency for general and further education and training, commissioned a study to assess public claims that the 2003 senior certificate exam actually signaled a drop in standards: that is, that the rising pass-rates in recent years (especially the last two years) were due to easier exams, rather than a dramatic improvement in the educational system.[4]

Among the other factors it analyzed, the Umalusi project assigned the national subject-area exams (known as "papers") to one of three levels of "conceptual challenge." The Umalusi researchers looking at the subject with the largest number of registrations, English Second Language Higher Grade (with 355,377 candidates enrolled in 2003), concluded that "the nationally set paper in the subject is becoming easier—or, in the jargon of the examiners, becoming 'more accessible.' "[5] The researchers cited as evidence a dramatic decline in the number of questions at more challenging levels, from 34 percent of items judged as challenging and 37 percent as very easy in 2001, when the pass rate was 68.9 percent, to a mere 4 percent of items judged as challenging and 65 percent as very easy in 2003, when the pass rate, perhaps unsurprisingly, rose to 73.3 percent.

Similar findings were reported by the research groups dealing with the other national papers. At least partly as a result of the adverse public reaction to Umalusi's findings, the examinations have since become marginally more demanding, accompanied by a drop in the pass rate to just below 2002 levels, a rate still believed to be unrealistically high given the very low levels of performance revealed by internationally benchmarked assessment studies such as TIMSS and PIRL, as described subsequently.

The seriousness of the situation needs to be emphasized: in a context of underqualified teachers[6] and poorly resourced learning environments, examinations tend to define the curriculum and the educational standards. The fact that the difficulty of the only external examination students write in their whole school careers has been revised down to ever-easier (or perhaps "more accessible") levels may explain many of the difficulties these students face once they enter the higher-education system. This problem is particularly serious for teaching of the English language, since English plays a crucial role in South African education as both a classroom subject in its own right, and the language in which the majority of the country's school students do their learning.

This situation poses complex difficulties for admissions officials. First, it seems self-evident that public institutions of higher education need to design their curriculum to begin at the same level at which public secondary education ends. As Ian Scott demonstrates in a later chapter of this book, the current failure and dropout rates in higher education suggest that this need is not generally being acknowledged or effectively addressed. Commenting somewhat wryly on an analogous situation in the United States, analysts Jamie Merisotis and Ronald Phipps note that "those halcyon days when all students who enrolled in college were adequately prepared, all courses offered at higher education institutions were 'college-level' and students smoothly made the transition from high school to college simply never existed. And they do not exist now."[7]

The very poor quality of South African schooling makes it highly unlikely that the majority of students entering the country's higher-education system will earn a quality degree in the normal allotted time. It is therefore incumbent on the higher-education system to facilitate access and offer a variety of curricular responses to this dilemma. It is clear, for example, that admissions criteria and procedures need to include placement functions—not simply pointing candidates toward a particular degree program, but toward a specific level and pace of study. Indeed, the placement issue is one of the most serious challenges to effective implementation of an affirmative-action-driven admissions policy, requiring constant attention both to steering at the time of admissions, and to ongoing curriculum development to meet the educational needs of diverse groups of incoming students.

Second, there is considerable evidence to suggest that senior certificate scores below 60 percent do not reliably predict future academic performance.[8] Since the great majority of educationally disadvantaged students who obtain an endorsement fall into this range, the difficulty is obvious: institutions of higher education have to select students on the basis of criteria they know to be unreliable, if they want to open their process up to educationally disadvantaged students.

There are a number of possible admissions responses to this problem. One is to implement alternative assessments or procedures that will help institutions to identify talented students whose potential is not adequately captured in their senior certificate results. Another is to establish differentiated entry requirements in the senior certificate for groups identified as disadvantaged. Both of these options are discussed later in this chapter. Irrespective of the response or combination of responses adopted, however, the generally poor quality of public schooling makes it essential that educators create strong links between the selection and placement processes.

The third of the three factors that complicate the South African admissions challenge is inequity within the schooling system.

Massive Inequities within the Schooling System
ᔆ

The Human Sciences Research Council (HSRC) has conducted three TIMSS studies in South Africa, in 1995, 1999, and 2003. The results of the 2003 study, seen in table 1, illustrate the generally low performance levels in the school system as a whole, as well as the particularly low levels observed in historically African, disadvantaged schools, known as DET schools (the apartheid-era Department of Education and Training system was designed to provide schooling for African students. It was severely underfunded, and the majority of its teachers were underqualified.). That serious inequities exist elsewhere—in the United States, for example—is cold comfort, especially in light of South Africa's constitutionally mandated requirement of redress.

Table 1 presents the average scores of students at the TIMSS-sampled schools, which are categorized according to the scheme used by the former racially based departments of education. While the average performance in former white schools is slightly below the international average (an outcome of great concern in its own right, since these schools consume a dis-

TABLE 1.   TIMSS 2003 Scores by Former Racially Based Departments

	Math Score	Science Score
Former African (DET) schools	227	200
Former White schools	456	468
National average	264	244
International average	467	474

Source: V. Reddy, *TIMSS 2003 Results: Fact Sheet 2* (Pretoria: Human Sciences Research Council, 2003), accessed at http://www.hsrc.ac.za/Research _Programme-Page-61.phtml.

proportionate share of resources and represent the apex of the South African educational system), average performance in African schools is significantly below White levels. Since the great majority of African students attend the formerly DET schools, the table makes clear the extent of the educational inequity.

A second source of evidence on the differences between schools comes from data supplied by applicants to the University of Cape Town who wrote the entrance tests developed by the Alternative Admissions Research Project (AARP) in 2006.

AARP is responsible for developing and administering an entrance testing scheme for educationally disadvantaged applicants whose final school results might not reveal their full potential. The project's tests evaluate core competencies in academic literacy, numeracy, and mathematics. What makes them particularly useful—as sources of information in their own right, or in combination with the senior certificate—is that they set out to test potential rather than, in the memorable phrase coined by Ronald Miller, simply "predicting the past."[9] Potential is tested through the introduction of carefully structured and sequenced opportunities within the tests, which elicit far wider ranges of performance than are achieved with traditional testing.[10] The AARP tests are used, in varying ways and for various purposes, by most of South Africa's institutions of higher education: in 2006 alone, approximately 100,000 tests were submitted by candidates seeking access.

As perhaps the most selective institution in the country, the University of Cape Town's applicants represent a particularly wide range of abilities and backgrounds, as can be seen from their AARP scores in table 2. The table compares student performance across school types, revealing dramatic differences.

If admissions offers were made only to the top two deciles of the overall group—that is, to those candidates obtaining a score of 72 percent or higher—then no DET graduates would have been selected. Clearly, some more relative measure is needed: at Cape Town, selection criteria during the 1990s stipulated that the top two deciles from each school type would receive an offer. Thus, ex-DET students with 50 percent and over in English language testing or 56 percent in mathematics would have been considered, along with graduates from historically advantaged schools with scores of 77 percent and over in English and 84 percent and over in math.

One difficulty posed by Cape Town's approach is that candidates scoring 50 percent on the Placement Test in English for Educational Purposes (PTEEP) do not have the same level of developed abilities as those scoring 75 percent. In the example already given, applicants with relatively low scores but high decile rankings are likely to be offered a place at UCT, but the place they will be offered is highly likely to be in a fundamentals or remedial program. To facilitate such decisions, two scores are reported for each candidate: one reflecting a decile ranking in the overall testing group (the candidate's tested knowledge according to an absolute measure) and the other a decile ranking in his or her educational category (the candidate's performance relative to peers). The difficulty lies in ensuring that admissions staff keep the very different information contained in these two rankings in mind during the hectic weeks when admissions decisions are being made.

The differences in performance among the school types listed in the table make it clear that school background must be considered in admissions. One possible solution, exemplified by Cape Town, is to rank students' results according to school type, and then select the top students from each ranking. This will ensure that disadvantaged students (still overwhelmingly black at this stage in South Africa's development) are not further disadvantaged by the need to compete on an unfair basis. The ranking could be done

TABLE 2. "Between School-Type" Performance Patterns, Alternative Admissions Research Project, 2006

| Deciles (lower boundary) | Placement Test in English for Educational Purposes (PTEEP) | | | Mathematics | | |
	Overall	DET Schools	Historically Advantaged Schools	Overall	DET Schools	Historically Advantaged Schools
1	77	57	79	84	66	91
2	72	50	77	75	56	84
3	69	45	75	66	50	81
4	66	41	72	56	47	75
5	61	37	71	50	37	69
6	56	34	68	44	34	66
7	51	30	65	34	31	59
8	43	28	62	28	25	53
9	33	23	57	22	22	41
10	12	12	28	3	0	19

Source: The data used to compile this table are taken from unpublished annexes to the AARP 2006 Annual Report: A. Visser, *UCT—General 2006 Writers for 2007 Intake,* University of Cape Town, Alternative Admissions Research Project (Cape Town: University of Cape Town, 2006).

Note: The "Overall" column shows the performance of all the students in the sample, divided into deciles. Deciles are obtained by ranking all the scores of a candidate pool, dividing the number of candidates by 10, and then reporting the scores of the candidates at each tenth interval. The table uses the lower boundary of each decile for ease of reading. The other columns show students' performance by school type. To do this, schools were grouped broadly into categories established by the pre-1996 examination authorities, on the grounds that the material conditions in the education system have not equalized systematically since then.

using senior certificate results or the results of alternative admissions tests—experience shows that some combination of the two is most useful. There is, however, some fluidity in school categorizations, which complicates the typology. The quintiles used by the state for funding purposes, which are based on socioeconomic status, could be useful against this uncertainty once they become available to institutions, but research by economist Servaas van den Berg suggests that the biggest differential in performance is found between the richest quintile and the other four. There is no simple linear relationship from poorest to richest.[11]

There is a simple measure of relative ability that compares students' performance only with those of their peers at the same school. Research suggests that this technique is both affordable and effective, and so could provide an equitable way of identifying talented students without any need to categorize their school of origin. In a 1999 study, I and two of my colleagues, Peter Dawes and Matthew Smith, examined the use of aggregate school-leaving examination scores to develop an equivalent to the American idea of a grade point average (or GPA). The American literature shows a strong correlation between such tests and subsequent academic performance, as well as between a student's high school record and subsequent performance. The majority of U.S. schools provide GPAs, making it possible for American colleges and universities to use them in combination with Scholastic Achievement Test (SAT) scores to admit students. Given the unreliability of internal assessment procedures at most South African high schools, however, one would have to develop other means for estimating a candidate's ability relative to that of classmates.

My colleagues and I used each individual's aggregate senior certificate score (the raw total of all the marks for all of her or his subjects) at a particular school to derive a rank for that school. We then assigned each individual a percentile score that revealed her or his place in the class rankings for that exam. The indicator was called the place-on-exam (PoE) indicator.

The study suggested that the PoE could be a useful indicator of subsequent academic performance at university. Strong correlations were found between the indicator and subsequent performance at the universities of Rhodes and Cape Town, for students from both advantaged and disadvantaged schools. Given the relative ease of use, as well as the contribution the indicator could make to equity of opportunity, we concluded by recommending that it be used as an additional source of information for selection purposes. Despite its promise, however, acceptance of the PoE has not been widespread, although plans are afoot to update the study and disseminate information on its use as an additional source of information.

Pervasive and Lingering Effects of Apartheid
∾
A major problem with using either school type or PoE ranking as a basis for selection is that the categories are not based on racial classifications, but on the type of school candidates attended. As such, an African candidate attending a historically White or private school would be ranked among the historically advantaged students, whereas an African candidate attending a historically DET school would be placed within the DET category. Since the historically advantaged rank is considerably more demanding than the DET group, this situation is only acceptable if we know for sure that the performance of African students in advantaged schools is competitive with that of their non-African peers, and has not been depressed or prejudiced by factors unrelated to innate ability. The method is not acceptable if we find that this is not the case.

In assessing whether the teaching and learning environment and experience is indeed equitable for all students, even where the overall schooling opportunity is nominally equal, researcher A. J. Visser of the Centre for Higher Education Development at UCT analyzed data from UCT applicants in 2003 for entry in 2004.[12] Visser found a significant difference in the performance of students from different population groups even when all of these students attended historically advantaged public schools. The intergroup differences can be explained in a number of ways: as the result of being educated and assessed in a language other than one's native tongue; of the length of time students have actually spent in the advantaged school sector; of the impact of institutional culture; of parental levels of education; or of issues related to being part of the first generation to pursue formal schooling. Some students also live in townships from which they have to travel long distances to school. Their parents may struggle financially to send their children to these schools, and are not necessarily in a position to provide the "cultural capital" that contributes to high educational achievement. Whatever the reason, Visser's data show that black students' performance does not compare favorably with that of their white peers in the same schools, at this early stage in South Africa's democratic history (see table 3). For example, white students on average achieve 42 entrance points on their senior certificate examination compared to 38.4 for black students. This difference is very significant for entry into high-demand courses such as engineering, health sciences, science, or law, and goes some way to explaining the preponderance of black students in humanities-related courses, and underrepresentation in the former group of courses.

The point is that exclusive reliance on school type as an indicator of educational disadvantage might well result in actively *disadvantaging* black students at historically advantaged schools. Put differently, any evaluation of these students that did not consider their race would without a doubt influence their chances of gaining admission to selective institutions.

Alternative Assessment Projects in South Africa

∾

The preceding discussion has focused on ways of interpreting and treating the scores achieved by students, using school type and "race" as the major variables to assist in achieving affirmative action goals in respect of admissions. However, several projects in South Africa have attempted to develop instruments and procedures that affect student performance and thus the scores on which students are assessed for admissions, rather than relying on score manipulations or differential treatment of scores. This work owes much to the pioneering studies of Feuerstein (1979) and Vygotsky (1978), who both attempted to investigate and measure what an individual could achieve, given appropriate mediation or learning environments.

The projects in this "dynamic testing" tradition that have been undertaken in South Africa have often been small scale, and closely tied to curriculum development initiatives. They are therefore difficult to evaluate in terms of their value for admissions. The Alternative Admissions Research Project, based at Cape Town, is the most promising of the projects for research into alternative admissions purposes because it is used, to some extent at least, by almost all higher-education institutions in South Africa, and therefore tests sizable numbers of candidates and recommends students for all programs. Its findings are thus somewhat independent of specific in-

TABLE 3. "Within School-Type," Performance Patterns (2003)

Population Group	Senior Certificate Points Score	PTEEP	AARP Maths Achievement Test
African	38.4	55.1	58.1
	($n = 1,125$)	($n = 513$)	($n = 359$)
Coloured	39.3	60.3	60.8
	($n = 917$)	($n = 487$)	($n = 300$)
Indian	42.8	63.4	68.8
	($n = 441$)	($n = 200$)	($n = 157$)
White	42.0	65.4	69.0
	($n = 3,725$)	($n = 1,483$)	($n = 772$)

Source: A. Visser, *Analysis of Admissions Indicators of ex-HoA Full-Time Applicants 2003–2005 by Racial Classification,* report commissioned by the Admissions and Progression Committee, University of Cape Town, October 2006.

Note: The points score is derived from the symbols obtained in the Senior Certificate examination. Degree programmes set their own minimum requirements, often doubling certain subjects, such as Mathematics and Science in the case of Engineering. Very crudely, the points score (with no weighting) for a student with a C aggregate (between 60 and 70%) is 36.

structional effects. In addition, because the test has not been used as a barrier to access—that is, since poor performance on the AARP assessments has not been used to reject applicants who would otherwise have been accepted—the sample is not as truncated as selection studies often are. Therefore, it is possible to compare the subsequent academic performance of students who had done well enough on the tests to have been recommended for admission on that basis, with the performance of students who performed poorly on the tests, but gained admission on the basis of their school-leaving results. Longitudinal research has shown that the former group outperforms the latter.[13]

The AARP testing approach is based on the development of tests that contain built-in instructional opportunities, provided through the technique of task scaffolding, where each task builds on the previous one, and where students are actively involved in constructing responses to carefully designed and supported tasks. Research into the approach demonstrates that this task scaffolding elicits performances from comparable candidates *different* from those elicited by more traditional approaches.[14] Importantly, from the point of view of selection, the task scaffolding does not simply make the test easier for all candidates—in fact, the gap between weaker and stronger candidates actually widens.

The AARP consistently makes the point in annual reports that good performance on either the AARP assessments or the senior certificate, or both, is a reasonable predictor of success in higher education. Since (as was demonstrated earlier in this chapter) too few black students achieve the competitive school-leaving results that would gain them admission into high-demand courses in selective institutions, this finding is of great value. To date many hundreds of students have gained admission to higher-education institutions on the basis of their performance on these tests, and their progress to graduation has been comprehensively monitored and reported.[15]

So, while more research is needed, as always, studies do suggest that alternative admissions procedures like these can provide a route into higher education for students seeking to overcome prior disadvantage, particularly if their educational needs are identified and met. The importance of thinking about admissions and placement together cannot be overstated, particularly in a setting like South Africa, which is characterized by generally low levels of educational attainment at the secondary level, and a high degree of continuing inequity in achievement.

Finally, then, it is clear that a number of issues need to be considered, and a number of approaches adopted, if higher education in South Africa is to succeed in admitting talented first-year students who represent all groups within the country. Until schooling improves, higher education will need to continue to learn to interpret what school-leaving examination scores mean by using school and individual biographical data, to develop tests and procedures that elicit different performances from those yielded by traditional achievement tests, and to develop appropriate curriculum routes that adequately meet the educational needs of students and place students into these routes if this placement is indicated.

NOTES

1. P. Govender, "The Making of Maths Stars," *Sunday Times,* January 7, 2007, 4.

2. N. Yeld, "Academic Literacy and Numeracy Profiles: An Analysis of Some Results from the AARP and TELP Tests of Incoming Students (2001/2002 Entry Years)," in *Into Higher Education—Perspectives on Entry Thresholds and Enrollment Systems* (SAUVCA-CTP Higher Education Admissions Project, 2003), 26, 46.

3. The name *Umalusi* is derived from the Nguni word *uMalusi,* which means "shepherd."

4. N. Yeld, M. Grobler, and C. Sekwane, "Investigation into the Examination of English Second/Additional Language by Selected Examination Authorities in the Years 1992, 1999, 2001, and 2003," research commissioned by Umalusi, Pretoria, 2004, 1.

5. Ibid., 15.

6. The difficulties faced by the national Department of Education in training teachers (in relation to both pre- and in-service training) are greatly exacerbated by the HIV/AIDS pandemic, which is now killing thousands of teachers and students training to be teachers each year.

7. J. P. Merisotis and R. A. Phipps, "Remedial Education in Colleges and Universities: What's Really Going On?" *Review of Education* 24, no. 1 (2000): 69.

8. H. D. Herman, "School-leaving Examinations, Selection and Equity in Higher Education in South Africa," *Comparative Education* 31, no. 2 (1995): 261–74; T. Barsby, W. Haeck, and N. Yeld, eds., *Accountability in Testing: The Contribution of Tests to Increased Access to Post-secondary Education,"* South African Association for Academic Development, Workshop Publication Series no. 2 (Cape Town: University of Cape Town, 1994); N. Yeld and W. Haeck, "Educational Histories and Academic Potential: Can Tests Deliver?" *Assessment and Evaluation in Higher Education* 22, no. 1 (1997): 5–16; N. Badsha, G. T. W. Blake, and J. G. Brock-Utne, "Evaluation of the African Matriculation as a Predictor of Performance in the University of Natal Medical School," *South African Journal of Science* 82 (1986): 220–21; N. Yeld, "Assessment, Equity, and Language of Learning: Key Issues for Higher Education Selection in South Africa," Ph.D. diss., University of Cape Town, 2001.

9. Ronald Miller, "Double Double Toil and Trouble: The Problem of Student Selection," *South African Journal of Higher Education* 6, no. 1 (1992): 98–104.

10. Yeld and Haeck, "Educational Histories."

11. S. Van den Berg, "How Effective Are Poor Schools? Poverty and Educational Outcomes in South Africa," Stellenbosch Economic Working Papers, June 2006.

12. A. J. Visser, "Analysis of Admissions Indicators of ex-HoA Full-time Applicants 2003–2005 by Population Group Classification," report presented to the Admissions Committee, University of Cape Town, October 2006.

13. Yeld, "Assessment, Equity."

14. For example, Yeld and Haeck, "Educational Histories."

15. Yeld, "Assessment, Equity."

Race and Class in the South African Higher-Education Sector

A Focus on the Undergraduate Experience

Crain Soudien

More than a dozen years after apartheid formally came to an end, almost every overview or assessment of education, whether it relates to the funding, planning, or evaluation of policies, has, in one way or another, had to respond to the persistent challenge of race.[1] But the manifestation of race as a phenomenon in South African education is much more complex than is popularly appreciated, and particularly in higher education.

Higher education was complicit with all other levels of schooling in the discrimination of the apartheid-era social, political, and economic environment. However, it is distinct as a result of the unique ways in which it has interacted with race, especially after 1994. While the ways in which race is experienced in the primary and secondary systems might reasonably accurately reflect its everyday nature, there are features of higher education that place race into a different relationship with everyday experience. Perhaps most important is the idea that social class, expressed in the form of individual achievement, configures the racial experience in distinctive ways. In the elite environment of selective higher education, social class is producing new and interesting racial demographics, but, more pertinently, also new ideas of how individuals within the system might understand race.

While some researchers have commented on the fragmentation of identity in South African higher education, they have so far paid insufficient attention to the ways in which these identities are formed.[2] The current chapter is intended to contribute an understanding of how racial identity can become a resource in individuals' contacts with educational institutions. It does not pursue the line of discussion familiar from the classic identity-formation literature about subject formation: who is attributing what identities to whom, and under what power relations. What it seeks to do, instead, is to highlight interesting new trends in how race is being experienced by South African undergraduates, and particularly black undergraduates. What does the racial experience look like for them? What are they saying when they invoke race?

My claim is that the experience of race takes on what might be called a "sublimated form" in the university. Locating race within the workings of higher education is difficult because, except in those most egregious situations where racism is blatant and unsophisticated, race's function is hard to recognize or name. So, for example, achievement and failure—both for individuals and for groups or communities—is hard to account for in strictly racial terms. While the institutional character of a university is key, and some forms of racism might be stronger in some institutions than others, the agency of individuals, principally black people in this instance, also plays a significant role in race's sublimation. This interaction can be very difficult to understand, and so is often interpreted through proxy devices, such as language use, family background, or school of origin. We have yet fully to engage with the substance of people's experiences in the university, however, and this stands as a challenge to any discussion of affirmative action, which as a policy tends to rely on essentialized understandings of what race is all about.

The Undergraduate Experience

∾

The recent literature on the South African undergraduate experience has highlighted the persistent racism experienced by black students. Reitumetse Obakeng Makobela's study of students at the University of Stellenbosch, a prestigious historically Afrikaans university in the Western Cape, Rochelle Woods's work on black students at the University of the Witwatersrand, also a leading historically English-speaking Johannesburg-based university, and Jonathan Jansen's interaction with students at the University of Pretoria, one of the country's largest and most important historically Afrikaans universities, provide important descriptions of black students' experiences with discrimination.[3] Institutional climate surveys and independent attitudinal surveys confirm the depth and extent of the problem.[4] There is also a recognition on the part of many universities that racist behavior persists in their institutions.

As Rochelle Woods has demonstrated, young black students feel that they are the subjects of racism and that this racism has affected their social, cultural, and academic well-being. This racism is sometimes overt but more often takes a form described by black students as intolerance on the part of white students and lecturers for their languages and cultures.

Racism is undoubtedly real. But accepting that fact at face value obscures some of the important ways in which the growing population of black students is settling into the academy. As in the United States, even though South African students experience racism in the formerly white universities, they are nonetheless choosing these institutions over those that had been especially established for them during apartheid. We must, therefore, look beyond general statements to explore how young black students, in particular, are thinking through their experience.

In developing this analysis we must embrace the apparently contradictory statements that students often make in institutional climate surveys. While surveys such as these paint a vivid picture of young people's racial frustrations, subjects may simultaneously feel an intense desire to feel at home. The education specialist Reitumetse Obakeng Makobela quotes a student from the University of Stellenbosch: "just look at Stellenbosch (the town)—it's White, White, White. Where do I go to socialize? I can't go to Kyamandi (the local Black township); those people look at us like we are strangers."[5] There is an intense desire on the part of the students to fit in and be accepted.

One must not underestimate the weight and substance of students' racial grievances. The pain with which they are conveyed is deep. In the University of Cape Town's 2004 survey, for example, the evidence was clear, as sociologist Zimitri Erasmus has remarked, that "black students are having to do all the racial work in the institution."[6] White students, black students felt, were not required to do any reflecting on their situation. Rather, whites' cultural orientations meshed perfectly with those of the institution, while black students felt that faculty were discriminating against them because of their language. As one student explained,

> there was like a four-page scenario that you had to read so that you can actually get to the question. By the time I was on page 2, I didn't actually know what I had read on page 1, because the words they are using are just too much. . . . even the other lecturer . . . agreed that it was ridiculous.[7]

Another said that she had noticed "with certain lecturers, because we were all Black, she . . . made you feel very stupid, that you are coming from a disadvantaged background, so . . . you don't know anything."[8] While there certainly were students who commended their lecturers for their sensitivity, there were others who were overwhelmed by the scope of knowledge that their lecturers took for granted: "you're so scared cause they gonna laugh at you if your English is not good and you end up just sitting there and not asking anything, sometimes it make me feel as if I am suffocating."[9] Feelings of inferiority and worthlessness were pervasive.

Black students also frequently spoke of their concerns about informal segregation at the University of Cape Town. Dining halls, residences, and even certain courses were color-coded. A Cape Town student commented on the divisions at a campus restaurant:

> There's Nescafe Coffee Shop. It used to be White dominated, I swear to God, if you go there, they look at you funny and you gonna feel like I don't belong here. I shouldn't even be here . . . even the staff who are serving you are a bit concerned about "what you are black, why are you here?" Two, even the residences, like Liesbeck [sic], has Black students only.[10]

It is clear from white students' statements that they struggle to comprehend the experiences of their black fellow students. As the data gathered by Cooper shows, many white students resent what is perceived to be the unfair advantage enjoyed by their black peers in the allocation of places at the university and in the job market.[11]

As powerfully as the evidence conveys the difficulties experienced by black university students, it is also characterized by the pervasive refrain of "making it"—of surviving and even succeeding in the institution. It is through students' aspiration to improve themselves that the understanding of race is transformed from an experience of helplessness and apathy to what one might understand as the mobilization of agency. In thinking about their racial identities, students' externally oriented drives and aspirations—their middle-class dreams—interact with the character-forming influences of higher-education practice. The interaction produces complex attitudes toward themselves, their fellow students and mentors and the institutions in which they find themselves.

One of the themes consistently evoked in the testimony of UCT students is their yearning for an improvement in their status. Extracts from the 2004 UCT Institutional Climate Survey testify to this yearning:

- Why UCT? Yeah, I was the best so you go to the best. [black male]
- Everybody goes to UCT as it is where standard of learning is highest. [black female]
- You should see how people's eyes widen when I pull out my student card when going to clubs. [Indian female]
- I think that people back home in Durban are impressed by the fact that I am a UCT student. [Indian male]
- Being one of the leading African institutions; the graduates that come out of this university especially the commerce graduates are generally held in high regard in the business community. [Indian male]

The very fact that they are at university makes some students think twice about how they might present themselves. Having been accepted into the institution sometimes induces a feeling of ambivalence about racial identity. Anger is a common trope, but there is also often a desire to exchange racial identities for class standing. Take, for example, this remark from a black male student at UCT

We should not use the fact that we are black for under-performing. UCT has got very high standards. If you want to get 50 and get to Honours then why don't you go to UWC [University of the Western Cape]? You are welcome to do that. UCT has always had high standards. I mean that is why we are here, because of the prestige. . . . So guys who are complaining about the standards, and that they are failing, then they must go to the previously black institutions.[12]

Black students continue to regard themselves as blacks, but as a special kind of black.

Some scholars have suggested that "black African students may equate low passing grades with academic success."[13] While a great deal more work needs to be done on this subject, it may be that black students are experiencing university through some combination of race and class lenses which demonstrate that the supposedly homogeneous category "black" is actually constituted in interaction with other factors. But students are also aware of the criticism that they will elicit by choosing to attend a privileged university. They become conscious of how their actions may alienate them from their communities and their histories.

At the same time, and complicating the picture, the internal influences of higher-education practice can moderate external self-interest. Academic courses help students look beyond the binary and categorical forms of everyday knowledge to appreciate the relativity of opinions, cultures, and societies. The possibility offered by the academic experience, which is not experienced by everybody in the same way, is that of self-transformation. Students emerge out of these experiences with optimistic and positive self-understandings.

It is well known that all university students, irrespective of their backgrounds, enjoy similar opportunities for self-construction. In the South African context, these opportunities exert a considerable impact on race and racial identity. Jonathan Jansen, for example, describes the process of conversion among white female students at the University of Pretoria, as they develop durable and robust friendships across color lines.[14] The university experience has the potential to bolster the confidence of black students, especially those enrolled at formerly white institutions, just as it does for other students, but it also unsettles their perceptions of their racial identities. This sentiment was expressed strongly in the 2004 UCT survey, as well as in a survey conducted at the University of Stellenbosch, where a senior student whom the researchers describe as deeply engaged in matters of identity negotiation at the university commented:

I've started looking at diversity with greater depth . . . and the funny thing is, when you sit and look at people you just assume that they're alike, but

even in homogeneous groups you'll find people from completely different backgrounds and they view the world differently.[15]

Similarly, a third-year student says,

> I have grown to realize through what I have been taught about God, fe-
> males and males, [that] the world is not necessarily what it is and that
> what I believe in is not necessarily true or wrong—not everything is black
> and white. . . . I have learnt that human beings are not passive; they ques-
> tion things, its roots and how things become universally accepted.[16]

The identities with which students arrived at university change. There
are, needless to say, many instances in which the convergence of external
and internal forces produces a deep sense of alienation. One student at
UCT told Hoadley that she "wasn't gonna stay at home and be like the rest
of the people around that place."[17] And a University of Stellenbosch student
told Liebowitz and coauthors that

> the other problem I have is my family. It's difficult even at this stage to
> sort of communicate and socialize with them because I've outgrown
> them in every possible way and when I do communicate with them I al-
> most have to pretend or be someone else simply because they are telling
> you "you want to be white."[18]

More positively, there are students who adapt well to the institution and
hold on to their identities in a way that affirms both their past and their future. A number of students in the 2004 UCT and 2005 Stellenbosch studies
talk of how their lives have changed and how they have come to learn to live
with others around them. Their self-conceptions are strong. There are also
students who go through deep transformations. A student named Linda, in
a 2006 study, holds on to her coloured identity, but refuses the facile ways in
which it is transacted in one of her classes:

> I put up my hand (in one of the lectures) and said "Um, I'm sorry, I don't
> like the use of the word, coloured, in class," and he was like, "But, but, but
> . . . we use it all the time." And I said, "Then, no, you should change it, this
> is the place where you change words. A university changes words." And
> then afterwards he was so scared. Every time he used the word . . . he
> searched me out. So this is what university has done for me.[19]

Other students experience less extreme changes, settling relatively smoothly
into the academic identity of their discipline. As one student, whose race is
not described, told researchers Kapp and Bangeni,

each day I find more and more evidence within myself that I am at that point where I moved from being in my discipline, to where I am my discipline. This is evident in my speech, thought, and ways I approach certain things, whether in academic or formal setting.[20]

Conclusion

ᨠ

Government concerns about higher education's incomplete transformation are not misplaced. Racism remains a problem in many South African institutions. But a study of racism's symptoms only leads to a partial understanding of the issue. In order to better appreciate the complexity of race as it is experienced by students, the higher-education system itself must be understood as an intensely complex sociological phenomenon. The sector's apparent resemblance to other areas of everyday life, with respect to how race operates and is experienced, may seem at first to belie this claim of complexity. The forms and much of the substance of the everyday experience of race—expressed as racism and the ancillary feelings of superiority and inferiority that go with it—are present as teaching and learning takes place. But the character of the university, it needs to be recognized, produces particular identity outcomes, particularly amongst people who have existed on the margins of privilege, who work with their identities and have their identities worked upon in a range of interesting ways.

In understanding the South African university one must come to terms with how external and internal factors influence the individual's understanding of race in particular ways. The desire for social mobility creates forces that often have the effect of weakening students' identification with their communities of origin. There are students who reject the idea of "home" as it is embodied in the lives of their parents. But, more significantly, there are many who choose to move on from the starting point of home. This evolution cannot easily be presented in a simple vocabulary of racial categories. And it is further complicated by the professional identities and vocabularies these students take on as social scientists, engineers, medical doctors, and the like. These identities may still have a racial component, but in an attenuated form. It is important, therefore, to come to terms with the extent to which young people use the status of their university or their disciplinary identity to explain who they are. One sees in this act of reaching a sublimation of their racial identities, and an emphasis on the new social class into which they are moving.

How these developments are managed within the changing policy environment of higher education is an unresolved and pressing question. While there undoubtedly remain many black people for whom race continues to be pivotal, the important phenomenon of weakened racial identity and the stronger allegiance to status must be taken into consideration, especially in the context of a higher-education system that relies on affirmative action and its relatively fixed notions of race.

NOTES

1. See for example, S. Brown, *Money and Morality* (Cape Town: Institute for Justice and Reconciliation, 2006); G. Steyn, and P. de Villiers, *Higher Education Monitor: The Impact of Changing Funding Sources on Higher Education Institutions in South Africa* (Pretoria: Council for Higher Education, 2006); Council for Higher Education (CHE), *South African Higher Education in the First Decade of Democracy* (Pretoria: CHE, 2004).

2. See particularly B. Liebowitz, S. Daniels, A. Loots, R. Richards, D. Sebrandt, and I. van Deventer, "What Do Students Say about Their Experiences of Studying at Stellenbosch University—Report Back from the Identity, Teaching and Learning Research Project," paper presented at the Interdisciplinary Colloquium, Cape Town and Stellenbosch, South Africa, March 30–31, 2006. For an important exception, see U. Hoadley, "Social and Academic Integration of Young Women Studying Science and Engineering," unpublished paper, 2007.

3. R. Makobela, "'Selective Inclusion': Transformation and Language Policy at the University of Stellenbosch," in *Apartheid No More*, ed. R. Makobela and K. King (Westport, CT: Bergin and Garvey, 2001); R. Woods, "'Oh Sorry, I'm a Racist': Black Student Experiences at the University of the Witwatersrand," in Makobela and King, *Apartheid No More*; and J. Jansen, "Race, Education, and Democracy after Ten Years: How Far Have We Come?" unpublished paper prepared for the Institute of Democracy in South Africa, 2004.

4. University of Cape Town (UCT), "Same River, Different Boats: Report on 13 Focus Groups with UCT Students," report prepared for the Student Climate Survey, 2004; UCT, "The Way Forward with the Student Climate Survey: Report to the Transformation Management Advisory Group," 2005; University of the Witwatersrand, "Success at the University of the Witwatersrand: Report of the Working Group on Retention and Throughput," overview report for council, Johannesburg, 2002; A. Cooper, "Research Report on Student Responses at the University of Cape Town about the Tutorial Space as a Site for Identity Development," unpublished report, Cape Town, 2005; J. Graaff, "The Challenge of the Social Sciences: The Impact of Sociology in First Year Students," paper presented at the Interdisciplinary Colloquium, Cape Town and Stellenbosch, March 30–31, 2006; R. Kapp and B. Bangeni, "Positioning (in) the Discipline: Undergraduate Students' Negotiation of Disciplinary Discourses," paper presented at the Interdisciplinary Colloquium, Cape Town and Stellenbosch, March 30–31, 2006; S. Daniels and R. Richards, "Speaking the Same Language? Afrikaans in Teaching and Learning at Stellenbosch University," paper presented at the Interdisciplinary Colloquium, Cape Town and Stellenbosch, March 30–31, 2006; and B. Liebowitz, H. Adendorff, S. Daniels, A. Loots, S. Nakasa, N. Ngxabazi, A. van der Merwe, and I. van Deventer, "The Relationship between Identity, Language and Teaching and Learning in Higher Education in South Africa," *Per Linguam* 21, no. 2 (2005): 23–37.

5. Makobela, "Selective Inclusion," 69.

6. Z. Erasmus, unpublished talk presented at a meeting of the Vice Chancellor's Group on Racism at the University of Cape Town, June 2006.

7. UCT, "Same River, Different Boats," 20.

8. Ibid., 22.

9. Ibid., 23.

10. Ibid., 30.

11. Cooper, "Research Report."

12. UCT, "Same River, Different Boats," 19.

13. J. Sennett, G. Finchilescu, K. Gibson, and R. Strauss, "Adjustment of Black Students at a Historically White South African University," *Educational Psychology* 23, no. 1 (2003): 114.

14. Jansen, "Race, Education," 5.

15. Liebowitz et al., "Relationship," 33.

16. Kapp and Bangeni, "Positioning (in) the Discipline."

17. Hoadley, "Social and Academic Integration."

18. Liebowitz et al., "Relationship."

19. Graaff, "Challenge of Social Sciences," 7–8.

20. Kapp and Bangeni, "Positioning (in) the Discipline."

Benefits and Barriers

Racial Dynamics of the Undergraduate Experience

∽

Sylvia Hurtado

The history of American higher education is punctuated by efforts to integrate its predominantly white institutions, and by the emergence of separate institutions to serve specific ethnic groups, including African Americans and American Indians.[1] While the latter, minority-serving institutions are an important part of the country's higher-education system, the racial dynamics on the campuses of predominantly white four-year colleges and universities remain particularly complex. Several large-scale studies are now beginning to reveal more about the process of stratification by race, income, and ability, about the experiences of different racial or ethnic groups on college campuses, and about the barriers and benefits to educating a more diverse student population. Research points to the value of making diversity a central element of higher education's educational and service mission, and is beginning to shatter myths that have long justified palpable resistance to diversity. The purpose of this chapter is to share what we have learned about students and their experiences with diversity on college campuses, counter myths meant to legitimize the current hierarchy of institutions, and enumerate the features of diverse learning environments that can help us achieve the just and equitable society to which we aspire.

Student Diversity Experiences and Beliefs

∽

Although America has seen some progress toward the desegregation of high schools since *Brown*, entering college freshmen have still been largely socialized in racially and economically homogeneous environments. A 2006 national survey of entering freshmen at four-year colleges and universities revealed that almost 57 percent of African Americans had grown up in predominantly nonwhite neighborhoods, and that they were the group least likely to be represented in predominantly white schools or neighborhoods.[2] In contrast, almost 75 percent of the white students surveyed had attended a predominantly white high school and more than 87 percent had grown up in predominantly white neighborhoods. Close to one-third of the Asians and Latinos surveyed (31.4 percent and 38.5 percent, respectively) grew up in completely nonwhite neighborhoods. They were nearly as likely as African Americans to attend mixed-race high schools. This suggests that a significant proportion of entering college students have had relatively little experience with diversity before coming to college, and know very little about the backgrounds and culture of different racial or ethnic groups. Yet entering students entertain high expectations despite these differences, with almost 65 percent of freshmen stating that they expected to socialize with someone of another racial or ethnic group while in college.[3]

Research is beginning to show how precollege environments can influence the quality of cross-race interactions once a college student is on campus: white students from predominantly white precollege environments were less likely than students who had grown up in more diverse environments to report positive cross-race interactions during the first two years of university.[4] In other words, in the absence of significant experience with diversity in high school, the cycle of segregation tends to reproduce itself.[5] This is evident in the fact that white students who grew up in predominantly white environments and joined a sorority or fraternity were less likely than their peers to report positive cross-race interactions while in college. On the other hand, participation in diversity cocurricular activities and living with people from different backgrounds were important predictors of positive cross-racial interactions during the first two years of college for all students. Furthermore, white students from predominantly white environments who attended universities with relatively higher percentages of students of color tended to report frequent positive cross-race interactions (e.g., they had intellectual discussions outside of class, shared personal feelings and problems, or had meaningful and honest discussions about race outside of class).[6]

In general, African Americans, Latino/as, and Asian Americans were more likely to report frequent positive cross-race interactions than white students.[7] Two college experiences proved critical for predicting the quality of cross-race interactions for African American students: the opportunity for intensive dialogue between students of different backgrounds in classrooms, and an expression of personal interest in their development from a faculty member. Latinos benefited from participation in academic support programs, which build confidence in academic skills and are associated with positive cross-racial interaction experiences. Asian Americans who participated in leadership training during college reported much more positive interactions with other groups. These results indicate that distinctively different college experiences can have an impact on specific racial/ethnic students' intergroup relations.

For many students today, however, the civil rights movement is a part of history, overt instances of discrimination are few, and many of the racial micro-aggressions experienced by minority students go unreported to campus officials. Figure 1 shows data from national, annual surveys of entering freshmen at four-year colleges and universities, during the time period in which states and campuses ceased considering race as a factor in their admissions. Nearly half of the freshmen entering during this period agreed with the statement that affirmative action in college admissions should be abolished, though since the *Grutter* decision the percentage opposing affirmative action appears to be declining. It is important to note that the other two opinion items in the figure are almost mirror images of each other. The proportion of students who declared it their personal goal to help promote racial understanding reached its high point in 1992, at 46.4 percent. This was the year that four white police officers were acquitted by a predominantly white jury of charges related to the Rodney King beating. Media coverage of the incident, the court case, and the ensuing uprising in South Central Los Angeles captured national attention. Since 1992, however, the percentage of students declaring racial understanding an important personal goal has declined, with only a slight increase in recent years, to 34 percent in 2006. Similarly, the proportion of students reporting that racial discrimination is no longer a major problem in America was lowest in 1992–93, at 12.5 percent, with steady increases up to 22.7 percent in 2004, and then slight declines again to 19.1 percent in 2006. These numbers indicate that many entering college students are simply oblivious to the persistence of racial oppression and privilege. American freshman accept legitimizing myths that justify inequality, and lack an awareness of either widening socioeconomic gaps or the value of specific policies for addressing them, and remain unaware until they come into contact with diverse peers, or participate in diversity education in college.

The Outcomes of Informal and Campus Facilitated Experiences

⤳

Sparked, in part, by concern about the elimination of affirmative action in higher education, many researchers are investigating whether and how diversity might affect learning environments. Diversity has been measured by counting individuals (also known as structural diversity), by measuring the frequency and quality of informal interactions, and by evaluating student participation in campus-facilitated diversity experiences. That is, learning about diversity often involves both a knowledge base (e.g., about the histories of diverse groups) and also an experiential base. Engagement with diversity can help enhance students' thinking, values, and dispositions.

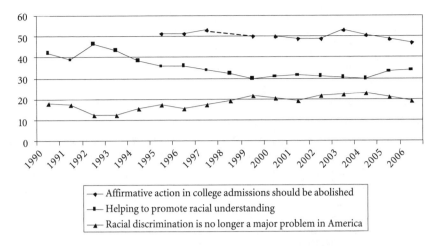

Fig. 1. Freshmen views of racial diversity issues, 1990–2006. *Note:* Responses show the percentage who agree "somewhat" and "strongly." The "helping to promote racial understanding" survey item is a personal goal, reflecting those responding it was "very important" or "essential." (Data from CIRP Annual Freshmen Survey, Higher Education Research Institute, UCLA.)

A few key studies have helped us establish the link between diversity and educational outcomes. The large-scale replication studies completed in preparation for the *Grutter* and *Gratz* cases raised the bar considerably for such work, prompting more attention to theory, method, and measures. Psychologist Patricia Gurin, also a contributor to this volume, and her colleagues developed the theoretical grounds for our understanding of how diversity influences learning, by establishing that we all are comfortable in our habits, routines, worldviews (even stereotypes) until we encounter people and experiences that cause disequilibrium or discontinuity.[8] Encounters with new types of people, perspectives, and situations force us to abandon our routines and think more actively—though in some cases these encounters give rise to anxiety, causing the individual to retreat from difference, at least temporarily. Gurin and her colleagues tested their theory and replicated the results among African American, white, Hispanic, and Asian American students; across multiple types of campuses and in a single campus context; over four years of college attendance (controlling for students' initial predispositions at college entrance) and nine years after college entry. Informal interaction with diverse peers affected *all* students' intellectual engagement and academic skills, and positively influenced the active thinking skills of both white and Asian American students. The effects of informal interaction with diverse peers on civic engagement and engagement with racial or cultural issues were even more impressive. Overall, the authors conclude that the independent effects of informal interactions in the college environment are too significant to dismiss, and that such learning cannot solely be acquired through a diversity-oriented curriculum, in the absence of a diverse peer group.

In a subsequent study, I found consistent results for the quality of students' cross-race interactions during the first two years of college. Positive interactions with diverse peers were a significant influence on 17 out of 25 possible outcomes, including complex thinking, perspective-taking (the ability to see one's work from someone else's perspective), pluralistic orientation (skills needed for a diverse workplace), ability to recognize inequality or oppression, interest in poverty issues, and belief in one's ability to create social change.[9] This confirms some of the research on diverse close friendship groups, in which group members demonstrated greater self-confidence, motivation, educational aspirations, and commitment to racial equity.[10] In contrast, students who reported negative interactions with diverse peers scored lower on 16 of the outcomes. They were more likely to report discomfort with diverse peers, and to believe that their values fundamentally differed from those of other racial or ethnic groups. Negative interactions with diverse peers also heightened one's identification with others from one's own racial category. In short, students who were not exposed to diversity during college were less likely than their peers to be prepared to function in a diverse world.

Analyses of campus-facilitated diversity education showed that students who took diversity courses in the first two years of college scored higher on 19 of the 25 outcomes, and those who participated in extracurricular diversity events were higher on 17 of the 25. This suggests that both classroom and nonclassroom diversity education has a significant impact on a wide range of educational outcomes. Opportunities for intense discussion with students from different backgrounds had a unique effect on students' perspective-taking skills, pluralistic orientation, and belief that conflict can enhance democracy. When students gain experience in holding civil discourse on difficult issues, they can acquire important skills for living and working in a pluralistic society. Engberg reviewed findings on the reduction of racial bias from numerous studies of multicultural courses, diversity workshops, peer-facilitated interventions, and community service programs on college campuses.[11] Though his study found great variability in the rigor of these intervention studies, most of them found some reduction in racial prejudice. This is somewhat surprising, since such interventions tend to be short term, and their effects are only likely to persist for so long, if not accompanied by more general changes in campus practices and attitudes about diversity.

In an experimental study on several campuses, researcher Anthony Antonio and his colleagues found that the presence in small working groups of racial and minority-opinion members, and the members' self-reported cross-racial friendships and classmate relationships all positively affected students' integrative complexity (a measure of complex thinking).[12] The thinking among the group members was more complex when different ideas were introduced by minority members.

Some critics have questioned whether racial diversity necessarily leads to differences in ideas. However, a number of studies have shown that student-body diversity is actually reflective of more diverse thinking: the racial composition of the student body is associated with greater variance in student opinion on such issues as racial inequality, the death penalty, and the treatment of criminals.[13] Further work is beginning to show that a college's racial composition is associated with more frequent interactions among diverse peers during college, which, in turn, is associated with leadership and a pluralistic orientation after college.[14] Thus, diversity among one's peers has the greatest effect when students are encouraged to engage with each other and share their perspectives. The ability to do so is largely contingent on environmental factors (dormitories, classes, and programs) as well as the larger institutional context and climate for diversity.[15]

Student Perceptions of the Campus Racial Climate

∽

All of the research on diversity in higher education suggests that the maximization of student learning depends on opportunities for favorable interaction. Not all campuses have such favorable climates, and in their absence racial incidents and student unrest may result.[16] Student perceptions of the racial climate are associated with their understanding of wider sociohistorical events, as well of their institution's historical legacy of exclusion, structural diversity, and interactions among campus groups.[17] These perceptions, in turn, directly affect student educational outcomes. Several studies have confirmed that student perceptions of racial hostility are associated with difficulties in college adjustment and a lower sense of belonging or attachment to the campus among all student groups (minority students in particular).[18] Perceptions of discrimination have a direct effect on students' academic and intellectual development and their success during the first year, as well as an indirect negative effect on grade point averages.[19] Social psychologist Shana Levin and her colleagues found that negative perceptions of campus climate led members of different racial or ethnic groups to favor in-group friends, rather than expanding their friendships to members of other groups.[20] That is, racial and ethnic clustering appeared to be a protective mechanism for students who encountered hostility along these dimensions. Clearly, student perceptions can have a strong impact on the likelihood of cross-group interaction, which not only affects social and academic integration, but also may negatively influence the individual's own learning outcomes. Most climate issues are subtle, and micro-agressions are less likely to be reported to campus authorities. Overt conflict as well as more subtle forms of discrimination are more likely on campuses that have not begun the process of institutional transformation.

Faculty Perspectives

✑

Faculty opinion, too, plays a significant role in a campus's racial climate, and in shaping student attitudes toward diversity. The Faculty Survey, administered by UCLA's Higher Education Research Institute, is based on the responses of over 40,670 full-time, undergraduate teaching faculty at 421 colleges and universities nationwide. It reveals a widespread belief among faculty that diversity is important for learning in higher education, and that it does not require compromise in student quality.[21] According to the survey, over 90 percent of undergraduate teaching faculty agreed with the statement that a racially or ethnically diverse student body enhances the educational experience of all students. Agreement ranged from 85 percent among Native American faculty to 96 percent among African American faculty. Only 24.1 percent of faculty believed that promoting diversity leads to the admission of too many underprepared students. Although the legitimizing myth of declining excellence as a result of diversity is often voiced by opponents of affirmative action, the majority (over three-quarters) of American faculty think that their institutions can become more diverse without compromising on quality.

However, underpreparedness remains an issue in a system that is moving toward universal access, and simultaneously relegating responsibility for remediation to less elite institutions. More than half of all faculty (55.5 percent) report that working with underprepared students is a source of stress. The percentage is highest at two-year colleges (68 percent) and lowest at private universities (33.5 percent). Indeed, many students attend community colleges to remedy deficiencies in their high school education. Many immigrants also elect to attend community colleges in order to learn English (one community college in New York state reports that their students speak 78 different languages). While some Americans view community colleges as "second chance" institutions for students who may eventually acquire a baccalaureate degree, only 11.1 percent of community college faculty feel that their institutions reward them for working with underprepared students. Some contend that community colleges are part of the socioeconomic sorting mechanism that directs lower-performing students toward

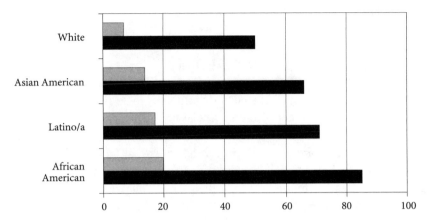

□ There Is a Lot of Campus Racial Conflict Here

■ Racial and Ethnic Diversity Should be More Strongly Reflected in the Curriculum

Fig. 2. Faculty perceptions of institutional diversity: Climate and curriculum, by race and ethnicity (percent who agree "somewhat" and "strongly"). (Data from the 2004–05 Faculty Survey, Higher Education Research Institute, UCLA.)

sub-baccalaureate degrees and occupations, while at the same time their convenience and low cost attract higher proportions of low-income students, nontraditional students, Latinos, and Native Americans.[22] Native Americans have established their own two-year tribal colleges that do not rely on state funding but are eligible for federal institutional grants because they serve large numbers of underrepresented students. Historically black and Hispanic-serving institutions (that have a minimum of 25 percent Hispanic enrollment) are also eligible for federal institutional grants, with the submission of a plan to enhance student success.

Faculty are also divided on how far their institutions have progressed toward achieving a more diverse learning environment. Slightly more than half (53 percent) of undergraduate teaching faculty believe that racial and ethnic diversity should be more strongly reflected in the curriculum at their college. Figure 2 shows that 85 percent of African American, 71 percent Latino/a, and 66 percent of Asian American faculty agreed with this statement, compared to only 50 percent of white faculty. Faculty of color are more than twice as likely as white faculty to report a prevalence of racial conflict on campus: 20 percent of African American, 17 percent of Latino/a, and 14 percent of Asian American faculty report difficulties with the racial climate on their campus, compared to only 7 percent of whites. Less than half of all respondents felt that recruiting more minority students (48 percent) or diversifying the faculty and administration (46 percent) were priorities at their institution. It is not that institutions have achieved their diversity goals; rather, it is more likely that faculty have observed other priorities taking precedence.

Diversity of Faculty

∾

Researchers have shown that faculty diversity improves classroom dynamics, by challenging students to cross social boundaries and requiring that they reexamine their views about different racial/ethnic groups.[23] For example, Anthony Antonio found in a 2002 study that faculty of color are more likely to place a greater importance on the affective, moral, and civic development of their students than their white colleagues.[24] Such faculty were also more likely to engage with diverse local communities as part of their research and public service. This finding suggests that faculty of color place a strong emphasis on students' preparation for life in a diverse society, that they have a broad view of their educational goals, and that they model civic behaviors through their own direct links with their communities. In terms of pedagogy, faculty of color are more likely to engage students in classroom dialogue and provide additional readings on race and ethnicity issues that challenge student's preconceived ideas of minority groups.[25] Because faculty tend to stay at institutions for many years—many more years than do the leaders of their institutions—the diversification of faculty at predominantly white institutions has a long-term impact on both the institution and the students it educates.

Elements of Progress

∾

Although South Africans have only more recently begun their institutional transformation, I was struck on a recent visit by the similarity of legitimizing myths employed to justify inequality. Years of research have begun to uncover how these myths operate at both the social and individual levels. We have begun to shatter some of the most egregious, which impede the creation of diverse learning environments. Although the American system of higher education has a long way yet to go, we are steadily improving our understanding of the benefits of, and barriers to, diversity in undergraduate education.

Myths are deeply embedded in organizational and individual thinking, however; and we will have to pay more attention to campus racial dynamics and transformational strategies if we are to make real progress. Along with increasing the diversity of students, faculty, and administrators, we must seek changes in normative attitudes, interactions, and beliefs.[26] Many campuses have marginal or short-lived diversity initiatives that ignore their institution's legacy of historical exclusion—a legacy that pervades the campus's policies, practices, and hiring procedures, as well as the general environment. But we also see evidence of real change in new patterns of interaction across academic units, among students and faculty; in the emergence of shared language and concepts; in new conversations and modes of inclusion; in the abandonment of old arguments or legitimizing myths that maintain inequality; and in new relationships with a variety of stakeholders.[27] The most successful leaders emphasized the importance of deep cultural change to institutional transformation. Campuses operating under race-neutral policies, meanwhile, have begun to reexamine their assumptions about talent in order to broaden their criteria for identifying it in an unequal society—essentially going beyond traditional criteria to take into account inequality in students' access to educational opportunity.

But the future is not entirely rosy. Not only are American institutions of higher education becoming more stratified by race and income, but their students are also entering college with little awareness or understanding of diversity, inequality, or oppression. Because learning about diversity occurs both inside and outside the classroom, it is essential that colleges and universities foster interactions among groups and improve their diversity education. Although educators have developed some strategies for this purpose, student service administrators are not always skilled in managing intergroup relations, and faculty are almost never trained to handle classroom conflicts that might arise from intense discussions, divergent perspectives, or deeply held views tied to students' racial or ethnic identities.[28] This suggests that staff and faculty training is important to create the safe spaces in which mutually beneficial student interactions are most likely. Leaving interracial student interactions to chance amounts to leaving learning to chance. Intentional educators seek to maximize the learning potential of diverse campus environments to prepare students for achieving and sustaining a more just and equitable society.

NOTES

1. J. D. Anderson, "The Evolution of Historically Black Colleges and Universities," in *Mind on Freedom: Celebrating the History and Culture of America's Black Colleges and Universities,* ed. S. Crew and L. G. Branch (Washington, DC: Smithsonian Institute, 1996); J. D. Anderson, "Race in American Higher Education: Historical Perspectives on Current Conditions," in *The Racial Crisis in American Higher Education,* ed. W. Smith, P. G. Altbach, and K. Lomotey, rev. ed. (Albany: SUNY Press, 2002); M. Peterson, R. T. Blackburn, Z. F. Gamson, C. H. Arce, R. W. Davenport, and J. R. Mingle, "Black Students

on White Campuses: The Impacts of Increased Black Enrollments," Institute for Social Research, Ann Arbor, MI; W. Stein, "Tribal Colleges: 1968–1998," in *Next Steps: Research and Practice to Advance Indian Education,* ed. K. G. Swisher and J. Tippiconic (Charleston, WV: ERIC Clearinghouse on Rural Education and Small Schools, 1999).

2. J. H. Pryor, S. Hurtado, V. B. Sáenz, J. L. Santos, and W. S. Korn, *The American Freshman: Forty Year Trends* (Los Angeles: Higher Education Research Institute, 2007).

3. Ibid.

4. V. B. Sáenz, "Breaking the Cycle of Segregation: Examining Students' Pre-college Racial Environments and Their Diversity Experiences in College," Ph.D. diss., University of California, Los Angeles, 2006.

5. J. H. Braddock, "The Perpetuation of Segregation across Levels of Education: A Behavioral Assessment of the Contact-Hypothesis," *Sociology of Education* 53 (1980): 178–86.

6. Sáenz, "Breaking the Cycle."

7. V. B. Sáenz, H. N. Ngai, and S. Hurtado, "Factors Influencing Positive Interactions across Race for African American, Asian American, Latino, and White College Students," *Research in Higher Education* 48 (2007): 1–38.

8. P. Gurin, "Expert Report of Patricia Gurin, in the Compelling Need for Diversity in Higher Education," *Gratz, et al., v. Bollinger, et al.,* No. 97-75321 (E.D. Mich.) and *Grutter, et al., v. Bollinger, et al.,* No. 97-75928 (E.D. Mich.); P. Gurin, E. L. Dey, S. Hurtado, and G. Gurin, "Diversity and Higher Education: Theory and Impact on Educational Outcomes," *Harvard Educational Review* 72 (2002): 330–66.

9. S. Hurtado, "The Next Generation of Diversity and Intergroup Relations Research," *Journal of Social Issues* 61 (2005): 595–610.

10. A. L. Antonio, "Diversity and the Influence of Friendship Groups in College," *Review of Higher Education* 25, no. 1 (2001): 63–89; A. L. Antonio, "The Role of Interracial Interaction in the Development of Leadership Skills and Cultural Knowledge and Understanding," *Research in Higher Education* 42 (2001): 593–617; A. L. Antonio, "The Influence of Friendship Groups on Intellectual Self-Confidence and Educational Aspirations in College," *Journal of Higher Education* 75 (2004): 446–71.

11. M. Engberg, "Improving Intergroup Relations in Higher Education: A Critical Examination of the Influence of Educational Interventions on Racial Bias," *Review of Educational Research* 74 (2004): 473–524.

12. A. L. Antonio, M. J. Chang, K. Hakuta, D. A. Kenny, S. L. Levin, and J. F. Milem, "Research Report: Effects of Racial Diversity on Complex Thinking in College Students," *Psychological Science* 15 (2004): 507–10.

13. M. J. Chang, "An Exploratory Study of the Role of Race in Selecting a Student Body with a Broader Range of Viewpoints," *Promoting Inclusion* 5 (2002): 4–13; M. J. Chang, M. Seltzer, and J. Kim, "Diversity of Opinions among Entering College Students: Does Race Matter?" paper presented at American Educational Researcher Association Conference, Seattle, 2001.

14. U. Jayakumar, "Can Higher Education Meet the Needs of an Increasingly Diverse Society and Global Marketplace? Campus Diversity and Cross-Cultural Workforce Competencies," Ph.D. diss., University of California, Los Angeles, 2007.

15. J. F. Milem, M. J. Chang, and A. L. Antonio, *Making Diversity Work on Campus: A Research-Based Perspective* (Washington, DC: American Association of Colleges and Universities, 2006).

16. S. Hurtado, "Campus Racial Climates: Contexts for Conflict," *Journal of Higher Education* 5 (September/October 1992): 539–69.

17. S. Hurtado, J. F. Milem, A. Clayton-Pederson, and W. A. Allen, *Enacting Diverse*

Learning Environments: Improving the Campus Climate for Racial/Ethnic Diversity in Higher Education (San Francisco: Jossey-Bass, 1999).

18. S. Hurtado, D. F. Carter, and A. Spuler, "Latino Student Transition to College: Assessing Difficulties and Factors in Successful Adjustment," *Research in Higher Education* 37 (1996): 135–57; S. Hurtado, J. C. Han, V. B. Sáenz, L. Espinosa, N. Cabrera, and O. Cerna, "Predicting Transition and Adjustment to College: Biomedical and Behavioral Science Aspirants' and Minority Students' First Year of College," *Research in Higher Education* 48 (2007): 841–87.

19. A. Nora and A. F. Cabrera, "The Role of Perceptions of Prejudice and Discrimination on the Adjustment of Minority Students to College," *Journal of Higher Education* 67 (1996): 119–48; Hurtado et al., "Predicting Transition and Adjustment."

20. S. Levin, C. Van Laar, and J. Sidanius, "The Effects of Ingroup and Outgroup Friendships on Ethnic Attitudes in College: A Longitudinal Study," *Group Processes and Intergroup Relations* 6 (2003): 76–92.

21. J. A. Lindholm, K. Szelenyi, S. Hurtado, and W. S. Korn, *The American College Teacher: National Norms for the 2004–2005 HERI Faculty Survey* (Los Angeles: Higher Education Research Institute, 2005).

22. S. Brint and J. Karabel, *The Diverted Dream: Community Colleges and Educational Opportunity in America, 1900–1985* (New York: Oxford University Press, 1989).

23. A. L. Antonio, "Faculty of Color Reconsidered: Reassessing Contributions to Scholarship," *Journal of Higher Education* 73 (2002): 582–602; D. Humphreys, *Higher Education, Race, and Diversity: Views from the Field* (Washington, DC: Association of American Colleges and Universities, 1998).

24. Antonio, "Faculty of Color Reconsidered."

25. S. Hurtado, "Linking Diversity with Educational Purpose: How the Diversity Impacts the Classroom Environment and Student Development," in G. Orfield, ed., *Diversity Challenged: Legal Crisis and New Evidence* (Cambridge, MA: Harvard Publishing Group, 2001).

26. A. Kezar and P. D. Eckel, *Leadership Strategies for Advancing Campus Diversity: Advice from Experienced Presidents* (Washington, DC: American Council on Education, 2005).

27. Ibid.

28. Hurtado et al., *Enacting Diverse Learning Environments.*

Diversity, Dialogue, and
Democratic Engagement

୬

Patricia Gurin, Biren (Ratnesh) A. Nagda,
and Akua O. Campanella

We have repeatedly acknowledged the overriding importance of
preparing students for work and citizenship, describing education as
pivotal to "sustaining our political and cultural heritage" with a
fundamental role in maintaining the fabric of society. This Court has
long recognized that "education . . . is the very foundation of good
citizenship." For this reason, the diffusion of knowledge and
opportunity through public institutions of higher education must be
accessible to all individuals regardless of race or ethnicity. . . . Effective
participation by members of all racial and ethnic groups in civic life
of our Nation is essential if the dream of one Nation, indivisible, is to
be realized. . . . In order to cultivate a set of leaders with legitimacy in
the eyes of the citizenry, it is necessary that the path to leadership be
visibly open to talented and qualified individuals of every race and
ethnicity. All members of our heterogeneous society must have
confidence in the openness and integrity of the educational
institutions that provide this training.
                                        —*Grutter v. Bollinger*

As we have seen by now, Justice Sandra Day O'Connor, writing for the majority in *Grutter v. Bollinger*, stressed the connections between education
and democratic legitimacy. Since the creation of public higher education
institutions in the first quarter of the nineteenth century, education has
been an essential tool for achieving effective citizenry. Thomas Jefferson, in
founding the University of Virginia in 1823, argued that citizens are educated, not born. Of course, his vision of democracy encompassed only
those who were defined as citizens at the time: namely, white men with
property. But he is nevertheless an important figure in the coevolution of
higher education and civic preparedness.

Like America's other great public institutions, the University of Michigan, from its founding in 1817, embraced the mission of imparting knowledge for the betterment of society. But did the now-famous affirmative ac-

tion cases *Gratz* and *Grutter v. Bollinger* actually settle the last remaining disputes over the relationship between higher education, diversity, and democracy? There is still considerable controversy about whether higher education is the appropriate forum for teaching citizens how to see themselves from others' points of view—an experience that some see as essential to the full development of a healthy civic consciousness.[1] We believe that the debates both leading up to and following from the *Grutter* and *Gratz* decisions encourage, rather than settle, questions about higher education's role in preparing a diverse and critical citizenry.

Critics of affirmative action argued at the time of the lawsuits that preparation for citizenship is *not* the business of higher education. The National Association of Scholars, which submitted an amicus brief in support of the plaintiffs, argued that the democracy outcomes included in psychologist Patricia Gurin's expert report on the educational value of diversity—cross-racial understanding, better preparation of students for an increasingly diverse workforce and society, and participatory citizenship—were not relevant educational goals, and simply represented a liberal, politically correct framing of Michigan's defense of affirmative action.[2] Associate Justice Scalia, in his dissent to the majority opinion in *Grutter,* joined this critique, adamantly discounting the democratic benefits of diversity claimed by Michigan:

> This is not, of course, an "educational benefit" on which students will be graded on their Law School transcript (Works and Plays Well with Others: B+) or tested by the bar examiners (Q: Describe in 500 words or less your cross-racial understanding). . . . If properly considered an "educational benefit" at all, it is surely not one that is either uniquely relevant to law school or uniquely "teachable" in a formal educational setting.

We would counter that it is indeed higher education's unique responsibility to prepare citizens capable of understanding different cultural and life experiences, of thinking critically about inequalities both at home and abroad, and of collaborating across differences to achieve a multicentric vision of democracy. Furthermore, it is not enough to merely bring diverse students together in one place. Institutions of higher education must foster learning opportunities that help students understand and work with "difference and connection, self and community, one and many."[3] They must expound a vision of the world in which difference and democracy are compatible.

To reconcile what have sometimes been posited as the opposing forces of diversity and unity, to consider ways in which diversity can be mobilized for greater equality and justice, we must first answer two questions:

1. What vision of democracy should guide our educational efforts?
2. What kind of education can promote citizenship that simultaneously values diversity and equity?

We will present an illustrative educational practice—intergroup dialogue—that leverages diversity as an educational resource with an explicit focus on achieving a more equitable society.

What Vision of Democracy?

~

American thinking about democracy is dominated by two major theories. The liberal model conceives of democracy mainly as a way for individuals to express their preferences, interests, and demands in an electoral system. The goal of the liberal model is to assure that leaders, rules, and policies will represent the majority of citizens.[4] This conception is focused on the individual: private pursuits take priority over the common good, and constitutional rights are individual rights. This is the guiding model in most contemporary Western democracies. A contrasting model, variably referred to as deliberative, strong, or participatory democracy, conceives of democracy as a system in which every member of the community participates in self-governance[5] by deliberating through public talk about policies affecting the common good.[6] This conception involves the individual as an active participant in a larger commons, someone who is both shaped by and shapes the larger collective.

Different in their understanding of the relationship between private and public, individual and collective, these two models are nonetheless similar in their failure to consider who the private individuals may be, and whose voices should be heard in collective reasoning about the common good. In the liberal tradition, individuals are interchangeable, whereas deliberative democracy does not acknowledge that culture, race, ethnicity, or religion gives particular voices privilege over others. Instead, it assumes that everyone is equally free to speak up and participate in the deliberative process. Both types of democracy are color-blind, then, each in their own way.

The critics of affirmative action also claimed to be color-blind. By invoking Martin Luther King's wish that his children be judged not by the color of their skin but by the content of their character, affirmative action opponents contended that considering race was not only legally but morally wrong because it subverts the ideal of color blindness. The author and activist Jeff Hitchcock calls color blindness "a noble response to the previously dominant philosophy of white supremacy. It stood against a proud and openly acknowledged racism and defeated it. . . . But," he adds, "color blindness of today is not the same as the color blindness of the mid-twentieth century."[7] Justice Ginsburg made this same distinction in her dissenting opinion in *Gratz*. Arguing that "government decision-makers may properly distinguish between policies of exclusion and inclusion," she wrote:

> Actions designed to burden groups long denied full citizenship stature are not sensibly ranked with measures taken to hasten the day when entrenched discrimination and its after effects are extirpated. To say that two centuries of struggle for the most basic of civil rights have been mostly about freedom from racial categorization rather than freedom from racial oppression is to trivialize the lives and deaths of those who have suffered under racism.

Sociologist Eduardo Bonilla-Silva[8] delineates four dominant types of modern color-blindness, which hold that (*a*) only minimal, if any, racial disparities still exist; (*b*) the few that exist are caused by cultural deficiencies in certain racial groups and not by structural constraints that unfairly impinge on different groups; (*c*) obvious patterns of racial segregation simply reflect the natural tendency of people to prefer to associate with similar others; and (*d*) meritocracy assures equality if individuals, assumed to play on a level field, take advantage of opportunities and work hard. He sees in the color-blind approach of opponents to affirmative action a new kind of racism, which may not be embedded in intentional prejudice but nonetheless produces racist outcomes because it promotes opposition to reformative social policies.

How can we deal with race and other dimensions of diversity without ignoring them? Diversity and democracy's compatibility is not self-evident, nor are we just now confronting diversity's implications for civic life for the first time. In her book *Fear of Diversity,* political scientist Arlene Saxonhouse details the ancient Greeks' debates about the impact of diversity on capacity for democracy. According to Saxonhouse, Plato envisioned a city-state in which unity and harmony would be based on the shared characteristics of a homogeneous citizenry—a conception of democracy that has prevailed in the United States. Plato's pupil, Aristotle, however, contended that a democracy based on a type of unity that incorporated difference would be more likely to thrive than one based on homogeneity. What makes democracy work is equality among citizens who are peers (at the time, this only included free men, not women or slaves), who hold diverse perspectives, and whose relationships are governed by freedom and the rules of civil discourse. It is discourse over conflict, not unanimity, Aristotle believed, that helps democracy thrive.[9]

We seek a vision of democracy that is compatible with diversity, one that is not color-blind. While the color-blind approach assumes that talking about race or any other group difference will foster intergroup prejudices, new work in social psychology and political science shows instead that color-conscious strategies are at least as, if not more, effective than color blindness when it comes to reducing racial prejudice and promoting robust problem-solving among groups.[10]

But does attention to color consciousness and diversity necessarily lead to democratic practices that are inclusive, effective, and just? We contend that imbalances in power must be considered as well. Among the accomplishments for which the late social and political philosopher Iris Marion Young was well known was her critique of deliberative democracy for failing to explicitly attend to inequality and imbalances of power. In what she calls communicative democracy, Young attends not only to social and cultural differences, but to how power enters speech itself. She is openly critical of the idea that people from diverse backgrounds can simply be brought together without first defining the rules of engagement in a way that promotes genuine equality of communication:

> In many formal situations the better-educated white middle-class people moreover often act as though they have a right to speak and that their words carry authority, whereas those of other groups often feel intimidated by the argument requirements and the formality and rules of parliamentary procedure, so they don't speak, or speak only in a way that those in charge find "disruptive." Norms of assertiveness, combativeness, and speaking by the contest rules are powerful silencers or evaluators of speech in many actual speaking situations where culturally differentiated and socially unequal groups live together. The dominant groups, moreover, often fail entirely to notice this devaluation and silencing, while the less privileged often feel put down or frustrated, either losing confidence in themselves or becoming angry.[11]

She prescribes three preconditions that she believes are necessary for effective communication across wide cultural and social differences: significant interdependence, equal respect, and agreed-upon rules for fair discussion and decision-making. "A richer understanding of processes of democratic discussion results," she informs us, "if we assume that differences of social position and identity perspective function as a resource for public reason rather than as divisions that public reason transcends."[12] This leads us to wonder: If education is the very foundation of democracy, what kind of education will teach students the practices of communicative democracy?

What Kind of Education? Education for What Kind of Citizenry?

∽

We turn now to an educational practice—intergroup dialogue (IGD)—that deals with diversity and imbalances in power while providing opportunities to bridge the divides. Intergroup dialogue is a face-to-face learning experience that brings together 12 to 16 students from two social identity groups: men and women; white people and people of color; heterosexuals, gay men, lesbians, bisexuals, and transgender people; and Christians and Jews. The facilitated dialogues continue over a sustained period (usually weekly for at least 10 to 14 weeks). IGD explicitly engages diverse groups of students in exploring the similarities and differences of their social experiences, helping them to understand the impact of systemic inequalities and privileges and to interrogate societal issues.[13] IGD frames learning as a group-conscious and dialogic process, which encourages students' awareness of their own group identities, while also helping them to bridge differences.[14]

Three educational elements identified by researchers Philip Mazzocco and Daniel Newhart (2006) to counter color blindness are evident in intergroup dialogue: (*a*) education about the importance of groups in influencing inequalities; (*b*) analysis of group-based inequalities as structured systems; and (*c*) consideration of different perspectives on public issues.

Group Bases of Inequalities

IGD is explicitly about diversity and color (group) consciousness. The method attends to the diversity of social group *membership,* and not just diversity of the participants' *opinions and perspectives.* Unlike a color-blind approach, IGD uses awareness of difference and identity as a resource for deepening personal and social understanding. Difference is not conceived of as a static barrier to positive intergroup relations but as a group dynamic, which can be harnessed in order to strengthen intergroup relations. Students in IGD, in a dialogic process of continual sharing and inquiry, are encouraged to recognize their social memberships, including racial, gender, sexual, and other identities. In conjunction with readings and in-class activities, these students explore each other's lives and assess how their life opportunities have been shaped by their group memberships, rather than thinking of themselves merely as autonomous individuals.

Structural Analysis of Inequalities

IGD students go beyond a multicultural celebration of difference and diversity to identify social injustices and prepare themselves to act as agents of change. This approach contextualizes diversity and identity as elements of power inequality, rather than just personal distinctions. Institutional racism, patriarchy, and other systemic inequalities are seen to structure relations among group members both inside and outside the dialogue group. Through sharing their own experiences, discussing course readings, and participating in class activities, students connect their individual and common experiences to these larger systems, thereby personalizing the significance of these inequalities for their daily lives and choices.

Consideration of Different Perspectives on Public Issues

IGD also examines how identities and imbalances in power play an enduring role in people's perspectives on public issues. The approach encourages deep inquiry into contentious public policy issues—such as affirmative action, abortion, or gay marriage—and more personally conflictual issues—such as interracial dating, gender and body image, or harassment of various sorts. Students examine these issues from multiple perspectives, and with a critical eye: How do group memberships and power differences play a part in these issues? How are issues of privilege and power acted out in these exchanges? What are the personally and institutionally responsible ways to participate in solutions? What public policies might help address the inequalities? Grappling with these questions in public and personal contexts brings home the realities of group consciousness and inequality.

Together, these three elements of IGD illustrate how the method helps enrich discussions of diversity and democracy with an awareness of the inequalities that hinder democratic engagement. They move us from color blindness to color consciousness, and from a focus merely on diversity to a critical analysis of power and inequalities. Critical analysis by itself, however, is not enough to ensure democratic engagement across group differences. We believe that it is crucial for students to openly discuss how these systems of inequalities affect them personally, and to understand how those inequalities affect others similar to or different from themselves. Thus, IGD incorporates two other elements that distinguish its value for communicative democracies: (*a*) a dedicated focus on building communicative relationships as a way of bridging differences; and (*b*) an effort to foster a sense of joint responsibility through alliance-building, but without erasing color/group consciousness.

Bridging Differences

Democracy is often seen as an entity rather than a living process. Following a line of argument popularized in the work of political theorist Benjamin Barber, we believe that democracy is enacted as a process, and that relationships can meaningfully bind diverse participants to a common democratic enterprise. Dialogue as a communicative process fosters empathetic connection and understanding through inquiry and mutual respect. As opposed to debate, a contest of ideas resulting in a winner and a loser, dialogue values different experiences, in the hope of integrating them into new understandings. In dialogue, democracy is enacted through communicative exchanges among diverse individuals. Listening and speaking, inquiring and revising, reflecting and reshaping one's perspectives *in relation to others* are all part of dialogic engagement. Without this face-to-face dialogue across differences, our understandings of the world will remain idiosyncratic and constricted.

Alliance Building

Finally, IGD is explicitly committed to helping students build alliances and accept joint responsibility for solving problems and promoting justice. Communicative exchanges are not simply talk for talk's sake, but a means for mobilizing individuals and collectives for personal and social change. IGD's group-conscious approach asks students to interrogate their own identities and social positions, as well as to understand those of other participants. Members from more privileged groups reflect on how they can use their positions to promote change. Members from less privileged groups reflect on how they can resist the status quo and empower themselves to bring about change.[15] Members of both groups consider how to collaborate across their differences. In essence, the social identities of the groups are not forsaken, but reconstrued to promote understanding, collaboration, and a shared social identity as fellow humans.

Final Thoughts

∾

Affirmative action can be understood as serving many purposes, only one of which—the cultivation of diversity in higher education institutions—was invoked by the University of Michigan's defense of its admissions policies before the Supreme Court. Too often the advocates of affirmative action in education focus only on the numbers: that is, on how affirmative admissions procedures increase the number of students from underrepresented groups who attend highly selective institutions. We agree that this effect is vitally important, both because it provides underrepresented groups with access to the highest quality education available, and also because, to paraphrase Justice O'Connor, the democratic legitimacy of our institutions is visible to all.

But we must remember that it was concern for equity, and not diversity, that provided the original justification for affirmative action policies in Executive Order 11246, signed by President Lyndon Johnson in 1965. Equity was also a core feature of the arguments offered by the intervenors (high school and law school students of color) in *Grutter* and *Gratz*. Their arguments, which stressed the constitutionality of using affirmative action in higher education to redress past and current discrimination, were not accepted by either the district or circuit courts. The University of Michigan believed—correctly, it turned out—that an argument based on Justice Powell's diversity rationale in *Bakke* was the only defense of affirmative action in admissions that was likely to be successful. As a result, the effectiveness of affirmative action policies at selective institutions like Michigan is often measured in hard numbers.

But numbers, as we hope we have demonstrated in this chapter, are not enough, especially when the goal is to increase democratic engagement. Simply putting students from various racial, ethnic, and cultural backgrounds together in one place does not insure that they will learn from each other, or that diversity will benefit the education of all students. Rather, diversity must be actively utilized so that students with different life experiences, and different points of view that reflect those experiences, actually interact with each other, challenge each other's perspectives, and learn how to bridge differences and perceive commonalities.

We hope to convey a larger lesson about affirmative action in higher education. Higher education must find ways to leverage diversity for educational benefit without abandoning the original intent of affirmative action—the pursuit of equity in society. Intergroup dialogue does this. At the broadest level, its philosophical underpinnings connect diversity and equity, showing them to be mutually influential. A focus on diversity by itself ignores power and inequity. Attention to equity by itself does not capitalize on diversity as an educational resource. At the level of practice, intergroup dialogue also integrates diversity and equity. It helps students learn from the experiences and perspectives of diverse peers while it presses them to understand how inequity is institutionally created and maintained. It prepares them for citizenship in a diverse democracy in which they can provide leadership for more equitable social policies.

NOTES

1. R. Post, "Introduction: After Bakke," in *Race and Representation: Affirmative Action*, ed. R. Post and M. Rogin (New York: Zone Books, 1998), 13–27.

2. P. Gurin, "Selections from the Compelling Need for Diversity in Higher Education, Expert Reports in Defense of the University of Michigan," *Equity and Excellence in Education* 32, no. 2 (1999): 37–62; P. Gurin, E. L. Dey, S. Hurtado, and G. Gurin, "Diversity and Higher Education: Theory and Impact on Educational Outcomes," *Harvard Educational Review* 72 (2002): 330–66; T. E. Wood and M. J. Sherman, "Is Campus Racial Diversity Correlated with Educational Benefits?" *Academic Questions* 14, no. 3 (2001): 72–88.

3. R. Guarasci and G. H. Cornwell, *Democratic Education in an Age of Difference: Redefining Citizenship in Higher Education* (San Francisco: Jossey-Bass, 1997).

4. I. M. Young, *Intersecting Voices: Dilemmas of Gender, Political Philosophy, and Policy* (Princeton: Princeton University Press, 1997).

5. B. R. Barber, "Public Talk and Civic Action: Education for Participation in a Strong Democracy," *Social Education* 1989:370.

6. Young, *Intersecting Voices*, 61.

7. J. Hitchcock, *Lifting the White Veil: An Exploration of White American Culture in a Multiracial Context* (Roselle, NJ: Crandall, Dostie and Douglass Books, 2002).

8. E. Bonilla-Silva, *Racism without Racists: Color-Blind Racism and the Persistence of Racial Inequality in the United States* (Lanham, MD: Rowman and Littlefield, 2006).

9. H. F. Pitkin and S. M. Shumer, "On Participation," *Democracy* 2 (1982): 43–54.

10. On reducing prejudice, see P. J. Mazzocco and D. W. Newhart, "Color-Blind Racism and Opposition to Progressive Racial Policy: A New Scale and Supportive Findings," unpublished manuscript, 2006; J. A. Richeson and R. J. Nussbaum, "The Impact of Multiculturalism versus Color-Blindness on Racial Bias," *Journal of Experimental Social Psychology* 40 (2004): 417–23. On problem solving, see S. E. Page, *The Difference: How the Power of Diversity Creates Better Groups, Firms, Schools, and Societies* (Princeton: Princeton University Press, 2007).

11. Young, *Intersecting Voices*, 65.

12. Ibid., 67.

13. X. Zúñiga, B. A. Nagda, M. Chesler, and A. Cytron-Walker, *Intergroup Dialogues in Higher Education: Meaningful Learning about Social Justice* (San Francisco: Jossey-Bass, 2007).

14. B. A. Nagda and P. Gurin, "Intergroup Dialogue: A Critical-Dialogic Approach to Learning about Difference, Inequality and Social Justice," in *New Directions for Teaching and Learning*, ed. M. Kaplan and A. T. Miller (San Francisco: Jossey-Bass, 2007), 35–45.

15. B. A. Nagda, "Breaking Barriers, Crossing Boundaries, Building Bridges: Communication Processes in Intergroup Dialogues," *Journal of Social Issues* 62 (2006): 553–76.

Institutional Culture and Diversity
Engagement and Dialogue in a South African University

∽

Martin Hall, Dorrian Aiken, and Nazeema Mohamed

Universities are complex institutions where people congregate to teach and learn, conduct research, take part in public events, and administer the day-to-day processes by which the institution reproduces itself. These activities contribute to a unique culture that shapes the relationships between members of the campus community (see "Nothing Is Different but Everything's Changed," by Martin Hall, in Part IV of this volume). Affirmative action is designed to transform such cultures by countering the injustices of discrimination—particularly those based on race, gender, and ethnicity—with accelerated and focused policies for change. But such policies can just as readily be undermined by the persistence of those very prejudices that are making life intolerable for the excluded. Very often, success or failure will depend on everyday slights or acceptances, scowls or smiles, greetings or snubs—the actions that James Scott has termed "everyday transcripts" of domination and resistance, or inclusion and acceptance.[1]

South Africa's University of Cape Town is still recovering from a long history of segregation and prejudice. The intervention program the University has devised to overcome this prejudice can be compared with Gurin, Nagda, and Campanella's account in this volume of the intergroup dialogue approach, which was designed to promote the recognition of diversity and the value of critical citizenship at an American university.

Perhaps the most obvious contrast between these two programs is the difference in their national-historical context: in America, the national impetus for civil rights is already a half-century behind us, whereas in South Africa, the end of apartheid was recent enough that many current university faculty and staff spent the formative years of their careers within a segregated system. In particular, then, such programs in South Africa must address "whiteness" and its assumptions of entitlement to positions of power and influence within institutions such as universities. These distinctions do not allow us to rely on universally applicable policies. Instead, we must ask new questions in each case: What sort of interventions work best? How can we measure their effect? Or would it be better not to intervene at all?

The 1997 White Paper, which has done so much to shape the post-apartheid reconstruction of South African public universities, acknowledges the significance of institutional culture in affirmative action efforts.[2] One of universities' primary purposes, it explains, is to "contribute to the socialization of enlightened, responsible and constructively critical citizens," who "help lay the foundations of a critical civil society, with a culture of public debate and tolerance which accommodates differences and competing interests." The paper saw much need for improvement in this area, both within individual institutions and in their relationship to the community at large: "to strengthen the democratic ethos, the sense of common citizenship and commitment to a common good."

All of this depends on what is really only a very general definition of "institutional culture." The pressing question of South African higher education is whether we can define the term more specifically, in order to permit targeted interventions with measurable results. Can we break this broad category up into individual domains—architecture and the physical plant; curriculum; service learning; working conditions and professional development; organizational structure, and others—that can be targeted for interventions?

In the rest of this chapter we describe one such intervention at the University of Cape Town. Khuluma (Zulu for "speaking out") is a program of three-day staff workshops that addresses race-based stereotypes of superiority and inferiority, directly tackling the recent legacy of segregation.[3] The largest exercise of its kind in a South African university, with more than 600 participants over an eighteen-month period, Khuluma tests the ability of a university to improve its institutional culture through planned and direct intervention and raises questions for future policies of this kind.

Institutional Climate

∾

UCT's Khuluma program was prompted by a survey of the university's institutional climate, carried out in 2003. The results of this survey were buttressed by several surveys of student views and have been further reinforced by the findings of a second institutional climate survey that was carried out in 2007.[4] A reading of the institutional climate—understood as the manifestation of institutional culture at a specific point in time—enables us to see where interventions can be targeted, and to devise measures for tracking change over time. Here, we focus on surveys of staff opinion and subsequent interventions; clearly student opinion is of equal importance in seeking a full understanding of the dynamics of institutional culture,

Both the 2003 and 2007 institutional climate surveys were based on anonymous questionnaires, to which all categories of employees were invited to respond. The aggregate results reveal durable institutional perceptions and attitudes, which can legitimately be termed "culture." These cultural measures reveal two major, intersecting fault lines: employment status and race.

Employment status places administrative, professional, and support staff on one side of the line, and faculty on the other. The former are more likely to be dissatisfied with their conditions of service, and more likely to feel that they are treated unfairly. For their part, faculty often express dissatisfaction with the quality of work performed by "the administration." This was a prominent theme in the 2003 results, and again in 2007, when the survey was carried out shortly after a strike by the administrative employees' union over working conditions.

In the South African workplace, dissatisfaction about employment status is invariably coupled with race because apartheid created labor aristocracies. Continuing skills shortages, the skewed nature of the education system, and the close relationship between race and class continue to reproduce these aristocracies, no matter what the overt policy of the institution.[5] Thus lower-paid, lower-status administrative and support jobs tend to be held by black staff—particularly Africans: the more senior the position, the more likely it will be occupied by a white person. The 250 or so members of Senate (the body charged with academic governance of the university, predominantly full professors and chairs of academic departments) are overwhelmingly white and male. Despite the rhetoric of change, at UCT this demographic pattern remained stable from 2003 to 2007. There were no significant shifts within the various employment categories, and some 40 percent of all new appointments to the staff were white people, which is just over four times the representation of whites in the South African population as a whole.[6]

Here is a black (African) woman administrator commenting in the 2003 institutional climate survey:

> They figured that because of the colour of my skin I could not cope with a challenging job, and I quote "Shame, we heard that you are struggling in that office, how are you doing now?" I dealt with these comments accordingly. Afterwards I was known as a rude person. But I did not care. When you are black you are expected to perform immediately even if the environment is still new, but when you are white everybody understands that you are still new, therefore your colleagues should be patient. Again, I asked for R100 in change from a white colleague, her response was, I do not have change but shame I can lend you some money if you want. She took out two twenty rand notes!

The respondent's anecdote captures the legacy of generations of race-based segregation in a few words. By expressing pity and offering a loan, the white coworker positions her black colleague as a domestic worker asking a favor from the mistress of the household.

A second respondent offered a similar observation:

> Blacks are always observed with suspicious eyes. For example, things like keys, stationery etc. are moved from accessible places to a highly secured place, once a Black person comes in the office.

Not surprisingly, when asked whether they have been treated differently in the workplace because of their race, a large majority of black staff in all categories of employment reply that they have.

In contrast, about half of white men and women in all job categories believe that their employment conditions are race-blind. This comparative silence of white employees on affirmative action and its consequences is striking: while black staff openly express their concern about the pace and adequacy of change, white staff generally remain silent. As one of us commented in reference to the 2003 institutional climate survey, "the silence of white staff on the employment equity policy and on student access, issues, redress, diversity and affirmative action is deafening in the reports submitted and it is critical that these areas are explored as there are clearly issues regarding fairness, equity and vulnerabilities that have to be dealt with."[7]

Only one white staff member took advantage of the anonymity afforded by the 2003 survey to complain that she felt her professional advancement was being threatened:

> Frequently when applying for a position at a higher grade (or occasionally even at the same grade but which promises to be more interesting) I have been told that I am wasting my time—that the position has to go to a person of colour, presumably to fit in with employment equity plans. It is extremely disheartening and discouraging, even though understandable to some extent. But if that is not racial discrimination what is?

Taken together, UCT's 2003 and 2007 institutional climate surveys show that the workplace is understood by the university's employees as a set of strong stereotypes, defined predominantly by interlinked factors of race and employment status. In broad terms, black staff believe change is slow and insufficient, while white staff see transformation as either complete (because they do not believe that employees are treated differently on the grounds of race) or as discriminating unfairly against them.

Khuluma

❧

Such outcomes confirm what is already intuitively apparent—that institutions grounded in a system of unfair racial discrimination will carry that legacy forward, even in the face of official efforts to ensure equity. To be effective, in other words, interventions cannot just be policy decrees: they have to address stereotypes of superiority and inferiority, and have to be scalable to the institution as a whole.

One of the early influences on the design of the Khuluma intervention was IBM's diversity task force initiative, one of the few such programs implemented across a large institution that has been comprehensively described and analyzed.[8] IBM's initiative was rooted in the work of eight task forces, each comprising about twenty members from pre-identified staff constituencies: Asians, blacks, gays/lesbians/transgender individuals/bisexuals, Hispanics, white men, Native Americans, people with disabilities, and women.

IBM's objective was to legitimize these fixed identities as a way to foster corporate diversity, which was then to be measured through increased sales to the company's diverse customer base. The University's objective, in contrast, was to challenge the salience of an equivalent set of South African identities (White, African, Coloured, Indian), to undermine assumptions about the relative superiority or inferiority of these categories, and to show that racial identity is a socially constructed phenomenon. To follow the IBM model by celebrating diversity, without an open and critical discussion of its past and present consequences, could have further entrenched the unwanted stereotypes.[9]

For these reasons, UCT decided to look for a more appropriate model. We settled on a program used to improve race relations in the United Kingdom, based on the trainer and consultant Ashok Ohri's "Ideologies of Superiority."[10] In South Africa this approach had been pioneered by ProCorp, an agency specializing in institutional transformation.[11] It starts from the observation that all people may harbor assumptions that shape attitudes and prejudices. When those assumptions are accompanied by positional power, they often result in discrimination, either direct or indirect. The ProCorp program uses experience and reflection to undermine stereotypes and encourage participants to challenge their internalized assumptions about superiority and inferiority. This approach, in other words, is aimed at developing respect for difference, and at breaking down the structure of the stereotypes themselves. It has become part of an emerging field of "critical whiteness" studies in South Africa, which complements the work of critical intellectuals such as Fanon, Biko, and Mangani by showing how the racially defined White minority created and used the ideology of white superiority to entrench their political, social, and economic dominance.

Khuluma was rolled out as a partnership between UCT and ProCorp. In mid-2006, staff were offered an open-ended series of three-day workshops, each designed to accommodate twenty participants working with two trained facilitators. The objective—not always achieved—was to have an equal number of black and white participants, a reasonable balance in terms of gender, and at least five participants who were in middle or senior management positions (and who were therefore capable of translating their workshop experiences into workplace action). While some workshops were requested within organizational units (and were therefore seen as part of a larger team-building effort), others straddled faculty/administration lines. The composition of the Khuluma workshops thus confronted the two dominant fault lines evidenced in the 2003 and 2007 institutional climate surveys: the racial divide, and that which separated administrative and professional work on the one hand from academic work on the other.

Each Khuluma workshop is held off-campus, at a venue that allows for easy interaction either as a plenary session or in smaller groups. The first day starts with introductions, in which the participants identify their position within the university's organizational structure of the university. Each is then asked to describe a person or an event that particularly influenced their thinking about race and racism. The facilitators detail the structure of the workshop, its purpose, expectations, and terms of participation, including guarantees of confidentiality and the aim of creating a "safe space," in which freedom of expression is possible. In the first exercise, participants recall and analyze a personal experience in which they were subject to discrimination and then describe a second situation in which they were the one doing the discriminating. The objective of this first day is to identify the "ideology of superiority" and understand how it functions in the ways in which we make choices as individuals.

The second day opens with an open reflection on the workshop so far, in which both positive and negative points of view are heard. Participants are then divided into a white group and a black group, which are sent to separate rooms. The groups are asked to identify and discuss the ways in which white people develop and apply negative stereotypes of black people. They then reconvene in plenary session to summarize and compare the results of their discussions. This leads into discussion about the results of this exercise, and its justification as part of the workshop. Here, the objective is to shift attention to the consequences of our actions on others, the victims of discrimination.

The third day again opens with a retrospective evaluation of the previous day's work, before moving on to assess the relationship between one's individual experience and role within the university. How does institutional culture play a role in sustaining the ideology of superiority? The workshop ends with comments and reflections on institutional change.

Twenty-seven Khuluma workshops had been held by the end of 2007, totaling 626 participants, of whom 31 percent were faculty and 69 percent administrative, professional, and support staff. Among faculty participants, the highest proportional attendance was from law, the health sciences, commerce, and engineering. Administrative, professional, and support department participation was variable, and tended to depend on whether the opportunity for participation was created by departmental leadership; in some departments, all staff attended workshops.

Evaluation

While the challenges of institutional transformation in South Africa are well known, Khuluma took participants into uncharted territory. ProCorp's challenge to the ideology of superiority had been well tested in other settings, and in early pilots at UCT; but there was no precedent for an intervention on this scale in a South African university. Consequently, we decided to commission an independent evaluation of the program's effectiveness as it was rolled out. An ethnographic approach allowed us to consider multiple perspectives: that of the university management launching the Khuluma, of participants' perceptions and experiences, and of their overarching observations about the program. UCT's Department of Social Anthropology was commissioned to carry out the study.[12]

More than 90 percent of the Khuluma participants polled were positive about the experience.[13] Participants had been prepared to invest considerable trust and emotional energy in the process, despite the fact that the experience could often be personally upsetting and even traumatic. Many respondents believed that participation should be compulsory for all university staff. The evaluation report summarized this investment as a "hunger" for the opportunity to speak out about what was so often left unsaid in the workplace.

Individual perceptions of the program's benefit depended in part on the respondent's work circumstances. Thus, for one participant:

> I went into this thing with the view that I'm not . . . in any sense consciously racist in any sense. I don't make those kinds of pre-judgements. But the simple fact is I do, because of the upbringing and that kind of thing. I would like to think that it never gets to the stage where it would

be overt, but I can't ignore the fact that sub-consciously it's going to be there.

While for another:

> I don't need a sensitised agenda. I'm fully aware of the race and gender issues and all the "isms" that there are around, and I don't need to spend two days going through that process. So for me there was nothing constructive.

The evaluators concluded that the experience changed a number of participants' views, and altered their behavior in small but significant ways. Almost everyone who commented on Khuluma saw the program as having improved their relationships with their professional colleagues. Greeting, and being greeted, was often commented on:

> You know, you always see them storming past . . . one guy, I never used to greet. Now I would go out of my way and say "HELLO! How are you?" you know, that person will turn around and the greeting you get back is so amazing. Whether he's doing it from the heart, that's his baby. But it made me feel good.

> That white manager upstairs who never looked at me before in the parking lot now greets me.

These and similar small changes are significant interventions in the daily institutional culture. One participant commented to the evaluation team on the "internal conversations" she has with herself about her white colleagues. While she was confident in her identity as a black Muslim woman, the Khuluma experience made her aware that she judged people in ways that she would not have wanted to be judged herself.

This personal framing of transformation hints at the possibility of lasting change. Consider, for example, this participant recalling her experience as a victim of racial discrimination:

> You don't realise what you actually, how you were affected; how deep it runs. You think it's all in the past, but it's out there. It just needed that trigger to surface it again. But I think it did me some good. You don't forget things like that. They're still there. But I can manage it.

At the same time, though, the experience of the Khuluma workshops was unsettling for some participants, who found what the evaluation termed "conceptual assaults to personal identity" threatening and unsettling in a way that could not be brought to closure within a three-day workshop format. This is in itself not surprising—it would be superficial to assume that internalized ideologies of inferiority or superiority could be washed away in three days of talk. A few respondents—university staff who are not South African—felt a strong sense of xenophobia. And some younger staff members, who had joined the workforce after the end of legislated segregation, believed that the program's emphasis on the past made it irrelevant. The breadth of responses, negative as well as unambiguously positive, raise questions about the connection between an intervention such as Khuluma and institutional mechanisms for counseling and personal support. Should a program such as this be part of a wider network of continuing support for members of the university community?

Participants also asserted the importance of momentum. Individuals could feel that they had benefited personally while simultaneously expressing frustration at not seeing individual awareness matched by institutional transformation:

> It's bigger than the individual, but it's also bigger than the department. Responsibility is personal, departmental, and across the whole university.

> There is still nowhere you can go to, to voice your opinion. Like we did in the last general meeting, we put up a suggestion box. But there is no person, say you had a problem, that you can actually go to and talk, who will handle these problems. So that support is not there as far as transformation goes.

In the words of the evaluation report,

> It seems that informants feel that Khuluma did "transform" them: but that it is left at the level of the individual, or small groups of individuals and, because it is not taken further, it cannot begin to "transform" UCT. Thus, though participants will mention how relationships at work may have changed after the workshop, there is a sense that it needs to be much larger than this: that Khuluma should be a doorway of sorts to a shift in UCT's institutional culture, and that this is not yet happening.

Looking Forward

It is reasonable to claim that UCT's Khuluma program has helped answer the challenge posed by the 1997 White Paper, which encouraged universities to "contribute to the socialization of enlightened, responsible and constructively critical citizens," and to "help lay the foundations of a critical civil society, with a culture of public debate and tolerance which accommodates differences and competing interests." As we know from the surveys of institutional climate, the university will not be able to generate social benefits to its fullest capacity unless the question of racial division is addressed. Khuluma has provided a structured opportunity for people to talk about these issues.

The Khuluma evaluation describes this opportunity as "a psychotherapeutic assumption of an intermediary zone where recovery, healing, rebuilding and re-empowerment can occur." The evaluation report sees this as storytelling in the tradition of South Africa's Truth and Reconciliation Commission (TRC) and similar encounter group activities:

> Story-telling is posited to play an important role in restoring the victim to his/her status as a social person, helping people find empowering themes or "plots" in their own lives. Thus, the speaking self equates with the healed self. . . . Almost without exception Khuluma participants described listening to the stories of others as pivotal to the success of Khuluma.

Storytelling and everyday interactions such as forms of greeting and recognition of competence and ability are good examples of the saliency of what James Scott calls the "everyday transcripts" in which culture is written. The reflections of Khuluma participants show how these everyday experiences come together to constitute institutional university culture. We must appreciate their importance, and the ways in which the past shapes their present manifestations if we are to make the most of opportunities for meaningful change.

The Khuluma program is distinguished from both the IBM model and the intergroup dialogue approach described by Gurin, Nagda, and Campanella in this volume by its focus on critiquing the assumption of white superiority, rather than on the values of diversity and inclusion. This difference is seen at its sharpest in Day Two of the Khuluma model when, in an environment that simulates forced racial segregation, all participants are asked to recall the ways in which those assumptions of white superiority work as a mechanism of oppression. In this, Khuluma breaks decisively with what in South Africa would be termed the "Rainbow Nation" tradition—encounter sessions that encourage whites to value the culture of those who are not white. By developing a critique of "whiteness," Khuluma shifts what Zimitri Erasmus ("A Future Beyond 'Race': Reflections on Equity in South African Higher Education," in Part IV of this volume) calls the burden of "race work." We see this as a key distinction, with considerable potential for future transformative efforts in universities and other institutions.

This approach, however, also comes with a potentially fatal weakness: a tendency to assume that the job is done once everyone has participated in the workshops. The challenge for a South African university, and also perhaps for an American university promoting the benefits of intergroup dialogue models, is "What next?" Thus, Khuluma participants express what at first appears to be a contradiction: a sense of personal achievement in liberating one's self-awareness, combined with a sense of frustration—edging towards anger—that the university as an institution is not keeping pace with the demand for change. Further strengthening of interventions such as Khuluma will show that, rather than being a contradiction, this dual sentiment is a logical and natural sign of the need for further work, such as that described in this chapter, coupled with a strategic assessment of the objectives of the university as a whole—with the way in which it is positioned as a public institution contributing to progressive change. Getting comprehensive, "joined-up" policies such as these into place will be one of the great challenges of the next 25 years.

NOTES

1. James C. Scott, *Domination and the Arts of Resistance: Hidden Transcripts* (New Haven: Yale University Press, 1999).

2. Republic of South Africa, "A Programme for the Transformation of Higher Education (White Paper 3)," *Pretoria Government Gazette* (18207), 1997.

3. See http://www.uct.ac.za/about/intro/transformation (accessed March 20, 2009).

4. University of Cape Town, "UCT Organizational Climate Survey 2003" and "UCT Institutional Climate 2007 Report."

5. See David L. Featherman's introduction to this volume and Martin Hall's "Nothing Is Different, but Everything's Changed."

6. University of Cape Town, "Employment Equity Report," 2007.

7. Nazeema Mohamed, "Response of the University Community to the Institutional Climate Survey," University of Cape Town, June 2004.

8. David A. Thomas, "Diversity as Strategy," *Harvard Business Review* (September 2004): 98–108.

9. Jane Bennett, Africa Gender Institute, University of Cape Town, personal communication.

10. See, for example, Paul Cumo, Ashok Ohri, and Basil Manning, *Community Work and Racism* (London: Routledge and Kegan Paul, 1982).

11. ProCorp was founded in South Africa in 1997 by Margaret Legum, political economist and change activist. The approach has been further developed by social psychologist Dorian Aiken.

12. H. Macdonald, M. Gebhuza, S. Bologna, and S. Morreira, "Feeding Hungry Souls: An Ethnographic Study of a Climate Intervention Strategy at UCT," Department of Social Anthropology, University of Cape Town, 2007.

13. The evaluation was based on documentary sources and analysis of 47 interviews, two focus groups, and 24 email responses. Sixty-six out of 71 (93 percent) informants were positive about their experiences of the Khuluma workshops, 2 undecided, and 3 extremely negative to the point they would not recommend the workshop to another person.

Who Is "Getting Through" in South Africa?

Graduate Output and the Reconstruction
of the Formal Curriculum

༄

Ian Scott

The major achievements of South African higher education in the postapartheid era have included the establishment of a unified system and substantial growth in access. The authorities have developed policies aimed at improving the quality, equity, and efficiency of educational outcomes, which are centrally important to South Africa's development. Unfortunately, those outcomes—particularly measured in terms of graduate output—are not meeting the overlapping needs for equity and development. Only systemic intervention, particularly curriculum reform, will enable the country's higher-education system to successfully accommodate student diversity. Capacity to accommodate diversity is in turn essential to the effectiveness of affirmative action in providing educational opportunities.

What Does South Africa Need from Higher Education?

༄

In order to assess the ability of the higher-education system to meet present and future needs, we must first be clear about what those needs are. The importance of higher education in the contemporary world is widely recognized, especially in less-industrialized countries such as South Africa. Social and economic development create a demand for high-level skills and knowledge. While higher education can make many types of critical contributions to this process—through research and community engagement as well as education—the government's concerted efforts to achieve economic growth have created a particular need for skilled graduates. The shortage of key skills is commonly acknowledged to be a major obstacle to development.[1] Such shortages are not new but have recently been highlighted by the growing need for international competitiveness as well as social stability.

There is some controversy about the nature of the demand for skills. Clearly, universities cannot limit themselves to servicing the needs of the economy. The central point, however, is that graduate output matters to national well-being. As South Africa's Council on Higher Education noted in a 2004 report on the first decade of postapartheid education: "Without . . . expanding opportunities for both young and adult learners, sustainable growth will be difficult, and competitive participation in the global economy well-nigh impossible, to achieve."[2] And absent such development, the social goals that affirmative action is meant to achieve will be very difficult to attain. The first question we should ask in any study of "getting through" is, therefore, How well is higher education meeting South Africa's need for high-level human resources?

Interwoven with the demands of development are a number of critical reasons to pursue equity in higher education, most of which are reflected in this book: that diversity enriches students' learning and preparedness for society; that the country needs to make full use of the talent in all its population groups; and that inclusiveness in higher education is increasingly important to social and political stability. For these reasons, our second question should be, Who is benefiting from higher education in South Africa?

These two questions reflect postapartheid higher education's central challenges, which have been experienced in practice as competing demands. The tension between equity and development has long been recognized in South Africa.[3] Addressing these twin imperatives productively is key to the success of affirmative action in promoting prosperity, social justice, and stability in the new democracy.

South Africa's Higher-Education Structures

∾

The recent major restructuring of South African higher education has forced the merger of many public institutions. But despite the appearances of new institutional forms, some fundamental features of the old system remain. For example, some institutions are still largely dedicated to vocational education and training, and the divide between vocational and academic education has scarcely changed. There are also persistent disparities in resources and the profile of the student intake. Although most students are still educated in public institutions, the number of private institutions has grown.[4] Thus, while the system is not formally stratified, it is characterized by considerable diversity in history and mission.

The basic qualifications framework of South African higher education dates back to the early twentieth century, with its origins primarily in the Scottish system. The core undergraduate qualifications are three-year academic bachelor's degrees and career-focused National Diplomas. While some professional qualifications require postgraduate study, most (including basic qualifications in engineering, law, and health sciences) are attained through specialized four-year bachelor's programs. This framework has significant implications for the success rate in "getting through."

In contrast with American liberal arts degrees, South African undergraduate programs require early specialization. Even in the most general degree programs, 60 percent or more of the curriculum is occupied by major subjects, with little space or incentive for students to explore a variety of disciplines. Since most students' qualifications end with their first degree, they typically have to make critical career choices while still in high school.

Student Performance Patterns: What Is Higher Education Achieving in South Africa?

∽

Measures of Student Progression

South Africa has made substantial gains in equity of access, at least partly because of a range of affirmative action interventions in student selection and admissions.[5] On the intake side, black enrollment has more than doubled since 1993, reaching 60 percent of total enrollment by early in this decade.[6] But one has to ask how these gains translate into graduate output.

The national data needed to answer this question were not available until recently. South Africa's Department of Education (DoE) recently concluded the first sectorwide longitudinal studies of first-time-entering undergraduates, covering the 2000 and 2001 cohorts. These studies track the progression of an entering cohort for up to five years, until the students qualify or leave their original institution, and the resulting data have enabled more in-depth analysis of student performance and graduate output.[7] The study paints a disturbing picture. After five years, the year 2000 cohort of approximately 120,000 students had progressed as shown in table 1.

We do not yet have the ability to track students who change institution, so the "left without graduating" category also includes students who transfer, estimated by the DoE at about 10 percent of that category's total. Final

TABLE 1. Performance of First-Time-Entering Students after 5 Years

Graduated	30%
Left original institution without graduating	56%
Still registered	14%

Source: I. Scott, N. Yeld, and J. Hendry, "A Case for Improving Teaching and Learning in South African Higher Education," *Higher Education Monitor Number 6* (Pretoria: Council on Higher Education, 2007).

Note: Percentages show the performance of 2,000 first-time-entering student cohort after 5 years for the whole higher-education sector.

completion rates have been estimated on the somewhat optimistic assumption that 70 percent of transferring and still registered students will eventually graduate. On this basis, the final 2000 cohort completion rate would be 44 percent, representing a loss of some 65,000 students in an environment of scarce skills.

These overall figures include distance-education students, who commonly have above-average attrition rates. However, even in the best-performing subsector—the so-called contact degree programs—only 50 percent of students had graduated after five years.

Disaggregating the figures by subject and qualification type gives us a more nuanced view. The study separately analyzed key subject areas, including engineering, the mathematical and natural sciences, law, languages, and business/management, which are known as Classifications of Educational Subject Matter, or CESMs. Among the main findings from this breakdown, two points stand out:

- In the subject areas analyzed across all first degrees—including highly selective professional programs and excluding distance-education students—completion rates after five years were generally 50 percent or lower, and there were only two cases in which the estimated final attrition rate was below 40 percent.
- After five years, two-thirds of students pursuing National Diplomas had left their original institutions without graduating. In none of the subject areas analyzed would the final completion rate exceed 50 percent.

While this poor performance may be attributable to various socioeconomic and educational factors, its significance for development is particularly obvious when seen against the background of the current patterns of participation in the higher-education system, as discussed in what follows.

Participation Rates

Despite overall growth in the higher-education sector, South Africa's gross participation rate—that is, total enrollment (of all age groups) in higher education as a percentage of the total 20–24 age group—has remained low. The national target, benchmarked against countries at a comparable stage of economic development, is 20 percent, but the rate has for a number of years fluctuated in the neighborhood of 15 percent to 16 percent.[8] Of greater concern are the disparities between population groups, as shown in table 2, calculated from 2005 enrollments.

The low black participation rate has major implications (since the performance patterns of black and coloured students are in many respects sim-

TABLE 2. Gross Higher-Education Participation Rates

White	60%
Indian	51%
Coloured	12%
Black	12%
Overall	16%

Source: I. Scott, N. Yeld, and J. Hendry, "A Case for Improving Teaching and Learning in South African Higher Education," *Higher Education Monitor Number 6* (Pretoria: Council on Higher Education, 2007).

Note: Participation rates are total enrollment in 2005 as a percentage of 20–24 age group.

ilar, for the sake of brevity this chapter focuses on the black group, which represents the great majority of the population). Unless most of the academically talented members of this group have somehow remained outside the system, it must be assumed that a high proportion of the current black intake—which is predominantly in the top decile of the black group overall, in terms of prior educational attainment—has the potential to succeed in higher education. This directly challenges the perception that equates underpreparedness with lack of ability, and the consequent view that many students in the intake are not university material. Instead, the disparities in participation must be regarded as the backdrop against which we should consider the issue of equity of outcomes.

Who Is Getting Through?

One answer to the question of who is benefiting from higher education can be found in the data shown in table 3, which measure racial disparities in the completion rate after five years in "three-year" degree programs at the contact universities.

The professional programs show similar patterns. In virtually all of the subject areas analyzed at the first degree stage, the black completion rate is less than half of the white rate. As a result, despite black enrollment growth, there are still fewer black than white graduates in these programs. The racial disparities are much smaller in the National Diploma programs, but completion rates there are very low across the board. Since the great majority of the students in these programs are black, the figures reflect high losses of black students in key skills areas.

In short, we are still very far from realizing equity of outcomes. Taking account of participation rates, overall attrition exceeding 50 percent, and the below-average black completion rates, only about 5 percent of black South Africans in the 20–24 age group are succeeding in the country's system of higher education.

Following are several key observations that arise from the analysis of performance patterns:

- The evidence indicates that the higher-education sector is not meeting national graduate needs overall, and that the benefits of higher education are still highly unevenly allocated along racial lines. The system is thus failing in its two main developmental missions, described by Minister of Education Naledi Pandor as to promote "economic growth and ... social cohesion."[9]
- It is clear that student performance in higher education continues to reflect the apartheid legacy of racial inequalities and educational disadvantage. The question is whether and how we can accelerate our efforts to surmount the past, especially in light of the pressing demands of development.
- Although the black student intake has strong academic potential, it is evident that the system as a whole is not succeeding in accommodating diversity, and that lack of equity of outcomes is the primary contributor to underperformance in the sector as a whole. This systemic deficiency applies to current cohorts, but even more so to future intakes. The participation and throughput rates show that substantial growth in graduate output must come predominantly from the black and coloured groups, but these are the groups that are least well served by the current system. Thus, the equity and development agendas are converging: the effective accommodation of diversity has become an imperative for reasons of economic as well as social development.
- The 2000 cohort patterns are corroborated by the 2001 study, and are in line with long-standing experience in a number of institutions. South African higher education has struggled to address overall student performance, and equity in particular, for several decades.[10] While there

TABLE 3.   Graduation Rates after 5 Years

Subject Area	Black (%)	White (%)
Business/Management	33	72
Life and Physical Sciences	31	63
Mathematical Sciences	35	63
Social Sciences	34	68
Languages	32	68

Source: I. Scott, N. Yeld, and J. Hendry, "A Case for Improving Teaching and Learning in South African Higher Education," *Higher Education Monitor Number 6* (Pretoria: Council on Higher Education, 2007).

Note: Percentages given show graduation rates after 5 years in general academic first bachelor's degrees (3-year programs), by selected subject area and "race" for first-time-entering students excluding distance education.

will no doubt be fluctuations, the underlying patterns are persistent and will not change spontaneously. The question, then, is what it will take to substantially improve them.

The Need for Systemic Change

∾

Although affective and material factors clearly play a role in the difficulties experienced by so many South African students—especially black students—analysts have argued since at least the 1980s that key academic problems are largely systemic in origin, the consequence of discontinuities between secondary schooling and the structures and assumptions of higher education.[11] Though only a small, select proportion of the black population gains access, the great majority of these black entrants continue to be severely disadvantaged by the school system and are underprepared for mainstream higher-education programs. For these students, despite their talent, the divide between schooling and the traditional entry level of higher education is unrealistically wide, and encompasses issues reaching well beyond subject matter. The resulting "articulation gap" has been recognized in posttransition higher-education policy as a key obstacle to equity of outcomes.[12] Its effects are particularly apparent at the entry level of many higher-education programs but are often manifested in later years as well. Problems of this kind exist in many countries, but are acute in South Africa (and other developing countries) because educational disadvantage particularly affects the majority population groups. This has implications for teaching at all levels.

The indicators of this systemic discontinuity include shortages of qualified candidates for many programs, disproportionately high first-year attrition, and, in particular, strikingly low rates of graduation within the regulation time allotted for degree and diploma completion. Sector-wide, fewer than one in three contact students complete their program in regulation time. And this generally low figure masks major discrepancies by race, with black students making up only 25 percent of regulation-time graduates in key subject areas at the universities, pointing to the racially disproportionate effects of the articulation gap.

The performance patterns as a whole suggest that the current system is not working effectively for the majority of students, and that it is particularly failing to help the most underrepresented groups—black and coloured students—realize their potential. The gains that have been made in equity of access are thus being neutralized at the outcome stage.

Many in the academic community attribute student underperformance virtually exclusively to individual deficits, and regard improvement of the

K–12 school sector as the only viable solution. The need to address the shortcomings and inequalities of South Africa's primary and secondary schools is not in dispute; but the question is whether higher education can and should make a substantial contribution toward a solution through its own curricula and practices. While there is strong resistance to changing the way things are done in higher education, there are two broad arguments for innovation:

- First, our expectations of school improvement must be subject to on-going assessment of the extent to which such improvement is likely to be achieved. Researcher Nan Yeld has concluded that continuing poor performance and the scale of development challenges in the school sector indicate slim prospects for significant improvement in outcomes.[13] Her analysis vindicates faculty criticisms of student preparedness, but at the same time warns that higher education cannot rely on improvement in external conditions to solve its performance problems.
- The higher-education sector has an obligation to review the appropriateness of its methods for meeting the country's needs. Despite major changes in the student intake, particularly in terms of their linguistic and educational backgrounds, the system is still dominated by curriculum structures and teaching approaches that were established decades ago, for a very different and largely homogeneous student body. In light of this, we must ask whose interests it serves to maintain the status quo.

More than a decade after political transition, South African higher education's legislative framework, governance, and funding have all undergone radical change, but the sector still faces the challenge of aligning its core educational practices with the country's developmental needs and realities. The central challenge is to enable talented students from very different educational backgrounds, with very different levels of preparedness, to realize their potential. The scale of the challenge, measured in current performance patterns, points to the need for systemic intervention. Curricular reform will be necessary in order to accommodate student diversity and facilitate responsible affirmative action, and is thus a key element of the system's contribution to transformation.

Towards Systemic Curriculum Reform

∾

Cultural diversity is widely accepted as enriching, but in the South African context diversity of educational background arises from social inequality, and obstructs equity. This latter form of diversity represents a central challenge that mainstream provision has not met.

As outlined by Yeld (in "Admissions Policies and Challenges," in Part III of this volume), the patterns of inequity in higher education are rooted in the stark disparities in the performance of different segments of the school sector, suggesting that simply "teaching better" within the existing higher-education framework is not enough. Yeld's analysis bears out a long-standing tenet of Academic Development (commonly abbreviated to "AD," the term as used in South Africa refers broadly to higher-education interventions designed to advance equity) that the full diversity of students' educational backgrounds cannot be effectively accommodated within the country's traditional curriculum structures. The pervasiveness of the articulation gap requires a systemic response, in the form of alternative curriculum frameworks that can meet diverse learning needs.[14]

This idea first emerged in the 1980s, when loopholes in apartheid legislation enabled the "open" universities—historically white institutions that embraced nonracial ideals—to admit black students in small but increasing numbers. Although these students were among the highest achievers from the then-black segment of the secondary school system, they did not perform well in regular higher-education programs, even with concurrent support from supplementary tutorial instruction. It became evident that the standard assumptions of first-year curricula about prior learning—in terms of both academic skills and subject-area knowledge—were not valid given black students' educational backgrounds. Clearly, different educational approaches were going to be required if these students were to realize their high potential. This awareness led to the development of "foundational" entry-level tracks designed to enable talented but disadvantaged students to develop a firm academic foundation. The key attributes of foundational courses are, inter alia, that they are not bound by the parameters and assumptions of traditional first-year courses, and are thus able to build on students' individual strengths; that they make strong but realistic academic demands; and that they allow time for the development of concepts and skills. Rather than characterizing foundational work as "remedial," educators see it as providing talented students with essential learning opportunities that mainstream education fails to offer.

As understanding of the curriculum challenge grew, efforts to integrate the foundational and mainstream tracks led to the development of what are now called "extended curriculum programs," which increase the duration of a regular undergraduate program, usually by a year, to incorporate foundational provision and allow greater flexibility in progression through the curriculum. In the face of persistent inequalities, these extended programs have become a central means of pursuing equity. Their use has spread, and their design has become increasingly sophisticated, linking foundational and traditional coursework in innovative ways. While sector-wide research on the impact of these efforts remains to be done, institutional studies show that such programs play a crucial role in fostering black student access and success, not least in scarce-skills areas.[15]

Following are amongst the important lessons that have been learned from AD experience:

- Educational disadvantage continues to affect the majority of the population. Consequently, higher education cannot admit students only on the basis of conventional achieved performance, if the dual goals of development and equity are to be met. Admissions policies must recognize academic potential. Such policies are not enough in themselves, however, and must be complemented by curriculum structures that meet the learning needs of talented but underprepared students. Otherwise, widening of participation is simply neutralized by attrition downstream.

- Systemic intervention is necessary to address this challenge. While a large proportion of the black students in incoming cohorts are underprepared for traditional programs, many are high achievers in their group and thrive on foundational provision. The differentials in prior learning are such, however, that the necessary foundational learning opportunities cannot be provided within traditional first-year courses, and require an alternative curriculum framework that allows time for building academic foundations. When this provision is made, many apparently marginal students are able to demonstrate their full potential and successfully complete their studies. This has been shown to be true in even the most selective programs and universities.[16]

- AD experience thus confirms that the traditional, unitary curriculum does not successfully accommodate diversity among the current intake, let alone allow for the increased diversity needed for future development. The range of educational backgrounds that has to be allowed for within South African higher education is arguably as wide as or wider than that managed by the highly diversified American system (with the added complication that the primary language of instruction in South Africa is not the first language of the majority of students),[17] so it is understandable that the sector is under pressure.

- South Africa's qualifications framework, with three-year degrees and diplomas as the core programs, is in itself an obstacle to accommodating diversity. One of the main reasons for the need for extended programs is the rigidity of the standard three-year programs, which allows

virtually no space for flexibility in teaching approaches, no ability to accommodate students entering from different starting points, and no
opportunities to select appropriate entry levels in key subjects (just as
American freshmen might take precalculus if they need a stronger
foundation in math) or to experiment with a range of subjects in their
formative years. Since the framework requires that programs raise students to an internationally accepted exit standard within just three
years of completing secondary schooling (which itself is typically not
strong), it is not surprising that mainstream curricula assume high levels of preparedness, and are ill-suited to accommodating nontraditional
constituencies. It is unlikely that any unitary structure could cater fully
to South Africa's diverse intake, but an extra year of study would create
much greater opportunities in many programs.

While alternative curricula have produced encouraging successes, they
exist mostly on the margins, serving perhaps 10 percent of the intake. It is
therefore important that we consider the implications of the AD experience
for mainstream higher education.

The focus on curriculum structure is not intended to underrate the
significance of knowledge and content issues. However, since curriculum
structure so strongly influences our ability to teach and learn, an evaluation of
curricular frameworks must be seen as an essential first step towards improving outcomes and making room for deeper qualitative change. Failing this, the
success of affirmative action in higher education will be seriously limited.

Curriculum Reform for Whom?

∾

If we need to offer different curricular frameworks in order to accommodate diversity, we have to ask whether the need for these options applies to
all institutions, or whether institutional differentiation would be an alternative solution. For example, could a college sector (comparable to the
American community colleges or British further education colleges) take
primary responsibility for dealing with underpreparedness, possibly
through an intermediate qualification like the American associate's or
British foundation degrees, while leaving the mainstream framework un-
touched? Or should institutions be formally tiered, as they are in America,
which reduces educational diversity in individual universities and enables
the top-tier schools to pursue traditional teaching and scholarship?

South Africa's institutions of higher education have long been diversified
in their missions and roles, and arguments in favor of formalized differentiation arise periodically.[18] The issues involved are complex, and a detailed

analysis is beyond the scope of this chapter. However, I would offer a few brief caveats about the value of institutional differentiation as a central strategy for accommodating diversity.

- Diversity of mission can clearly be a strength, but in South Africa formalizing functional differentiation would be likely to intensify racial stratification. If entrants were channeled in accordance with their level of secondary attainment, the great majority of black students would be relegated to colleges or lower-tier institutions, counter to our equity goals. South Africa needs to avoid the problems depicted in Astin's critique of aspects of the American system three decades ago:

> The initial handicaps of less prepared students are simply exacerbated by the hierarchical public system in which open admissions are limited only to the lowest tier in the system—the community college. . . . In essence, hierarchical public systems match the weakest students with the most limited educational opportunities.[19]

- Articulation arrangements can facilitate student mobility between tiers, but this solution would still force talented but underprepared students (who could well be in the top decile of the majority population group) to negotiate indirect routes and pass through additional admission filters in order to gain access to the higher-tier universities and thus to the professional and other highly selective programs where increased black participation is most needed. By contrast, experience with AD shows that such students can thrive in extended programs when admitted directly into their university of choice.

In the interests of equity and growth in high-skills areas, we must recruit students with good potential from all sectors of the population into all categories of institutions, as long as their potential is consistent with the demands of the programs in question. Given ongoing inequalities, this means we must cater to differential levels of preparedness in all major programs. Colleges and universities predominantly concerned with teaching have an important role to play in increasing participation of underrepresented groups, but their work is not a substitute for efforts by all South African institutions to increase their capacity for accommodating diversity.

Implications for the Mainstream

∾

In contrast with the state of affairs in most developed countries, in South Africa educational inequalities disadvantage the majority of the population, and the majority of the intake are not being well served by the current system. The performance patterns show that only an unrepresentative minority of the intake can successfully navigate the traditional curriculum. The inflexibility of the curricular framework thus constrains the sector's capacity to accommodate diversity and generate successful growth.

Structural curriculum reform needs to be undertaken systemically, not confined to the margins or remanded to a layer of "teaching-only" institutions expected to bear the greater burden of disadvantage. As an interim measure, extended programs need to be recognized alongside the traditional forms, as part of the mainstream. Substantively, however, the scale of the challenge also calls for reconceptualizing that mainstream, by inter alia establishing a four-year degree as the core of a more flexible framework that can accommodate the diversity of the intake, and provide space in which the student body as a whole can attain the skills and attributes needed for success in the contemporary world.

In contrast with countries with stable, well-established systems of higher education, in South Africa the circumstances of the demographic majority create a need and opportunity for transformative change. Decisions about curriculum taken over the next few years could have far-reaching effects on the system's shape and capacity. To reconfigure the qualifications framework would be a major undertaking; but such a transformation is warranted by both the evidence and the high stakes involved.

In summary, affirmative action in admissions to higher education is essential for economic growth as well as for social justice and development. However, it comes at a cost. If we are to ensure that it is responsible and effective, affirmative action requires investment, not only of funds but more importantly of will, energy, and creativity in developing an educational process that can unlock the talent present in all South Africa's ethnic and class groups. Curricular reform would thus be a key expression of affirmative action with a significant impact on overall outcomes, more generously and equitably distributing the full benefits of higher education.

NOTES

This chapter draws on research commissioned by the Council on Higher Education (CHE) for the Improving Teaching and Learning for Success Project of the Higher Education Quality Committee (I. Scott, N. Yeld, and J. Hendry, *A Case for Improving Teaching and Learning in South African Higher Education. Higher Education Monitor No. 6* [Pretoria: Council on Higher Education, http://www.che.ac.za/documents/d000155/index.php, 2007]). Thanks are due to the CHE, the Department of Education and Jane Hendry of UCT.

1. Haroon Bhorat, "Higher Education and the Labor Market in Postapartheid South Africa," in this volume; Joint Initiative for Priority Skills Acquisition (JIPSA),

http://www.info.gov.za/asgisa/jipsa.htm, 2006; P. Moleke, *Inequalities in Higher Education and the Structure of the Labour Market* (Cape Town: HSRC Press, 2005).

2. Council on Higher Education, *South African Higher Education in the First Decade of Democracy* (Pretoria: Council on Higher Education, 2004), 19.

3. H. Wolpe, S. Badat, and Z. Barends, *The Post-secondary Education System: Beyond the Equality vs Development Impasse and Towards Policy Formulation for Equality and Development* (Cape Town: Education Policy Unit, University of the Western Cape, 1993).

4. G. Kruss, "More, Better, Different? Understanding Private Higher Education in South Africa," in *A Contested Good? Understanding Private Higher Education in South Africa,* ed. G. Kruss and A. Kraak (Pretoria: Boston College and PROPHE Center for International Higher Education, 2003), 19–32.

5. N. Yeld, "Admissions Policies and Challenges," in this volume.

6. Council on Higher Education, *South African Higher Education,* 66–67.

7. The analysis outlined in this chapter comes from research commissioned from UCT's Centre for Higher Education Development by the Council on Higher Education. The samples of 2000 cohort data are intended to illustrate key patterns. For the full study, see Scott, Yeld, and Hendry, *A Case for Improving Teaching and Learning.*

8. South African Department of Education, *National Plan for Higher Education* (Pretoria: Department of Education, 2001).

9. N. Pandor, "Education Key to Improving Economic Growth and Promoting Social Cohesion," edited extract from address by Minister of Education Naledi Pandor, *Cape Times,* September 7, 2005.

10. I. Bunting, *A Legacy of Inequality—Higher Education in South Africa* (Rondebosch: University of Cape Town Press, 1994); D. Cooper and G. Subotzky, *The Skewed Revolution: Trends in South African Higher Education, 1988–1998* (Cape Town: Education Policy Unit, University of the Western Cape, 2001).

11. M. C. Mehl, "Academic Support: Developmental Giant or Academic Pauper?" *South African Journal of Higher Education* 2, no. 1 (1988): 17–20; J. Hofmeyr and R. Spence, "Bridges to the Future," *Optima* 37, no. 1 (1989): 37–48; I. Scott, "Tinkering or Transforming? The Contribution of Academic Support Programmes to 'Opening the doors of learning and of culture,'" *Aspects* 7 (Pietermaritzburg: University of Natal, 1986).

12. South African Department of Education, "Education White Paper 3: A Programme for the Transformation of Higher Education," Government Gazette No. 18207, August 15, 1997; South African Department of Education, *National Plan for Higher Education,* 2001.

13. Yeld, "Admissions Policies and Challenges."

14. South African Association for Academic Development (SAAAD), "Facilitating Academic Development as a Key Element of Transformation in Higher Education," submission to the National Commission on Higher Education by the SA Association for Academic Development, 1995.

15. For a more detailed account of the evolution of equity-related interventions, see I. Scott, N. Yeld, J. McMillan, and M. Hall, "Equity and Excellence in Higher Education: The Case of the University of Cape Town," in *Equity and Excellence in American Higher Education,* ed. W. G. Bowen, M. A. Kurzweil, and E. M. Tobin (Charlottesville: University of Virginia Press, 2005).

16. C. Sikakana, "An Academic Development Programme Has Enabled Students from Disadvantaged Backgrounds to Qualify as Doctors," report to the Faculty of Health Sciences, University of Cape Town, 2006.

17. See, for example, L. Thesen and E. van Pletzen, eds., *Academic Literacy and the Languages of Change* (London: Continuum, 2006).

18. Council on Higher Education, *Towards a New Higher Education Landscape: Meeting the Equity, Quality and Social Development Imperatives of South Africa in the 21st Century* (Pretoria: Council on Higher Education, 2000); M. Makgoba, "Differentiation for Education," *Mail & Guardian,* September 23, 2006, 8–14.

19. A. W. Astin, *The Myth of Equal Access in Public Higher Education* (Atlanta: Southern Education Foundation, 1976).

Defining the Problem of Equity in Teaching Elementary School Mathematics

Jennifer Lewis and Deborah Loewenberg Ball

This volume is concerned with the undergraduate university program and how it prepares its graduates to work in diverse societies. Our chapter focuses on a special subset of undergraduate students—those who go on to enter K–12 teaching as a profession. The impetus for this chapter is the recognition that although there are many ways in which adults engage in the life and work of a diverse society, one that is both central and often taken for granted is the work of teaching young people. Many university faculty members are unaware of how many students in their classes eventually become K–12 teachers and thus the extent to which they themselves are in fact engaged in the education of future teachers. As teachers work with youth, they represent the adult society for which young people are preparing. Teachers have the power to extend opportunity and expand individuals; they can also through their actions and interactions restrict both. In their role, teachers hold substantial power to affect society. Teachers are, of course, also profoundly shaped by their experience in that society. It is on this duality that our chapter focuses. We ask the question: How might undergraduate education contribute to a more equitable society by training those who will teach the next generation?

In this chapter, we examine how the preparation of undergraduate teacher candidates for a just and diverse society entails the design of practice-based pedagogies, which represent a significant departure from the typical undergraduate curriculum. We look in on a moment from a mathematics lesson in a third-grade classroom to illustrate the demands of teaching for equity, and how such examples of classroom practice can be the basis of a pedagogy that prepares teachers for diverse learners. We argue that teaching for a more equitable and just society demands a deliberate pedagogy of teacher education, one that is both centered on the practice of teaching and framed by theories drawn from the social sciences and the academic disciplines.

A Practice-Based Pedagogy

⤳

Professional schools are concerned with what their graduates will do when they leave the university. Professional practice depends not only on skilled performance but also on the perspective enabled by a broad education. Teacher education seeks to prepare people for the complexities of the work they will do as teachers, and to do that work competently. This, we think, is served by a pedagogy based on practice, one that entails the use of typical problems that arise in the classroom, their "diagnoses" and treatment. This practice-based pedagogy would need to specify the work of teaching for equity, since if teaching in general is underspecified, as Glazer[1] and others have argued, then the work of teaching in a diverse society is even less understood. As an example of this practice-focused teacher education design, we look to snippets of real practice to illustrate the complexity of considerations and demands of teaching in a diverse society, and to show how such snippets can be the basis for a practice-based teacher education that is concerned with teaching for a just and diverse society.

Consider the experience of the third-grade teacher in the following example. She is teaching a multicultural group of eight-year-olds who are working on the following mathematics problem:[2]

a. I have one dozen small raisin cookies. If I want to share them equally with my family at supper tonight, how many cookies would each person get? How do you know?

b. How would this work out in YOUR family—how many cookies would each person get if YOU had a dozen cookies to share with them? How do you know?

The children copy the problem into their notebooks and, after some clarification, begin to work on solutions. Some of the children come from families with two, three, four, or six members, and so are easily able to divide the 12 cookies into an appropriate number of equal shares.

Cassandra, on the other hand, comes from a five-member family. This makes the problem challenging, because the class is just beginning to study fractions. Her discomfort about solving the problem is heightened by the fact that she is older and taller than her classmates, having been held back a grade earlier. In a class in which over half the pupils are from countries other than the United States, she is also one of only three African American students.

What happens in such little moments will shape who Cassandra becomes, and how she behaves. Her actions, in turn, will shape how others in the class see her—and perhaps, by extension, how they see other African Americans. How should the teacher respond?

Just a few minutes into this third-grade mathematics lesson, we see how a teacher has to navigate the issues of identity, family, fairness, and academic competence, among others. The university introduces undergraduates to theory and research on such issues, but it is not at all clear how this knowledge bears on actual instruction: in practice, teachers have to draw on a multitude of resources, but which resources matter most here? What might a teacher education student learn from watching a videotape of Cassandra and investigating the accompanying materials (her written work, the teacher's plan, photographs of the chalkboard, etc.)?

Our undergraduates can see—literally and figuratively—how the challenges of a diverse society manifest themselves in classroom life. They can learn to interpret what children and teachers do through multiple lenses—through a disciplinary lens such as mathematics, through the lens of sociocultural theories, or through a policy lens, to name just a few possibilities. A multimedia recording of Cassandra's classroom allows the professor to stop the action, so that his or her students can deliberate their next moves in light of these varying interpretations. Absent such opportunities, students are often unable to connect the world of ideas to the world of practice, or only learn on the fly, with no opportunity to reflect on the efficacy of their actions.

The Demands of Teaching in a Diverse Society

❧

Cassandra's teacher had many moves she could have made in our story. She could have let one of the other students go first; she could have presented Cassandra's solution herself; or she could have explained that the problem was more difficult for children with five people in their family.[3] But for a teacher committed to classroom equity, none of these options serve the goal of supporting the learning of *all* students. What would a teacher need to know in order to help Cassandra learn the mathematics needed to solve this problem—and, in a broader sense, to be able to perform competently in a public setting where mathematics is taught and learned? What skills and dispositions, in other words, as well as knowledge, do teachers need to help all children succeed? And what role can undergraduate education play in developing these capacities?

We will return to Cassandra's story later. For now, we must simply remember that similar dramas are playing out in classrooms across America every day, often invisibly. Education has tremendous, unique potential to help close the achievement gap between white students and students of color, between middle-class students and those living in poverty. But too often it instead perpetuates inequality.[4] To reverse this tendency, our system for educating new teachers has to accomplish two tasks: first, it must help educators-to-be to understand the challenges of a diverse society; and second, it must impart both the awareness and the skills they need to make schooling more equitable.

A History of Equity in Teaching Elementary School Mathematics

∾

In America, educational achievement has long been correlated with race, ethnicity, class, and gender. The roots of this injustice lie buried in our past and entangled in our present, permeating classrooms, schools, and all of society. Bowles and Gintes argue that inequality is so tightly woven into the fabric of schooling that both teachers and students are (perhaps unwittingly) complicit, and urge their readers to consider how teachers can effect change in such a stratified and unequal system.[5]

Complementing this analysis, sociologist Dan Lortie argues that the teaching profession tends to attract people who liked school themselves, and who implicitly accept the educational practices they grew up with. These experiences exert a major influence on how they behave as teachers. That is, their "apprenticeship of observation" imbues them with ideas about what teachers should do, and about what good teaching looks like. As members of society, these teachers are also "apprenticed" to commonly held ideas about race, class, and gender. Teacher education, according to Lortie, is a weak intervention on the powerful impressions and sense of knowledge that teachers bring from their own experience as students.[6] The warrants for knowledge are more often personal than professional, as finding "what works for me" dominates much pedagogical reasoning.[7] Lortie's analysis of teaching suggests important ways in which the very nature of the occupation and socialization into its practice may reinforce, preserve, and reproduce inequality.

Lortie's observations about the occupation of teaching, and its strong tendencies toward continuity, can be extended: Not only do teachers experience an apprenticeship of observation in schools, but, in addition, living in this society provides a powerful cultural apprenticeship with race, class, and gender. Teachers bring with them beliefs and attitudes, knowledge and patterns of action and interaction, values and perceptions that are the product of this apprenticeship. If teachers are to be able to teach all students, professional education must be able to intervene effectively, in some cases, and make profitable use, in other cases, regarding these attitudes, knowledge, and skills.

As Lortie argues, however, professional education is a relatively weak treatment compared with the lessons of a lifetime. Nor does the strong individualistic ethos of the profession do much to challenge these prejudices.

Nowhere is this pattern of inequity harder to address, or professional culture harder to change, than in mathematics teaching and learning, where inequality manifests itself in consistent disparities in achievement scores.[8] Because mathematics plays a key role in determining who will have access to college, funding, and a high-status career, this inequality leads to the exclusion of students from minority and other nondominant groups—either because their schools do not offer advanced mathematics courses or because tracking plays into a self-fulfilling prophecy of low expectations.[9] This underrepresentation is most evident in university faculties, in advanced course enrollments, and in mathematics and mathematically based professions such as engineering, physics, and computer science. This observation has led Moses and Cobb to refer to mathematics education as the "new civil right."[10]

The work of Bowles and Gintes, Lortie, Moses and Cobb, and others makes it clear that in order to create a more just and equal learning environment, teacher-educators must help their students connect the challenges of actual classroom instruction to theories of learning and diversity that they may have read about in their coursework.[11]

A Pedagogy of Practice: Contexts as Equity Work in Mathematics Teaching

∾

Let us now return to Cassandra's third-grade classroom. How might a teacher-educator use this classroom example—a videotape of the class, as well as copies of transcripts, the children's work, and the teacher's field notes—to prepare future teachers?

Take, for example, the numerous theories about "contexts," or real-life situations. There is a great push for the use of such real-life examples in mathematics teaching, in part because they make abstract mathematical concepts seem more relevant and immediate to the learner. This argument is especially common in discussions of mathematics learning among less privileged children, for whom math supposedly seems distant and irrelevant.

Teacher education students read a great deal about such ideas. They read policy documents that advocate the use of real-life contexts in mathematics, and they see this policy translated into curricula populated by story problems. Their instructors paint pictures of children working on such story problems, and of teachers using them to teach high-level mathematics.

But these traditional forms of teacher education cannot replicate the experience of working with real children. Policy documents, curricular materials, and portrayals of teaching are composed from words that someone else has chosen. The messiness that ensues in the classroom when children's feelings are at stake, when there are disparities in children's knowledge and experience, or when race, class, and gender differences come into play, are hard if not impossible to represent in lectures or textbooks. A future teacher's ability to disrupt the reproduction of inequality in the classroom[12] can only be learned from professional training centered on practice.

By "practice" we do not mean the field experiences that are standard fare in current teacher education. Such experiences often confirm, rather than challenge, prior assumptions about race, class, gender, and children's ability to learn. Instead, we mean practice that can be queried using students' liberal arts knowledge. It may involve fieldwork in real schools, but it may also involve using records of practice: the videotapes, transcripts, and other documentation mentioned earlier. Unlike field experiences, students can pause on a record, query ideas and assumptions, insert questions of social (or mathematical or linguistic) import, consider alternatives, project children's learning, and the like.

These instructional designs allow teacher education students to tackle, with the help of their instructors, the taken-for-granted practices in school that perpetuate inequality. We have noted in particular a number of commonly accepted teaching practices—which we refer to as "defaults"—that we think have implications for equity in the mathematics classroom.[13] The use of contexts, for example, is a default strategy for connecting academic learning to pupils' experiences. But a closer look reveals that relying on contexts can widen and intensify inequality, rather than reduce it.

But recognizing such defaults, and acting wisely in instruction, will involve more than reading about them. Knowing how to act in ways that advance equitable outcomes demands a pedagogy for teacher education that brings together ideas from theory and research, the mainstays of the liberal arts curriculum, with the particulars of practice, the heart of professional training.

Consider the experience with Cassandra in her third-grade classroom. The encounter with practice through the example of Cassandra's work could help prospective teachers understand how contexts introduce a host of issues that so-called bare mathematics does not. As Jill Adler[14] has pointed out, the use of contexts forces us to confront questions about the universality of experience: about whether what may seem to one person a "basic" or "natural" problem (for example, about dividing cookies equally among family members) may in fact highlight differences in background or experience that lead to the subtle reproduction of inequality.[15]

These nuances become evident on videotape: by pausing the tape and poring over transcripts, a new teacher can see how subtle considerations about family, fairness, access to resources, and public persona come into play. These issues may seem easy to solve through abstract declarations of belief about diversity, but when viewed in the classroom setting their complexity becomes apparent.

Despite these challenges, the use of contexts is not optional. First, mathematics comprises a set of tools for framing, reasoning about, and solving problems in familiar settings—that is, in context. Second, mathematics teaching relies on students' prior knowledge and experience to help them make connections to new situations and concepts. Third, nonmathematical contexts can help structure otherwise abstract mathematics learning. For example, the cookie problem could be understood as a "real-life" (i.e., applied) problem. But it could also be a means for structuring a lesson about the abstract concept of division with a fixed dividend and a variable divisor (the number 12, sharing equally, different numbers of people).

Thus, the use of contexts in mathematics instruction is not just nice, but necessary. Its unexamined use, however, is problematic when viewed from a perspective of equity and an awareness of privilege. Student teachers need to be sensitized to such problems if they are to succeed in fostering equitable classroom achievement. Pedagogical designs for this kind of work include use of "records of practice" such as videotape, transcriptions of talk, curriculum materials, children's work, and teacher's field notes. The object of study in this pedagogy is not the records themselves, but the reconstruction of practice using constructs from students' liberal arts classes. Ideas about equality, equity, and the value and challenge of diversity in the classroom that come from readings and lectures become lenses through which practice can be judged. Unlike traditional pedagogy, there is little to be imparted by the instructor. Teacher education students are not empty vessels to be filled with ideas about equity. Rather, they are budding practitioners who need to be able to make inferences and judgments, as well as act, using such ideas as tools for their work.

As we do in teacher education, we return again to examples from practice to stay grounded in what our students will need to *do*. In the cookie problem, we would want teacher education students to notice, for example, that the teacher will have to use the concept of *family* carefully. Teachers assume that inclusion of family in the curriculum involves children's lives in ways that make mathematics meaningful and engaging. Mostly true—but family structures vary enormously in twenty-first-century America, often in ways that are entangled with racial and class identities, and exercises like the cookie division may expose student sensitivities. Several students in Cassandra's class live in single-parent homes, for example. Others have extended or nuclear family members who live at home intermittently. Prospective teachers may have encountered ideas about the fluidity of family structure in their sociology and psychology courses, but applied professional learning involves seeing how effective teachers are able to acknowledge these differences while still imparting mathematical knowledge. By observing records of practice, teacher education students may also see that the cookie problem is fraught because it involves food, and because it depends on a commonly understood definition of *fairness,* or what it means to share cookies equally. The understanding of such factors can vary tremendously across ethnic, cultural, and social lines.

Courting Diverse Interpretations of Practice

∾

We step back now to consider how a university education might prepare teachers for the challenge of using contexts in mathematics in ways that are sensitive to issues of equity. To answer this question, we consider what a teacher would need to know in order to teach Cassandra. They would first need to know mathematics: not only the mathematics other college students learned in university, but a specialized version that will help the teacher convey mathematics to children.[16] In our example, the teacher would need to recognize that the cookie problem is a partitive division problem, so that she could help her students set up strategies for working on the problem, or identifying where they went wrong. The teacher would also have to be fluent in her thinking about how best to represent this division problem—able to recognize that round cookies may be difficult for a child to divide into even fifths in a drawing, and that rectangular objects might be easier to manipulate.

Clearly coursework can help teachers ready themselves for the demands of their work. But typical university coursework is often insufficient to the task. And teaching also demands dispositions: the disposition, for example, to consider that context has equal potential to become a help or a hindrance in equitable math instruction. So how can universities fully prepare students for the demands of teaching?

This particular mathematics problem demands a kind of sensitivity to children's varied definitions of "family" and an inclination to be inclusive when children choose to count different relations as family members. It requires a way of being in the world that systematically looks past one's own experience, of not blindly presuming shared experience. Knowing that food has cultural and socioeconomic valences for children is also dispositional.

Skillfully navigating through children's conceptions of fairness requires a disposition to be open to the difference between the complex social concepts of "fairness" and "sharing," and the mathematically cleaner notion of "equal." Noticing and interpreting these issues requires multiple sets of eyes on watch. Not every student will see each of these; not every student comes with training, life experience, and personal background that render these issues readily apparent. Being able to apprehend the different meanings of family or fairness, to take two issues from our current examples, would depend on a pedagogy that invites multiple voices to comment on the Cassandra vignette. Undergraduates of varying backgrounds and prior experiences can contribute an array of insights if the design for this work includes collaborative discussion of the records of practice at hand. This, too, is part of the necessary pedagogy.

Courses in "multicultural education" or "social foundations of education," too, aim to cultivate beliefs and dispositions about the effects of race, ethnicity, and social class in schooling. Such classes often focus on educating for democratic participation, on race as a social construct, and on the role of privilege in determining academic success. Even if undergraduates' beliefs are in fact changed by reading about and discussing such issues, those changes will not necessarily help them to *act* when confronting inequality in real-life situations. Content knowledge and disposition are necessary but insufficient for skilled teaching. Cassandra's teacher needs to know how to help her approach the mathematics problem and systematically consider the many different paths to a solution.

The skills and dispositions described here will not likely be acquired in the university classroom alone. They are more likely developed in some interaction of teachers' field experiences, coursework, and personal histories. And the skills and dispositions that arise out of this mix do not emerge automatically. Consider, for example, the cultural and personal resources needed in teaching. These resources depend on a nuanced and self-conscious set of cultural sensitivities and competencies that are not automatically developed by growing up in one's own environment, whatever that may be. University education can help to develop such competencies through deliberate exposure to cultural experiences that stretch and challenge the assumptions, perspectives, and practices tacit in one's own experience. Immersion in other societies or milieus can help, if introduced in ways that bear on instruction, and contribute to these skills and dispositions. But this involves a conscious pedagogical design that brings such experiences to bear directly on experience in ways that are made public and accessible for all to learn from. Engaging with records of practice such as the videotape of Cassandra working on the cookie problem creates for teacher education students a virtual environment of practice in which teachers can craft possible teaching moves, in the company of peers and an experienced instructor.

Undergraduate Education and the Preparation of Teachers
∿

We take the special case of teacher preparation in this chapter as an argument for the importance of diversity in the undergraduate curriculum more generally. We do so for a number of reasons.

First, teachers constitute the largest occupational group in the United States, and therefore deserve attention both for the education they receive and the education they produce. Because a university degree is required as a foundation for teaching in the United States, the lessons that teachers absorb during their college years will influence the education of children like Cassandra. The role of undergraduate education in shaping the effects of K–12 teaching for equity in a diverse society therefore warrants direct attention.

Second, because teacher education programs combine liberal arts and professional curricula, a great deal can be learned about undergraduate education as a whole by focusing on this particular area of specialization. Cassandra's teacher in the vignette we have presented needs to possess both pedagogical skills and also enough mathematics expertise that she can help students like Cassandra learn to navigate new challenges successfully.

Third, teachers play a pivotal role in the creation and maintenance of a just society. Because the challenges and imperatives of diversity are central to effective teaching, as we have seen, understanding how we prepare teachers gives us a useful perspective on the broader challenges of life in a diverse society. Although we do not believe that teachers should shoulder this obligation alone, their contributions do shape learners' lifelong opportunities for achievement and participation. It would have been easy, for example, for Cassandra's teacher to pass over the halting solution she offered in favor of a more polished response from one of her classmates. Indeed, Cassandra herself suggested that another girl be allowed to demonstrate her solution instead. But the commitment to equity requires that the teacher help Cassandra craft a solid explanation that she can confidently present to the class, participating as a full and equal member.

Finally, we are interested not only in what university students learn to think about, but how they learn to act. Teacher performance is a limited but significant measure of what undergraduates learn to think and do. Cassandra's teacher may have a host of ideas about equity in a diverse society. She may be committed to ensuring all children's access to rigorous academic work. But she also may not have the tools necessary to act on these beliefs. The undergraduate experience for preservice teachers combines their liberal arts education—ways to think—with their professional training—ways to act. Thus, the study of teacher education serves as a window onto the university's more general contribution to young people's ability to think about and act on notions of equity in a diverse society.

The liberal arts curriculum and experience form, unacknowledged, the major part of teachers' preparation for teaching. Prospective teachers study academic content that they will be responsible for passing on to their pupils. They encounter unfamiliar people and ideas. Most undergraduates are living and studying outside their communities of origin for the first time. Their assumptions and dispositions will be confronted and challenged as they develop into young adults who inhabit and shape our society. But while undergraduates are enjoying one of the greatest opportunities our society can offer—an education—their beliefs about the meritocratic nature of advancement and opportunity may be reinforced as privilege begets more privilege. The university experience can, in other words, unwittingly perpetuate the reproduction of inequality.

The demographic and intellectual diversity of higher education also creates a special opportunity for social change. It is not enough merely to pay tribute to the value of diversity; nor even to deliberately create a diverse educational community. Learning to be an agent for equity in a diverse society requires *intentional* education: challenge, discomfort, surprise, support, and reflection. The undergraduate education, in both its liberal and professional aspects, holds much possibility if it is consciously used toward these ends.

Education or Teacher Education?

∾

We close with one final observation. Our focus here has been on how undergraduate education can become a force for change through its effect on future teachers: that is, on undergraduate education as *teacher* education. But learning does not end after childhood, and it is no mere afterthought to suggest that our adult lives are also replete with "teachers" of a less formal sort: parents and grandparents; aunts, uncles, and cousins; religious leaders, community members, coaches, and friends. A society in which more adults used these teaching opportunities to encourage young people to value diversity and increase equity would be a better one—one that did not waste human potential, but instead expanded the meaning of the "public good."

Undergraduate education could become a more intentional force, preparing adults to assume responsibilities in the next generation. Undergraduate study could include opportunities to learn about culture, social and educational inequality, and the development of young people. It could provide experiences that make undergraduates more aware of how culture and social status shape who they are, and how they can prepare themselves for life in a diverse society. Undergraduate education is poised on the interface of youth and adulthood, affording it enormous possibility for growing a society in which children are supported and raised more equitably.

NOTES

This work has been supported by grants from the National Science Foundation (REC #0126237) and the Spencer Foundation (MG #199800202). The opinions and arguments herein are the responsibility of the authors. We acknowledge Jill Adler, Jo Boaler, Imani Masters-Goffney, and Keisha Ferguson for their influence on our thinking about these issues in the context of our collective efforts as teacher-educators. We also thank Courtney Cazden for encouraging us to move in this direction with our work, and Carol Lee for inspiration and focus.

1. J. Glazer, "Education Professionalism: An Inside-out View," *American Journal of Education* 114 (2008): 169–89.

2. The episode used in this chapter comes from an archive of records of an entire school year where one of the authors, Deborah Ball, taught a third-grade mathematics class. The archive consists of video records of lessons, audiotapes, digitized copies of the students' written work and the teachers' notes and plans. These records were collected though generous funding from the National Science Foundation in 1989. All names are pseudonyms, standardized across published analyses of these data, and selected to be culturally similar to the children's real names. For example, Cassandra, an African American child, was given a name chosen from among other moderately common African American girls' names.

3. M. Henningsen and M. K. Stein, "Mathematical Tasks and Student Cognition: Classroom-Based Factors that Support and Inhibit High-Level Mathematical Thinking and Reasoning," *Journal for Research in Mathematics Education* 28, no. 5 (1997): 524–49; J. Hiebert and D. Wearne, "Instructional Tasks, Classroom Discourse, and Students Learning in Second-Grade Arithmetic," *American Educational Research Journal* 30 (1993): 393–425; L. Resnick, ed., "Do the Math: Cognitive Demand Makes a Difference," *Research Points* 4, no. 2 (2006).

4. S. Bowles and H. Gintes, *Schooling in Capitalist America: Educational Reform and the Contradictions of Economic Life* (New York: Basic Books, 1976).

5. Ibid.

6. D. C. Lortie, *Schoolteacher: A Sociological Study* (Chicago: University of Chicago Press, 1975).

7. M. Buchmann, "Role over Person: Morality and Authenticy in Teaching," *Teacher's College Record* 87 (4): 529–43.

8. ABT Associates, "Prospects: The Congressionally Mandated Study of Educational Growth and Opportunity" (Cambridge, MA: Author, 1993); J. S. Braswell, A. D. Lutkus, W. S. Grigg, S. L. Santapau, B. Tay-Lim, and M. Johnson, *The Nation's Report Card: Mathematics 2000* (Washington, D.C.: National Center for Educational Statistics, 2001); P. A. Kenney and E. A. Silver, eds., *Results from the Sixth Mathematics Assessment of the National Assessment of Educational Progress* (Reston, Va.: National Council of Teachers of Mathematics, 1997); and E. A. Silver and P. A. Kenney, eds., *Results from the Seventh*

Mathematics Assessment of the National Assessment of Educational Progress (Reston, Va.: National Council of Teachers of Mathematics, 2000).

9. J. Oakes, *Keeping Track: How Schools Structure Inequality* (New Haven: Yale University Press, 2005).

10. R. P. Moses and C. E. Cobb, *Radical Equations* (Boston: Beacon Press, 2001).

11. D. L. Ball, M. H. Thames, J. L. Lewis, H. Bass, and E. Wall, "Inattention to Equity in Teaching Elementary School Mathematics," paper presented at the Annual Meeting of the American Educational Research Association, Chicago, 2003.

12. Ibid.

13. Ibid.

14. J. Adler, "Lessons from and in Curriculum Reform across Contexts?" *The Mathematics Educator* 12 (2002): 2–5.

15. Ibid.

16. D. L. Ball, H. C. Hill, and H. Bass, "Who Knows Mathematics Well Enough to Teach Third Grade, and How Can We Decide?" *American Educator* 5, no. 3 (2005): 14–17, 20–22, 43–46.

PART IV ᕦ The Next Twenty-five Years

Introduction to Part IV, *Martin Hall*

The chapters in this section look through the present to the future. Thus the chapters by Stuart Saunders and by Naledi Pandor and Nasima Badsha start from South Africa's legacy of legislated segregation and look to what has been required to address it in the interests of social justice. Pandor and Badsha's perspective is that of unfolding public policy and a series of measures intended to address student access, equity in staffing, funding, and planning at the level of the national system of higher education. Saunders, while equally aware of the public policy environment, addresses the question from the vantage point of a university leader first trying to circumvent segregationist laws and, once a democratic government was in place, addressing the need to accelerate change in the interests of redress.

Richard Riley and Judith Winston take a matching approach for U.S. higher education. Starting with the effects of the GI Bill, passed after the end of the Second World War, they track subsequent key legislation and court rulings and from this platform look forward to the needs of the new century. They argue that, given the combination of economic and security demands and the changing demographics of the American population, government cannot afford to ignore the pressing need for effective affirmative action. Michael McPherson and Matthew Smith look back to a later benchmark—the Civil Rights Act—and forward through the rhetorical dissection of the implications of Justice O'Connor's opinion in the Supreme Court's ruling.

McPherson and Smith conclude that "the greatest fraud perpetrated by opponents of affirmative action is their claim that the struggle for racial justice ended with the Civil Rights Act. The struggle that began with abolition continues today in the fight against the overwhelming inequities that still correspond to race. The principal virtue of the '25 year' statement, however it was intended, is that it provides perhaps the best opportunity since the Civil Rights Act to renew our commitment to eradicating racial disparities." Taken together, these four chapters look to a future that is grounded in the challenges of the past, and do so from the complementary standpoints of legislators, administrators, and university leaders.

The second cluster of chapters in this part looks from the past to the future in terms of race and gender—the organizing axes of identity that give definition to affirmative action and equity policies. Elaine Salo points to the dangers of relying only on the metrics of race and gender in tracking transformation. Consideration needs to be given to the cultural transformation needed to attract and retain those who are so necessary to diversify the institutional cultures of higher education. Salo argues that insufficient attention has been paid in South Africa to the "quotidian processes" that determine how minorities manage within the institution. Future success will depend on the ability to be appropriately critical of the ways in which the dominant culture of a university works against transformation by continuing to marginalize and exclude women and minorities. Abigail Stewart and Danielle LaVaque-Manty pick up the same theme for U.S. higher education by looking close-up at the ways women are marginalized and excluded from the mainstream discourse of science. They hope that, in 25 years, "inclusive" excellence will be an obsolete concept, because academic excellence will by definition be inclusive. However, the research that they review tends to show that stereotyping by means of race and gender schema is deeply entrenched, suggesting that corrective policies may be needed well beyond Justice O'Connor's notional threshold.

Glenn Loury comes to the question of race from a different perspective, using the analytical techniques of the economist to appraise the status of policies now, and into the future. Seeing affirmative action as a policy endeavor intended to achieve the democratic construction of elites within a social context of diverse identities, he opposes blind egalitarianism while supporting affirmative action policies because they are an efficient way of achieving desirable goals.

In the final chapter in this part, Zimitri Erasmus looks beyond liberal humanism and essentialism to the abolition of racism through confronting race as a question of politics and power. Taking South Africa as her canvas, she argues against both those who claim that it is a requirement of democracy that we become "race blind" and also against those who argue that the cultural construction of race is an inevitability. Erasmus rather makes the case for a progressive movement towards antiracialism through political engagement with entrenched power. These she sees as issues that defy the implementation of equity as a bureaucratic process involving quotas, targets, and similar concerns. Instead, she sees equity and antiracial interventions as requiring interactive and dynamic interventions from which new questions and new challenges will emerge.

Looking Back

❧

Stuart Saunders

White colonial power came to South Africa in 1652 when the Dutch East India Company established a Dutch settlement in what is now Cape Town to provide fresh meat, vegetables, and fruit for their ships en route to and from the East. The enslavement of blacks was not banned by the British until 1840, and antiblack discrimination was the norm from the seventeenth all the way through the late twentieth century.

It was in this context that the South African College, or SACS, was founded in 1829. It became the University of Cape Town (commonly referred to as UCT) in 1918. After a period in the city the university moved to the slopes of Table Mountain in the Cape Town suburb of Rondebosch, where it now resides on a large estate left to the nation by Cecil Rhodes.

In his biography of Rhodes, *The Founder,* Robert Rotberg writes, "Rhodes never wavered in his espousal of a great South African university, based near Cape Town along the warm eastern side of Table Mountain. He dreamed of an Oxford-like teaching institution which would attract pupils from all the white settlements south of the Zambezi, and arouse in those students an enthusiasm which would sustain closer union." The young white men who attended his university would, he proclaimed, "make the union of South Africa in the future." He did not mention black South Africans, and was silent, too, on the subject of women students. Interestingly, though, women were first admitted to degree studies at SACS in 1886, well before they were accepted at most other universities in the world.

The Cape Town campus was theoretically open to all races until 1959, but the number of people of color enrolled was always very small. In the second volume of *The History of the South African College,* published in 1918, William Ritchie wrote:

> There can be no doubt that the college was open to all alike without distinction on colour or creed and this had been acknowledged by the college authorities on several occasions, more particularly when the Corporation of Cape Town made their annual grants in favor of the college. Theory and practice, however, are not always easy to harmonize, and, in view of the strong prejudices which are held by many on the question, the cases where application has been made to the college or school have al-

ways been a source of considerable embarrassment to the council. There has never been any positive prohibition to their admission and from time to time one or two coloured students have attended, and, in one case at least taken a degree with credit, but, naturally, with a view to the general interest of the institution, there has never been any great encouragement extended to these students. A rather unusual case occurred in this year (1915) when the son of a native chief applied for admission to the inter-mediate class after passing the matriculation examination, but after some very friendly negotiation the applicant saw that is was better on the whole to seek instruction elsewhere.[1]

The coloured graduates of the 1930s included people of great distinction, such as the socialist activist, organizer and founder of the National Libera-tion League Cissy Gool, and Richard van der Ross, who went on to become rector of the University of the Western Cape and South Africa's ambassador to Spain; but overall black enrollments remained small.

Racial discrimination became further entrenched after the election of the National Party to power in 1948. A series of laws were enacted to intro-duce more stringent racial segregation in all spheres of life, culminating in the 1959 Extension of University Education Act, which classified UCT in the newly created category of "white universities," while designating the Uni-versity of the Western Cape for coloured students, the University College of Durban–Westville for Asians, the University College of Zululand for Zulus, the University College of the North for Sothos, and creating a university college for Tswanas. Somewhat later the Medical University of South Africa (known as Medunsa) was established as a medical school for blacks, while the well-established University of Fort Hare was reserved for Xhosas. To their great credit, a number of black academics and other members of staff at Fort Hare resigned in protest.

Tom Davie, the vice-chancellor of UCT, led the opposition of the so-called open universities to this draconian legislation. The movement was spearheaded by UCT and the University of the Witwatersrand, commonly known as Wits. Davie defined what he called the four essential freedoms of a university as the rights "to determine for itself on academic grounds who may teach, what may be taught, how it shall be taught, and who may be ad-mitted to study" (interestingly, Justice Felix Frankfurter of the U.S. Supreme Court subsequently used this same definition in his opinion in the 1957 free-speech case *Sweezy v. New Hampshire*).

The protests at UCT culminated in a march of staff and students in aca-demic dress through the city, led by the chancellor, the former South African chief justice Albert van der Sandt Centlivres, and his acting vice-chancellor, Professor R. W. James.

As an undergraduate, I was disturbed by the restrictions placed on UCT's students of colour, and as a young medical graduate I was appalled by this apartheid legislation and identified very closely with Davie and the protestors. But their efforts were to no avail. The 1960s and 1970s saw some increase in black enrollments, but black students still could not fully participate in campus activities, and were barred from everything from dances to football teams. The university was also subject to the Group Areas Act, which designated where people of each defined racial group could live, and by the Immorality Act, which forbade interracial sexual relations or marriage. Under government pressure the vice-chancellor at the time, J. P. Duminy, imposed a policy of integration inside the classroom and segregation outside. It was a policy that had the support of the majority of white South Africans.

Of course, the classrooms were not entirely safe from segregation either. Black medical students could not attend the postmortem examination of a white corpse, examine white patients, or attend operations on white patients. When I became head of medicine at UCT and Groote Schuur Hospital (GSH), the university's main teaching hospital, in 1971, GSH was still segregated. Coloured and Indian doctors who wished to specialize had to undertake their training at the New Somerset hospital, another hospital in the UCT system, which lacked many of the advanced facilities that GSH could boast.

The policy was fundamentally wrong. So I approached Bryan Kies, who was then just starting his training as a specialist (he is now a professor at GSH), and told him I wanted him to work in my ward at GSH. He would have to eat in the ward and sleep in my office, however, because the Group Areas Act forbade him access to the doctors' bungalow. He agreed, and Jerry van Aswegen and a number of others followed him. I had not spoken to my peers or the hospital authorities about this. The coloured and Indian doctors eventually started eating in the doctors' bungalow. I knew that we had made a major breakthrough when the medical superintendent, Dr. Burger, told me that the housekeeper of the doctors' bungalow had threatened to resign if coloured doctors were allowed access there, and he told her to do so. Burger's successor, Dr. Reeve Sanders, was also a great help in this regard. We started to integrate the intensive care wards by arguing that we did not have enough trained personnel to sustain them otherwise. A number of UCT faculty members played important roles, and eventually all the wards became integrated, with students and staff working everywhere irrespective of their color.

Questions were raised in Parliament. The superintendent received complaints from Johannesburg, but the integration proceeded successfully. It would have been difficult for the authorities to close the hospital, since it was the only fully integrated public hospital in South Africa at the time. From all this I learnt that with determination the discriminatory laws and regulations could be overcome in certain circumstances.

After I was elected vice-chancellor in 1980, Alan Pifer, then the president of the Carnegie Corporation of New York, asked me about my goals. I told him that I wanted to ensure that when I retired, the majority of students at UCT would be black. When I took up the vice-chancellorship there were 11,038 students at UCT. Of these, 9,719 were white, 959 coloured, 256 Asian, and 104 African. Any nonwhite student had to have a ministerial permit to attend UCT. Indeed, this was only the first of five requirements for black students to succeed at UCT. The other four were an admissions policy capable of identifying students with academic potential; adequate housing; financial aid; and support (also known as development) programs. Most black students at the time suffered serious financial problems, many came from an inferior and inadequate school system, and none had ever been allowed to reside in a university dormitory: UCT was located in a designated "white" area, and the only blacks who were allowed to sleep there were servants. To live in a black township, often in a temporary shack, with no privacy, sharing with several others a room that doubled as living room, study, and bedroom, with no electricity and a long commute to campus, was a huge academic disadvantage. One student was studying in a chicken run!

I was determined to deal with these problems in a way that would permit black students greater access to UCT, and improve their chances for success. We dealt with the access challenge by using every possible ploy to get around the permit system. Eventually, the actions of UCT and other English-speaking universities imposed too great an administrative burden, and the government introduced legislation creating a quota system. UCT and Wits led resistance to the move. The bill officially became law in 1984, but the supervising minister, Gerrit Viljoen, asked to see me and told me that it would only be applied to programs in quantity surveying (what Americans know as construction project management) and medicine, quotas being necessary in these two fields in order to "protect" the segregated institutions of Medunsa and Fort Hare! Viljoen explained that the government had come to realize how unacceptable quotas were to us at home, as well as internationally.

I think this was the first time the apartheid ideologues gave any ground. From then on we admitted applicants irrespective of race, and soon we achieved the goal that I had chosen as the title of my 1981 inaugural address: "Scholarship and Not Ethnicity." In 1995, the year before my retirement, UCT enrolled 14,877 students, of whom 42 percent were black and 43 percent were women. The first-year class was 52 percent black. We had gone from 104 African students in 1981 to 3,489 African students by 1995, and 6,319 black students total. The average annual increase in African student enrollments was 24 percent, compared to an overall student body growth rate of just 2.1 percent.

South Africa's school-leaving examinations were notoriously poor indicators of university success, prompting the education scholar Nan Yeld (also a contributor to this volume) to lead a group in developing additional tests in English and mathematics, which subsequent studies have shown to be more reliable measures of academic potential. Many students who would have been considered marginal candidates for admission at best gained entry after being tested under the new regime, and were successful in university. The same tests are now also taken by any student seeking admission to a South African medical school, and are likely to be used still more widely in the future.

To address the financial needs of students, and especially black students, in 1981 we allocated R1.26 million from UCT's budget and R3 million from other sources—mainly donors—for financial aid. This figure can be compared to our overall budget of R45 million. I made raising scholarship support for poor students my top priority in UCT's fund-raising campaign, and we were very successful (UCT also raised money in South Africa, the United Kingdom, the United States, and Canada). This kind of support was not a priority for most of the nation's universities, and certainly not for the Afrikaans institutions, who did not even allocate funds from their own budgets for this purpose. By 1995, we were allocating R9 million a year for student aid. Scholarships were means-tested, and in 1995 2,458 students received aid.

Once admitted to the university and provided with financial means, black students still had to succeed academically, of course, despite the very poor schooling many of them had received at the primary and secondary levels. So in 1980 we started an academic support program. This eventually became the academic development program, or ADP, which grew to employ more than 40 full-time staff and numerous part-time tutors by 1995. Again, most of the funds for ADP came from donors. We were criticized by those who said this was not a task for a university, but until the schools have improved sufficiently (and they have not done so by the time of this writing, and will not for some time) these programs will be essential. They have made success possible for many students to whom it would otherwise have been denied. Funds for this purpose were first allocated by the department of education in 2005—something I had been urging for over 20 years! There were few universities in the world at the time that made raising funds for student financial aid, ADPs, and student housing their top institutional priorities.

Shortly after my taking up office I told UCT's registrar, Mr. Len Read, that we would admit black students to the residences (dormitories). I did not seek permission from anyone to do this, not even the university council. The UCT official responsible for the residences refused my request for fear that he would end up in court and possibly jail, so I gave him a written instruction to do so. I think that was the only written instruction I gave during my time as UCT vice-chancellor (notably, Len Read sent me a letter expressing his full support for my action). In the event, we admitted the students without incident. Each year we admitted more black students to the residences.

It was extremely difficult for black students to find accommodation off-campus near the university because of apartheid's laws, and so it was imperative to ensure that as many as possible could live in the dormitories. At the beginning of each academic year we would go to extraordinary lengths to secure suitable accommodations by renting additional places wherever we could. White students had little difficulty getting convenient accommodation close to the campus. Blacks, meanwhile, could be accommodated in so-called international hotels (part of the madness of apartheid), and so we bought a hotel near UCT that we could use as a front if the police arrived. It is now a students' residence. Our policy was illegal, of course, but the police and the government took no action.

We also needed more beds, to accommodate the increasing number of black students. This was achieved by using donor money to buy two very large apartment blocks close to UCT, along with two smaller ones and the hotel. As of 1995, 2,610 African students were in residence on campus, a 3,575 percent increase since 1984.

We were much less successful in facilitating the professional advancement of black employees, especially among the academic staff. This was partly because many of the most talented black staff were still in exile in the 1980s. After 1990 (and especially after 1994) these same black elites were snapped up by business and government, often at salaries much higher than those available at UCT. In 1984, 97 percent of our professors and associate professors were white, 1 percent were African, and 21 percent were women. Eleven years later the numbers had barely budged: 92 percent were white, 4 percent African, and 24 percent women. This has lent some urgency to UCT's current efforts to improve staff diversity.

Looking back, we pursued a determined policy of affirmative action and moved substantially towards equity in admission, financial support, ADP help, and housing, thus helping to ensure success for many black students.

If I learned any one lesson from this experience, it was that the most important quality in a vice-chancellor or university president is leadership. It far outweighs the importance of management. I was pleasantly surprised by the university community's support for our efforts to achieve equity at UCT. If the issues are made clear and a value system is established, then you can take the necessary actions without difficulty, although they may at times be hazardous. An American visitor once asked me what strategy I had used to achieve our goals, and I replied that it was to bend the branch until it is about to break. Then you allow the branch to spring back just a little, so that when you start bending it again it bends a little farther, until you eventually get a tree with a completely different shape.

Looking Forward

∽

At the time of this writing, South Africa has sustained a constitutional democracy for more than a dozen years. While still young, the country's democracy has vigorously withstood challenges and will endure. We have a comprehensive bill of rights that stands as an example to the world, and a government that recognizes the importance of education. As of 2000, the South African government was devoting 25.8 percent of its expenditures to education, compared with 11.4 percent in the United Kingdom, 9.7 percent in Germany, and 17.4 percent in South Korea. As a proportion of GDP, South Africa budgets 5.5 percent for education, which is equal to the United Kingdom and compares favorably to Germany's 4.5 percent and South Korea's 3.8 percent. The nation's commitment to education is clear.

So what are the obstacles to achieving equity in higher education? One major limiting factor for many Africans is the poor quality of primary and secondary education, coupled with generations of political and social deprivation. While the previously exclusively white schools are now fully integrated and mostly of good standard, the vast majority of African pupils go to schools that were (and still are) exclusively black. Considerable government and private investment have not effectively raised the level of facilities in many black schools to even a basic standard. Those funds that are available are underutilized by some provinces, the result of their lack of capacity to deliver services. The numbers are telling: in 2002, 16 percent of teachers were unqualified. The figure was 7 percent in Gauteng province, 9 percent in the Western Cape, 32 percent in North West, and 19 percent in the Eastern Cape. The discrepancy is significant: Gauteng and the Western Cape have many more previously white schools than North West or the Eastern Cape. Aggravating this situation is the fact that many of the teachers in the African schools were educated under the apartheid-era system of Bantu education, and are generally not as well equipped to carry out their tasks.

Facilities are another huge problem. As of 2000, only 49.3 percent of South African schools had electricity, mainly those in the urban areas.

Nineteen percent had piped potable water. Only 34 percent of secondary schools had physical science laboratories, and a mere 12 percent had computers. Of the 500,000-plus pupils who wrote the final school-leaving examination in 2005, 305,774 passed the senior certificate examination; but of those who passed, only 86,531 achieved results high enough to qualify them for a university education

Of those who passed, only 32,112 (or 10 percent) passed mathematics at the higher grade level, and 45,652 (or 15 percent) achieved the same result in physical science. These are skills needed for engineering, medicine, and science, and at the better universities for business degrees, as well. Taken together with the fact that English is a second, third, or fourth language for many African students, and that their English teachers usually come from the same communities as the students, the lack of graduates with an adequate subject mix at an appropriate level is a major impediment to achieving equity in higher education. African students consequently have more difficulty in gaining access to the institutions with the highest entry standards and quality of education. Most of the African graduates who do win admittance are studying in the humanities, social sciences, and education. It will take a great effort and the wise use of resources over more than one generation to eliminate the bottleneck in the physical sciences.

Financial factors are also inhibiting the pursuit of equity, and the government has recently funded a National Student Financial Aid Scheme (NSFAS) to address the problem. A group of us, including economists and actuaries, gave the then-minister of education a position paper on this subject in 1997. It was clear then that R500 million was needed to fund the scheme. Only half that amount was allocated, and although the quantum has since exceeded R1.2 billion per annum, it is still inadequate. The scheme provides generous funding for anyone who meets the means test requirements, though a family contribution is required of those with formal earnings. So the poor get support; but those who fail to meet the means test get nothing. For example, a teacher grossing less than R170,000 a year (equivalent to roughly $25,000) gets no help even if she has three children at university.

Poor students, overwhelmingly African, struggle to fund their studies and either run up large debts or avoid paying their university fees, with the result that some universities have accrued large levels of student debt. The struggle to come up with tuition money and keep body and soul together does not help young people succeed in their studies. Poor students may feel obliged to pass scholarship money to poor relatives, further compounding the problem. Meanwhile, African students from the rapidly growing black middle class who have been to good (often previously white) schools are gaining access to the best institutions, but find that they do not qualify for financial aid because their family income is just above the threshold.

The third limiting factor is the shortage of academic development programs, which are either nonexistent or rudimentary at many universities. This institutional deficit diminishes students' chances of success.

The fourth factor is the mismanagement of higher educational institutions. On a number of occasions the minister has been forced to appoint an independent assessor to investigate administrative problems on various campuses, or has had to resort to appointing an administrator to replace incompetent university management.

Finally the level of poverty in South Africa, especially amongst Africans, burdens communities with poor housing, poor sanitation, and inadequate electrification. Poorly educated parents desperate to make ends meet have little time or experience to prepare their children for primary or high school, let alone higher education. And to this must be added the problem of AIDS and the abnormally high mortality rate among African teachers, together with the large numbers of AIDS orphans deprived of parental guidance or support.

Despite these problems there are grounds for optimism. The government is committed to adequate levels of educational funding of education, and South Africans as a whole—and especially Africans—place a high value on education. Many institutions of higher education are sound and some very good indeed, and more and more black students are gaining admission to and succeeding in them. South Africa has a strong democracy that has been under threat in recent times, including attempts to undermine the authority of the Constitutional Court and the judiciary as a whole. Vigilance and determination will be needed to protect it.

NOTE

1. W. Ritchie, *The History of the South African College, 1829–1918* (Cape Town: T. Maskew Miller, 1918).

The First Ten Years

The Role of Public Policy in Shaping Postapartheid Higher Education in South Africa

༾

Naledi Pandor and Nasima Badsha

Setting the Context

༾

The heavy hand of the apartheid state defined the structure and nature of education in South Africa for over four decades. The notorious Bantu Education Act of 1953 divided education along racial and ethnic lines and, in effect, excluded blacks from quality education and training at all levels. The cynically named Extension of the University Education Act of 1959 established and entrenched racially based, ethnic universities and formally restricted entry to universities in terms of race. It limited higher-education opportunity and eradicated nonracism at universities such as Fort Hare, which was restricted to Xhosa-speaking Africans.

Apartheid's legacy in higher education was a system characterized by gross racial and gender inequalities in student participation rates and staffing patterns, and major disparities between historically black and white institutions in terms of geographical location, infrastructure, and facilities, as well as teaching and research capacity. The prime focus of the historically black universities was to meet the skills needs of the civil service in the so-called homelands, with the result that professional areas such as engineering were entirely neglected.

The transition from apartheid to democracy compelled higher education to consider its role in the country's reconstruction and development. The imperatives of the new Constitution and the policy and legislative frameworks that stemmed from it helped set the agenda for this enterprise.

Given the huge disparities in access and opportunity, it is not surprising that redress and equal rights became "the central demand in education reconstruction," to quote one influential report of the time.[1] However, by the early 1990s, the debates in South Africa, as elsewhere, had expanded to include an examination of higher education's contribution to economic development. The tension between these two goals of equity and development—which poses particular challenges to South African policymakers

contending with gross structural inequalities and resource constraints—
also demanded attention. In the event, a number of policy analysts, including Wolpe and Badat, argued persuasively that equity and development
should be pursued simultaneously, to support the consolidation of democracy in South Africa.[2]

A rich and intense policy process, built on foundations laid by the progressive movement in the early 1990s, has unfolded over the past decade to
mediate this balance.

The National Commission on Higher Education (NCHE) was established by Nelson Mandela in February 1995 to advise the first democratically elected government on the reconstruction and development of
the higher-education sector. The NCHE identified two sets of considerations in this process: "firstly, the profound deficiencies of the present system
which inhibit its ability to meet the moral, social and economic demands of
the new South Africa; and, secondly, a context of unprecedented national
and global opportunities and challenges."[3]

The NCHE's propositions informed the Education White Paper 3 of
1997, which along with the Higher Education Act and the Ministry of Education's implementation plan, the National Plan for Higher Education of
2001, continues to serve as the policy framework for renewal of higher education more than a decade later.

But what role, precisely, has the South African government played in
shaping higher education in the years since the adoption of the Higher Education Act? And what impact has public policy had on efforts to meet the
dual objectives of educational equity and development?

Student Access and Success
∾

One of the central goals identified by the White Paper is the achievement of
equity in the composition of both faculties and student bodies in higher education:

> The principle of equity requires fair opportunities both to enter higher
> education programmes and to succeed in them. Applying the principles
> of equity implies, on the one hand, a critical identification of existing in-
> equalities which are the product of policies, structures and practices
> based on racial, gender, disability and other forms of discrimination or
> disadvantage, and on the other a programme of transformation with a
> view to redress. Such transformation involves not only abolishing all ex-
> isting forms of unjust differentiation, but also measures of empower-
> ment, including financial support to bring about equal opportunity for
> individuals and institutions.[4]

The Council on Higher Education (CHE), the statutory advisory body to the minister of education on higher-education policy, reiterated this widely held view when it stated in a 2004 report that "the extent to which higher education promotes or frustrates equity and access will have a direct bearing on social and class stratification, and the nature of the labor market."[5]

It is important to state that in the late 1980s and early 1990s, even before the government intervened, various universities started to respond to pressure to widen and expand access, particularly for first-generation students. Some of these institutions were driven by a clear commitment to social justice, while others were forced to rethink established practices by growing demands for social change, driven by the student movement and civil-society formations. The historically English-speaking universities in particular established alternative admissions and academic support programs to facilitate access of black students who, in the main, would not have qualified for entry under standard criteria. Considerable sums of money were also raised from foreign donors (including some of the major U.S. foundations) for student scholarships.

In many of the former "homeland" universities, meanwhile, this same period was characterized by strife over the legitimacy of institutional governance and management. Still other institutions, like the University of the Western Cape, identified themselves with the liberation struggle and opened their doors to large numbers of academically underprepared students, straining their capacity and limited resources.

One of the government's early priorities after 1994 was to facilitate the access of the previously marginalized, particularly black and women students but also other socially disadvantaged groups. The state's key instrument was a loan scheme established through the National Student Financial Aid Scheme (NSFAS) Act of 1999. The Scheme provides government-funded loans to academically able students who lack the financial resources to pursue a higher education. It is open to all South Africans, with eligibility determined through a financial means test. Loans are repayable (with interest charged at rates far lower than commercial bank loans) once students have graduated and in the workforce. Part of the loan may be converted into a scholarship if the student maintains a sufficiently high level of academic performance. Funds generated from the repayment of loans are recycled into the Scheme. Repayment rates compare favorably to those in similar programs in other countries.

The NSFAS has enabled close to 500,000 students to pursue opportunities in higher education. Despite the significant investment ($1.2 billion since 1999), funding for the Scheme is still inadequate to meet the full needs of students from poor communities. And tuition increases are now particularly affecting the ability of students whose family incomes put them outside of NSFAS's eligibility criteria but not within reach of bank loans to pursue higher-education studies.

The South African government has initiated discussions with the country's commercial banks about increasing their role in student loan financing. A new partnership between government and the financial services industry is also encouraging families to save for higher education, by offering matching public funds as an incentive.

Discussions are now under way about whether the Scheme should be targeted toward high-priority fields, reflecting market demand for particular skills. Full scholarships for students in teacher education and social work have also been introduced, in order to encourage enrollments in these fields. The recipients are expected to work in public service after graduation.

By 2006, 55 percent of all students in higher education were women and 75 percent were black, compared to 43 percent women and 53 percent black student enrollments in 1993. The higher-education sector as a whole has grown more than 50 percent in roughly the same time. However, these figures mask a number of persistent inequalities:

- The overall participation rate (16 percent) remains racially skewed, with the participation rates of white and Indian students being approximately 60 percent and 50 percent respectively, while that of African and coloured students is around 12 percent. In 2002, the National Plan for Higher Education set an overall participation rate target of 20 percent in the "long-term, i.e. ten to fifteen years." This target still stands.
- Black and women students remain underrepresented in postgraduate studies, particularly at the doctoral level. This, in turn, affects the size and diversity of the candidate pool for academic and research positions. South Africa, like many other countries, is faced with the aging of its most productive researchers. In the South African case this trend is complicated by racial and gender inequities, such that the bulk of research output is being generated by (aging) white male researchers.
- Although gains have been made in the numbers of black and female students enrolled in undergraduate engineering, science, and technology programs, the numbers are still cause for concern. This can be at least partially attributed, as Jonathan Jansen and others point out elsewhere in this volume, to the limited pool of school leavers who possess the requisite passes in mathematics and science to qualify for these fields of study.
- A cohort study of first-time students entering public higher education (both on-campus and distance education) in 2000 found that over a five-year period only 30 percent of the intake had graduated, another 14

percent remained in the system, and a full 56 percent had left without graduating, representing a loss of 65,000 students from this cohort.[6] Even more disturbing was that in all fields of study and qualification types the black student completion rate was less than half of that for white students, and the total number of black graduates was less than the number of white graduates. In their own contributions to this book, Jonathan Jansen, Ian Scott, and Nan Yeld discuss some of the factors that seem to contribute to this retention problem, which may include student preparedness; institutional culture and the failure to embrace racial and gender diversity; and insufficient student financial aid.

Clearly, and despite the significant gains that have been made, we are not attaining equity of outcomes. Nor are system outputs yet keeping up with the demands of economic growth and the expectations of society at large.

The government has responded to this challenge in three ways: through funding, planning, and quality assurance.

Funding

∾

The state has set aside funds to support academic development initiatives at all public institutions of higher education. These initiatives provide students from educationally disadvantaged backgrounds with access to foundation courses and other interventions that can support their transition into higher education, particularly in relation to their proficiency in academic language, mathematics, and science. This funding has only been available for four years, and its full impact on graduation rates is yet to be quantified.

The funding also enables institutions to test curricular reforms that may help to improve graduate output. There are strong arguments for degree and course structures that better meet the needs of the majority of students, who take longer than the minimum time allotted to complete their degrees. The Ministry of Education and the Council on Higher Education have encouraged debate and research on these efforts. The ministry has also approved a new Higher Education Qualifications Framework that we hope will stimulate the academic community to take the lead in curriculum innovations.

The government is also investing considerable resources in improving the quality of the secondary-school graduate pool, especially in mathematics and science. Focus schools have been established to provide support in these areas, and are complemented by programs for teachers' continuing professional development.

The government's new higher-education funding plan, which has been in place since 2004, also makes provision for addressing historical disadvantage through "institutional factor grants." These grants provide additional support to institutions with large proportions of disadvantaged students. In the absence of reliable information on students' socioeconomic status, race is used as a proxy for disadvantage in the allocation of funds.

Most recently, in order to address skills shortages in the engineering field, the government earmarked funding that enables designated institutions to increase the quantity and quality of their graduates by supplying additional faculty, infrastructure, and other resources. Institutions were selected to receive this incentive funding on the basis of their track record in recruiting and graduating black students, among other factors.

Planning

∽

A policy vacuum during the period from 1994 to 1997 permitted uncoordinated institutional growth. Growth at some institutions came so quickly that it outstripped available resources and directly threatened quality. This unplanned growth could not be fully funded through state subsidies, particularly since it was not matched by increased graduate outputs. Instead, the government responded by launching a series of consultations with the country's higher-education leadership, eventually leading to individual agreements with universities about the numbers of students (categorized into broad fields and levels of study) that would be annually funded by the public purse. The principal considerations during negotiations were the institution's capacity to enroll and graduate additional students, particularly in national priority areas of human resource development (including science, engineering, technology, business science, and information and communications technology) and in postgraduate studies. Early indications are that this "enrollment planning" exercise will be an effective tool for governing the size and shape of the public higher-education system, thus enhancing its effectiveness.

One of the consequences of planning growth is that not all qualifying students can be accommodated in their university or academic program of choice. This is particularly the case in areas of study, such as medicine, where numbers have to be restricted and the competition for spaces is intense. Given the historical legacy of apartheid, the vast majority of places would be taken up by whites and Indians, who are already overrepresented in the profession, if academic performance were the sole selection criterion.

Universities have responded to this dilemma by identifying and recruiting talented African and coloured students who can be shown to possess the potential for success, but who may have earned lower marks in their school-leaving examinations than their white and Indian contemporaries. As in America, so too in South Africa have challenges arisen to universities' selection policies and procedures. However, in South Africa, quite unlike America, higher education has had recourse to a Constitution that makes provision for redress, and so has been able to successfully defend its efforts. In light of the skills shortages produced by the country's growing economy, as well as their desire to promote student diversity, South Africa's higher-education leaders have committed themselves to securing the resources needed for responsible growth, better enabling the system to meet the needs of all its students.

Thanks to a major recapitalization program, the South African government has also been able to modernize its Further Education and Training (FET) colleges. The FET colleges, which are spread throughout the country, provide students with relatively low-cost education and vocational training in areas such as information and communications technology, engineering, tourism, agriculture, and design. The institutions cooperate closely with industry partners, particularly in curriculum development and the provision of student work experiences and internships. The FET colleges are spread throughout the country, offering students affordable postsecondary education opportunities with the prospect of moving on to diploma or degree programs, particularly at the universities of technology (formerly known as technikons). Such transitions are not yet commonplace, but will be encouraged through a variety of enabling policies and funding programs.

Staff Equity
᧞

Although this chapter has focused on students, faculty equity is also an area of concern. Prior to 1994, as one CHE report explained it, employment patterns in higher education "reflected broader patterns of the apartheid division of labour."[7] Unlike the relatively rapid improvements achieved in student access, the transformation of the race and gender composition of academic staff has come slowly at best. As the CHE explained, "progress in this regard is inhibited by a combination of factors. One factor is structural, which limits the pool of available and suitably qualified black, women and disabled academics and senior management and administrative personnel. The other is institutional and academic disciplinary culture, which, combined with micro-political dynamics, further constrains efforts to achieve staff equity."[8]

As mentioned earlier, this problem is exacerbated by the ageing of the academic workforce. The production of a new generation of academics has been impeded by challenges including the low level of academic salaries, the competing lure of more profitable private- and even public-sector employment, and the opportunity costs of postgraduate study for black students.[9]

The government has responded to these challenges with efforts, driven in part by the Ministry of Science and Technology, to increase the pool of postgraduates through the provision of scholarships and research opportunities, as well as through renewed investment in research through the establishment of research chairs, international partnerships, and other, related programs.

Institutional Redress

ᔈ

South African higher education has undergone a radical and large-scale restructuring. Mergers and incorporations have reduced the number of institutions from thirty-six to twenty-three. A widespread desire to address the inequalities of apartheid resulted in, amongst others, the merger of a number of historically black and white institutions, and in demands for greater efficiency and effectiveness.

While the full impact of this restructuring is yet to be fully assessed, it has already stimulated the injection of new resources into the system: in particular for the renewal of infrastructure, such as student accommodation and teaching and learning facilities, and especially at the historically black campuses. The new institutional landscape comprises traditional universities, universities of technology that focus on technical and vocational higher-education programs, and comprehensive universities that combine traditional university programs with technical and vocational higher education. It includes one large distance education institution, the University of South Africa (UNISA), which has a particularly important role to play in enhancing access for students from across the country, and which is also playing an increasingly important role in providing opportunities to students from other parts of Africa.

Conclusion

ᔈ

In the first decade of democracy, South African higher education was characterized by major advances in equity, and particularly in student access. These gains were achieved by inspiring all the key stakeholders to join in a shared commitment to a set of broad policy objectives, in particular the quest for a higher-education system representative of the county's demographics. The government has largely played its guiding role in ensuring student access by establishing enabling policy frameworks, as well as funding incentives and planning models. Quotas and sanctions have not been necessary, thanks largely to a sector-wide consensus about the need for redress.

Yet greater equality of outcomes is still needed. The government will have to evaluate progress and review policy and implementation strategies accordingly. Alongside this requirement, the need to secure additional resources to meet the increasing demand for student financial aid remains a priority. Without these resources, the further expansion of the system is likely to be constrained.

As we have indicated, progress towards the transformation of the race and gender composition of academic staff in higher education has been slow and remains a challenge for the sector. This is an area that will clearly require more focused attention in the coming period.

NOTES

1. National Education Policy Investigation (NEPI), "Report of the Post-secondary Education Research Group," National Education Co-ordinating Committee, 1992.

2. S. Badat, H. Wolpe, and Z. Barends, "The Post-secondary Education System: Towards Policy Formulation for Equality and Development," in *Changing by Degrees: Equity Issues in South African Tertiary Education* (Rondebosch: University of Cape Town Press, 1994).

3. National Commission on Higher Education (CHE), "Report of the Commission on Higher Education (NCHE): A Framework for Transformation," 1996.

4. South African Department of Education, "Education White Paper 3: A Programme for the Transformation of Higher Education," July 1997.

5. CHE, "South African Higher Education in the First Decade of Democracy," November 2004.

6. I. Scott, "Undergraduate Student Performance Patterns and Some Implications for Curriculum Reform in Higher Education," policy seminar for the Ministry of Education, October 2006.

7. CHE, "South African Higher Education," Section 4.1.2.

8. Ibid., Section 4.2.4.

9. Ibid., Section 4.2.4.4.

The Role of Public Policy in Shaping Higher Education in the Twenty-first Century

Achieving Diversity, Excellence, and Equity in the Academy

❧

Richard W. Riley and Judith A. Winston

Diversity in Higher Education: A National Security Imperative

❧

During this first decade of the 21st century, Americans have become more aware than ever of our vulnerabilities. We have become anxious—some might even say obsessed—about our national and personal security, and with good reason, perhaps, in light of the tragedy the nation experienced on September 11, 2001. We now live in a world rife with unstable and dangerous places, where the United States has become the focus both of longing and discontent. Those same places often are characterized by the poverty, limited rights for women and girls, and limited access to education and opportunity that often result from chaotic social and economic conditions. By comparison, America's social, economic, and educational systems appear to be thriving. On the other hand, a number of other countries once considered technologically and educationally inferior to the United States are now outpacing us by producing greater numbers of well-prepared professionals in the sciences, information technology, engineering, and other high-value skill areas. Thanks to the evolution of the Internet and related technologies, those professionals now can put their skills to use anywhere in the world without having to leave their home countries.

The unequal attention of many Americans to these two phenomena has lulled them into a false sense of security, in that they fail to recognize that in some fundamental respects we are losing our global competitiveness.[1] The country cannot afford to fall into the illusion that our system of higher education can maintain its reputation without substantial new investments in public education, as well as the development and implementation of creative public policies that expand access to higher education.

National security cannot and should not be regarded as a function solely of our military might and reach of our diplomatic skills. Our national well-being is also a function of our ability to nurture effectively our children and young adults. We must close the wide gaps in school achievement and college attendance that exist between affluent children on the one hand and poor children and children of color on the other. And we must work simultaneously to eliminate racial, ethnic, and cultural isolation among students in postsecondary institutions.

The Next 25 Years and the Critical Role of Government in Ensuring Equal Access to Educational Opportunity

⌒

Over the next 25 years, members of racial and ethnic minority groups will become a larger and larger segment of the American population. By the middle of the 21st century, almost half of all Americans will be people of color; and no single racial or ethnic group will constitute a national majority. Moreover, Americans of color are disproportionately poorer than their white fellow citizens. But, historically, students from these communities generally have not been well served by our public education system. Unless our public schools, colleges, and universities change dramatically by midcentury, a disproportionate percentage of America's adults and children of color will be poor, undereducated, and unprepared for productive employment. Fewer adults will be able to contribute significantly to our tax base, and more will have to seek government assistance to meet basic health and social service needs. These conditions, should they continue unabated, will pose a grave threat to our domestic and global security.

When confronted with challenges to the country's economic and education status, the federal government traditionally has responded vigorously. After World War II, Congress enacted the Servicemen's Readjustment Act of 1944, better known as the GI Bill, the first of two major higher-education laws enacted in the course of the twentieth century. The second, the Higher Education Act (HEA), has been amended by Congress every five or six years since it was enacted originally in 1965. Both laws have channeled substantial financial assistance to public and private higher education, opening postsecondary education to many who otherwise would have been shut out.

The GI Bill provided an unprecedented level of federal support to the 16 million veterans of World War II. In addition to funding college education or vocational training for 7.8 million veterans, the bill provided subsidized home and business loans. Unfortunately, its benefits were not equitably allocated to African American or women veterans, although many were able to use the education support to attend segregated colleges or acquire job training that helped move them into a more secure economic position. At the height of its implementation in 1947, 49 percent of all college admissions were veterans.[2]

The government's motives in implementing this policy were not entirely altruistic. The battle to preserve and extend democracy during and after

World War II exposed a number of vulnerabilities in our system. States in the South and the District of Columbia maintained racially segregated schools and other public institutions as a matter of law, and our Cold War enemies often pointed to this fact as belying our commitment to democracy. Meanwhile, the Soviet Union was threatening to outpace us in science, math, and technology, demonstrating its capacity by launching *Sputnik,* the first satellite propelled into space. The *Sputnik* launch very quickly increased interest in American science and math education.

In 1958, federal support for higher education was further expanded by the passage of the National Defense Education Act, NDEA. The act enhanced research facilities and provided graduate fellowships and low-interest loans designed to inspire students to enter fields like science, mathematics, engineering, and foreign languages that were vital to our country's advancement. The NDEA not only created the foundation for our modern student financial aid system and laid the groundwork for HEA, it transformed the American higher-education landscape without federal meddling or impinging on the traditional bounds of academic freedom. Importantly, campuses all across America no longer were viewed as the exclusive preserves of the elite and the most well-connected citizens.

The Higher Education Act of 1965, a direct descendant of the NDEA, created the student grant and loan programs that still provide the bulk of all government financial aid for postsecondary students. This aid historically has been targeted to the neediest students and was intended to expand significantly access to higher education. In 2003–4, 72 percent of all dependent, low-income undergraduates were recipients of federal student aid, with grants averaging $3,700.

Through the GI Bill, NDEA, and HEA, the federal government has provided students—and, indirectly, postsecondary institutions—with necessary financial support. All three served the nation's critical policy objectives: returning veterans were able to convert their military experience into educational attainment and to contribute more effectively to civic life and the economy; critical technological and scientific research was funded and professionals were trained to carry on that work for the benefit of the nation as a whole; and access to higher education was greatly expanded for students who otherwise would have faced great difficulty in winning admission and paying tuition. In the process, America built the greatest system of higher education in the world.

Notably, the government achieved this result while respecting educators' freedom to set their own education policies. Governments can and should attach accountability provisions to their education aid programs, ensuring that the funded programs are effective. But, at the same time, students must be permitted to choose the school and program that best fits their interests and needs, and educators must be allowed to establish the mission and programmatic emphasis of their institutions.

Federal and state education policies, while reacting quickly to external national security threats, have not been as quick to respond to the equally important domestic threat posed by governmentally sanctioned racial segregation and discrimination in the public schools. After World War II and during the Cold War, Communist regimes around the world attempted to exploit that threat for their own purposes, arguing that racial segregation demonstrated that America failed to practice the democratic and egalitarian principles that it espoused.

However, early in the 1930s, a significant effort was initiated by civil rights advocacy organizations, notably the NAACP and its Legal Defense and Educational Fund, to pursue legal challenges to end school segregation and racial inequality in education. That effort culminated in the 1954 unanimous Supreme Court decision in *Brown v. Board of Education.* The legal foundation for the *Brown* decision was laid, for the most part, in cases brought against institutions of higher education. In these postsecondary school cases, the Supreme Court whittled away at the "separate but equal" doctrine asserted in 1896 by the infamous *Plessy v. Ferguson.* During the period leading up to *Brown,* the Court came to recognize the illegitimacy of racial segregation in public schools, as well as the long-term social, economic, and educational disabilities engendered by that segregation. Moreover, the disabling consequences were not limited to the black students who were educated in underresourced schools. In 1950, in *McLaurin v. University of Oklahoma,* a predecessor to *Brown,* the Court described the broader national consequences of racial segregation and, in so doing, foresaw our 21st-century predicament. The plaintiff in *McLaurin* was a young black man enrolled in Oklahoma's graduate school of education. He was forced to sit behind a barrier in the classrooms, the library, and the cafeteria, and he was shielded from his white fellow students.

In declaring this racial and physical isolation unconstitutional, Chief Justice Vinson, writing for the majority, declared:

> Our society grows increasingly complex, and our need for trained leaders increases correspondingly. [This] case represents . . . the epitome of that need, for he is attempting to obtain an advanced degree in education, to become, by definition, a leader and trainer of others. Those who will come under his guidance and influence must be directly affected by the education he receives. Their own education and development will necessarily suffer to the extent that his training is unequal to that of his classmates. State-imposed restrictions which produce such inequalities cannot be sustained.

A public policy that segregates by race denies all affected students the benefits of a racially diverse education outcome and, further, makes it all the more difficult for them to live and function effectively in a global community that is culturally, racially, and ethnically diverse.

Brown v. Board of Education declared the legally enforced segregation of students in public schools to be unconstitutional. That declaration did not end school segregation, nor did it remedy the many decades of unequal education received by generations of black Americans. The country has been struggling to right those wrongs, and steady progress has been made in many places. Nevertheless, inequities in education quality and resources continue. As the University of Michigan affirmative action cases have demonstrated, all too many students of color, who have excelled in under-funded, underequipped, and educationally inferior public schools, are at a disadvantage when competing against better-prepared white students for admission to selective postsecondary institutions. In addition, students of color generally do not have the advantage conferred by "legacy" status, be-cause their parents and close relatives were excluded from many of these same institutions by virtue of their race, ethnicity, or economic circumstances. The power of federal and state governments to expand access to education has been critical to the country's progress. However, this authority has been exercised incrementally, fitfully, and sometimes only reluctantly.

The slow pace of school desegregation helped prompt the enactment and enforcement of Title VI of the Civil Rights Act of 1964. Title VI prohibits the federal government from providing federal financial assistance to private or public schools, colleges, or universities that are racially segregated or illegally discriminate on the basis of race, color, or national origin. Eight years later, Congress similarly was moved to forbid the exclusion of women and girls from education programs and activities, by enacting Title IX of the Higher Education Amendments of 1972.

The executive branch of the federal government, charged as it is with the interpretation and administration of these important provisions, has, with limited exceptions, strongly enforced them. The effort to achieve compliance has been balanced between carrots and sticks. For example, the U.S. Department of Education traditionally has offered colleges and universities technical assistance to bring their programs into compliance, without needing to impose sanctions such as lawsuits or terminations of federal funding. Even more importantly, the federal government has used its authority to make the case for why it is in the national interest to end racial and ethnic isolation and promote affirmative action in colleges and universities.

Two examples may be instructive in this regard. In 1978, the U.S. Supreme Court in *Bakke v. Regents of the University of California at Davis* found against the University's race-conscious admissions program, by requiring that public institutions of higher education apply strict standards to evaluate and justify any use of race in their policies. The decision was seen by many in higher education as a death knell for efforts to improve racial and ethnic diversity, particularly in elite institutions and professional schools in areas such as medicine and law.

Recognizing the danger of increasing gender, racial, and ethnic segregation in higher education, the executive branch under President Carter undertook a painstaking analysis of the competing opinions in the case. It was determined that many federal programs that used affirmative action provisions to increase the number and percentage of minority students and women in the academy could be revised in a manner that might withstand a constitutional or Title VI challenge. This effort to fortify programs that expanded access and opportunity was undertaken in a manner that also ensured that nonminority students were not unduly burdened. It was motivated by the executive branch's belief in the national importance of diversity as a prerequisite to educational excellence for all students.

Our second example is from the early 1990s, when the first in a wave of lawsuits were filed challenging the constitutionality of the Carter-era affirmative action programs, which adhered to the principles outlined by Justice Powell in *Bakke*. These included scholarships for minority students, used not only by colleges and universities but also by education and civic organizations to foster diversity.

The legitimacy of one such affirmative action program was questioned in 1990 by a federal civil rights official. Michael Williams, the assistant secretary for civil rights in the U.S. Department of Education, wrote to the organizers of the Fiesta Bowl in Tempe, Arizona, when they proposed to offer a scholarship for minority students to the two universities competing in the bowl that year. Mr. Williams indicated that Title VI of the Civil Rights Act prohibited the awarding of financial aid or other benefits on the basis of race, color, or national origin. College officials and others believed this change represented the government's backtracking on its Carter-era guidance. The retrenchment left many institutions vulnerable to legal attack and appeared to call their eligibility for federal financial assistance into question. In 1994, however, the U.S. Department of Education issued policy guidance that mirrored in fundamental respects both the judgment of educators and the position later articulated by the U.S. Supreme Court in *Grutter*, which showed, albeit in the context of financial assistance, that a properly constructed and properly administered admissions program that takes race into consideration could withstand scrutiny under Title VI and under the Constitution.

The 1994 minority scholarship policy, like the later opinions in *Grutter* and *Gratz*, articulated the grounds on which an institution of higher education could pursue a race-conscious program without offending the Constitution or Title VI. At the same time, the government made clear that such policies must be subjected to rigorous examination, in order to ensure that race be used only to the extent necessary to achieve the compelling education goal of diversity.

Federal initiatives like the foregoing ought to be complemented by action at the state and local level to meet the multifaceted challenge of expanding access to, and graduation from, postsecondary institutions by poor students and students of color. Just as important as expanded access for individuals is the goal of having successive generations of students experiencing educational and social interactions across racial, ethnic, and cultural lines. State initiatives banning affirmative action in state-supported colleges and universities already have been enacted in California, Washington, and Michigan, and they are gaining momentum elsewhere. Public universities in these states, formerly buoyed by the Supreme Court's approval of race-conscious admissions programs in *Grutter*, now find their institutions losing ground in the struggle to achieve meaningful levels of diversity.

These three states have long recognized that affirmative action programs are only partial measures. The real, long-term solution lies in urgently needed but long-delayed improvements to our public elementary and secondary school systems, which enroll large numbers of poor students and students of color. The leadership of governors and state legislators is essential to guarantee poor students and students of color the quality public education that will permit them to compete with affluent white students graduating from private and well-resourced schools. Education policy successes at the state level are on the rise, as states adopt and implement rigorous state achievement and performance standards.

What often is needed is the sheer force of leadership. Such was the case in the state of South Carolina a few years ago. As one of us wrote at the time:

> Governors can focus the attention of the people on an issue, explain what it is, and then move the state toward an equitable solution. To do this effectively, they must take time to understand their roles and how they personally fit into the situation before deciding on a course of action. By setting the tone and coordinating their effort, they can crystallize the acceptance of a solution.... By using the governor's office as a catalyst for change, the governor's office was able to spark a grassroots reform effort ... that resulted not only in passage of nationally recognized education legislation but also a penny sales tax increase that many political experts predicted [would never be successful].[3]

This penny sales tax initiative was enacted in South Carolina in 1984 to support a $240 million effort to improve the public schools. To get it passed, the governor barnstormed the state and rounded up business and civic leaders. He hired a public relations firm to market the "penny-for-education" idea and set up a toll-free comment number. At the time, the state ranked forty-ninth out of fifty states in spending on education, and its SAT scores were among the nation's worst. With the support provided to schools by the penny tax, the state was able to improve SAT scores and move its rank in per-pupil spending up to forty-first. Even so, 23 years later, there remain large gaps in achievement between affluent white students in South Carolina and their poor African American and Latino counterparts.

The "Sheer Force of Leadership": Making Education a National Security Priority

∾

Any significant improvement of our public schools will require a coordinated and collegial relationship between the federal government and the states. Revisions to the current Elementary and Secondary Education Act, known as No Child Left Behind (NCLB), and a substantial increase in appropriations for its implementation may provide the vehicle for that movement. However, in light of the persistent inequities that are hallmarks of urban and rural schools, it is highly unrealistic to project that the achievement gap can be closed in twelve years, as the law currently requires. It even may be overly optimistic to suggest that the gap will be closed in 25 years, as proposed by Justice O'Connor in *Grutter*. Even with forceful leadership and a creative public policy approach at all levels of government based on the professional judgments of educators, our government still will be challenged to achieve and sustain the necessary education reforms. There is no more important challenge.

Among the reforms that ought to be incorporated into NCLB are provisions to improve teacher education. The law should create bold incentives for attracting academically outstanding high school students to the teaching profession. Special intensified outreach should be made to such students from high schools in poor and racially isolated communities. Many of them will be students of color and poor students, who will enhance diversity on the campuses that successfully recruit them. Colleges of education with improved teacher-training programs should receive incentives for prioritizing admission opportunities and scholarships for students who agree to become after graduation teachers for at least five years in poor urban and rural public schools. These incentives might include funding to pursue an advanced or professional degree at the end of the five-year term.

Provisions also should be included to ensure that public school teachers are held accountable for the academic performance and achievement of their students. This provision should be matched by policies that recognize teachers as the professionals they are. Their salaries should be commensurate with those paid to doctors, lawyers, and other essential professionals, with bonuses for those who consistently raise student achievement above expectations.

The inevitable question of how to pay for these improvements and incentives must be answered and the funding found. If Americans understand that these efforts are designed to secure the nation's future, much as our military and homeland security forces do, they surely will find the funds and make the necessary sacrifices. Among the sacrifices that ought to be considered are the tax cuts that have gone to the wealthiest Americans. These should be rescinded, with one-third of every recovered tax dollar used to support the aforementioned teacher education programs and incentive scholarships.

If the federal government, supported by state and local authorities, acts quickly enough, we may come close to achieving Justice O'Connor's ambition. Whether her statement is a deadline or a prediction, Justice O'Connor has set us an extraordinary, but not impossible, challenge. It is extraordinary because of the achievement gaps that exist and the traditionally slow pace of change in the public school system. It is extraordinary, too, in its suggestion that we may face a deadline in our use of race and ethnicity to improve diversity in institutions of higher education, even when that diversity serves a timeless and compelling education interest. It is achievable, however, if policymakers not only are willing to use the sheer force of their leadership, but exhibit the foresight to understand the considerable costs to our national security and global stature should we fail.

NOTES

1. T. Friedman, *The World Is Flat: A Brief History of the Twenty-first Century* (New York: Farrar, Straus and Giroux, 2005), 329–34.

2. www.gibill.va.gov/GI_Bill_Info/history.htm.

3. R. Riley, in *Education Governors for the 21st Century,* report by the James B. Hunt, Jr. Institute for Educational Leadership and Policy, commissioned by the Wallace Foundation, 2005, 10.

Racial Disparities and the
Next Twenty-five Years

The Continued Need for Affirmative Action

∾

Michael S. McPherson and Matthew A. Smith

At the end of her majority opinion in *Grutter v. Bollinger,* Justice O'Connor made the provocative statement that in 25 years affirmative action may no longer be necessary: "[I]t has been 25 years since Justice Powell first approved the use of race to further an interest in student body diversity in the context of public higher education. Since that time, the number of minority applicants with high grades and test scores has indeed increased. . . . We expect that 25 years from now, the use of racial preferences will no longer be necessary to further the interest approved today."

Although the decision shielded the narrow use of race in admissions from equal protection clause challenges for the time being, the reactions of affirmative action supporters to Justice O'Connor's statement have ranged from laudatory to deeply critical. The justice herself has on several occasions, including in this volume, offered her own interpretation of the statement. But Supreme Court justices, even more than other authors, lose control over the interpretation of their words once they are released to the world. Indeed, because the words of Supreme Court justices are enforced as law and are used to order our society, we have just as much at stake in them as the justices themselves. This is especially true in the case of affirmative action, which affects not just the quality of American higher education but also the prospect of a racially equitable society. With so much at stake, it is not surprising that Justice O'Connor's provocative statement should be interpreted variously. We believe that reviewing some of these interpretations is a useful heuristic for consideration of the significant empirical, legal, and moral issues regarding affirmative action.

We emphasize at the outset that our analysis rests on two ideas: first that the essential goal of affirmative action is substantive racial equality; and second that racial disparities in America are so broad and pernicious that such equality is highly unlikely in the next 25 years. By substantive equality, we mean that black Americans should not enjoy only formal equal access to the whole range of life options our society has to offer, which happens when there are no formal bars to success, but actual equality, which happens when Americans of all races have equal probabilities of gaining access to life options and of being successful in their life choices. So defined, substantive equality is a familiar and widely accepted norm. The second idea underlying our analysis, that we are so far away from substantive equality, is more controversial. We believe that Justice Ginsburg said it well in her dissent in *Gratz v. Bollinger* (the companion case to *Grutter* that found the Michigan undergraduate racial "points" system unconstitutional):

> [W]e are not far distant from an overtly discriminatory past, and the effects of centuries of law-sanctioned inequality remain painfully evident in our communities and schools. In the wake "of a system of racial caste only recently ended," . . . large disparities endure. Unemployment, poverty, and access to health care vary disproportionately by race. Neighborhoods and schools remain racially divided. African-American and Hispanic children are all too often educated in poverty-stricken and underperforming institutions. Adult African-Americans and Hispanics generally earn less than whites with equivalent levels of education. Equally credentialed job applicants receive different receptions depending on their race. Irrational prejudice is still encountered in real estate markets and consumer transactions. "Bias both conscious and unconscious, reflecting traditional and unexamined habits of thought, keeps up barriers that must come down if equal opportunity and nondiscrimination are ever genuinely to become this country's law and practice."

The injustices that began to be corrected with abolition and the Civil Rights Act still persist, albeit more subtly, in America. Eradication of these injustices is our goal, and affirmative action in higher education is essential to achieving that goal.

Indeed, a dearth of racial minorities on college campuses, particularly at elite research universities and liberal arts colleges, would be an especial setback in the pursuit of racial justice precisely because our system of higher education is so strongly linked to social mobility and status. Strong empirical research demonstrates the importance of a college degree in the labor market. For example, between 1980 and 2004, the median salary for males with a bachelor's degree grew from $46,300 to $50,700 while the median salary for those without a degree fell from $38,800 to $30,400. During these 24 years, the salary differential between the two groups grew from $7,500 to $20,300.[1] And even beyond the isolated economic effects of degree attainment, the importance of racial representation in higher education on the perception of race should not be underestimated: "If elite colleges and professional schools lack any significant number of minority students, they revive the dangerous symbolism of an entrenched, racially-defined underclass."[2] Affirmative action has long and correctly been seen as integral in the campaign to end racial disparities.

And while 25 years may sound like a long time in the context of government policymaking, it is a far shorter time in the contexts of demographic, life-cycle, and institutional change. This is particularly the case because learning itself is hierarchical: research in a host of social sciences has shown that educational disparities that manifest themselves in early grades (even before preschool) persist over long periods of time and may ultimately affect life prospects. The result is that if even one level of the educational ladder produces unequal outcomes between black and whites students, affirmative action in higher education might still be needed years down the line. As James Heckman puts it, "Early family environments are major predictors of cognitive and non-cognitive abilities. Research has documented the early (by ages 4 to 6) emergence and persistence of gaps in cognitive and non-cognitive skills."[3] So even if schools and other social institutions (particularly early-family interventions) are able to produce equal outcomes for black and white students, affirmative action in higher education will still be needed for those students who previously passed through the system. For example, if outcomes between black and white preschoolers were equalized in the year 2028, affirmative action in higher education may still be needed through the year 2040 to assist those students who graduated from preschool before 2028.

Justice O'Connor and Stewart J. Schwab's chapter in this volume argues persuasively that vast improvement in the earlier education of minority students is essential to bringing those students to the doors of colleges with preparation equal to that of white applicants. But we already know that thousands of students are beginning their educational careers in conditions of deep inequality, and we have little reason for confidence that improvements in later years of schooling—if they even happen—will have the power to overcome those early gaps. It is worries on this score that lead us to explore the interpretation of her "25 year statement" more closely.

The first issue we will consider is the statement's legal status: whether it should be taken as a dictum (that is, a personal pronouncement lacking legal force) or as having legal effect. Given the context of the remark, we believe it is best taken as the former, and clearly this is Justice O'Connor's view. In an interview to the *Chicago Tribune* the day after *Grutter* issued, she cast her remark in that light: "I hope it looks as though we don't need artificial help to fill our classrooms with highly qualified students at the graduate level. And if we do our job on educating people, we can reach that goal."[4]

Of course, whether future courts will actually treat the "25 years" phrase as a dictum or a statement of greater legal significance remains to be seen. Justice Thomas construed the remark as having legal import in his dissent, when he characterized the majority opinion as "preferring to grant a 25 year license to violate the Constitution"—a reading that treats O'Connor's comment as a binding sunset clause, rather than a personal statement.

In any case, its legal status will ultimately be determined by the courts. It is entirely plausible that the present, more conservative Supreme Court would overrule *Grutter* outright, without addressing the remark. Indeed in the most recent affirmative action case, *Parents Involved in Community Schools v. Seattle School District No. 1,* the Court took an implicit step in this direction when it refused to find the educational benefits of racial diversity, in the context of primary and secondary education, a compelling state interest. As Justice Breyer put it in his dissent: "In light of this Court's conclusions in *Grutter,* the 'compelling' nature of these interests in the context of primary and secondary public education follows here a fortiori." That a majority of the Court failed to recognize the import of *Grutter* strongly undermines it.

Alternatively, one could imagine that conservative appeals courts (or the Supreme Court itself) might end affirmative action in their jurisdictions in 2028 by invoking the statement in support of an argument that affirmative action has proven too ineffective to justify its costs. Or, conversely, a more liberal court could cite the statement and the continued need for affirmative action at that time as a reason to redouble the effort. There are a variety of ways that the courts could use the "25 year statement" to further or hinder affirmative action. This is one, but not the only, reason why the interpretation of the statement is worth considering.

So how is the statement best interpreted? While there are many possible interpretations, four are worth investigating explicitly: (1) an expression of hope; (2) a prediction or empirical forecast; (3) a goal and call to arms; or (4) a deadline providing an outer limit for affirmative action, "25 years or else." As detailed previously, Justice O'Connor has said she meant the statement as the first interpretation, an expression of hope. However, the statement also plays some predictive role: it was conjoined with the observation that racial disparities have diminished somewhat in the last 25 years; and unless it is to be taken as purely inspirational, there must be at least some plausibility to the claim that affirmative action will not be needed after the next 25 years.

As we have already indicated, we think it is unlikely that, even under favorable conditions, affirmative action won't be needed by 2028. This is not because we doubt the efficacy of affirmative action; it is just that policies to change educational results are inherently generational, and 25 years seen in that light is just too short a time. Predictions are fundamentally empirical: they are a forecast that x will be the case at time t. To be credible, then, they must be based on empirically reasonable premises about why x will be the case at *t*. The closest the majority opinion gets to this is its statement that since the *Bakke* decision, "the number of minority applicants with high grades and test scores has indeed increased." As many observers have noted, this remark fails to recognize that tremendous disparities still exist between the races, and that such disparities are only slowly diminishing, if at all. Consider Courtland Milloy's sardonic comments from his column in the *Washington Post:*

> The year is 2028. The last vestiges of nearly 400 years of slavery and apartheid in America have disappeared. When identically qualified blacks and whites try to buy a house, rent an apartment, or obtain a mortgage, the results are the same for both groups. Racism is dead. There are more black men in college than in prison. A quality public education is available to all—regardless of race, creed, color or income. No child has been left behind. All is well. This is the future implied in Monday's Supreme Court ruling . . . What a wonderful year 2028 would be.[5]

Of course, Milloy's incredulity is hardly dispositive. In an essay titled "Was Justice O'Connor Right? Race and Highly Selective College Admissions in 25 Years," economists Alan Krueger, Jesse Rothstein, and Sarah Turner extrapolate past trends to estimate the higher-education admittance rate for black students under a racially blind admissions standard in the year 2025.[6] While there is certainly no guarantee that past trends will continue, their work provides an excellent framework for evaluating the statement as a prediction.

Using SAT scores as a reasonable proxy for the likelihood of admission to highly and moderately selective private institutions as well as flagship public universities, Krueger, Rothstein, and Turner estimate the admission percentage of black students in the year 2025 based on the continued narrowing of both the income gap between black and white families (since students from higher-income families consistently have higher SAT scores) and the SAT gap between blacks and whites from families with similar incomes. Assuming that these trends do indeed continue—an optimistic assumption, given that the SAT gap between blacks and whites widened during the 1990s, rather than narrowed—they conclude that under a racially blind admissions policy black students would not be admitted to higher-education institutions in 2025 at the rates they are today: blacks presently make up approximately 17 percent of all admitted students, while the most optimistic predictions suggest that they would make up only about 12 percent in 2025. The authors' more realistic predictions set the number closer to 7 percent.

Where interpreting the statement as a prediction runs up against the slow rate at which racial disparities diminish, the third possible interpretation, the idea that the statement was intended to establish a goal, sits rather uneasily with the role of Supreme Court justices in our constitutional process, perhaps especially so for a generally conservative and federalist justice like O'Connor. The Court often emphasizes that its legitimacy depends on its acting as a legal, rather than political, institution. To quote just one of its statements on the subject, from *Planned Parenthood v. Casey:*

> The Court's power lies . . . in its legitimacy, a product of substance and perception that shows itself in the people's acceptance of the Judiciary as fit to determine what the Nation's law means, and to declare what it demands. . . . The Court must take care to speak and act in ways that allow people to accept its decisions on the terms the Court claims for them, as grounded truly in [legal] principle, not as compromises with social and political pressures having, as such, no bearing on the principled choices that the Court is obliged to make.

In short: judges interpret laws; they do not impose or advocate for policies. Indeed, they would be ill-equipped to do so, lacking both the moral legitimacy that comes from popular election—taken as expression of the general will—and the means to enforce or promote their judgments. To quote *Casey* again: "the Court cannot buy support for its decisions by spending money, and, except to a minor degree, it cannot independently coerce obedience to its decrees."

Taking the "25 years" statement as a call to arms would be to suggest that the Court was calling for increased attention to racial equality, and by extension the policies that promote it. To exhort an end is to exhort the means necessary to that end. Given the role the Court plays, such a political call is rarely made overt.[7] The question before the Court was merely whether the Michigan Law School's consideration of race in its admissions was acceptable under the equal protection clause. To take the 25-year statement as an overt goal would thus be inconsistent with the Court's role. Naturally this point applies only to the statement within the context of *Grutter* qua legal case. In her own writings since the decision, Justice O'Connor has made clear her own commitment to "willing the means" to bring about the changes that would render affirmative action obsolete.

The fourth possible interpretation is the "deadline" option, which suggests that Court was establishing the year 2028 as a definitive end point for affirmative action: if affirmative action succeeds by that time, then racial categorization will be obsolete; if it does not succeed by then, it will have conclusively failed and its continuance would be unjustified. This is the interpretation favored by Justice Thomas, in his argument that the statement is a 25-year grant to violate the Constitution, and by some other commentators.

The problem with this interpretation, from the standpoint of supporters of affirmative action, is that it requires an analysis of why affirmative action would be constitutionally proper now, but will have become improper 25 years hence. Put another way, to take the 25 years as a deadline, we must fill in the "or else" in the phrase "25 years or else," and we must do so in constitutional terms. The justices cannot simply decide that they are sick of a program, or that it has had its chance.

Of course, there are obvious reasons why the Court would be unwilling to grant a permanent constitutional sanction to racially based affirmative action programs: "racial classifications," as the Court held in *Grutter,* "however compelling their goals, are potentially so dangerous that they may be employed no more broadly than the interest demands. Enshrining a permanent justification for racial preferences would offend . . . [the] fundamental[s of the] equal protection principle." Ideally, race should never be a basis for discrimination. The evil against which the majority opinion was trying to protect, then, is the permanent entrenchment of racial discrimination, which would itself become insidious were it allowed to extend beyond the narrow interest by which it is currently justified in affirmative action. But in order to regard the statement in *Grutter* as a deadline, something must inexorably change over the course of 25 years (otherwise it wouldn't have the certitude required to be a "deadline"), such that race-conscious programs will no longer be constitutionally acceptable.

In principle, it could be argued that the interest that justifies the program now—namely, educational diversity (which was the exclusive justification in *Grutter*)—will cease to justify the program by 2028. Or, in other words, racial diversity and the creation of a diverse student body and global leadership will no longer be compelling state interests. But this answer is clearly inadequate. There is no reason to think that racial diversity will in fact matter any less in 25 years, and even opponents of affirmative action would be hard pressed to describe how racial diversity could be important now but not later. Absent such a reason, to admit that racial diversity matters now, as *Grutter* does, is also to concede that it will matter 25 years from now.

Alternatively, a deadline could be motivated by the expectation that affirmative action policies will have been decisively proven either effective or ineffective. If colleges and universities have completely succeeded in advancing the goal of racial equality, then presumably affirmative action will no longer be needed. Conversely, if such policies have had little or no effect, then one could argue that they can no longer be justified as a constitutionally acceptable means to a socially desirable end. Both of these possibilities are untenable, however, because they require a significant departure from the narrow holding in *Grutter,* which specifically eschews racial equality

and the amelioration of injustice as constitutionally acceptable justifications for affirmative action. Both possibilities, moreover, would need to
meet thresholds that are by no means guaranteed in the manner required
by a preset deadline: to declare affirmative action a success would require
that racial disparities will have been eradicated; similarly, to declare
affirmative action a failure would require more than just slow progress, it
would require a stark and unmistakable lack of progress.

Last in this list of reasons for a "deadline" interpretation, it could be that
racial diversity will be achievable through the use of proxies for race (e.g.,
community and socioeconomic characteristics), instead of race itself. But
proxies have a poor track record. As Justice O'Connor and Stewart J.
Schwab explain in their contribution to this volume, states have had limited
success in achieving racial diversity through indirect methods. For example, California's flagship public universities, UCLA and Berkeley, have seen
both a percentage and absolute decline in the number of black students
since the state's 1995 ban on outright consideration of race. The underlying
problem is that the numbers work against the effectiveness of proxies: for
example, while black people are much more likely to be poor than are white
people, the majority of poor people are white. Proxies are at best a crude replacement for race-conscious standards; the most effective way to achieve
racial diversity is by considering race, not resorting to indirect measures.

Thus, none of the circumstances necessary to support a deadline interpretation is convincing. However, it is worth noting a somewhat more limited variation on the deadline idea: the statement could be a signal to future
courts to review the decision and the constitutional calculus (a simple, non-
binding recommendation), rather than a deadline for the success of
affirmative action. This is consistent with the textual warnings that race-
conscious programs should have a termination point, so that they will not
become entrenched; but it does not require an explanation for why the constitutional calculus would have changed by 2028. The result could be welcome pressure to make progress quickly—making it more a "hope" than a
"deadline"—but there remains the risk that for an unsympathetic court, "25
years" could help lay the groundwork for pulling the plug.

Justice O'Connor's dictum has had a remarkable effect in focusing attention on affirmative action. Whatever the challenges of interpretation, we
are finally interested in the question: can the discussion of the next 25 years
inspire progress toward the overarching goal of ending racial disparities?
We are struck by the fact that a number of commentators—who may in
some cases have been dismayed by a statement that could be read as a slow-
motion death sentence for affirmative action—have found ways to draw inspiration from it.

For example, *Boston Globe* columnist Derrick Z. Jackson characterized the statement as a forecast or prediction based on "supreme optimism," and ended with an exhortation to make it a reality:

> Actually, it is not a bad thing in the abstract for O'Connor to proclaim we can kill affirmative action 25 years from now. The only thing that can bring her words to life is an assault on white bonus points just as deadly as the one just concluded on black and brown bonus points. Anything less will ensure that our system of racial caste will endure.[8]

Glenn Loury, another contributor to this volume, takes the statement as goal, coincidentally also in the *Boston Globe:*

> Although the legal significance of such a speculation is uncertain, the fact that this statement appears in the opinion at all should serve as a clear warning to supporters of affirmative action. We must not rest on our laurels. This recent victory may well be our last, and its benefits may be short-lived. Unless over the course of the next generation the dramatic underrepresentation of blacks and Hispanics among top academic performers is remedied, their access to selective institutions of higher education may one day be severely curtailed. It is therefore essential that we begin to make significant and sustained progress on closing the racial test-score gap . . . our [black and Hispanic] families and communities must accept our share of the responsibility to address this situation. We have essentially one generation to get this done. There's not a moment to waste.[9]

The most overt example of the statement-as-deadline is an actual deadline. In 2005, the Ford Foundation offered to match the funds of regional groups working to end the need for affirmative action. The program was called the Fulfilling the Dream Fund Challenge, and summoned activists to help bring about substantive equality within 25 years—a number chosen based on the statement in *Grutter.* As the prospectus put it:

> At the core of the Fulfilling the Dream Fund is a simple proposition: If the U.S. fully intended to eliminate racial and gender disparities in education and employment within the next 25 years, what would be needed now? The Fund's goal is therefore to help redefine how the U.S. thinks about, talks about, and achieves racial and gender inclusion, and how to re-align these aspirations with the country's core democratic values.

One result of this was the Minnesota Dream Fund, a coalition of foundations from Minnesota that accepted Ford's challenge and is devoted to eradicating the need for affirmative action by 2030 (25 years from its inception). Its activities include coalition building among existing minority organizations, legal advocacy, research on existing disparities and methods of amelioration, and communication initiatives designed to promote affirmative action and minority education.

We think, however, that a general word of caution is in order when interpreting the statement as a deadline. There is certainly no question that the work the Ford Foundation has stimulated is timely and admirable; the more effort in the pursuit of racial justice, the better. That said, interpreting the statement as a deadline has the potential of eventually undercutting the very efforts it seeks to promote. After all it is possible, depending on the fluctuating composition of the Supreme Court, that affirmative action may be around in 25 years. Taking the statement as a deadline—if it actually is not—risks labeling as "failure" what may really be limited but real success, and thereby providing an unintended warrant for those who may wish to use such a deadline to press for an end to affirmative action in 25 years. And it is a regrettable truth, at least in our view, that even with determined efforts—at least efforts on a scale that our society appears at all prepared to contemplate—we face a struggle that is going to have to last a lot longer than 25 years. The idea is to make as much progress as possible in 25 years without irreversibly committing to a goal that may be unreachable in that time frame.

All of which makes it worth reemphasizing that we go well beyond the majority opinion in *Grutter,* and perhaps even most commentators in this volume, by insisting on affirmative action's role in ending systemic and continuing racial injustice. The majority opinion in *Grutter* rests on the very narrow claim that the need for racial heterogeneity, unreachable under a racially blind system, furthers a compelling state interest in educational diversity. We agree that diversity of many kinds is educationally valuable, and that racial diversity is of special importance, even a compelling state interest. But we go further in tying the importance of racial diversity to the deep and continuing racial inequalities in our society.

The best argument for singling out race as a component of educational diversity is the fact that race was made to matter, and still matters in America. It is no coincidence that the categories currently understood as contributing to educational diversity (race, gender, ethnicity, and sexual orientation) all point toward groups that have been socially disadvantaged. Racial inequalities in particular persist to a staggering degree. A focus on educational diversity derives much of its force from these inequalities, and the social aim of eliminating race-based inequalities thus seems to us a necessary and the strongest justification for affirmative action.

Much work remains to be done. The greatest fraud perpetrated by opponents of affirmative action is their claim that the struggle for racial justice ended with the Civil Rights Act. The struggle that began with abolition continues today in the fight against the overwhelming inequities that still correspond to race. The principal virtue of the "25 year" statement, however it was intended, is that it provides perhaps the best opportunity since the Civil Rights Act to renew our commitment to eradicating racial disparities. Interpreting it as a prediction, an overt call to arms, or a deadline are all fine as long as they stimulate our collective endeavor for racial justice.

NOTES

1. U.S. Department of Education, National Center for Education Statistics, *The Condition of Education 2007*, 157 (salary statistics are in 2004 dollars).

2. K. M. Sullivan, "The Future of Affirmative Action: After Affirmative Action," *Ohio State Law Journal* 1998:1039.

3. J. J. Heckman, "Skill Formation and the Economics of Investing in Disadvantaged Children," *Science* 312, no. 5782 (June 30, 2006).

4. J. C. Greenburg, "O'Connor Voices Hope for Day Affirmative Action Not Needed," *Chicago Tribune*, June 25, 2003.

5. C. Milloy, "A Ruling Not Entirely of This Reality," *Washington Post*, June 25, 2003, B1.

6. A. B. Krueger, J. Rothstein, and S. Turner, "Was Justice O'Connor Right? Race and Highly Selective College Admissions in 25 Years," in *College Access: Opportunity or Privilege?* ed. M. S. McPherson and M. O. Schapiro (New York: College Board, 2006).

7. Of course the line between personal asides, procedural realities, and political exhortation is a delicate matter. The justices' comments in decisions, particularly dissents, can be ambiguous. For example in *Lawrence v. Texas*, 539 U.S. 558, 605 (2003), Justice Thomas emphasized that he would vote to repeal Texas's sodomy law "were [he] a member of the Texas Legislature." Similarly, in her strongly worded dissent in *Ledbetter v. Goodyear Tire Co.* (2007), Justice Ginsburg argued that the Court's interpretation of Title VII is inconsistent with the statute's broad remedial purposes, noting, "Once again, the ball is in Congress' court. As in 1991, the Legislature may act to correct this Court's parsimonious reading" (at 71). However, if our analysis of the Court's role is correct, such observation will tend not to be couched in the exhortative tone implied by a "call to arms." That is the case with both the preceding quotations: Justice Thomas brought up the silliness of sodomy laws to illustrate that merits are independent of constitutionality (not to exhort the Texas legislature in one direction or another); and Justice Ginsburg's quote is primarily procedural, emphasizing what Congress "may" do, rather than what it should do.

8. D. Z. Jackson, "What About the Bonus Points for Whites?" *Boston Globe*, June 25, 2003, A19.

9. G. C. Loury, "Affirmed . . . for Now the Supreme Court's Decision Made Affirmative Action Resoundingly Legal. Now Comes the Hard Part—Making It Unnecessary," *Boston Globe*, June 29, 2003, D1.

Beyond Equity Committees and Statistics

⌒

Elaine Salo

South African institutes of higher education have begun to make racial, cultural, and gender diversity an acceptable goal of good management. More than a decade has passed since the 1998 Employment Equity Act ushered in a host of affirmative action policies, and the debates over their relevance have, it seems, become less fraught with time. Ten more years hence, we hope, most South African universities will reflect such great diversity that sensitivity to the issue, especially in relation to student enrollments and faculty employment, will be commonplace. However, we can only achieve such a "naturalization" of diversity if we move beyond the current focus on statistics to actually transform the processes of institutional culture.

By now, most managers in South African higher education seem to accept that diversity is a prerequisite to the production of knowledge. The postapartheid era's formal protections of citizens' rights to equality have, together with national education legislation, set out the basis for policies that ensure increased access to higher education for previously marginalized groups, including black women.

Institutions such as the University of Cape Town have created employment equity and transformation committees at virtually every level of management. They assist in the design of student enrollment and employment equity plans; submit these plans, along with implementation strategies, to the South African Department of Education; and assess their success in achieving enrollment and employment targets for defined groups, including blacks, women, and the disabled. Their plans, replete with table after table of data describing individuals' exact disciplinary, professional, and economic status within the university, have become a regular feature on the agendas of faculty boards and other management bodies.

Yet it appears that the goals of increased student and staff diversity are more elusive than was originally appreciated. In particular, universities have found it difficult to retain students and staff from the communities in question.[1] The shortfall suggests that in our haste to implement equity policies, educators have focused too exclusively on getting the numbers right without due consideration for the importance of cultural transformation. Such transformation is necessary if one wants not only to attract but also to retain diverse constituents. Cultural transformation means greater sensitivity to the manner in which everyday social interactions reproduce gender and racial biases. We know a little about the quotidian processes that facilitate long-term staff retention, but not enough. We need to more effectively identify the factors that obstruct development of a hospitable environment for underrepresented groups, such as black (specifically African) women. This chapter will examine the experience at the University of Cape Town in order to illustrate the specific challenges that institutions have to overcome in "naturalizing" diversity.

I use the term *diversity* rather than *affirmative action* because in the new South Africa "affirmative action" is too often taken to mean that one is employed on the grounds of one's (nonwhite) race and (nonmale) gender, rather than on the basis of one's qualifications. In short, for many South Africans, affirmative action has come to connote inferiority.

In a March 4, 2007, column in the *Sunday Times,* the prominent South African business reporter David Bullard argued that affirmative action prevented the appointment of skilled employees. Many qualified black employees perceived affirmative action as an insult, Bullard claimed, because it implicitly suggested that these individuals were unable to compete as equals against white applicants. Bullard's analysis rests on two erroneous assumptions: First, he was working within an extremely narrow conception of merit; and second, he contrasted race and merit, implicitly suggesting that white male candidates were only hired on merit and other candidates on the basis of affirmative action. In Bullard's version of events black, disabled, and women candidates were only hired as affirmative action appointees; a process that, he implied, could not be meritorious. Such a rigged analysis leads to the apparently natural conclusion that affirmative action automatically leads to mediocrity.

This line of argument, of which Bullard is only one exponent, fails to question the processes that create homogeneous workplaces. It does not place a central value on workplace diversity, or on employees' ability to negotiate cultural, racial, and gender boundaries—a higher-order social skill that fosters collaboration. By contrast, our globalizing era will ultimately marginalize homogenous workplaces.

A History of Recognition for Diversity

ᴄ◡

The University of Cape Town (UCT) has a long history of resisting racial discrimination in education. Even during the heyday of apartheid, when it was officially considered to be a white-only university, UCT still managed to admit a minority of black students, albeit under the constraints of the despised permit system. In certain arenas, faculty members pushed the envelope in their efforts to provide support for black students: UCT economists Francis Wilson and Dudley Horner, for example, provided mentoring for black researchers through their Southern African Labour Development Research Unit. The unit offered junior scholars like myself the rare opportunity to work with senior specialists, producing high-quality research that oftentimes informed the activism of trade unions and antiapartheid groups.

Cape Town was also the first institution in the country to appoint a black woman vice-chancellor, Dr. Mamphela Ramphele, in the early 1990s. The institution's formal symbols have changed in subsequent years: graduation ceremonies have integrated (albeit unevenly) African forms of affirmation and celebration alongside European-style ceremonies. The institution's mission and logo locate it within the African context, and attempt to recognize its linguistic and cultural diversity. Works of art, commemorative plaques, and building names reflect the university's contradictory colonial, English, and African origins, and bear the names of prominent South African men and women of all races. All of these symbolic transformations are emblematic of deeper shifts in racial and gender relations.

Cape Town's numerous equity and transformation policies also generally recognize the importance of diversity in terms of race and, more recently, gender and ability. At the time of writing 60 percent of the University's senior management is black at this erstwhile white-only institution. But this equates to only three out of a total of five senior managers. At the next level down the org chart, at least 50 percent of faculty deans are women. But the apparent transformation effects fade away as one digs down deeper into the ranks of academic and support staff, with the few African women professional academics mostly clustered in the lower tiers.

Statistics as Explanation and Statistics as Description

∿

These statistics seem to suggest that Cape Town has achieved significant diversity among its senior echelons. But examination of the university's Employment Equity Plan reveals a failure to recruit staff members from the targeted groups. Statistics such as these often reflect what the writer and scholar Pumla Gqola calls a facade of apparent, rather than actual transformation.[2] Gqola insists that actual transformation demands a critical analysis of the processes behind the numbers, and the active cultivation of an environment that supports members of underrepresented groups.

Statistics on the race and gender of UCT academic staff indicate that, as of April 2006, 71 percent of the staff was white, and 29 percent was black. This can be compared to April 2004, when 80 percent was white and 20 percent was black.

While the institution was able to increase the racial diversity of its academic staff between 2004 and 2006, it has not been able to do the same for gender diversity. Forty-five percent of academic staff were women in 2006, compared to 55 percent men: a ratio that has remained more or less constant since April 2004.[3] Looking further into the data, gender diversification has benefited the employment and advancement of white women more than black women, because the former group already possessed the educational skills needed to take advantage of new equity provisions. Statistics indicate that black women constitute 8 percent of the total number of permanent academic staff at UCT, while African women constitute a mere 2 percent.[4]

To ensure that diversity is prioritized, UCT's Employment Equity Plan suggests that transformation committees be established at all levels of governance to gather statistics and monitor changes in staff and student profiles. This empirical focus, while important, tends to freeze dynamic processes into mere measures. Diversity itself is reduced to a tally of particular bodies at a particular moment, and the work of deepening it is limited to the formation of bureaucratic structures. Instead, we need to give more careful consideration to the reasons for the relative absence of particular groups from higher education; and to the processes needed to ensure the equal mobility of these groups up through the full hierarchy of academic employment.

The extent of black—and specifically African—women's representation in the academy is an important signifier of deepening transformation in higher education more generally, and in South African society at large. Consequently, if we wish to ensure equity in higher education, then we need to mitigate the gendered, racial, and socioeconomic biases that impede these women's access to and retention by institutions of higher education.

Where Are the African Women Students and Academic Staff?

∽

According to data compiled by researcher Louise Morley and her colleagues, the nationwide enrollment of women students in South Africa reached a healthy 53 percent by 2003.[5] At UCT, women constituted 51.2 percent of all undergraduate students, 45.4 percent of postgraduate students, and 50.4 percent of all students by 2004. Morley and her coauthors do not track these women by race, but they do note that the enrollment figures reflect regional, racial, and socioeconomic disparities. One can safely assume that the data included only a small number of relatively privileged black women students. Morley and her colleagues also note that women were for the most part concentrated in the social sciences and humanities, with only a very small number in engineering and commerce.

Among academic staff, the picture is even more troubling. The number of permanent African women academics remains disappointingly small, currently only 2 percent of the total faculty.[6] Even if we count all permanent black women academic staff, including African, Coloured, and Indian women, they still only constitute 8 percent of the total. Including temporary academic staff improves the picture slightly, raising African women's representation to a total of 5 percent of all academic staff. But, again, closer examination indicates that most black women work in the lower ranks of the faculty, as senior lecturers, lecturers, and tutors, where they bear the bulk of the responsibility for teaching and student consultations, leaving little time for the writing, research, and publication that would be necessary to advance their careers.

Widening African Women Students' Access and Ensuring Retention
∾

Numerous studies have identified the structural constraints impeding African women's access to higher education: national cuts in educational investment; girls' low enrollment rates in primary and secondary education; racial discrimination (e.g., apartheid); violence and civil war; and the lack of a supportive familial and community environment, combined with normative notions of femininity.[7] Universities cannot dismantle these structural constraints singlehandedly. But in a country where the state has enacted policies to correct past injustices and undo unequal power relations, institutions like UCT have to help minimize these constraints or even eliminate them altogether.

Louise Morley and her colleagues emphasize the need to cultivate links between schools and universities, so that girls in secondary school are encouraged to qualify and apply for admission.[8] Cape Town maintains a network of relationships with schools in black communities. That program needs to be monitored and evaluated, especially with regards to its effect on young black women. This may require involving women academics in the project, as well as accomplished alumni who can serve as guest speakers at the partner schools. As role models, these women not only embody the possibilities of tertiary education but also challenge norms that limit young women's ambitions to motherhood and domesticity.

The link program could also incorporate an auxiliary research component for graduate students in education and the social sciences, allowing UCT to track the efficacy of their efforts. A program that is attentive to gender and directs students not only to fields of study but also to possible funding sources will ensure a pool of potential applicants, especially from targeted groups such as African women. We also need better monitoring and evaluation of the university's internal initiatives. If the University is trying to increase admissions of African women students from impoverished backgrounds, for example, to what extent is this effort coordinated with the availability of scholarships and other relevant forms of financial support?

Undergraduate and graduate students have different types of financial need, and we have to do more to understand how women students pay for their tertiary education. Some programs, such as the Mandela Rhodes Scholarships, take account of race and gender in their support for postgraduate students. But more could be done to support black women, for example by hiring them as funded junior researchers on large research projects. Academics that do make such hires should be rewarded for it through a points system that figures into tenure or funding decisions. Furthermore, any such project should incorporate mentoring-through-participation as a central element of its operations.

Nor should we limit our definition of support to questions of financial aid. Mentoring opportunities, which are widely recognized as a central factor in women's professional success, should be extended to African women students, as well.[9] UCT's Extended Degree Programme (EDP), to cite one case, offers intensive faculty mentoring to applicants who otherwise fall just short of the standard requirements for admission. These students—many of whom hail from disadvantaged communities—are admitted on the condition that they complete their degrees over four years instead of three, and work closely with their mentors. In my experience the EDP students tend to succeed when intensively mentored. If so, then the program should be expanded to meet the needs of other target groups, including African women.

Gendering the Disciplines and the Curriculum

ᴥ

African women students, like their other women peers, tend to be concentrated in traditionally feminized disciplines within the humanities and the social sciences. Yet, even there, many academics are unwilling to regard gender as a central analytical concept or a legitimate subject of academic inquiry. Philosophers of science such as Donna Haraway and anthropologists like Emily Martin have argued convincingly that scientific knowledge is often produced through a research lens that is colored by gendered assumptions. Their research suggests that gender works through subtle processes that render bias invisible, especially to the field's practitioners. Such a bias alienates women from the scientific disciplines and reinforces their masculine identity.

Approximately 26 percent of the students registered in UCT's Faculty of Built Environment and Engineering in 2003 were women. Once again, data on their racial breakdown were unavailable, but we can safely assume that black and specifically African women would constitute a minority within a minority.

It is known that women often have to break with notions of gender-appropriate fields and careers just to apply to study any of the sciences.[10] Yet admission is only the first of many hurdles. Research suggests that the particularly masculine culture in the sciences creates a hostile environment that actively alienates those women who do choose to pursue a scientific education.[11] This culture tends to be reinforced by the overrepresentation of men as students, teachers, and researchers, as well as by masculine imagery and language used in the curricula. The fact that few of the male scientists tend to be African reinforces the gender bias with a sense of racial exclusivity, as well. Women in the sciences often have to face questions about their gender identity and sexual orientation, including crude stereotypes that "only butch women and lesbians do science." Ironically, characteristics such as self-discipline, diligence, and perseverance that are associated with academic achievement are considered to be feminine, so that academic underachievement is, paradoxically, considered to be a positive masculine trait. Such stereotypes undermine both women's and men's academic performance.

There are at least three measures that can help overcome such biases. First, the architects of degree programs should require all incoming students to take interdisciplinary courses in women's and gender studies or sociology, in order to introduce them to critical thinking about gender, race, and ability. Postgraduate courses in the feminist philosophy of science, too, can help students think critically about gender stereotypes and influence.

Second, universities should encourage postgraduate research projects that acknowledge the gendered nature of science, and that support African women as scientific researchers and knowledge producers. The research on African women in science is sparse, and African women's writing and publication in this field is insignificant, making the need for their representation all the more urgent. South Africa's National Research Foundation actively supports such projects, but we need to think more creatively about specific projects that affirm women scientists' gender and racial identities.

Third, and finally, women's organizations in the sciences should also step up their efforts to counter masculinist bias. At UCT, organizations such as Women in Science and Engineering (WISE) provide a supportive environment for women students. But women, and especially black women, need to be more fully supported in their efforts to form mentoring networks. These women should be regarded not as victims but as agents in the unmaking of gender bias in their field. An increased presence of professional women academics would also help fuel a transformation in the predominantly masculine culture. The need for a greater gender and racial balance among teachers and researchers cannot be overemphasized. The research is replete with case studies that illustrate how minority representation in the ranks of particular fields can positively influence the ambitions of younger generations.

Creating an Organizational Culture That Is Sensitive to Gendered and Racial Differences

❧

Organizational culture is expressed in the quotidian aspects of university life, and is often an expression of wider power relations. These everyday practices relay the minutiae of power through subtle acts of discrimination.[12] Women students and staff alike are subjected to such biases as a result of trivial decisions about how they dress, what spaces they occupy at which times of day, when and from whom they request assistance, and even which bathrooms they use. Black and African women's experiences are further nuanced by race, so that they constantly have to fight the perception that they are out of place in the academy. An African woman academic can only courteously reply that she is not an undergraduate student or a member of the cleaning staff so many times before the experience begins to erode her confidence or will to continue. In the absence of efforts to counter these biases, individual women face a lonely struggle as they constantly have to legitimize their authority to their students and colleagues. Further research is needed into the corrosive effects of such battles on women's health.

Gender-based violence is now openly acknowledged as a particularly insidious feature of institutional culture. At UCT this problem is addressed through the Discrimination and Harassment Office and the formulation of a sexual harassment policy. At the time of writing, Professor Jane Bennett, a senior staff member in the Women and Gender Studies department and a specialist in gender-based violence, is leading a committee in formulating the institution's sexual harassment policy. Her committee's work signals an institutional awareness that gender-based violence impedes the academic advancement of women of all races, and also of members of the lesbian, gay, bisexual, and transgendered and intersexed communities. UCT needs to ensure that these efforts are well supported, so that well-intentioned policies do not founder upon the sands of neglect.

Even the experience of sexual harassment is differently tinged by race.

For example, historian Yvette Abrahams has described how her own experience as a junior academic teaching the historiography of gender and colonialism at UCT ran into a novel form of sexual harassment.[13] Abrahams was charged with teaching course materials about Sarah Baartman, famously known as the African Venus, that contained explicit images of the Baartman's genitalia. Abrahams argued that while she found these images an outrage to herself and the other black women in her class, nonblack participants and the course convenor failed to understand their objections. She cites this experience as evidence of the manner in which gender and racial regimes of power are naturalized in the academy, even in the new millennium, so that even when black women have a physical presence in the academy, this agency is negated by their continued stereotypical representation—in this case, as a mute, sexually exotic object.

African women are found in the most junior academic positions across UCT's academic departments. Yet their very experiences on the academic periphery provide them with valuable insights about how marginal individuals experience academic curricula and pedagogical styles. Unfortunately, these women are often overlooked as collaborators who could help advocate for diversity and tolerance in the classroom—often because they are considered too inexperienced or junior to provide valuable advice.[14] Senior academic staff often do not consult junior staff members, such as postgraduate tutors, about their teaching practices and curriculum content. Yet these junior tutors and assistant lecturers are often the first individuals whom students encountered in the classroom. In her work, Pumla Gqola reflects upon her own contradictory position as a UCT tutor, teaching course themes that she had played no part in selecting, and yet having to convince undergraduates of their relevance. Suitable development programs are needed to break through this impasse. Staff training, mentoring, and empowerment play a particularly important role in supporting junior staff members' professional careers

UCT offers an array of programs and initiatives that support the academic staff's research. These include a research fund targeted for academics at various levels of professional development; regular seminars on the use of information and communications technology; and an excellent system for disseminating research information to colleagues. Senior academic staff are also expected to consult with their junior departmental colleagues about professional plans and progress. These systems need to be monitored and expanded to include mentoring focused on writing and submitting fundable proposals; formulating and managing research budgets; setting up national and international research networks; and familiarizing junior researchers with the publication process.

Balancing Work and Personal Lives

ᑑ

The masculine culture of the academy renders invisible women's multiple roles as professionals, spouses or partners, mothers, and daughters, and thus, too, the numerous competing priorities that demand our time and energy. Solitary activities such as writing and research often effectively isolate professional women. When one adds family responsibilities to this heady mix, then it is clear that few women have time to socialize after working hours, when they could advise each other about effective strategies for juggling family and professional responsibilities. In many cases women academics are forced to forgo travel to international conferences, or applications for fellowships abroad. Yet, as Morley and her colleagues have argued, these international networks are a key feature of a successful career in the academy.[15]

One does find a few institutional supports at UCT, such as the childcare center, that assist professional women in managing their competing roles and responsibilities. The center was established only after a long struggle by the student women's movement of the 1980s. Other women cope by "choosing" to remain single or childless. But why should women have to forgo the emotional, psychological, and, even economic benefits that partnerships and offspring may bring? Women follow a different academic career track, marked by gendered changes in the life cycle; and this must be acknowledged.

Women, especially black women, cannot leave their professional futures to fate while they wait for employers to create institutional support structures. If we do, then we only acquiesce in our own marginalization. As I write this, some of us have begun assembling the building blocks of a professional network for black academic women. Such efforts help us assert our agency and work within existing institutions to support our professional development.

Conclusion

ᑑ

It is time that we institutionalize diversity's benefits. In order to ensure that individuals of all backgrounds can work productively in an environment of gendered, racial, cultural, and linguistic diversity, we need to move beyond a focus on equity committees and statistical profiles. Instead, we need to begin three simultaneous processes that will help us entrench diversity as both ideology and practice.

First, we must recognize the broad structural constraints that limit African women's access to higher education, and initiate or reinforce efforts to mitigate these forces. Second, we need to foster an atmosphere of sensitivity to the gendered and racial needs of African women, as one of our most underrepresented groups. In focusing on this group's needs, we ensure a broader sensitivity to inherent racial and gender biases, creating an enabling environment for all black women and men. The campaign to create such an enabling environment should encompass the following efforts:

- We should ensure that equity policies and practices articulate with each other at all levels of the institution.
- Senior management should strengthen and support disciplinary efforts to negate the corrosive effects of sexual harassment and racism.
- Universities must retain and strengthen their links with high schools in disadvantaged areas, to encourage the recruitment of black, specifically African, women.
- Universities should also retain and expand funding sources that support African women.
- Existing academic support programs should incorporate African women as peer mentors.
- The disciplines should be gendered throughout the curriculum. This could include making women and gender studies courses part of every discipline, including the sciences and engineering.
- Senior academic supervisors should encourage research projects that affirm women—specifically African women—as knowledge producers. Similarly, they should support research that critically examines classroom pedagogies and promotes more inclusive approaches that support participation by minority students.
- Academic staff should open the curriculum-planning process to include the opinions, advice, and active participation of junior teaching staff, many of whom are black women.
- Staff development programs should incorporate career-counseling methods that are sensitive to an individual's gender and race. This could include supporting organized efforts by staff and students to overcome their own marginalization.

All of these processes would help foster institutional sensitivity to gendered and racial diversity. If such efforts are sustained over time, we may eventually reach a point where diversity of both gender and race has become normal.

NOTES

1. M. Hall, address to the Humanities Faculty, University of Cape Town, 2006.

2. P. D. Gqola, "Language and Power, Languages of Power: A Black Woman's Journey through Three South African Universities," in *Hear Our Voices: Race, Gender, and the Status of Black Women in the Academy,* ed. R. Mabokela and Z. Magubane (Pretoria: University of South Africa Press, 2004).

3. University of Cape Town, Employment Equity Plan 1, April 2007–March 31, 2010.

4. N. Mohammed, "Imbokodo: The Rock," *The Monday Paper,* August 7, 2006.

5. L. Morley et al., "Gender Equity in Higher Education: An Examination of Sustainable Interventions in Selected Commonwealth Universities," unpublished end-of-project report to the Department for International Development, 2005.

6. Mohammed, "Imbokodo."

7. On disinvestment, see T. Manuh, "Higher Education: Conditions of Scholars and the Future of Development in Africa," *CODESRIA Bulletin* 3 and 4 (2002): 42–48; D. Mkude and B. Cooksey, "Tanzania," in *African Higher Education: An International Reference Handbook,* ed. D. Tefera and P. Althbach (Bloomington: Indiana University Press, 2003). On discrimination, see F. Wilson and M. Ramphele, *Uprooting Poverty: The South African Challenge* (Cape Town: David Philip, 1989). On violence, see D. Mazurana, "Reintegrating Girls from Fighting Forces in Africa," *Insights Education* 3 (2004): 6. On normative femininity, see K. Adeyemi and N. Akpotu, "Gender Analysis of Student Enrollment in Nigerian Universities," *Higher Education: The International Journal of Higher Education and Educational Planning* 48, no. 3 (2004): 361–78; and J. Kwesiga, *Women's Access to Higher Education in Africa: Uganda's Experience* (Kampala: Fountain Series in Gender Studies, 2002).

8. Morley, "Gender Equity in Higher Education."

9. M. Eliason et al., "Mentoring Programmes: A Shortcut for Women's Academic Careers?" *Higher Education in Europe* 25, no. 2 (2000): 173–79.

10. E. Byrne, *Women and Science: The Snark Syndrome* (London: Falmer Press, 1993); Morley et al., "Gender Equity."

11. See, for example, D. Bebbington, "Women in Science, Engineering and Technology: A Review of the Issues," *Higher Education Quarterly* 56, no. 4 (2002): 360–75; J. Philips and K. Hausebeck, "Just beneath the Surface: Rereading Geology, Rescripting the Knowledge-Power Nexus," *Women's Studies Quarterly,* special issue, 28, nos. 1 and 2 (2000).

12. Gqola, "Language and Power"; Mabokela and Magubane, *Hear Our Voices;* Morley et al., "Gender Equity."

13. Y. Abrahams, "'Ambiguity' Is My Middle Name: A Research Diary," in Mabokela and Magubane, *Hear Our Voices.*

14. Gqola, "Language and Power."

15. Morley et al., "Gender Equity."

Achieving Critical Mass

The Future of Gender and Higher Education in the United States

∽

Abigail J. Stewart and Danielle LaVaque-Manty

One of the questions feminist scholars are routinely asked by deans and colleagues in other fields is, "How long will we need a women's studies program?" (or psychology of women, or gender history, etc.). The assumption is that the field in question is only needed on a temporary basis, to redress a problem in the way knowledge was once produced. Perhaps, one should ask whether all policies designed to promote gender equality in U.S. universities should eventually become obsolete: after all, equality is the goal; policies are only a means to that end.

Many institutions around the country are considering ways to make themselves more hospitable to women faculty by improving their policies on dual-career hiring, family leave, and the tenure clock. At the same time, admissions policies and funding for graduate and undergraduate students are being reevaluated, both by those who believe that affirmative action has already accomplished enough—or even too much—and those who believe it has hardly even begun to have the impact it should. This pair of trends raises the question: how will we know when the policies we are striving to keep or create have made themselves redundant? Perhaps they'll become so irrelevant in the coming years that we'll forget about them, until they reemerge as amusing anachronisms, like Michigan's 1897 law against using obscene language in the presence of women and children, which was repealed in 2002 after it was used to prosecute a man who uttered several profanities in front of a woman and her two children after falling out of his canoe.[1] On the other hand, it might be helpful to know what criteria we should use to judge whether educational equality has been established, and when equality-promoting policies have become moot. What would need to change in the next 25 years for gender equity to be achieved?

Space constraints lead us to focus on the area within higher education that we know best, namely, academic science and engineering. The sciences, in contrast to many social science and humanities disciplines, have resisted the idea that the race or gender of faculty or students should be taken into account in admissions, hiring, or interactions in classrooms, faculty meetings, and labs. Let us regard the academic woman scientist, then—at whatever stage in her career—as our canary in the coal mine. When she can breathe easily, then we can all relax and declare the environment healthy for everyone.

Let us consider the further possibility that our woman scientist is African American. As the legal scholar Kimberlé Crenshaw has noted, because African American women exist as both women *and* people of color in a world that demands a single dominant identity, their interests and experiences are frequently marginalized within both groups.[2] We hope that using an African American woman scientist in our examples will help us keep both race and gender in view. What would need to have happened, 25 years from now, to make the university as hospitable for our scientist as it is for her white male colleagues?

One thing we know is that she would have to have colleagues or classmates who look like her. Research shows that all of us employ gender and racial "schemas"—stereotypes about what men and women are like, and about what members of different ethnic and racial groups are like—that lead us to overvalue the job performance of men and undervalue that of women, and to overvalue the performance of whites and undervalue the performance of racial and ethnic minorities.[3] For example, a study conducted by psychologist Rhea Steinpreis and her colleagues found that both male and female psychology faculty were significantly more likely to recommend hiring "Brian Miller" than "Karen Miller" for faculty positions in psychology, although "Brian" and "Karen" had identical CVs, with the sole difference being the candidate's name at the top of the page.[4] The fewer women or minorities there are in a hiring pool, in a classroom or on a faculty, the more gender and racial schemas are relied upon, and the greater the extent of the resulting evaluation bias.[5] In addition, Thompson and Sekaquaptewa have found that solo status—that is, being the only member of one's social category within an otherwise homogeneous group—has a negative effect on the performance of members of disadvantaged groups.[6] Being the only man in a pool otherwise composed of women has no effect on a man's test results; and being the only white woman in a group otherwise composed of women of color does not affect a white woman's performance; but being the only woman in a group otherwise composed of men or the only woman of color in a group otherwise composed of white women causes the solo from the disadvantaged group to underperform. Psychologist Claude Steele has argued that results like these are the result of "stereotype threat," the sense that negative stereotypes are relevant to success in such situations.[7]

Evaluation bias and solo status lead women and minorities to "leak" out of science and engineering, whether because of few opportunities, poor performance, undervaluation, or because of frustration and dissatisfaction. The best remedy for evaluation bias is an increase in the number of women and minorities present in relevant settings.[8] When women constitute approximately a third (or more) of workplaces, they are more satisfied and accepted, perhaps because a critical mass has been reached. At this point, the salience of gender or race is minimized (although not absent), and the proportion of women in the pool is more likely to remain stable, instead of continuing to drop.

It is not as easy to establish a critical mass of women or men of color in science and engineering settings as it is to do so with white women. Many more white women than people of color earn graduate and undergraduate degrees in these fields.[9] And focusing on our African American woman scientist leads us to ask another question—what would count as critical mass for her? To what extent would the presence of white women alleviate the evaluation bias she confronts? To what extent would the presence of African American men help? And what about women from other racial and ethnic backgrounds? To what extent are they enough like her to count?

A qualitative study conducted by the University of Michigan's NSF ADVANCE project during the summer of 2006 asked 26 science and engineering faculty of color what role they thought their race or ethnicity had played in their lives at Michigan, whether they thought other people there found their race or ethnicity to be important, and, if so, how.[10] Asian American women were more likely than women from other backgrounds to say that they believed people paid more attention to their gender than their race. African American faculty, both men and women, were most likely to say that others found their race to be salient, and Native American and Latino/a faculty suggested that their racial-ethnic identity was both a positive and negative factor in their relationships with others. There was a wide variety of responses within each racial-ethnic group, but these modest trends suggest that race is not salient in the same ways for all groups. Faculty from all four groups mentioned that they perceived a tendency by white faculty to pigeonhole them, but the pigeonholes into which they felt they were expected to fit were not identical.

In response to a question about what kinds of actions might be more or less feasible for faculty of color than for white faculty, some participants responded in terms of race-ethnicity, and some also responded in terms of gender. However, the most common responses to these questions focused on faculty members' sense of being highly visible representatives of their groups. For example, one Asian woman indicated that "you cannot have an excuse if you're a woman; you don't want anyone to cut you slack." An African American woman indicated that you "don't want to publicize any failures, because it's always 'well, you know, if she were a different color.'"

Speaking for many, one faculty member said, "I'm mindful that everything I do is viewed not as an individual but as a representative." In contrast, as one respondent noted, "White males can get away with a lot more. Because they are almost ubiquitous, they are almost anonymous."[11] In their work on solo status, Thompson and Sekaquaptewa found that the differing effect of solo status on high- and low-status groups can be attributed in significant part to the members of the lower-status group feeling burdened by this expectation that they represent their group.[12]

The question of what demographic balance would be required to alleviate this sense of constant visibility and its accompanying disadvantages remains open. However, it is clear that being the only member of an underrepresented group is extremely disadvantageous. This is true for students, as well as faculty, and should be taken into account in a wide range of educational settings. In her 1997 book, *Re-engineering Female Friendly Science*, Sue Rosser points out that the possibility of achieving a critical mass of women or underrepresented minorities can easily be influenced either positively or negatively by instructional choices that might seem unimportant at first glance, like how to allocate students to groups when asking them to do group work. In a class of 20 students, in which four are women, where should the women be placed when the class breaks into four groups of five? It might seem egalitarian to put one woman in each group, so that there is no group that consists only of men, but in fact such an approach would leave each woman isolated and maximize each group's tendency toward evaluation bias and each woman's risk of underperforming. But neither is it ideal to put all of the women together and draw attention to the existence of a "special" group within the class. The best solution might be to pair the women, putting two each into two groups. This would avoid isolating any of the women students or singling them out as a minority within the class. But what if only one of the women students is African American? As Rosser notes, "While assigning an African American woman to a group whose other members consist only of white men clearly constitutes isolation, questions arise about whether the African American woman is still isolated when another woman (not African American) or an African American male is assigned to the group along with the white males."[13]

The problems of critical mass and evaluation bias can be self-perpetuating. How can critical mass be achieved in the face of evaluation bias and a leaky pipeline? And how can evaluation bias and pipeline leaks be prevented in the absence of critical mass? Which is the chicken, and which the egg? But some programs have in fact been successful, not only at keeping women and underrepresented minority students in the science and engineering pipeline, but also at bringing more students in. At Carnegie Mellon, for example, attention to trouble spots in the curriculum and gender stereotypes in the climate, along with attempts to reduce the social isolation of female students through networking dinners and a Big Sister / Little Sister program, increased the percentage of women among incoming computer science majors from seven in 1995, to 42 in 2000.[14] Similarly, the creation of Minority Engineering Programs (MEPs) has greatly increased the retention of underrepresented minority engineering students at 18 universities in California (and subsequently at other institutions as well). The MEP model is based on three elements that enable students to work collaboratively: the clustering of students in course sections, a freshman orientation, and a student study center.[15] The idea behind clustering is not that some sections will be minority-only—remember Rosser's concerns about how to distribute women among groups—but that each cluster section will have a significant number of minority students. The orientation and study center elements further contribute to the acquisition of academic survival skills and to crucial community-building among minority students.

In a study of women in physics and astronomy published in 2005, Rachel Ivie and Kim Ray found that women most often exit the physics pipeline at the transition point between high school and college: women as a percentage of physics students dropped from 47 percent in high school in 1997, to 23 percent of bachelor's degrees in physics four years later.[16] The University of Michigan has long maintained two introductory sequences in physics, one a calculus-based version that typically begins the path toward a physics degree, and the other an algebra-based version that is regarded as less appropriate for physics majors or scientists of any type. More than half of the students in the algebra-based sequence but less than a quarter of the students in the calculus-based sequence are women. Thus, even those women who do take physics at the university level often follow a path that leads them away from physics degrees, starting from the very beginning of their college careers. In response, the UM physics department has created a third introductory sequence, Physics for the Life Sciences, which is calculus-based but likely to appeal to women, many of whom plan to major in life science fields. This sequence is still in its experimental stage, being taught for the first time during the 2006–7 academic year, but already more than half of the students in the first cohort are women.

It remains to be seen how many of these women will choose to pursue physics or other science degrees; but creating a curriculum more appealing to women has worked at Carnegie Mellon, where researchers have noted how a curriculum that emphasizes the real-world applications and impact of technology is more engaging for some female students than one that focuses on technology for its own sake.[17] In addition to creating an introductory course that focuses on the breadth of the discipline and the range of uses of computer technology (instead of simply cultivating programming skills), Carnegie Mellon offers an advanced course that integrates all students into a single software development team, encouraging cooperative learning and applied understanding, along with other courses that use interdisciplinary teams and skills to accomplish projects for real clients. This kind of curriculum change is perhaps not something that can be required—such policies are likely to conflict with the tenets of academic freedom—but it may be cultivated through incentives and the dissemination of research findings about efforts that have succeeded in retaining women and underrepresented minorities.

At the faculty level, a proactive approach to recruitment can help build a critical mass of women and underrepresented minority faculty. For example, faculty hiring committees can be educated about the nature of evaluation bias, encouraged to design job descriptions in a way that invites applications from members of underrepresented groups who are more easily found in some academic fields than in others, required to stop relying only on familiar networks comprising primarily white men, and required to submit written evaluations of candidates brought to campus for interviews rather than relying on holistic, subjective impressions.[18]

In one of a series of papers on the topic "Making Excellence Inclusive" published by the American Association of Colleges and Universities in 2005, Damon Williams, Joseph Berger, and Shederick McClendon suggest that, rather than worrying that excellence and inclusion are mutually exclusive ideals, we should understand that "diversity is a key component of a comprehensive strategy for achieving institutional excellence—which includes, but is not limited to, the academic excellence of all students in attendance and concerted efforts to educate all students to succeed in a diverse society and equip them with sophisticated intercultural skills."[19] The onus here is on the institution to serve all constituents equally, rather than on women and members of underrepresented minorities to conform to norms that have been established by a long history in which white male students and faculty were the primary if not the only group of interest. By this light, when the academic progress of white women and members of underrepresented minorities is slowed by evaluation bias and by underperformance resulting from solo status and a feeling of being excessively visible and scrutinized, it is the university's responsibility to change that situation.

It is our hope that, 25 years from now, "inclusive" excellence will be an obsolete concept, because academic excellence will by definition be inclusive—the modifier will have become redundant. We'll know that this has been achieved when studies like those summarized by Valian and conducted by Thompson and Sekaquaptewa show that evaluation bias no longer exists, when our African American woman scientist and her peers (because she will have peers) report that their work-life experiences are not systematically worse than those of their white male colleagues, and when the alignment between gender schemas and fields of study seems quaint to our children, who wonder where we got such old-fashioned ideas.

NOTES

1. American Civil Liberties Union, "Cussing Canoeist Conviction Reversed in Michigan," http://www.aclu.org/freespeech/gen/10917prs20020401.html (2002).

2. K. Crenshaw, "Mapping the Margins: Intersectionality, Identity Politics, and Violence against Women of Color," *Stanford Law Review* 43, no. 6 (1991): 1241–99.

3. V. Valian, *Why So Slow? The Advancement of Women* (Cambridge: MIT Press, 1999); B. F. Reskin, D. B. McBrier, and J. A. Kmec, "The Determinants and Consequences of Workplace Sex and Race Composition," *Annual Review of Sociology* 25 (1999): 335–61.

4. R. E. Steinpreis, K. A. Anders, and D. Ritzke, "The Impact of Gender on the Review of the Curricula Vitae of Job Applicants and Tenure Candidates: A National Empirical Study," *Sex Roles* 41 (1999): 509–28.

5. J. Yoder, "2001 Division 35 Presidential Address. Context Matters: Understanding Tokenism Processes and Their Impact on Women's Work," *Psychology of Women Quarterly* 26 (2002): 1–8.

6. M. Thompson and D. Sekaquaptewa, "When Being Different Is Detrimental: Solo Status and the Performance of Women and Racial Minorities," *Analyses of Social Issues and Public Policy* 2, no. 1 (2002): 183–203.

7. C. M. Steele, "A Threat in the Air: How Stereotypes Shape Intellectual Identity and Performance," *American Psychologist* 52 (1997): 613–29.

8. P. R. Sackett, C. L. Z. Du Bois, and A. W. Noe, "Tokenism in Performance Evaluation: The Effects of Work Group Representation on Male-Female and White-Black Differences in Performance Ratings," *Journal of Applied Psychology* 76 (1991): 263–67.

9. National Science Foundation Division of Science Resources Statistics, *Women, Minorities, and Persons with Disabilities in Science and Engineering: 2004*, NSF 04-317 (Arlington, VA: NSF, 2004).

10. A. J. Stewart, D. LaVaque-Manty, and D. Rios, *Experiencing Michigan: Accounts by Faculty from Underrepresented Minorities,* accessed at http://www.umich.edu/~adv proj/ncid/NCIDqualstudyreport_final.pdf.

11. Ibid., 7.

12. Thompson and Sekaquaptewa, "When Being Different Is Detrimental," 198.

13. S. V. Rosser, *Re-engineering Female Friendly Science* (New York: Teacher's College Press, 1997).

14. J. Margolis and A. Fisher, *Unlocking the Clubhouse: Women in Computing* (Cambridge: MIT Press, 2002).

15. R. B. Landis, *Retention by Design: Achieving Excellence in Minority Engineering Education* (Los Angeles: UCLA, 2005).

16. R. Ivie and K. N. Ray, *Women in Physics and Astronomy, 2005* (College Park, MD: American Institute of Physics, 2005).

17. Margolis and Fisher, *Unlocking the Clubhouse,* 131.

18. A. J. Stewart, D. LaVaque-Manty, and J. E. Malley, "Recruiting Female Faculty Members in Science and Engineering: Preliminary Evaluation of One Intervention Model," *Journal of Women and Minorities in Science and Engineering* 10 (2004): 361–75;

D. G. Smith, "How to Diversify the Faculty," *Academe* 86, no. 5 (2000): 48–52; D. G. Smith, C. S. Turner, N. Osei-Kofi, and S. Richards, "Interrupting the Usual: Successful Strategies for Hiring Diverse Faculty," *Journal of Higher Education* 75, no. 2 (2004): 133–60; C. S. V. Turner, *Diversifying the Faculty: A Guidebook for Search Committees* (Washington, DC: American Association of Colleges and Universities, 2002).

19. D. A. Williams, J. B. Berger, and S. A. McClendon, *Toward a Model of Inclusive Excellence and Change in Postsecondary Institutions* (Washington, DC: American Association of Colleges and Universities, 2005).

Democracy and the Choosing of Elites

Glenn C. Loury

Racial affirmative action is at a crossroads. For over 30 years, its critics and supporters have been competing for the moral high ground via lawsuits and ballot initiatives, in the state and federal legislatures, and before varied courts of public opinion. Supporters were encouraged recently by a pair of landmark Supreme Court decisions (*Gratz* and *Grutter*) declaring in no uncertain terms that the U.S. Constitution's Fourteenth Amendment—which guarantees the equal protection of the laws to all persons—does not require public colleges and universities to be "color-blind" in their admissions policies. Justice Sandra Day O'Connor's words could not have been more definitive: "The Court endorses [the] view that student body diversity is a compelling state interest that can justify using race in university admissions."

Nevertheless, the future of affirmative action in the United States is extremely uncertain. In reaching its qualified endorsement of racial affirmative action, the Court relied heavily on the advice of business, academic, and military leaders whose friend-of-the-court briefs asserted the importance of racial diversity in their respective domains. Yet it is clear that the Court remains troubled by the use of racially discriminatory methods to attain the compelling public goal of racial diversity. Looking to the future, Justice O' Connor declared: "Race-conscious admission policies must be limited in time and the court expects that 25 years from now, the use of racial preferences will no longer be needed to further the interest approved today." The Court's affirmation of racial preferences notwithstanding, it is likely that heated debate over affirmative action policies will continue for some time.

The stakes for American higher education could not be greater. University administrators, public and private, are virtually unanimous in their view that blacks and Hispanics need to be present in meaningful numbers among the ranks of those being inducted by these institutions into the upper ranks of American society. Elite education is the primary site in American life where access to influence and power is rationed. For this reason, the significance of *Gratz* and *Grutter* reaches beyond the ivory tower. Evidently, if blacks and Hispanics are to achieve anything approaching equality of influence and standing in this hierarchical society, they must gain access to its meritocratic institutions.

For this reason, the spring selection rituals by which fortunate young people are designated for admission to prestigious colleges and universities are vitally important political acts. These rituals are publicly visible, high-stakes civic exercises, and their perceived fairness contributes importantly to the legitimacy of our social order. Supporters of affirmative action recognize that the presence of more than a token number of blacks and Hispanics at selective colleges and universities is necessary to ensure both the perception and the reality of fairness. In other words, the racial diversity of a society's selective colleges and universities demonstrates the genuinely democratic character of the processes by which that society constructs its elite classes.

So, the debate over racial affirmative action in higher education is really a dispute about the meaning of racial justice. At stake in this argument is the determination of what it means for us to deal fairly with one another in this country today, given our unlovely racial past. Through their practice of affirmative action, elite educational institutions are publicly endorsing the view that, precisely because of the way race has distorted American history, the aggressive pursuit of racial diversity is essential for creating a just society today, and this will continue to be the case for the foreseeable future.

Comparing the United States and South Africa

～

Of course, the United States is not the only nation where affirmative action-like policies engender controversy. Neither is higher education the only venue where policies of this kind are employed. Whenever productive or developmental opportunities are rationed in a population, the question of who is selected for those opportunities takes on great importance. When choosing which employees to hire, candidates to slate, or firms to patronize, governments and businesses often confront intense public demands for more diversity in the ranks of the chosen. As a result, regulations intended to achieve this end—under the rubric of "affirmative action," or "positive discrimination," or, less neutrally, "reverse discrimination"—have been adopted in societies throughout the world.

Consider a few examples. In nations with sharp sectarian divisions— Lebanon, Indonesia, Pakistan, Iraq—political stability can hinge on maintaining ethnic balance in the military ranks, or on distributing coveted political offices so that no single group enjoys disproportionate influence. Amid rioting and civil unrest, France has been struggling to design policies that ensure greater diversity in various elite venues. Elsewhere in Europe, political parties have mandated that female candidates be adequately represented on their electoral lists. After widespread ethnic rioting erupted in

1969, Malaysia adopted its so-called New Economic Policy, creating quotas and preferences for ethnic Malays in government contracting, employment, and education. In India, "scheduled castes and tribes" enjoy preferred access to university seats and government jobs by constitutional mandate, though amid fierce controversy. In postapartheid South Africa "Black Empowerment" policies have been enacted in the public and private sectors to ensure that wealth is distributed more equitably in society. Though these programs vary in their details, all are a form of affirmative action. The comparative study of affirmative action policies—in the United States and South Africa, for instance, as exemplified in this volume—promises to be tremendously fruitful.

This chapter discusses conceptual issues raised by the practice of affirmative action in these two countries. In so doing, I have three goals in mind: (1) to suggest what I hope will be a useful definition of the problem; (2) to propose an analytical framework for the study of some key issues raised by affirmative action policies; and (3) to show how this framework can be applied to some important practical questions that have arisen in both societies.

A Universal Definition of the Problem

∿

I suggest that we think about affirmative action as *a policy intended to achieve the democratic construction of elites within a social context of diverse identities.* There are three key elements of this definition: democracy, hierarchy, and identity. It is very important, I believe, to be explicit about the fact that this policy entails selecting the members of elite cadres. It is an unavoidable reality that those venues where affirmative action policies are most needed (and most controversial) will also be the places in society that are the most exclusive. These are the settings where people of varying abilities and aptitudes compete for a chance to move to the front of the pack, and where not everyone can be presumed to be equally qualified to exploit the opportunity. Inevitably, therefore, a rationing problem lies behind every exercise of affirmative action. An economist cannot help but think about affirmative action as an instance of the more general problem of efficiently allocating scarce resources.

But my proposed definition is not just a manifestation of disciplinary bias. Rather, it appears to be an objectively correct way to think about the problem. We are deciding who is to be admitted to a course of study; who will be offered a job; who will win a government contract. We have social objectives that we hope to advance (efficiency, diversity, fairness, institutional legitimacy), and a number of alternative ways to pursue those objectives. Rationality would seem to require that our decisions should be guided by careful assessment of those alternatives.

To talk about affirmative action is inevitably to talk about elitism. The democratic impulse that one encounters in so much affirmative action advocacy exists in profound tension with the fundamental fact of hierarchy. Studying an advanced, technical curriculum in the university presupposes the acquisition of certain skills that not everyone possesses. The organization chart of a large corporation is never perfectly flat. Rather, it is pyramidal, with the higher ranks characterized by fewer positions and more responsibilities. Again, not every aspirant will be capable of making the most of a promotion up the organizational ladder.

A failure to recognize this inherent tension between democracy and hierarchy can lead to confusion. For example, a person may say, "Aha! The way to engender more diversity in our educational institutions is to do away with selective admissions, and replace it with an open-door policy." Yet, in order to pursue such a nonselective policy, it is typically the case that one must sacrifice maintenance of high academic standards.

Understanding that affirmative action inevitably entails a conflict of objectives enables us to recognize the necessity of trade-offs. One historically important way in which liberal societies have dealt with the contradiction between elitism and democracy is through the principle of "careers open to talents." The notion is that individuals should have an equal opportunity to show themselves sufficiently talented to warrant a scarce and coveted position. Rather than assigning such positions on the basis of nepotism, or favoritism, or the influences of family and wealth, the matter should be decided according to the abilities and talents of the contending parties. That is the ideal. This view acknowledges that there is going to be inequality at the end of the day, and it justifies that inequality by reference to underlying disparities in the talents and aptitudes of those competing for higher positions in society.

Elitism and hierarchy are built into the very structure of our modern societies. The complex, hierarchical, multifaceted institutions and organizations that generate the benefits of modern life draw on the specialized talents of those who work within them—talents that must be developed over long decades of disciplined self-application. Even avowedly egalitarian political movements cannot amount to much without leadership. As a result, those who would set the agenda of such a movement immediately encounter the problems of inequality. Someone must be in charge, and, for the sake of the movement, one wants the most gifted leaders in those top positions; someone must be the public spokesperson for the organization and, again, one wants the best public speakers, and so on.

Unfortunately, one often encounters a kind of blind egalitarianism among affirmative action advocates that denies this reality. Our problem—to achieve the democratic construction of elites in a social context of diverse identities—is actually a lot harder than it may appear. Determined to be democrats, we must nevertheless also be elitists, if we are to be effective. What is more, it is no longer possible to make all careers open to talents once you accumulate a history in which race and ethnic identity have been important determinants of access to power. After slavery, Jim Crow segregation and racism more generally, we cannot say that American careers have been open to talents. In South Africa it is similarly obvious that, as a historical matter, careers have not been fully open to the talents of the most gifted individuals. This history has had detrimental effects on the human development of those who were treated unfairly. This debilitating historical legacy heightens the conflict between the imperatives of democracy, on the one hand, and the inevitability of hierarchy in modern social life, on the other.

A Framework for Analysis

~

In both the United States and South Africa, affirmative action policies, more often than not, aim to benefit "disadvantaged" social groups. They entail the presumption that those preferred are unable to compete on an equal basis, because of a preexisting (if not innate) social handicap. But the fact of historically unequal development creates a situation in which greater diversity cannot be achieved without lowering standards, distorting human-capital investment decisions, or both. Given that the supply of opportunity is limited, and not all elements of the population have been equally free to acquire useful skills by some elements of the population, diversity can be a costly commodity. The relevant problem then becomes understanding how these costs should be conceptualized, and how they can be minimized.

One principle of economics that can be enormously useful to our thinking about this problem is the idea of *efficiency:* a policy is desirable to the extent that no alternative policy can achieve as many valued goals while incurring fewer undesired consequences. There are four points worth emphasizing in any discussion of efficiency in this context: First, one must be clear about one's objectives. Second, one must know which alternative policies are feasible. Third, once clarity is achieved about goals and available alternatives, then one has to pay attention to the facts, which are hard to get and difficult to interpret. Finally, one must understand the difference between color blindness or race blindness on the one hand, and indifference to racial disparities on the other.

So, what goals are we pursuing in our institutions of higher education?

What are the alternatives to conventional affirmative action that are available in our pursuit of those goals? What questions of fact are most critical for evaluating the benefits and costs associated with these alternatives? And, how should we think about the distinction between color blindness and indifference?

1. The pursuit of affirmative action can have several goals. Diversity is a particularly common aim in educational settings. Institutional legitimacy, as mentioned earlier, is another.

Ultimately, social hierarchy must be justified if it is to be a stable arrangement. People are exercising influence over others; they are enjoying prerogatives; they are differentially sharing in the fruits of social cooperation. That has to be made to seem appropriate, or else those on the short end of the arrangement are likely to object. Moreover, when social inequality takes the form of racial hierarchy, and when this occurs in a setting of gross historical racial injustice, the need for such legitimacy becomes all the greater. The notion of merit, of careers freely open to the most talented, is in my view too thin a philosophical reed upon which to rest such a project of justification. I am not saying here that merit is irrelevant. I simply hold that it is not the only relevant factor.

Let me give an example: graduates of Boston's elementary public schools attend a variety of high schools throughout the city. Some of these schools are better than others. Some so-called exam schools are much sought-after, admitting students based on their performance on a standardized exam. The famous Boston Latin Academy is one such public institution. Now, one way to conceive of the objective being pursued in this admissions process is that the institution simply wants to reward the city's smartest kids by giving them a private-school education at taxpayer's expense—a system into which all students in the city have the same chance (via an outstanding exam performance) for admission. But there can be many other ways of conceiving the institution's objectives. For instance, the goal might be to find students to whom the greatest value would be added by attending such an elite institution. Or it might be to ensure that students at each feeder school who excel relative to their peers there are given a chance to achieve even greater heights, despite the fact that in absolute terms they may have performed less well than lower-ranked students at another school.

My point here is not to take sides in a contest over which objective is the correct one. I merely want to convey the idea that such disputes over objectives can be deep and interesting arguments. It is far from self-evident which would be the objectively "best" institutional goal in any absolute sense.

Consider another example. The public university must go to the state legislature for funds. Representatives in the legislature have a complex set of responsibilities, and their objectives need not coincide with those of the faculty, students, or alumni of that university. It is not at all clear how much weight these democratically elected representatives should give to their stewardship of public funds, versus the rather more elitist concerns of those who teach and do research in a state's flagship university. Indeed, establishing the objectives that a public university should pursue in a democracy is an extraordinarily complex problem. Simply to declare that the goal must be to admit absolutely the "smartest" students without considering the alternatives carefully is, in my opinion, to engage in a callow bit of moral reasoning.

The legitimacy of institutional conduct is one objective to which racial diversity can contribute powerfully—just ask the generals, admirals, and academy commandants of the U.S. military who submitted briefs in the *Grutter* and *Gratz* cases on behalf of the University of Michigan's position. That is precisely how they argued for the view that the Supreme Court ultimately affirmed—that racial diversity is a compelling public objective, the pursuit of which could constitutionally warrant the use of racial preferences. They realize that, given the very minority-heavy bottom end of their military hierarchies, it is crucially important to cultivate racially diverse leadership cadres, in order to preserve good order and discipline within the ranks.

2. Thinking about efficiency in the practice of affirmative action also requires us to be clear about alternatives. Given our goals, what exactly are the alternatives by which we might achieve them? In the short run, conventional affirmative action—by which I mean naked racial preference—is clearly the most efficient way to achieve any given degree of racial representation. The argument for this conclusion is not rocket science. It simply involves observing that if, absent any kind of affirmative action, all applicants above some performance threshold would have been admitted, and if more racial diversity is desired, then the most efficient way to gain more diversity is to ration out those in the nonpreferred group (say, whites) who are closest to but above the line, and to ration in those in the preferred group (say, blacks) who are closest to but below the line. This is just common sense; with a limited number of seats and a goal to enhance racial diversity, the best way to achieve it is to exclude the least promising whites from those who would otherwise have been admitted, and to admit the most promising blacks from those who would otherwise have been rejected. Doing so, of course, would result in a racial preference (because some whites would be rejected who have performed at a higher level than have some blacks who would be accepted). So, if the efficient increase of racial diversity was the

only concern, then a naked racial preference would be the best policy to achieve that goal.

3. Here is another economist's point: Affirmative action is not an all-or-nothing proposition. What matters most when assessing the efficiency of affirmative action policies is the size of effects at the margin. In layman's terms, the key question is "How much?" We need to know what difference it makes if we aim to get 7 percent minority admissions in the freshman class of an elite university, rather than 8 percent or 6 percent. What typically matters is not the global declaration that "affirmative action must do this or that." More relevant is assessment at margin: that "a little bit more of affirmative action costs us this or that."

These are subtle empirical questions that cannot be answered off the top of one's head. The answers vary, depending on the details and circumstances of particular institutions and social settings. We desperately need more studies of these details before we can answer the key questions. We need clever people thinking hard about how to measure these effects. Public arguments about racial preferences are based on far too many generic proclamations, and far too little careful scrutiny of the facts pertinent to particular situations.

Applying the Framework
⤮

Goals versus Quotas

There is a belief on both sides of the affirmative action debate that it is possible to draw a meaningful distinction between "goals" and "quotas." Supporters of affirmative action typically endorse goals, but back away from quotas. Here is President Bill Clinton, in 1995, defending affirmative action in his "Mend It, Don't End It" speech: "Since President Nixon was here in my job, America has used goals and timetables to preserve opportunity and to prevent discrimination, to urge businesses to set higher expectations, and to realize those expectations. But we did not and we will not use rigid quotas to mandate outcomes." Likewise, in 2004 President George W. Bush leaned heavily on this alleged distinction when, in commenting on the Supreme Court's decision in the University of Michigan cases, he said: "I agreed with the Court ... that we ought to reject quotas. I think quotas are discriminatory by nature. . . . We also agreed with the finding that, in terms of admissions policy, race-neutral admissions policies ought to be tried. If they don't work, to achieve an objective which is diversification, race ought to be a factor. . . . I think it's very important for all institutions to strive for diversity, and I believe there are ways to do so."

This distinction between goals and quotas is dubious, because to implement either a goal or quota requires that a regulator credibly commit to some (possibly unspoken) schedule of rewards and penalties for an employer or an educational institution, as a function of observable and verifiable outcomes. The results engendered by either policy depend on how firms or educational institutions react to these incentives. If the penalty for bad results is sufficiently severe, then people will tend to say that a rigid quota had been imposed. If penalties for bad results are milder, then people will tend to view the policy as flexible goal has been adopted. Clearly, the difference is one of degree, not of kind.

Nor can one draw a sharp distinction between the use of numerical hiring goals and the enforcement of a regime of nonracial discrimination. When the agents who enforce antidiscrimination laws are less informed than potentially discriminating employers, any effective enforcement policy will have quota-like effects.

To understand this point fully, imagine that a government entity is trying to enforce laws against racial discrimination by auditing employers' hiring practices. Suppose that employers differ, both in their proclivities to discriminate and in the fraction of qualified minorities applying for positions in their firms. Assume that the auditor cannot perfectly observe either a firm's proclivity to discriminate, or all of the characteristics of its applicant pool, but can observe the rate at which minorities are actually hired at a firm. Under such circumstances, the auditor's observation of a low hiring rate for minorities will be consistent with two alternative interpretations: either the employer is a discriminator who rejected qualified minority candidates, or the employer is a nondiscriminator who happened to draw a small fraction of qualified minority applicants. Because an outsider can never perfectly distinguish between the two situations, their efforts to limit discrimination will on occasion be subject to error. Sometimes the employers who did not discriminate will be punished, and sometimes those who discriminated will not. As a result, even those employers who do not wish to discriminate for or against minority workers will nevertheless have an incentive to alter their hiring practices if they happen to draw an unusually low number of qualified minority applicants, because doing so will reduce their risk of being audited and undeservedly punished.

If these arguments hold, then in a legal environment that eschews affirmative action and requires only nondiscrimination, employers will nevertheless behave as if they faced an implicit quota. That is, they will adhere to a self-imposed hiring target that can be understood as their equilibrium response to the incentives created by imperfect auditing. So, a regulator enforcing antidiscrimination laws, who is less well informed than are employers about the qualifications of job applicants, will find that an effective enforcement regime must on occasion induce some departures from race-neutral hiring by the firms being regulated. What is more, these induced departures from race-neutral hiring will generally favor members of the groups being protected from discrimination—which is to say, such protective actions by the firms will be hard to distinguish from racially preferential affirmative action.

A similar false distinction often encountered in the affirmative action debate is that between racial preferences, on the one hand, and the mere enhancement of efforts to attract qualified minority candidates, on the other. Some opponents of affirmative action reject preferences but argue that race-targeted recruitment and outreach efforts (as exemplified by the phrase: "Please alert us to qualified minority candidates") are acceptable, so long as all applicants are judged by a common, race-independent standard. Likewise, some supporters of affirmative action argue that to prefer a minority applicant whose qualifications are roughly the same as a nonminority competitor ought to offend no one. Both of these arguments avoid the hard truth that targeted outreach will generally lead to an equilibrium in which the targeted applicants of a given skill level enjoy wider job options, more bargaining power, and, consequently, greater remuneration than comparable nontargeted applicants.

The Effect of Affirmative Action on Incentives

ᔔ

It is theoretically possible that affirmative action could undercut the incentives to acquire skills in a targeted group, since a preferential policy might make it possible for those individuals to achieve their goals without incurring the cost of skill acquisition. On the other hand, affirmative action could also enhance skill-acquisition incentives in a targeted group by creating a situation in which opportunities previously thought to be out of reach come to be perceived by the preferred party as attainable, and thus worth the expenditure of additional effort. Those who support racial preferences tend to downplay adverse incentives, while those who oppose preferences similarly downplay enhanced incentives.

Both assertions are unfounded. It is useful to think about affirmative action as a form of market regulation, which induces a shift in the demand for the services of individuals at various skill levels from an affected group. For example, in a labor market context affirmative action policy may cause firms to hire and promote minority applicants at a certain level of skill, even though similar non-minority applicants would not be hired or promoted. Thus, economic theory suggests that the impact of such a policy on incentives for skills acquisition depends on the relative magnitude of these demand shifts, and on labor supply elasticities at various levels of skill. If regulation caused firms to bid up the rewards to the highly skilled in the targeted group by more than the rewards to the less skilled, then skill-acquisition incentives would be enhanced. Alternatively, if the demand for various skill grades within a preferred group were to shift in such a way that the less skilled gained more than the more skilled, then skill-acquisition incentives would fall. Thus, the incentive effect of affirmative action policies depends (in what could easily be a counterintuitive way) on the specific environments into which racial preferences have been introduced.

Indeed, it is not difficult to show that the incentive effects of affirmative action can depend crucially on the aggressiveness of the policy. When the affirmative action goal is modest, it can be met by raising the prospects of high quality minority applicants without elevating the chance that an unqualified candidate would be selected—thereby enhancing incentives. Alternatively, if the goal is highly ambitious, then to achieve it may require employers to hire grossly unqualified minority applicants, which would lower the incentives for minority applicants to invest in skills.

This suggests that affirmative action, even when adopted to counter employment discrimination by race, can embody an awkward trade-off: highly aggressive plans risk undercutting incentives, while more modest plans may not eliminate discrimination. One obvious compromise would be to ratchet up affirmative action goals over time. If a modest but not insignificant affirmative action goal was initially enacted in such a way that the first stage of the plan could be satisfied by drawing only on qualified minority applicants, then as these applicants were hired the incentive for minorities to acquire skills would increase. Later on, the affirmative action goal could be made more ambitious without moving incentives in the wrong direction, because employers would be able to draw on a larger pool of qualified minority applicants.

Blindness to Race versus Indifference to Racial Inequality

∽

The belief that to achieve a color-blind society we are best advised to use color-blind (or, as they are sometimes called, race neutral) means was the driving force behind two ballot initiatives in California: Proposition 209, which in 1996 successfully banned the use of affirmative action by state or local government (including state colleges and universities in their admissions decisions); and Proposition 54, which unsuccessfully sought in 2003 to ban state and local government from collecting information that would permit them to categorize students, contractors or workers by race. The public relations campaign for Proposition 54, led by Ward Connerly, proclaimed: "Asking citizens to check a race box on a school or job application form is demeaning to the growing millions of our citizens who are multiracial and multiethnic. It divides us as a people and forces Americans to pay more attention to immutable and meaningless characteristics like skin color and ancestry."[1]

Connerly's view is superficially plausible, even if one begins with the assumption that achieving racial diversity is a compelling government objective. After all, to abide by the color-blindness constraint in employee or student selection does not rule out the pursuit of greater representation for a disadvantaged group. Group-representation goals can be sought tacitly under color blindness: selectors can favor a targeted racial group by over-emphasizing the non-racial factors that are relatively more likely to be found among members of that group. For example, the states of California, Florida, and Texas now guarantee admission to their public university systems for all in-state high school students graduating in the top 4, 20, and 10 percent, respectively, of their senior classes (see "The Promise and Peril of the Texas Uniform Admission Law," by Marta Tienda and Teresa A. Sullivan, in Part III of this volume). Since high schools across these states have different racial populations, this policy will tend to cause university admissions to mirror more closely the racial composition of the state. We use the term *color-blind affirmative action* when referring to this kind of implicit racial preference.

Let us consider in more detail how color-blind affirmative action might work. Suppose that a college has the capacity to admit only a certain fraction of its applicants, and seeks to maximize the expected performance of those admitted. Assume for the sake of this illustration that expected performance is a linear function of a student's standardized test scores and their level of involvement in extracurricular activities. Then the college will admit an applicant if their performance exceeds some suitably chosen threshold. The weight the college gives to extracurricular activities relative to test scores in this admissions policy function will equal the ratio of the partial correlations of these variables with post-admissions performance.

Now, suppose the college believes that to follow this threshold policy would yield too few members of some racial group. Imagine that the level of extracurricular activities is distributed among applicants within racial groups in approximately the same way, but that the within-group test score distributions differ substantially between the races. Given this setup, a college could enhance racial diversity in a color-blind manner by placing more weight on extracurricular activities relative to test scores. That is, the college could practice color-blind affirmative action by valuing an applicant's traits in the admissions process not only because a variable might help forecast post-admissions performance, but also because that trait might be associated with an applicant's membership in the targeted racial group. The practice in California, Florida, and Texas—which guarantees admission to some students based solely on their high school class rank—is one way to implement such color-blind policy. Another method, recently enacted by Mt. Holyoke College in Massachusetts, is to make reporting of an applicant's test scores optional while committing to choosing some portion of the incoming class from among those who elect not to submit scores. It is important to note, however, that even though the targeted group may constitute only a small fraction of the overall applicant pool, the college would need to bias its evaluation of *all* applicants—minorities and non-minorities alike—in order to practice color-blind affirmative action in this way.

Such color-blind policies enhance racial diversity at the cost of lowering selection efficiency—colleges are now maximizing diversity, instead of choosing the highest performers. Of course, if this tradeoff were not necessary, then there would be no need to actively cultivate racial diversity. Even so, for a fixed distribution of traits, any color-blind affirmative action policy is less efficient than the optimal color-sighted policy calibrated to achieve the same degree of racial diversity.[2] In the short run, with applicants' traits given, the efficiency of color-blind affirmative action depends on how well one can proxy for race by using observable, non-racial characteristics that are not negatively correlated with a student's performance. If, for instance, a college could perfectly forecast an applicant's race by using some combination of the applicant's name and date of birth, then that college could implement an admissions policy which, in effect, set separate thresholds of expected performance for each racial group, while being able truthfully to maintain that all of its applicants have been evaluated relative to a common, non-racial standard. At some point, though, this effort to find perfect proxies for race ceases to be color-blind in any meaningful sense. In practice, since color-blind affirmative action generally shifts weight from academic characteristics to social characteristics, the policy will concurrently help Hispanics and low-income whites as well as blacks.

Moreover, color-blind affirmative action is likely to be inefficient over the long run, as well.[3] In any proper long-run analysis, the distribution of applicants' traits must be allowed to shift in response to the colleges' policies. Because color-blind policy works by placing unequal weight on non-racial traits, it creates a situation in which the incentive for students to acquire specific traits diverges from the relative importance of those traits to projected post-admission performance. For example, in states using a top-x-percent scheme, students have an incentive to enroll in high schools (or particular courses within a high school) at which they expect to perform relatively well. So, "top-x-percent" policies should be expected to alter the way that students and high schools of varying qualities are matched with one another. There is no reason to expect that such a shift will promote efficiency. Similarly, a policy that raises the weight on extra-curricular activities relative to standardized test scores in the admissions process will lower the pre-application incentives for students to acquire skills that enhance their performance on such tests. To the extent that such skills also enhance post-admission performance, the shift from color-sighted to color-blind affirmative action policies could create a less academically promising applicant pool.

In the *Gratz* and *Grutter* cases, I and some of my social science colleagues submitted a brief in which we considered in some technical detail the question of whether or not so-called race-neutral alternatives to conventional preferential affirmative action were more efficient or were of comparable efficiency. We tried to measure this with data, and concluded that the decision to keep the same representation goal but constrain oneself to racially neutral means for pursuing it would have very significant negative consequences for the efficiency of selection. Of course, if one can't use the most efficient way to pursue a goal, the cost of the goal goes up and with it the likelihood that one's ability to pursue that goal will be compromised. So, limiting institutions' means for pursuing diversity is bound to result in their producing less of that diversity, because it will make the pursuit itself more costly. So, anyway, an economist is obliged to say; but it also happens to be the truth!

Conclusions
∽

In conclusion, I wish to emphasize what I believe is a fundamental point: an aversion to *racial discrimination* (which leads many critics of affirmative action to argue that race-blindness must be the goal) does not exhaust the important questions of principle in this discussion. Indeed, I am prepared to argue that the question of discrimination is often a trivial moral issue, relative to the deeper questions of social justice that are at play. To restrict one's attention to asking whether all parties have been treated without regard to their racial identity is to leave out issues of enormous moral significance.

What I am saying is that there are, broadly speaking, two stances one can take: one can focus on the *procedures* used to make decisions about the allocation of opportunities; or, one can address oneself to whether the *outcomes* engendered by a given set of procedures are acceptable in light of widely held notions of fairness and equity. This is a question of race-indifference, not race-blindness. In my view, race-indifference is the more fundamental moral question.

Blindness versus indifference: a person exhibits indifference who says "We have various social outcomes, human beings experience them, and I really don't care about the racial identities of those human beings. I am concerned about individuals, period." Whereas a person exhibits blindness who says "How we treat individuals may depend on many of the traits they possess, but it can never legitimately depend on their racial traits." These are vastly distinct notions.

Consider an example from the criminal law: America's jails overflow with black prisoners. Now, one procedural question is: have prosecutors, juries, judges, and the police discriminated against blacks? Is that why so many are in jail? Let us suppose for the sake of argument that the answer, after thorough investigation, is "No, racial discrimination does not figure in the racial disparity of imprisonment in this country." Are we then done with the moral analysis? Have we resolved all questions of racial justice by determining that racial discrimination is not the culprit? When we see that our jails are full of young black men—and that this circumstance is having devastating effects on some of our most disadvantaged communities—does our assessment of the fairness of this situation turn only on procedural matters about what courts and lawyers and police officers do? Or does not this continuing manifestation of a palpably racist history raise questions of justice in some larger sense, to which we are obligated to respond? I submit that the latter is the morally superior stance, and I believe this analogy carries over pretty nicely into higher education.

Does an elite, privileged, rich institution, operating within an ongoing social enterprise whose history has been palpably unfair in racial terms—exhaust its concerns about justice by checking to see whether or not it has discriminated against any individual? I think not. In my view, the University of Michigan, the University of California, the University of Minnesota, the University of North Carolina and like institutions owe the citizens of their respective states a good deal more than taking the racial identification boxes off of their application forms.

The historian Ira Katznelson brilliantly illustrates this point in his recent book, *When Affirmative Action Was White.* The book calls our attention to the fact that much social policy has the effect of benefiting some groups and disadvantaging others. This has certainly been true in the development of social welfare programs in the United States. Katznelson shows that the basic institutions of the American welfare state—income support for the elderly; unemployment insurance; labor organizing regulation; benefits for the veterans of military service; housing assistance and aid to farmers—were all influenced in the years between 1930 and 1950 by subtle racial factors that did not usually manifest themselves as overt discrimination. Thus, farmworkers and domestic servants were excluded from many protections legislated for other workers in the founding laws of the New Deal. This was done largely at the behest of Southern members of the U.S. Congress, all Democrats, who feared that the new laws empowering labor could undermine racial hierarchy in the former Confederate states, where most blacks were living at that time. Likewise, Katznelson shows that the massive social benefits engendered by the GI Bill for those who fought in World War II flowed mainly to whites—in part due to the discriminatory ways in which these benefits were administered, but mainly due to the fact that fewer blacks qualified for benefits because they were excluded from military service except in segregated units, for most of the country's history.

I mention this as an example of how affirmative action often is not what it might seem to be. It is not simply about universities exercising a preference. It is also about how in a democracy we structure policies that have racially disparate consequences: policies, that is, like the War on Drugs—which is a response to a broad social malady affecting all races and classes, but which imposes its costs mainly on the marginal, male, minority city-dwellers who are the most likely recruits into retail drug trafficking. Katznelson's work shows that racial considerations had huge financial implications—on a trillion-dollar order of magnitude—for racial inequality in the country. So that, too, was a kind of tacit affirmative action—for whites—but it had little to do with racial discrimination as conventionally conceived.

The framework that I advocate for thinking about racial affirmative action would be sufficiently broadly gauged and historically aware to take such concerns into account. When debating this policy, we are actually deliberating over the instruments that will be used to select our society's elites, and the consequences for the character of our democracy that may ensue from our choices. One way of talking about this problem is to stand firm on the principle that we must avoid preferences by race. But I hold that this is an impoverished way of thinking, because there is room for ample discretion even within race-blind instruments. The New Deal could have been designed in many different ways, leaving black farmworkers in the South with more or less bargaining power, for instance. Such choices are not issues of racial preference. Rather, they are choices about the structure of the American state. Likewise, how we react to the social malady of drug use—whether we stress punitive responses or therapeutic—is a choice about how to distribute the social costs of our struggle against an important social problem.

Affirmative action is just one policy among many. It is not a site for the spiritual resolution of all the problems with which our tortured racial histories have left us. Nor is it an emblem of commitment to progressivism and social justice. It is a policy, the merits of which should be assessed based on an evaluation of its costs and benefits, relative to the feasible alternatives. We need not always do this, because it is not always a good idea. But sometimes this policy is the most effective way for us to respond to compelling problems of racial inequality that continue to confront us. Whether it is the most effective way now is an empirical question—a question of fact.

NOTES

1. Racial Privacy Initiative, 2002.

2. J. Chan and E. Eyster, "Does Banning Affirmative Action Lower College Student Quality?" *American Economic Review* 93, no. 2 (2003): 858–72; D. Epple, R. Romano, and H. Sieg, "Peer Effects, Financial Aid, and Selection of Students into Colleges and Universities: An Empirical Analysis," *Journal of Applied Econometrics* 18, no. 5 (2003): 501–26; R. Fryer, G. C. Loury, and T. Yuret, "Color-Blind Affirmative Action," NBER Working Paper no. 10103 (Cambridge, MA: National Bureau of Economic Research, 2003).

3. Fryer, Loury, and Yuret, "Color-Blind Affirmative Action."

A Future Beyond "Race"

Reflections on Equity in South African Higher Education

❧

Zimitri Erasmus

> And it is for my own time that I should live. The future should be an edifice supported by living men [*sic*]. This structure is connected to the present to the extent that I consider the present in terms of something to be exceeded.
> —*Frantz Fanon*

> The people . . . want to shatter the limits apartheid imposes, not simply on what you can do, but on what you can think.
> —*Albie Sachs*

There are two predominant perceptions of "race"[1] in South Africa today. In one, race is entirely irrelevant, and should be immediately removed from our vocabulary and policies. This view holds that a future beyond race is possible *now*, but for those who stubbornly choose to hold onto it. The other sees race as the only foundation of a hierarchy of inequality and suffering, which likely will remain central to our lives at least over the long term, if not for the rest of time. Proponents of this latter view generally find it hard to imagine a future beyond race. But race is not always *the* central axis of inequality in our lives. The impact of various inequalities and differences on people's lives is best seen in the intersection of race, class, gender, nation, generation and sexuality. An alternative conceptualization of race may be achieved through specific reference to equity policies and their implementation, and antiracialism in higher education more generally.

Evading Social Justice

❧

Liberal humanists hold race to be irrelevant in postapartheid South Africa, and invalid as a scientific or biological concept. They regard any use or recognition of the concept as itself a racist practice, and dismiss examinations of its material, social, and subjective significance as purposeless. Seen from their perspective, the South African government's attempt to address

334

historical inequalities in higher education through equity policies is nothing less than apartheid race classification in a new guise. Instead, the proponents of this view claim that appointments and admissions should be made strictly on merit, with all candidates competing equally for positions.

It might be true that in some cases, particularly with regard to candidates designated "white," implementation of these policies may assert biological legitimacy with little regard for applicants' political practice, and even less creative thought for joint appointments, in which willing white appointees could be employed temporarily to provide needed capacity-building and mentoring. Liberal humanists are not primarily concerned with such subtle cases, however. Instead, they are far more focused on promoting fair competition in a supposedly open market. They pay little or no attention to the sociohistorical reasons why perfectly competent and brilliant black candidates are rejected for lack of experience and seniority, in contexts where more senior scholars are already part of existing staff. These cases have not mattered much to those for whom race is irrelevant. One can cite many other examples to illustrate the discrepancy between aims and outcomes that arises from the narrow interpretation of policy in specific micro-contexts. The narrowness of such liberal-humanistic interpretations makes it ill-suited to advance us toward the main goal of equity policies: the politicization of race.

The liberal humanists' emphasis on race's *scientific* invalidity eclipses the *historical* associations between conventional definitions of merit and apartheid's pigmentocracy, a relationship that has effectively racialized recruitment pools and networks and rendered the market less open than suggested. Jonathan Jansen, a leading critical voice in higher education and a fellow contributor to this volume, asserts that middle-level management, particularly in the historically white universities and technikons, is adept at keeping certain administrative staff positions white and male, and others white and female.[2] Beyond—or, perhaps more accurately, beneath—the market lies what Jansen calls the "last frontier," the elusive institutional culture that renders the market less competitive.

Contrary to the liberal humanists' assumption, merit-based appointments and equity policies are not mutually exclusive. Equity policies make it possible for perfectly deserving and talented black people to excel while serving their institutions well in the process. Such policies make race a political matter, by deliberately creating opportunities that were denied during apartheid.

We have known for some time that race is not scientifically or biologically real. Nor, however, is it an illusion. To study its social enaction is to expose hierarchies of racialized power and privilege, and to witness the dehumanization of all racialized beings. These hierarchies have both material and subjective consequences. Simply eliminating the concept race from our vocabulary will not ensure social justice, nor will it contribute to the making of anti-racial subjects. Liberal humanists imagine that a postracial future awaits as soon as the category has been erased. They have demonstrated little thought for the long and painful effort required to provide redistributive and restorative justice, or to redirect technologies of power toward the creation of a new, nonracial humanity. While they claim that all people are members of one human race, they deny the work required to cultivate, against the history of colonialism and apartheid, a critical humanist politics.

Discourses of Victimhood and Entitlement

∾

The other main stream of thought, essentialism, is an unsatisfactory alternative. Essentialist approaches attribute to race a timeless centrality, one unaffected by differences in class, gender, sexuality, generation, or political persuasion, among others. From this perspective, solidarity with the national equity project for higher education is premised on racial sameness. Such membership is usually conferred only through judgments of authenticity or inauthenticity, often defined by origins, political loyalties, nationality, or degree of suffering during apartheid.

One such strain of thinking is characterized by a crude reasoning that matches hierarchies of suffering with hierarchies of entitlement. In South Africa, this reasoning sometimes translates into claims that individuals designated as African should be first in line for redress at all times, while those historically classified Coloured or Indian ought at all times to wait, and those designated white should at all times be excluded. This view is blind to context. For example, in provinces like Kwa-Zulu Natal and the Western Cape, where historically classified Indian and Coloured staff, respectively, dominate certain sectors of employment—particularly the administrative sector of higher education—it makes sense in most cases to prioritize black African candidates; but in other cases this practice might be neither just nor strategic. For example, in an institution in which black African students with significant wealth or privileged secondary schooling begin to predominate, it might make sense to consider the inclusion of eligible candidates from poorer backgrounds and less privileged schools, irrespective of race. Furthermore, in cases where suitable black African candidates are not available and a competent white person committed to transformation is willing to occupy a post and work toward mentoring a successor, it would be strategic to appoint this person.

Another strain criticizes equity policies by suggesting that they victimize whites. This line of argument is closely related to the one advanced in the *Grutter* and *Gratz* cases in the United States. It reveals little regard for a continued legacy of privilege, and, more importantly, little thought for the importance of unlearning white ways of being: an ingrained but learnt habituation to racialized power relations, constructed around a history of superiority and entitlement. This same rhetoric of victimhood also perpetuates the idea that those who were historically classified as Coloured were neither white enough to benefit from apartheid nor black enough to benefit from redress.

Arguing against a cult of victimhood and entitlement in his commentary on the merged North West University, Jonathan Jansen raises concerns about both "the failure to broaden democratization to include black vice-chancellor leadership in the former Afrikaans universities, and the presumption by black academics that by virtue of identity, such positions should be occupied by persons of color."[3] Elsewhere Jansen refers to the declining status of the South African professoriate as a consequence of "the growing malpractice in especially technikons and some universities to create a new class of (mainly) black professors" in response to pressures on technikons to become "universities of technology," and to a growing unease in relevant government departments about the continued predominance of older white scholars.[4] He argues that while such "malpractice" may help institutions achieve their short-term equity targets, it destroys the quality of scholarship for successive generations and damages the integrity of higher-education degrees and appointments. Jansen also points to a decline in the quality of the student body, particularly in historically black universities, as a consequence of increased admissions through administrative exceptions like senate discretion, rather than by admission criteria. Such exceptions, largely the consequence of a smaller pool of secondary school graduates, now constitute an estimated 15 to 20 percent of all admissions.[5]

Such appointments and admissions premised solely on racial membership rather than the scholarly achievement, potential, or prior learning of black candidates draw on essentialist conceptions of race. They do not actually serve the interests of those who supposedly benefit from them in the immediate term, nor do they contribute to the future health of higher education. Instead, they perpetuate racist myths about black incompetence and erode the confidence, authority, and motivation of young black scholars and potential scholars. In the process, they legitimize both liberal and conservative discourses against equity.

The discourses of victimhood and entitlement entail obedience to the logic of apartheid, and deference to familiar racial postures, both of which lend support to the power dynamics from which racialized society derives its stability. This submission to what Gilroy calls raciology—the essentialist and reductionist biological and cultural discourses that keep the idea of race alive—cannot help us unmake race.[6] Instead, it forecloses any possibility for reimagining the loyalties rooted in common political and practical projects, for beginning the process of making antiracial beings, and for building a postracial future. Essentialist approaches are blind to an emerging, albeit small and more privileged, generation of South Africans who are not yet racialized. In their concern for the most immediate, they sacrifice any consideration of the present as "something to be exceeded."[7]

"Race": A Political Matter

⌒

It is important to recognize that South Africans' stubborn and, in the case of the oppressed, hard-won investments in race are fueled by their uncertainty about the colossal changes in South African higher education since 1994. But such a recognition should not deter us from challenging the wisdom of such investments.

Liberal humanists and essentialists take an ahistorical, apolitical, and unimaginative approach to race. What is the alternative? The only way to address the inequalities and malpractices for which the category stands is to lift our conception of it out of the realm of biology and a primordial or familial notion of racial membership, into the realm of politics and power.[8]

What is politics? Mbembe sees it as the process of recovering our humanity in a "forward movement toward freedom."[9] For Fanon, it is "the tie that, despite or rather because of the separations and subjugations of the social world, binds unequal citizens into a community of ends."[10] In this conception, any investment in race—whether openly exploitative and discriminatory, sublimated and denied, or mobilized in the name of solidarity and liberation—draws on the same technology of power that fragmented humankind and led to our suffering in the first place. This "dermo-politics"[11] of race divides, rather than binds, us, making a politics of race—or submission to the category—a contradiction in terms.[12]

How, then, does one make race a political matter? In other words, how does one enable thought and living in defiance of both the category and its effects? First: it is important to recognize the historical and political conditions in which the concept emerged: European Enlightenment thought and the politics of 18th- and 19th-century imperialism. This history shows that the inequalities for which the concept stands were human made, and so can be unmade. Second: it is important to recognize the impact of this history of inequality on the present. Third: our analyses of the concept should account for and illustrate the workings of power embedded in its various uses, abuses, denials and political effects, thus revealing dynamics of privilege, subordination, and differential value. Fourth: these analyses need to challenge such power in ways that can be translated into practical politics, in other words, actions taken to build resistance to these workings of power. Examples of such actions include the creation and successful implementation of government and institutional policies specifically intended to intervene in the workings of power with a view to enabling the participation of all adults as peers in social relations.[13] Fifth: it is important that resistance strives toward unmaking *both* the inequalities for which the concept stands, *and* the concept itself. Once we begin to struggle out of racialized regimes of meaning toward new ways of seeing ourselves and thinking about the world—new repertoires for collective action. The process of politicizing race—namely the abolition of race as a form of social differentiation and a means for mobilization—nears its apex only once we begin to struggle out of racialized regimes of meaning toward new ways of seeing ourselves and thinking about the world, toward new repertoires for collective action. This requires us to think and live beyond "what is," toward "what can be." The struggle toward the demise of race does not permit either our acceptance of race or our escape from it. Instead, it emphasizes the work that must be done to liberate ourselves from racial thinking. There is no rest. In the process of its unmaking there is only a wrestling with race: its deep hurts, its inequalities and entitlements. Only in this way can we make race a political matter.

This abolitionism relies on the now commonly held theory of race as a social construct. To conceptualize race as socially constructed is to enable political action toward its demise. This is one of the challenges of higher-education institutions in South Africa. It entails creating a cultural and conceptual architecture designed for the cultivation of antiracial beings and practices. South Africa's history of nonracialism, its Constitution, equity policies, and legislation designed to abolish racial inequality are all part of the structural skeleton of this architecture. The University of Cape Town's policy against racial harassment (currently in the making), for example, and its attempts at building a community of transformative practice through its interventions against racism and racialization exemplify embryonic efforts in South Africa's higher-education institutions to foster antiracial practice and ways of being. If we can effectively build on this scaffolding, modifying it where necessary, it is possible that 25 years from now, race, if not entirely abolished from higher education, will at least be well along in its disintegration.

What are some of the questions that should guide us in these efforts? First: *Does this equity process recognize when and where race contributes to social injustice, and does it act to correct such injustice?* Second: *Is this solely racial injustice, or is it an intersection of injustices?* For example, the intersection of race and nationality often results in xeno-racism against Africans from elsewhere on the continent. Third: *Does this decision privilege racial over class-based injustices?* The privileging of race can turn equity from a principle of access for all, into a means of access to power and privilege for a few. Fourth: *Is this equity process primarily concerned with the color of a candidate's skin, or the candidate's relationship to a transformative project?* Fifth: *Is this equity process more concerned with who candidates are than with what they do?* Sixth: *Does the technology used in antirace interventions confront the social realities of race and racial injustice? How might this technology contribute to reinscribing or unmaking race? Does it treat race as a black-white binary, too skimpy to encompass its complexities, intersections, fluidity, and politics?* Finally: *Is political mobilization centered on social issues, or is it centered on imagined primordial affiliations?*

To answer these questions requires political imagination. These are issues that defy the implementation of equity as merely a bureaucratic process involving quotas, targets, and epidermal concerns. Instead, they require interactive, dynamic interventions from which new questions and challenges will emerge—processes that are by necessity fraught with difficulty. To be willing to embark on what seems unthinkable is to be courageous.

NOTES

This writing was enabled by funding from the Thuthuka Programme supported by the National Research Foundation and the University of Cape Town's University Research Committee.

1. To remind us of its offensive and derogatory nature, I put the word *race* in quotation marks at first use. Hereafter I eliminate the quotes to facilitate reading and rely, instead, on the reader's continued vigilance.

2. J. Jansen, "How Far Have We Come?" *Mail & Guardian,* August 13–19, 2004.

3. Ibid.

4. J. Jansen, "On the State of South African Universities," *South African Journal of Higher Education* 17, no. 3 (2003): 9–12.

5. Ibid., 10.

6. P. Gilroy, *Between Camps: Nations, Cultures, and the Allure of Race* (London: Penguin, 2000), 72.

7. F. Fanon, *Black Skin, White Masks* (London: Pluto Press, 1986), 15.

8. P. Gilroy, *There Ain't No Black in the Union Jack* (London: Routledge, 2005), xx.

9. A. Mbembe, quoted in M. Anderson, "Dreaming of a New Kind of Freedom," *Mail & Guardian,* April 30–May 6, 2004.

10. A. Sekyi-Otu, *Fanon's Dialectic of Experience* (Cambridge: Harvard University Press, 1996), 86.

11. Gilroy, *Between Camps,* 46.

12. Sekyi-Otu, *Fanon's Dialectic of Experience,* 87.

13. N. Fraser, "Social Justice in the Age of Identity Politics: Redistribution, Recognition, and Participation," in *Redistribution or Recognition? A Political-Philosophical Exchange,* ed. N. Fraser and A. Honneth (London: Verso, 2003), 101 n. 39.

Conclusions

The Challenge of the Next Twenty-five Years

Marvin Krislov

Oberlin College (where I now serve as the 14th president), a private liberal arts college in northeastern Ohio, made history in 1833 by becoming the first American college to admit students regardless of race or color. In 1837, Oberlin made history again by becoming the first coeducational college to admit women for a baccalaureate degree. Today, Oberlin's commitment to inclusion and diversity, particularly of underrepresented minorities and students from first-generation, poor, or working-class families remains key to its mission.[1]

The University of Michigan (where I served as vice president and general counsel from 1998 to 2007), a large public university with a highly selective campus in Ann Arbor, has also made inclusion of women and people of color a vital part of its mission for many decades. Its vigorous and public defense of affirmative action policies resulted in the 2003 Supreme Court decision in *Grutter* upholding the constitutionality of diversity considerations in admissions decisions. The University's actions made it the target for Ward Connerly's Proposition 2, a state constitutional amendment designed to eliminate consideration of race, ethnicity, or gender in public employment, contracting, or education.

Both Oberlin and the University of Michigan assert the value of diverse student bodies and diverse campuses. Both have employed policies that might be lumped under the heading of affirmative action—policies ranging from aggressive outreach and the recruitment of faculty, staff, and students to targeted summer programs and financial aid (including aid reserved for women in such areas as science and math), and extending to race- and gender-conscious admissions decisions. Proposition 2, which passed in 2006, has changed the University of Michigan's policies. The university eliminated its use of race and gender considerations midway through the 2006–7 admissions cycle.[2] By fall 2008, the first full admissions cycle under the new law resulted in a roughly 2 percent drop in the number of minority applicants and admissions.[3] With only one year's data, it is too early to predict whether Michigan will in fact experience significant declines like those seen on the Berkeley and UCLA campuses after California passed Proposition 209.[4] Such concerns have impelled Michigan's administration to intensify its recruitment and outreach, and to modify a number of targeted programs.[5]

Oberlin College, as a private institution in a state that has not banned affirmative action, has not had to deal with legal constraints like those imposed on Michigan. Instead, it and the University of Michigan contend with a different kind of constraint, one faced by most selective colleges and universities in the United States: the limited pool of highly qualified students from underrepresented minorities. Sophisticated, expensive recruitment and retention programs, including Posse and Questbridge, have helped generate a pool of capable minority students. Programs that might be called "affirmative action," including race-conscious admissions and targeted aid and summer programs, continue to operate at Oberlin, as at most highly selective private colleges and universities throughout the nation. Indeed, as it has been observed, one irony of the politicization of the college admissions game (and the bans imposed in California, Florida, Washington, and Michigan) is that the nation's private schools may have greater freedom to enroll diverse populations than do public institutions.[6]

Economic access is a further concern, since the high cost of higher education disproportionately affects students of color, particularly African Americans and Latinos. Both Oberlin and Michigan have led their peer institutions in admitting low-income students. However, recent analysis suggests that both institutions' percentages of low-income students (as measured by the number of Pell Grant recipients) declined during the period from 1983 to 2006: Michigan's from 21.8 percent to 12.7 percent, and Oberlin's from 20.2 percent to 12.5 percent.[7] It is not clear whether this decline was matched by commensurate increases in aid to working-class families or those with incomes above the Pell Grant level, although both institutions have asserted their commitment to aiding working-class families.[8]

Oberlin and Michigan are of course not representative of America's institutions of higher education. Both are highly selective, and boast national and international student bodies. Both are situated in parts of the Midwest with relatively small local Latino populations, and so must recruit on the coasts and elsewhere to attract diverse student bodies. Both institutions are considered financially well-off in their respective categories: they do not attain the level of wealth seen at peer schools like Harvard or Amherst, but they certainly are not struggling, either. Their histories illustrate American higher education's focus on diversity, particularly in student bodies. But their examples also suggest that challenges remain, even at those institutions that have prioritized student-body diversity. Affirmative action programs have traditionally been considered an essential tool for achieving this goal.

But will the political and legal challenges to affirmative action undercut such efforts, or will institutions find alternative ways to achieve Justice O'Connor's vision? How diverse will American colleges and universities be in the year 2028? Will they maintain roughly their current levels of diversity, even though underrepresented minorities will make up an increasing share of the college-age population? Will state initiatives like California's and Michigan's continue to spread, thus jeopardizing public institutions' affirmative action programs nationwide? For example, the election of 2008 featured several statewide initiatives modeled on Proposition 209 and Proposition 2. Several initiatives did not make it onto the ballot, while the Nebraska ban passed and the Colorado initiative failed, marking the first statewide initiative modeled on Proposition 209 that was defeated by the voters.[9] Does it matter whether faculty, staff, and students reflect (in some measure) the growing racial and ethnic diversity of the United States and even the world? If it does, then what policies should universities and relevant public and private agencies pursue to sustain that degree of representation?

American higher education will undoubtedly be more diverse in 2028 than it is at present. Community colleges and universities with relatively open admissions policies are likely to draw diverse student bodies, particularly in states with growing populations of people of color. A recent census estimate projects that by 2042, Caucasians will no longer constitute the majority in the United States.[10] What is unclear is whether the highly selective public and private universities will keep up with this trend, particularly when it comes to enrolling African American, Latino, and Native American students. Policies designed for this purpose—often categorized as affirmative action—have provoked heated political and legal debate. Although public discussion has focused on admissions, there are also many financial aid and outreach programs that focus on members of groups "underrepresented" in higher education. These efforts range from scholarships for women and underrepresented minorities to pipeline programs. The attack on affirmative action policies may well undercut them, as well. The California Supreme Court's ruling in *Hi-Voltage Wireworks v. San Jose,* for example, outlawed targeted outreach programs under Proposition 209.[11] University interpretation of this ruling led to the abolition of many scholarship and outreach programs throughout the state.

Many writers in this volume have discussed the Supreme Court cases of *Grutter* and *Gratz.* Unlike the South African legal context, where redress justifies "affirmative action" programs for minorities, American case law establishes that efforts at redress must, in most instances, be tied to identifiable victims.[12] The University of Michigan focused its legal arguments on the importance of student body diversity in providing excellent educational experience.[13] The arguments therefore drew on social scientific data and the validation provided by amici from the worlds of business, the military, education, law, medicine, and other sectors. To meet the strict scrutiny standards, the University needed to demonstrate both a compelling interest (diversity) and a narrowly tailored means (the admissions method). As discussed elsewhere, ultimately the Court found the interest compelling and divided on which method was sufficiently well tailored. *Grutter* determined that the law school admissions process was constitutionally sound; *Gratz* found the so-called point system in the undergraduate admissions process too mechanistic and therefore unconstitutional.

The University's arguments relied in part on the challenging demographics of the student pool. In those cases, the University of Michigan argued that two facts required continued consideration of race as one factor among many—the continuing residential separation of whites and Asians from most African Americans, Latinos, and Native Americans; and the relatively small number of highly qualified members of those racial and ethnic groups who apply to universities and colleges. Were either of these conditions altered, affirmative action policies would no longer be critical to achieving racial and ethnic student body diversity. For the moment, let us ponder whether either of these factors is indeed likely to change in the next quarter century.

First, will American public policy or market forces promote greater residential integration, thereby relieving American universities of their reliance on affirmative action to educate diverse populations? Most Americans express support for residential integration in public statements and opinion polls, yet their behavior tells a very different story.[14] Statistics show that residential segregation has actually *increased* in many American cities since 1954. In most parts of the country, communities are becoming increasingly racially stratified.[15] Professor Patricia Gurin, a contributor to this volume, and others have noted the importance of student diversity for fostering democratic values. Justice O'Connor's opinion for the Court noted this same link. Presumably, if Americans from various racial and ethnic groups lived in close enough proximity to interact in their daily lives, then higher education would bear a more equitable share of responsibility for helping students get to know individuals from different backgrounds. And colleges and universities would no longer have to rely solely on affirmative action policies to achieve diversity.

As things stand, however, existing segregative patterns make it difficult to imagine how federal, state, or local policies could significantly improve the situation, at least in the near future. Housing policies such as the Chicago Gautreaux Program that create low- or moderate-income housing in more affluent areas can be beneficial, but would need to be greatly expanded before they could have an appreciable impact.[16]

Since most Americans still go to public schools in their own neighborhoods, the country's public schools reflect its residential segregation. The proliferation of private secular and religious schools may well heighten the separation. In part to combat this trend and attract more students to their public school systems, many municipalities have introduced magnet and charter schools, which can draw students from across entire school districts, or, in some instances, even across districts. The Supreme Court case of *Milliken v. Bradley* established that districts cannot bus students across district lines to achieve racial balance (or integration) unless the district in question is found to have segregated its schools.[17] *Milliken* thus requires districts to devise voluntary systems for integration if the districts themselves were segregated in whole or in part. Magnet schools have allowed some integration by choice, but they depend on their given districts as a whole having integrated populations. Where a school system is largely homogenous while the surrounding areas are more integrated or have a very different majority population, policies promoting interdistrict transfers become necessary. For various political, economic, and social reasons, this form of district amalgamation or voluntary transfer often runs into strong local opposition (particularly from the group whose welfare would appear to suffer). Moreover, data suggest that the educational impact of charter schools is mixed.[18] Magnet schools may be more effective, but are by necessity limited in number. Moreover, the more competitive magnet schools may face the same pool problems faced by selective colleges.

In 2007, the Supreme Court curtailed the ability of K–12 schools to utilize race-conscious admissions processes. In a fiercely debated decision, a plurality of the Court, with Justice Kennedy concurring in the result, concluded that the Louisville and Seattle school systems had violated the equal protection clause by utilizing a tiebreaker (for the 10 public high schools in Seattle's case) or by adhering to racial group composition guidelines (for all public schools in Louisville).[19] Chief Justice Roberts's opinion found the diversity rationale compelling, but attacked the Seattle school district for not tailoring its program narrowly, because race itself was a determinative factor in school assignments. In Seattle, the student's race (white/nonwhite) operated as one of a series of tiebreakers in filling slots at popular high schools. By contrast, the chief justice noted that the Michigan Law School admissions plan that the Court had approved in *Grutter* provided individualized review of multiple factors, including race and ethnicity.

The Seattle and Louisville cases raised the question of whether a school district's effort to avoid segregation qualified as a compelling interest under equal protection law. Chief Justice Roberts's opinion explicitly rejects the notion that voluntary efforts to avoid resegregation justify considering race in school assignments—where the school system has eliminated the vestiges of discrimination, as in Louisville, or where the school system has never been found discriminatory in the first place, as in Seattle.[20] Justice Breyer, in dissent, accused the majority of violating the spirit of *Brown v. Board of Education*. For Breyer and his three fellow dissenters on the Court, the race-conscious plans served compelling interests and were narrowly tailored to integrate the public schools. He noted that the record before the Court lacked any specific evidence of a school board policy that ensured racial integration in public schools *without* race-conscious means.[21] In concurrence, Justice Kennedy suggested alternative methods such as "strategic site selection of new schools," targeted recruitment of students and faculty, drawing attendance zones, and tracking enrollments by race.[22] As Justice Breyer pointed out, none of these methods succeeded in either Louisville or Seattle.[23]

The Court's decision makes it even more unlikely that America's public schools will be racially integrated without significant social change. This conclusion does not even take account of the within-school segregation that may also occur because of academic tracking or social groupings.[24] While there may be school line-drawing efforts that do not raise the same constitutional concerns, such as bringing together groups from different socioeconomic backgrounds, it seems likely that racially segregated housing and schooling patterns will endure well past 2028.

What, then, to make of the second constraint necessitating affirmative action—the limited pool of highly qualified underrepresented minority students? The latest data show that the number of college-age minority students will indeed increase, but it is unlikely that their qualifications, at least as measured in traditional academic terms, will appreciably increase without significant changes. Indeed, the potential elimination of targeted pipeline programs (as occurred in California) cuts against any increase in the number of such students. College preparation is key. We could expect some increase in states with minority student growth, but the figures from California show that this trend does not necessarily translate into higher number of minority students admitted or matriculating to highly selective campuses. As recent data indicate, the graduation rates from urban high schools are still dismal.[25] The largest cities near the University of Michigan and Oberlin—Detroit and Cleveland, respectively—rank near the bottom of the nation's most populous cities in terms of high school graduation rate: Cleveland graduates 34 percent; Detroit a mere 24.9 percent.[26]

It is hard to imagine that by 2028 the increased flow of minority students moving successfully through the pipeline will be sufficient to eradicate the need for programs designed to increase their enrollment in the more selective colleges and universities. It may be that we will also continue to need initiatives to increase women's enrollment in science and medicine programs.[27] Recent studies suggest that the educational gaps between rich and poor and between whites and blacks and Latinos are widening, making it even more difficult for black and Latino families to move into the middle class. While the causes of this differentiation can be disputed, it is certainly tragic in light of the widely accepted correlation between educational attainment and economic success.

If we believe that students from diverse social and ethnic backgrounds should enjoy equal access to higher education, and we recognize that the current pipeline is inadequate to ensure such opportunities, then we come to the conclusion that more, not less, needs to be done to prepare young people from minority and low-income backgrounds for college. Community colleges will play an increasing role, and schools like Oberlin and Michigan may cultivate further partnerships with these institutions to expand access. Such programs will require significant support, both because students will require financial aid (and perhaps other forms of support) and because there may be gaps in preparation. The corporate, philanthropic, and public sectors should also redouble their efforts to support preparation, recruitment, outreach, and mentoring programs for minority and disadvantaged students. Colleges and universities will increasingly be called upon to support K–12 programs, which will stretch already-overtaxed higher education budgets. Such efforts might include tutoring, mentoring, and support program during the academic year, as well as special summer programs. Oberlin College, for example, has instituted a program whereby any admitted student from the local high school wins a free four-year tuition at the College. But even with all these efforts, it is still difficult to imagine that we could eliminate the need for so-called affirmative action by 2028.[28]

How should we measure the importance of a diverse student body? On the one hand, some might point to Barack Obama's success as proof that academic achievement and upward mobility are possible regardless of race.[29] President Obama is the product of three elite colleges or universities and we cannot know the extent to which affirmative action contributed to his success. But the opportunities he enjoyed are unfortunately still very far out of reach for most African American children.

Colleges and universities offer the best hope for advancement under the circumstances. Furthermore, as the dream of an integrated K–12 system fades in many parts of the country, higher education emerges as the one place where young people can still hope to encounter peers and mentors from different backgrounds. Ironically, my conversations with college students suggest that many of them do not think their high schools will be successfully integrated in the near future, and hope that their college years will provide that experience of diversity instead.

I teach an undergraduate course on the Supreme Court and public education, and in recent years I have been struck by how many students of both majority and minority backgrounds seem to feel that *Brown* is somehow passé, and that integration is a secondary goal for our public schools, if it is even a goal at all. Many of them believe that residential segregation has become so entrenched that the only policy worth pursuing is greater investment in public schools (even if we are largely separated racially and culturally). I find this widespread fatalism disturbing, and not simply because it makes me feel dated. Educational integration is, I believe, absolutely essential to the construction of a strong society.

The easy—and unfortunate—assumption these students make is that integration is useful only as a means to improve the lives of minorities. Taken to a logical extreme (but not an uncommon one), this line of thinking holds that efforts to achieve integration could be dropped as soon as race no longer correlates with, say, family income. But integration is also its own end. While it seems needless to march out its benefits, it is worth pointing out diversity's centrality to our notions of democratic society. In her *Grutter* opinion, Justice O'Connor famously found that race still matters in today's society, and that diversity in higher education keeps the ranks of our country's leadership open to people from all backgrounds. Importantly, she drew her arguments from amicus briefs submitted by the business community and the military, thus emphasizing that diversity's benefits are not theoretical but real. As her opinion for the Court goes on to declare, "Effective participation by members of all racial and ethnic groups in the civic life of our nation is essential if the dream of one Nation, indivisible is to be realized."[30]

Looking back to 1954, author and legal scholar Richard Kluger cited *Brown*'s influence on the "reconsecration of American ideals": that is, a set of values that looks beyond questions of whether separateness may be inherently unequal for minorities, to the fact that it is inherently undesirable for everyone.[31]

Alongside students' sense that the public schools will not be integrated in their lifetime, one finds an expectation that college and graduate school provide the only opportunities for diverse relationships. If true, this means that the inherent benefits of diversity flow only to society's most educated members.[32] Antiaffirmative measures or litigation may further limit these experiences. For instance, underrepresented (African Americans, Latinos, and Native Americans) minority enrollment on California's flagship campuses plummeted after Proposition 209 and has still not recovered to pre-209 levels, despite the state's growing minority population.[33] In Texas, affirmative action programs were reinstated after *Grutter*, but there is now a legal challenge to the so-called percentage plan.[34] While minority enrollment at some private colleges and universities may have grown sluggishly, the vast majority of college students actually attend public universities.

The benefits of educational diversity are thus being enjoyed by only a very narrow segment of society, and so long as only that small fraction is exposed to the benefits of diversity, programs that encourage diversity will be at risk. Indeed, in both California and Michigan the most highly educated voters strongly opposed efforts to ban affirmative action, while the majority of less-affluent voters tended to support them.

After the 2003 cases, we at Michigan hoped that the magnificent coalition we had assembled in response to *Grutter* and *Gratz*—business, military, nonprofits, higher education, K–12, the religious community, and others—would work together to tackle the enormous challenge of fostering diversity and racial equality. Yet we are far from overcoming these challenges, and most observers agree that the solutions now being offered at the K–12 level—magnet schools, vouchers, consolidation, accountability—whatever one thinks of them, will make a marginal difference at best because of resegregation and existing political boundaries. A good deal of experimentation has occurred, and while some efforts have been successful on a small scale, they do not show much promise on a systemic scale.[35] More dramatic solutions, including direct public involvement in higher education and K–12, have not excited much mainstream interest. Instead, many colleges and universities have begun announcing ambitious plans to increase socioeconomic diversity, most of which are predicated on offering grants instead of loans to students whose families fall below a certain income threshold. These programs may compensate for some of the harm done by Proposition 209 and its ilk, but, as has been widely noted, socioeconomic status is at best an imperfect proxy for race. The outlook is not bright, but there are reasons for hope.

Now is a critical time in the history of American education. We are reaching a point of agreement on the importance of diversity (or at least the repugnance of separation), but we remain deeply divided on how to achieve it. Leaders of higher education are asking, quite rightly: How can we address the needs and challenges of a fundamentally separate and unequal society, when that society itself is not prepared to invest significantly in the solutions?

The response is twofold: first, colleges and universities should employ whatever methods are consistent with their mission of encouraging the enrollment and success of diverse populations. These methods may be called "affirmative action" and might include admissions, aid, and outreach programs. The actions might include partnerships with community colleges and high schools. Second, college and university leaders should speak out about the importance of addressing inequities in our K–12 systems and the critically important role of higher education in economic advancement and democracy. As we did in the 2003 Supreme Court victory, colleges and universities should help make the case for greater commitment to programs that ensure opportunities for all Americans. Higher education in America must help provide the leadership to ensure diverse populations in our most competitive colleges and universities.

NOTES

1. *Oberlin College Online,* Oberlin College Goals and Objectives, http://catalog.oberlin.edu/content.php?catoid=10&navoid=177 (visited March 11, 2008).

2. Federal court litigation is currently considering the legal implications of Proposition 2. The Michigan Civil Rights Commission has issued a more permissive interpretation; the Michigan attorney general issued a more restrictive interpretation. "University of Michigan Enrollment up in 2007–8," November 1, 2007, press release at www.umich.edu. See also Michigan Civil Rights Commission, "'One Michigan' at the Crossroads: An Assessment of the Impact of Proposal 06-02," March 7, 2007; and E. Cose, "Killing Affirmative Action: Would Ending It Really Result in a More Perfect Union?" University of Southern California Institute for Justice and Journalism, 2006.

3. T. Martin, "University of Michigan Sees Fewer Minority Applicants," www.mlive.com, June 12, 2008.

4. This chapter focuses on undergraduate student bodies, although many concerns echo in graduate and professional schools. In the aftermath of Proposition 2, the University of Michigan Law School minority student population stayed relatively stable. The number of students is small, and it also should be noted that given the growing diversity of the American college-going population, one should actually expect minority populations to increase. D. N. Goodman, "University of Michigan Drops Affirmative Action for Now," *Washington Post,* January 11, 2003.

5. R. Erb, "Colleges Find New Ways to Retain Diversity," *Detroit Free Press,* December 10, 2007.

6. L. C. Bollinger, "Why Diversity Matters," *Chronicle of Higher Education* 53, no. 39 (2007): B20; see also P. Schmidt, "Justice O'Connor Sees 'Muddy' Future for Affirmative Action," *Chronicle of Higher Education* 53, no. 33 (2007): A28.

7. K. Fischer, "Wealthy Colleges Show Drop in Enrollments of Needy Students," *Chronicle of Higher Education* (2008), accessed at http://chronicle.com/weekly/v54/i34/5434pell_table.htm; see also "Enrolling Needy Students: How the Wealthiest Colleges Rate," chart from *Chronicle of Higher Education* 54, no. 34 (2008): A19.

8. For Michigan, it should be remembered that in-state students receive substantial break on tuition and fees (in 2006–7, the figure for in-state tuition was $9,723.38 as compared with $29,131.38 for out-of-state students). Moreover, needy in-state students may receive additional aid at Michigan, whereas need-based aid for out-of-state students is severely limited. At Oberlin, needy students may receive significant aid in the form of grants and loans. Beyond the scope of this chapter is the current debate concerning reducing loans as a form of aid, and providing greater subsidy for middle-class families, as Harvard and other schools have done. Some commentators have worried that the Harvard initiative may actually result in less aid to lower-income students, because of the

pressure on competitors to match the aid packages offered to middle-class students. S. Rimer and A. Finder, "Harvard Steps Up Financial Aid," *New York Times,* December 10, 2007. Maximum annual household income for a Pell Grant recipient at Oberlin College for the 2007–8 year was $68,000 (information from Robert Reddy, Oberlin College Office of Financial Aid, February 26, 2008). Maximum annual income for a Pell Grant recipient at University of Michigan for 2007–8 year was $177,000. It is not typical to be this high; however, certain circumstances determine eligibility (information from Margaret Rodriguez, University of Michigan Office of Financial Aid, May 1, 2008).

9. D. Frosh, "Vote Results Are Mixed on a Ban of Preference," *New York Times,* November 8, 2008; S. Hebel, "Colorado Becomes the First State to Reject Ballot Measure to Ban Affirmative Action," www.Chronicle.com, November 6, 2008.

10. S. Roberts, "A Generation Away, Minorities May Become the Majority in the U.S.," *New York Times,* August 14, 2008.

11. M. Cox, "Hi-Voltage Wire Works, Inc. v. City of San Jose," *Public Law Journal* 24, no. 2 (Spring 2001): 1, 3–4.

12. While scholarly debates about the reach of the Fourteenth Amendment's equal protection clause have generated considerable controversy, cases such as *Crosen* and *Adasand* point to the most exacting standard of judicial review—strict scrutiny—for affirmative programs and a narrow reading of the notion of ameliorative programs based on societal discrimination.

13. For a fuller discussion of these arguments, see P. Gurin, J. S. Lehman, and E. Lewis with E. L. Dey, G. Gurin, and S. Hurtado, *Defending Diversity: Affirmative Action at the University of Michigan* (Ann Arbor: University of Michigan Press, 2004).

14. Eisenhower Foundation, "What Together We Can Do: A Forty Year Update of the National Advisory Commission on Civil Disorders," 2008.

15. K. Drew, "Today's Battle in Classrooms: Resegregation," *CNN,* May 18, 2004.

16. F. Roisman, "End Residential Racial Segregation: Build Communities That Look Like America," http://www.hlpronline.com/Roisman.pdf. See also Eisenhower Foundation, "What Together We Can Do."

17. *Milliken v. Bradley,* 418 U.S. 717 (1974).

18. J. Betts and P. T. Hill, "Key Issues in Studying Charter Schools and Achievement: A Review and Suggestions for National Guidelines," NCSRP White Paper Series 2 (May 2006), accessed at www.ncsrp.org/cs/csr/print/csr_docs/states.htm on April 7, 2008.

19. *Parents Involved,* 551 U.S. at 2 (Kennedy), concurring.

20. Ibid., 28.

21. Ibid., 51 (Breyer), dissenting.

22. Ibid., 8 (Kennedy), concurring.

23. Ibid., at 52 (Breyer), dissenting.

24. For an insightful look at the role race plays in social groupings, see B. D. Tatum, *Why Are All the Black Kids Sitting Together in the Cafeteria? And Other Conversations about Race* (New York: Basic Books, 2003).

25. K. Thomas, "Report: Low Grad Rates in U.S. Cities," Associated Press, April 1, 2008, accessed at www.ap.org.

26. "America's Promise Alliance Launches National Campaign to Combat Nation's High School Dropout and College Readiness Crisis," press release, April 1, 2008, accessed at www.americaspromise.org.

27. Possible examples of target programs: The Women in Science, Dentistry, and Medicine Faculty Organization (WISDM), The School of Medicine Committee on the Status of Women and Minorities, and others found at http://www.womeninmedicine

.vcu.edu/; see also "NIH leads Effort to Help Women in Science and Medicine Fulfill Potential," *NIH News*, January 29, 2007, accessed at http://www.nih.gov/news/pr/jan2007/od-29.htm on April 7, 2008.

28. P. Schmidt, "Researchers Bemoan Lack of Progress in Closing Education Gaps between the Races," *Chronicle of Higher Education*, March 26, 2008 (Web).

29. See T. Strom, "Beyond Black Politics," *Wall Street Journal*, March 14, 2008 (Web).

30. *Grutter*, 539 U.S. at 309.

31. Kluger, R., *Simple Justice: The History of Brown v. Board of Education and Black America's Struggle for Equality* (New York: Knopf, 1975), 710.

32. C. King and M. Martin, "College: Diversity Drive Isn't Quotas," *ABC News Washington*, January 26, 2003; see also H. Greene and M. Greene, "The Importance of Diversity from Our Perspective—Brief Article," *Matrix*, September 2001.

33. Cose, "Killing Affirmative Action," 19–24 (also pointing out that minority enrollment at the less selective campuses has "caught up" to pre–Proposition 209 levels); see also P. Schmidt, "Study Challenges Assumptions about Affirmative Action Ban," *Chronicle of Higher Education*, February 8, 2008 (Web); J. Chapa and C. L. Horn, "Is Anything Race Neutral? Comparing 'Race Neutral' Admissions Policies at the University of Texas and Universities of California," in *Charting the Future of College Affirmative Action: Legal Victories, Continuing Attacks, and New Research* (Los Angeles: Civil Rights Project at UCLA, 2007); J. Hou, "Affirmative Action Ban Discussed," *Daily Bruin*, September 29, 2007.

34. S. Jaschik, "Affirmative Action Challenged Anew," *Insidehighered.com*, April 28, 2008.

35. J. A. Grozuczak Goedert, "*Jenkins v. Missouri:* The Future of Interdistrict School Desegregation," *Georgetown Law Journal* 76 (1988): 1867, 1882.

Nothing Is Different,
but Everything's Changed

∽

Martin Hall

Paul Simon's lyrics from "Once Upon a Time There Was an Ocean" express the paradox of unstoppable motion in combination with timelessness: the mountain range that was once an ocean; lives once still, now in unstoppable movement; the fragile reminders of a lost past and the sense of overwhelming change. Nothing is different, but everything's changed. Similarly, it is a paradox of the university that little changes with time and yet little is predictable. This is well illustrated by the recent history of the University of Cape Town. If one turned Justice O'Connor's "mirror to the future" to UCT circa 1980, one would be impressed by a sense of continuity with 2007. Architecture inspired by Jefferson's design for the University of Virginia and augmented by controversial modernist elements still appears against the backdrop of Devil's Peak and Table Mountain. Teaching is still taking place in tiered lecture halls and smaller seminar rooms. A few eccentrics persist with blackboard and chalk. The newer computer laboratories are tucked away in basements. There have been some new academic departments added, and some disciplinary casualties. But the qualifications on offer in 2007 are still largely the same as those from 1980, and a student whose studies were interrupted back then could still apply her academic credits when reregistering today. Graduation ceremonies have become more interesting with the addition of graduates from more than 90 countries, along with ululation, the blowing of the air-horns known as *vuvuzelas,* and a diverse dress code. But gowns are still worn and Gaudeamus mumbled, and the faculty still proceed in rank order, leading in the chancellor to convene the assembly.

Yet if anyone at a 1980 graduation ceremony had described the political order of South Africa as it really looks 25 years later, he would have been regarded as eccentric. Worse still, if he had made his predictions publicly known, he could have expected the attentions of the Bureau of State Security. In 1980, Nelson Mandela was still on Robben Island, and the ANC was in exile, internally weak and externally regarded as a terrorist organization. Racial segregation was in full force, as was job reservation, residential segregation, and the Immorality Act. The National Party appeared impregnable, buttressed (despite international sanctions) by Cold War policies of

Russian and Chinese containment. While Soweto and other townships had erupted four years earlier, the uprisings were widely thought to have been suppressed by police and military firepower, working in concert with an all-pervasive security apparatus. Despite an established tradition of principled opposition to apartheid, UCT was in 1980 still an overwhelmingly white institution, constrained by both enrollment and employment legislation and almost completely dependent on the state for financial support. Any suggestion that, 25 years later, South Africa would be known for its progressive Constitution, would be one of the few countries permitting gay marriage, and would have a seat on the United Nations Security Council would have been met with laughter.

This paradox—that nothing is different but everything's changed—makes more sense if we distinguish the university-as-institution from the university-as-practice. The former encompasses the regulations, customs, and physical structures that guard the gates of knowledge. The formal institution scrutinizes applicants, assesses and examines students, confers qualifications against preestablished standards, determines who can be considered a legitimate "knowledge worker," and validates the form and content of knowledge through guildlike academic disciplines.

The substantive university, in contrast, is volatile and pliable. It can be understood as a collection of what educators call communities of practice. These communities define academic, social, and political affinities and exclusions within the physical space of the formal institution and also—in conjunction with local communities or international organizations of similar knowledge specialists—beyond it.[1] The popular image of the ivory tower notwithstanding, the substantive university is profoundly affected by the wider society that it is both in and of.

The distinction between the formal institution and its substantive communities of practice is an analytic device, an artifact that helps us understand some of the complexities of higher education. In reality the two aspects are constantly interacting, creating institutions that can be monumental and predictable or transitory and volatile. What starts as a paradox—a puzzle amenable to solution—may end as a contradiction, in which the needs and aspirations of diverse communities of practice can no longer be met within the framework of a formal institution. For both South Africans and Americans interested in the future of racial diversity and equality, looking closely at the University of Cape Town allows us to ask whether the paradox of substantive change within a largely unchanging institution is likely to persist, or whether something unstoppable has been set in motion. Closer examination of three particular domains—admissions, the faculty, and the construction of knowledge—may help us to answer this question.

The core dynamic in UCT admissions for the last 25 years and also the foreseeable future is the relationship between race and class.

Until recently, South Africa's last half century has been largely treated as exceptional, its racial classification systems an aberration that should have been swept away in the processes of decolonization and civil rights reforms. White Afrikaner intransigence was in this view so intransigent that it left apartheid South Africa an international pariah for the last 20 or so years of its existence. To take but one example from my own experience as an archaeologist: the World Archaeological Congress, formed in 1986 around international opposition to South Africa, stated this opposition in its constitution without reference to other states that had also been criticized for human rights violations, such as the Soviet Union, Israel, and Argentina. While such issues of human rights are of undoubted importance, this exceptionalist point of view led too often to the conclusion that the South African problem had been solved once key symbolic and juristic milestones had been achieved: for example, the release of Mandela, the first democratic elections, and the ratification of a new constitution.

Recent scholarship, based on reasonable reconstructions of socioeconomic data from before the first nationally representative household surveys and censuses of the 1990s, has mapped out a more complex scenario than is possible from an exclusive emphasis on human rights.[2] This work is showing how persistent interracial inequality was, from the early 1970s onwards, accompanied by increasing intraracial inequality among Africans. Even as the state was introducing policies during the so-called late apartheid era that sought to modernize discrimination, a black middle class was emerging and distinctions developing between the unionized workforce and a growing rural proletariat that was structurally excluded from the labor force and geographically isolated in the Bantustans. Further research shows that, contrary to most expectations, these trends have continued and even accelerated since the achievement of formal freedoms in the 1994 elections.[3] Indeed, the first decade of democracy has seen widening general inequality; increasing inequality within demographic groups, to the point where Africans are almost as unequal as a group as the South African population is as a whole; growing unemployment, including a large number of people with no prospect of jobs and therefore outside the workforce; and increasing poverty, as measured by the recognized thresholds of one or two U.S. dollars per day, adjusted for parity.

Our increasing understanding of the interplay of race and class in South Africa is, in turn, challenging established approaches for seeking equity in university admissions. Current admissions policies are rooted in the mid-1980s, when, as Stuart Saunders describes in his contribution to this volume, a subset of South African universities began to actively defy apartheid policies and seek to admit significant numbers of black students. Because of marked disparities in the quality of prior education, these admissions policies have typically imposed achievement standards that differed according to the apartheid education department that administered a given applicant's school. This differential requirement was buttressed by alternative, scaffolded forms of admissions testing that made test outcomes less dependent on the test-taker's prior level of knowledge, as Nan Yeld outlines in this volume. South African high schools were still racially segregated through the mid-1990s—in practice if not law by the end of this period. As a result, race was a reasonable proxy for the quality of education available to an individual prior to university attendance: even middle-class African learners usually had little choice in schooling, and were still obliged to attend underresourced, apartheid-era schools.

This situation has changed to a degree since the mid-1990s. White schools (so-called Model C schools, named for a futile last-ditch attempt by the De Klerk government to protect white privilege immediately prior to the 1994 elections) have been increasingly desegregated, giving small but significant numbers of black learners access to well-resourced formerly white schools.[4] By 2005, many of them had received their entire secondary education in such schools. This has raised the question of whether these black university applicants are being unfairly privileged by affirmative action, particularly in the context of Black Economic Empowerment policy, which has fueled the emergence of a financially advantaged black "supraclass." This argument will be familiar to Americans, and, indeed, the South African debate often references the case against affirmative action in the United States.

But the South African and American cases are not identical, as Njabulo Ndebele emphasizes in his foreword to this volume. The African victims of apartheid form a large majority, and the burdens of national unemployment, poverty, and social marginalization are carried overwhelmingly by Africans. For this reason, the emergence of an African middle class and the widening of intragroup inequality within the African racial category does not affect the distribution of acute poverty, structural unemployment, and social exclusion. When the average income of the bottom decile of households is one hundredth of the top decile, the rising tide leaves the poor submerged.[5] Consequently, and despite the emergence of a black middle class over the last 25 years, statistical analyses show a clear correlation between poverty and educational attainment.[6]

A university admissions policy that took account only of school-leaving results would lead to a resegregation of universities, since the comparatively small number of African applicants from formerly white schools would be insufficient to allow an equitable admissions profile. The picture is further complicated by evidence that African students in formerly white schools score consistently lower than their white peers, despite equivalence of formal opportunity—a South African version of the U.S. black-white test score gap that is probably due to continuing discrepancies in social capital and the prevalence of "everyday" discrimination.[7]

The combination of a conspicuous and financially privileged black elite, on the one hand, and persistent and increasing economic marginalization of a large majority of black households, on the other, is already provoking calls for admissions reform from diametrically opposed political positions. The media report on claims, especially from white applicants and their families, that black applicants now have an unjustified advantage. Some of the plaintiffs are demanding an admissions system based solely on school-leaving results, while others are arguing for a combination of race-blind admissions for "Model C" graduates and weighting in favor of applicants from less privileged schools. At the same time, there is criticism from the opposite pole, including ANC-affiliated groups such as the ANC Youth League and the South African Students' Congress, that universities are failing the poor. These groups are calling for an explicitly pro-poor set of policies in which, among other changes, universities would need to base admissions on a combination of household income and the measured quality of prior schooling.

There are parallel movements within the ruling alliance of the ANC, the Congress of South African Trade Unions, and the South African Communist Policy to pressure government to move away from policies that create black elites toward economic and social inclusion. This was a major theme in the December 2007 ANC leadership elections, which saw President Thabo Mbeki deposed as ANC leader by a populist coalition led by Jacob Zuma. It would not be surprising if the government, perhaps using the lever of the public subsidy to universities, began pressuring universities to change their admission policies.

Financial aid is closely associated with equity in admissions. South African universities have minimal endowments, and ambitious policies to the contrary, this is unlikely to change over the next 25 years. There is little equivalent to the North American culture of philanthropy and only a small alumni donor base. Given that alumni loyalty is built up over lifetimes and even generations, this situation is unlikely to change by 2030. At present, South African universities produce financial aid from within their operating budgets or from bursary programs, with additional allocations from the National Student Financial Aid Scheme. Without this support, students from lower socioeconomic groups could neither afford tuition nor raise personal loans to cover such costs against potential earnings.

While we do not yet have systematic data from across South African higher education, it is probable that all universities in the country are already close to, or in excess of, their capacity to provide financial aid within the present system. Given the extent of inequality and poverty, any shift to a class-based admissions policy will only succeed if it is accompanied by a new approach to student financial aid. Were they to meet current academic requirements for entry, a large majority of South African households would qualify for full financial aid for university study on any reasonable definition of eligibility. Consequently, any shift to a class-based admissions system would bear major implications for the ways in which tuition and other costs are funded.

Policies that seek to achieve equity in admissions are also closely related to faculty recruitment and internal university policies for transformation. Universities are unusual institutions in that they develop and qualify their own human resources: there is a direct pipeline from undergraduate admissions to graduate recruitment to the hiring of junior faculty. Universities previously designated for specified races also face considerable pressure, both from within and without, to achieve equitable balances in the composition of their staff.

This pressure affects universities differently according to their history. Most obviously, previously white universities such as UCT still have overwhelmingly white faculty (combined with a gender imbalance that grows with increasing seniority). But the staffing profiles at other universities are also skewed as a result of the peculiarities of apartheid social engineering. For example, the University of the Western Cape was shaped by the apartheid-era Coloured Labour Preference Policy, which attempted to restrict the numbers of Africans living in Cape Town and its vicinity.

The internal impetus for change is sharpened by the Employment Equity Act, which requires all organizations with more than 50 employees to set targets for improving their staff representativity by race, and to annually report their progress against these targets to the Department of Labour. These trends add up to a considerable challenge for South African universities as they seek to improve the representativity, and therefore the diversity, of their faculty over the next 25 years.

In contrast with student admissions, the future of faculty recruitment and retention is somewhat more certain. South Africa has a small higher-education system offering limited employment opportunities for academic or specialized administrative staff. Faculty turnover rates are low and thus the opportunities for diversification are quite limited. UCT, for example, has a staff turnover rate through retirement, resignation, and unanticipated events of less than 10 percent per annum. Under South African labor law it is illegal to terminate staff contracts for the purposes of achieving diversity, contrary to widespread popular opinion among white South Africans that this happens. As a result, the profile of the faculty at a university such as UCT remains 90 percent or more constant on a year-to-year basis.

The effects of this inertia are compounded by the length of the pipeline connecting undergraduate admissions to faculty recruitment. It is at best a 10-year journey, and projects such the U.S.-based Mellon Mays Undergraduate Fellowship program (of which UCT is a member) have shown that it takes about 15 to 20 years to make a measurable impact on diversity through targeted recruitment, mentorship, and career tracking. Black faculty at South African universities are also actively recruited by other organizations seeking to meet their equity targets, some of whom are able to offer significantly higher remuneration. The government recruits from universities as do other university systems (South African higher education has contributed three vice-chancellors to universities in the United Kingdom in recent years). On top of all of this add the international mobility that is one of the attractions of the academic life. All of these factors together pose a significant hurdle to any effort to change the demographic profile of South African faculty.

Change will, therefore, be slow over the next 25 years. A significant number of the staff currently working at South Africa's universities will still be doing so 25 years hence, and it will remain difficult to meet objectives for employing black faculty for a decade or more. There is likely to be variability by discipline, as individual fields contend with the shape of their current graduate cohort, as well as competitiveness from peer institutions. For example, considerable progress has been made in undergraduate engineering education, and it is reasonable to expect that these advances will carry through to graduate student recruitment and the employment of junior faculty. In contrast, while medicine has been a target for admissions equity since the 1980s, and the profile of graduates has changed markedly, equity recruitment into postgraduate specialties like surgery has been negligible, with the result that the potential applicant pool for faculty positions among South Africans is almost completely white (and skewed by gender, as well). There is unlikely to be significant change in staffing equity in such fields over the next 25 years.

One underexplored opportunity to break out of the slow pattern of change may be found in the relationship between South African universities and the academic diaspora. South Africa has been hemorrhaging academic talent for half a century. Waves of young professionals left the country as apartheid policies began to bite in the early 1960s, and are now ending often-distinguished academic careers in other countries. Others left at key points in the history of state oppression: the Soweto uprising of 1976 and its aftermath, the successive and formal states of emergency after 1985. There are significant numbers of South African trained professionals in all English-speaking countries, and many informal networks that connect them with each other, and with family members who remained. Such networks have been central to economic revivals in a number of countries, including most recently China and India, and South African universities have yet to develop innovative approaches that will allow those who wish to retain or regain connections to do so in ways that contribute to change in South Africa, without surrendering complex material and social investments in their new countries of residence.[8]

A second factor, also underexplored, is the relationship between South African universities and universities elsewhere on the continent. This relationship is complicated both by inconsistency in current policy and tension between the objectives of labor legislation and the natural interests of universities. South African higher-education policy seeks to expand the community of scholarship by requiring that students from the Southern African Development Community be treated as if they were South African citizens. In contrast, labor legislation insists that only South African citizens be counted towards employment equity targets, and also precludes anyone who has attained citizenship since 1994, thereby counting out a significant number of intellectuals from other African countries who have made South Africa their home and taken South African citizenship. Again, South African universities have a natural interest in recruiting such scholars, who can bring fresh perspectives to their teaching and research and also serve as role models, particularly for graduate students—the faculty recruits of the future.

As with the diaspora, it is difficult to predict how this trend will change over the next 25 years. On the one hand little may happen. Xenophobia is entrenched and on the rise in South Africa, which imposes significant entry restrictions on nationals from other African countries. But there is also a chance that government policy will follow the Pan-Africanist inclinations of former president Thabo Mbeki, who made the construction of a sub-Saharan economic and aligned community a central pillar of his policy through two terms of office. These efforts, combined with appropriate incentives, could help strengthen the meaningful connections between South Africa's universities and others from across the continent.

In a country where many public institutions are sharply unrepresentative of the communities they serve, changing the demographic profile of students and staff is an important end in itself. It also benefits the work of organizations dedicated to the creation and dissemination of knowledge. From Kant's reflections on the relationship between what would today be called disciplines, to Von Humboldt's University of Berlin, the U.S. land-grant colleges, Paolo Freire's radical pedagogy, John Dewey's philosophy, experiential learning, and the efflorescence of new universities across Europe and Africa

in the middle of the last century, the modern university has served as a magnet for diverse forms of knowledge, expertise, and perspective. Universities with established high rankings in international league tables invariably attract talent from a wide, and often global, catchment. Leading American research universities would not be what they are if they had not recruited excellent students and faculty from India and China, and both countries are now benefiting enormously from the reverse flow of expertise.

Within this broader context, the end of segregation and the onset of diversification offer many opportunities for knowledge work in South African universities. In contrast with the private sector's emphasis on equity in admissions and employment, however, the campus discussion has barely begun. With important exceptions, there have been no broad public debates about the nature and direction of the curriculum, no equivalent to the American "culture wars" in the humanities, the public agonies about the competitiveness of the sciences in the United Kingdom, or the nationalist and Pan-Africanist debates that have enlivened intellectual discourse in other countries in Africa. In South Africa, questions about the role of indigenous systems of knowledge and their relationship to university curricula and research remain unresolved (dangerously so, given the risk of alienation of intellectual property). Issues of adult education, the formal recognition of prior experience, and lifelong learning have been given little more than a nod of recognition—a significant failure for a country that is home to so many midcareer adults who were prevented from realizing their innate potential because of earlier exclusion on the grounds of race, gender, or both.

Why this slowness to get to the heart of the matter? One reason is found in the contribution that university-based intellectuals have made to nation-building. The last apartheid government handed the ANC a nation with segregated institutions, an almost-bankrupt economy, and a failing grade on almost all measures of good governance. In the long process of reconstruction, the state has drawn on a wide range of resources, including, appropriately, the country's universities. Faculty have played substantial roles in commissions, research projects, and advisory roles in areas including education reform, public health, HIV and AIDS interventions, urban renewal, legal reform, economic policy, culture and heritage, and the framing of the new Constitution. They have taken on many of these tasks in addition to their home universities' requirements for teaching, research, and administration. The pressure of this dual burden has diminished their capacity for transformative work within the universities themselves.

A second reason is the intense institutional reconstruction that has followed the release of the National Commission on Higher Education's 1996 report, and, particularly, from the national working group that reported to the Minister of Education in 2000.[9] The national higher-education system has undergone an ambitious series of mergers, incorporations, and closures that have reduced the number of public institutions and created a new and little-understood hybrid of universities and technical colleges: the so-called technikons, or universities of technology. This restructuring has absorbed substantial resources, once again leaving little time or energy for curricular reform, and has probably encouraged traditionalism in core areas of knowledge work: when everything else is contested, established methods of teaching and research may appear to be a raft of stability.

The future of knowledge work is the most difficult to project over the next 25 years. While trends in the interaction of race and class are reasonably well understood, and the limitations on change in the demographic profile of staff are all too apparent, the "knowledge question" has only been partially explored. Will the established disciplines remain dominant, either capturing or excluding new forms of knowledge? Will universities take up the opportunities that the reversal of apartheid isolation has brought? Will the curriculum and the research agenda follow the lead of the West and the North, or will South African universities seek distinction by developing new forms of local knowledge that can inform global issues? Will there be a greater emphasis on adult education, prior learning, and continuing professional education? At present these are options for advocacy; their outcomes will be better judged in retrospect.

How could such substantive changes in admissions, the composition of the faculty, and the construction and dissemination of knowledge affect the nature of the formal institution—that edifice of regulations, customs, and monuments that is replicated through organizational arrangements, official certifications, ceremonies, and architecture?

Would a move from race to class preferences in admissions change the formal structures of the university? There is a tendency to assume not—to see this as a steady, evolutionary process in which the university's neoclassical facade has presided benignly over colonial, apartheid, and democratic eras alike, and will similarly preside over whatever the future will bring. Such an assumption warrants interrogation.

The university is one of a number of gatekeepers of class mobility. By recognizing the potential of students from lower socioeconomic groups and providing them with accredited qualifications, the university helps these graduates gain access to opportunities for better earnings and higher social status. In a country beset by extreme inequality, the stakes are high and the rewards potentially substantial. Increasing numbers of black South Africans have benefited from these opportunities over the last 25 years, but their achievements have little effect on the formal structures of the university and may indeed reinforce existing traditions. It is not in the interests of first-in-family graduates to devalue the qualification they have worked so hard to achieve. Twenty-five years ago, many UCT students did not bother attending graduation; with participation rates for white South African among the highest in the world, university education and graduation could be taken for granted. Such ceremonies are far more popular today among students and their families. The environment is more competitive for all students, and for first-in-family graduates the generational change in opportunity can be particularly profound.

This, however, is to assume that the gate is open and the road clear of major obstacles. But, as Haroon Bhorat points out in his contribution to this volume, South Africa is experiencing both a national skills shortage and rising graduate unemployment, the consequences of a serious mismatch between the requirements of the economy and the ability of universities to produce suitably qualified applicants. While this mismatch is partly attributable to shortcomings in higher education, the bulk of the problem stems from the crisis in prior schooling, and the inability of the public education system to provide an adequate education in mathematics and science. So the gateway becomes a barrier and the university a holding ground for unemployable young adults. Optimistic views of globalization hold that the rising tide lifts all ships. But other analyses see widening marginalization ahead, and an international labor surplus that will further reduce the opportunities for job creation in the developing world.[10]

A shift from race to class would also open up the question of academic standards. One of the more insidious aspects of apartheid education was the conscious decision to invest unequally in public schooling and teacher preparation. While the late-apartheid period saw accelerating investment in African schools, quality varies significantly to this day.[11] Universities such as UCT responded by creating academic development programs that have now been in place for more than 20 years, and which can demonstrate an acceptable statistical correlation between admissions decisions and eventual graduation rates.[12] However, it is not clear that such programs could be scaled up to manage a significant increase in first-time undergraduates from poorly performing schools. While the Department of Education's focus on school quality will result in improvements, they will come only with the entrance of new generations of teachers into the profession; at present, provincial authorities are experiencing difficulty in recruiting teachers for critical areas such as math and science. In the shorter term, universities seeking to change the class profile of their admissions may have to balance this goal against their current entrance standards.

It is unlikely that a shift from race to class preferences in admissions will leave the institutional structures of the university unchanged. Given South Africa's history of youth-led pushes for revolutionary change—epitomized in the Soweto uprising of 1976—continuing or worsening graduate unemployment may lead to a reradicalization of South African campuses in concert both with the labor movement inside the increasingly fragile governing alliance, and with nongovernmental organizations focused on poverty and social and economic marginalization.[13] If, in years to come, South African universities admit larger numbers of students from poor backgrounds who will not find opportunities for employment after graduation, these campuses will again become major sites for political activism and opposition, creating pressure for major changes in the systems of governance.

Pressure for change in these systems will also come from the need for a major expansion in student financial aid. As noted, this need cannot be met from existing resources, and is unlikely to come from endowment income because such endowments have yet to be raised. Instead, the impasse may lead South African higher education down one of two different roads toward change.

One route would be toward calls for greater state support through increased subsidy, dedicated grants, or a revised national grant and loan scheme. In essence, any major shift from race to class will considerably reduce the number of students paying tuition fees and mean that a majority of students will receive grants covering almost all of their costs. Given the growth of inequality and poverty, there is little middle ground. This, though, will come at the price of autonomy. While the 1997 Higher Education Act confirms that universities are autonomous entities with substantial control over admissions, curriculum, research, and other activities, a series of almost-annual amendments to the act has steadily eroded this autonomy by extending the minister of education's right to intervene in their affairs.[14] New forms of subsidy also allow the state greater control over universities through the funding of student places, level of funding by discipline, rates of graduation, and the nature and quantity of research outputs. The chaos of the apartheid-era higher-education arrangements has been replaced by a unitary, state-steered system. Given continuing concerns about the efficiency of South African universities and the returns they generate on the investment of public funds, it is improbable that the state would grant large amounts of additional funding for student financial aid without expecting a significant increase in control over the way this subsidy is used.

The alternative route would be for universities to hold out for autonomy and respond to the demand for more financial aid instead by reprioritizing budgets. In practice, this would be a trade-off between support for students and support for research. In contrast to their American peers, South African universities have few sources of support for their research activities and infrastructure. There is little technology transfer and industry-sponsored research. Income from intellectual property is too low to be worth

counting. In contrast again with the United States, where federal departments sponsor research across a wide range of disciplines, South African
agencies offer little in the way of contract research, and what little one finds
is subject to competition from specialized organizations like the Council
for Scientific and Industrial Research and the Human Sciences Research
Council. In order to increase financial aid funding within present budgets,
universities would have to raise their research overhead to a level that would
allow them to recover all research-related costs. This would have a severe
impact on investment in research infrastructure, and would lead to a reduction in research output and competitiveness.

Pressure on the status quo comes also from knowledge work. This is an
area of tantalizing possibility. For reasons outlined earlier, wide discussion
of the curriculum has been curtailed by other considerations. It is clear,
though, that big research benefits from network effects, and that interinsti-
tutional consortia can attract significant resources. South African universities are currently involved in regional and international collaborations in
medical research, astronomy, climate change studies, marine biology, food
security, and public health, among other areas. The South African diaspora
has the potential to heighten these effects. This international cooperation
could be coupled with a reevaluation of the value of local knowledge—an
asset available to the country's universities as a consequence of their location along the fault lines of rapid urbanization, key public health issues, and
the literary and artistic innovations that are so often fueled by diversity.

Will the interaction between these substantive changes and the formal
structures of the university end in a continuing paradox—in education
both changing and staying the same—or will the paradox give way to contradiction, in which forces pulling in different directions cannot be reconciled without a total restructuring of the university?

Again, it is edifying to reverse Justice O'Connor's mirror and look 25
years back into the past. The remarkable thing about South Africa's universities is that they survived apartheid with any credibility intact. Apartheid
legislation and policy effectively required that universities like UCT remain
a high-quality national resource while drawing its talent from less than 10
percent of the population: a tenth with common historical and cultural origins and a homogeneous social profile. The effects of this policy were
reflected directly in the proportion of national age cohorts attending university. A participation rate of more than 35 percent is generally regarded as
high, and has yet to be achieved by many developed countries. However, by
the late 1980s the participation rate for white South Africans was more than
80 percent.[15] The university system as a whole had ceased to be selective.
Had apartheid continued for another 25 years, we would undoubtedly have
seen a steep decline in undergraduate standards, a shortage of qualified

graduates, and a concomitant decline in the aptitude of entering faculty. By 2030, South African universities would have been doing little credible research, instead offering an extended high school education for those entering racially defined state administrations, or taking up jobs reserved on racial criteria in state-owned enterprises.

The South African university was saved from lapsing into such contradiction by a chain of events, beginning with the collapse of the Soviet Union and the end of the so-called red threat that barely sustained the apartheid regime. When Nelson Mandela accepted an honorary doctorate from Chancellor Harry Oppenheimer at the University of Cape Town in 1992, the formal structure of the institution was reaffirmed and the enduring paradox was secured instead.

Can this settlement hold into the indefinite future? Probably not. At least three forces may disrupt the continuum: a major shift in the admissions without an accompanying increase in employment opportunities; a significant loss of institutional autonomy; and the evolution of new forms of knowledge work. Any of these trends could be accelerated or impeded depending on circumstances. But why should we be any better at predicting the future than our forebears in 1980? The university of 2030 is at best a vague form, a mountain range glimpsed from the ocean, where perhaps nothing is different, but perhaps everything has changed.

NOTES

1. J. Lave and E. Wenger, *Situated Learning: Legitimate Peripheral Participation* (Cambridge: Cambridge University Press, 1991).

2. J. Seekings and N. Nattrass, *Class, Race, and Inequality in South Africa* (New Haven: Yale University Press, 2005); A. Whiteford and D. Van Seventer, "Understanding Contemporary Household Inequality in South Africa," *Studies in Economics and Econometrics* 24, no. 3 (2000): 7–30.

3. H. Bhorat and R. Kanbur, "Introduction: Poverty and Well-Being in Post-apartheid South Africa," in *Poverty and Policy in Post-Apartheid South Africa*, ed. H. Bhorat and R. Kanbur (Cape Town: HSRC Press, 2006), 1–17; H. Bhorat and M. Oosthuizen, "Evolution of the Labour Market: 1995–2002," in Bhorat and Kanbur, *Poverty and Policy;* J. Hoogeveen and B. Ozler, "Poverty and Inequality in Post-apartheid South Africa: 1995–2000," in Bhorat and Kanbur, *Poverty and Policy;* M. Leibbrandt, L. Poswell, P. Naidoo, and M. Welch, "Measuring Recent Changes in South African Inequality and Poverty Using 1996 and 2001 Census Data," in Bhorat and Kanbur, *Poverty and Policy;* and S. Van der Berg, "Public Spending and the Poor Since the Transition to Democracy," in Bhorat and Kanbur, *Poverty and Policy.*

4. N. Yeld, *Equity Assessment and Language of Learning: Key Issues for Higher Education Selection and Access in South Africa* (Cape Town: University of Cape Town, 2001); N. Yeld and W. Haeck, "Educational Histories and Academic Potential: Can Tests Deliver?" *Assessment and Evaluation in Higher Education* 22 (1997): 5–16.

5. Seekings and Nattrass, *Class, Race, and Inequality;* Leibbrandt et al., "Measuring Recent Changes"; Van der Berg, "Public Spending."

6. H. Bhorat and M. Oosthuizen, "Determinants of Grade 12 Pass Rates in the Post-apartheid South African Schooling System," *Secretariat for Institutional Support for Economic Research in Africa Working Papers* 6 (2006): 1–25; M. Louw, S. Van der Berg. and D. Yu, "Educational Attainment and Intergenerational Social Mobility in South Africa," Stellenbosch Economic Working Papers, September 2006; S. Van der Berg and R. Burger, "Education and Socio-Economic Differentials: A Study of School Performance in the Western Cape," Development Policy Research Unit Working Paper 03/73, 2003; S. Van der Berg, "How Effective Are Poor Schools? Poverty and Educational Outcomes in South Africa," Stellenbosch Economic Working Papers, June 2006; see also D. Conley, *Being Black, Living in the Red: Race, Wealth, and Social Policy in America* (Berkeley and Los Angeles: University of California Press, 1999).

7. Alvin Visser, personal communication and unpublished reports, Centre for Higher Education Development, UCT. See also A. Visser and M. Hanslo, "Approaches to Predictive Studies: Possibilities and Challenges," *South African Journal of Higher Education* 19, no. 6 (2005): 1160–76; Conley, *Being Black;* C. Jencks and M. Phillips, "The Black-White Test Score Gap: An Introduction," in *The Black-White Test Score Gap,* ed. C. Jencks and M. Phillips (Washington, DC: Brookings Institution Press, 1998), 1–54.

8. Friedman, T. *The World Is Flat: A Brief History of the Twenty-first Century* (New York: Farrar, Straus and Giroux, 2006).

9. National Commission on Higher Education (NCHE), *A Framework for Transformation* (Pretoria: NCHE, 1996); Republic of South Africa, *National Plan for Higher Education* (Pretoria: South African Ministry of Education, 2001).

10. M. Castells, "Information Technology and Global Capitalism," in *On the Edge,* ed. W. Hutton and A. Giddens (London: Jonathan Cape, 2000); D. Cohen, *Globalization and Its Enemies* (Cambridge: MIT Press, 2006); R. Kaplinsky, *Globalization, Poverty, and Inequality* (London: Polity, 2005).

11. Seekings and Nattrass, *Class, Race, and Inequality.*

12. I. Scott, "Balancing Excellence, Equity and Enterprise in a Less-Industrialized Country: The Case of South Africa," in *The Enterprising University: Reform, Excellence and Equity,* ed. G. Williams (Buckingham, UK: Open University Press, 2003), 40–53; I. R. Scott, N. Yeld, J. M. E. McMillan, and M. J. Hall, "Equity and Excellence in Higher Education: The Case of the University of Cape Town," in *Equity and Excellence in American Higher Education,* ed. W. G. Bowen, M. A. Kurzweil, and E. M. Tobin (Charlottesville: University of Virginia Press, 2005), 261–84.

13. R. Ballard, A. Habib, and I. Valodia, eds., *Voices of Protest: Social Movements in Post-apartheid South Africa* (Scottsville, South Africa: University of KwaZulu-Natal Press, 2006).

14. M. Hall, A. Symes, and T. M. Luescher, *Governance in South African Higher Education* (Pretoria: Council on Higher Education, 2002); M. Hall and A. Symes, "South African Higher Education in the First Decade of Democracy: From Co-operative Governance to Conditional Autonomy," *Studies in Higher Education* 30, no. 2 (2005): 199–212.

15. D. Cooper and G. Subotzky, *The Skewed Revolution: Trends in South African Higher Education, 1988–1998* (Bellville, South Africa: Education Policy Unit, University of the Western Cape, 2001).

Contributors

Dorrian Aiken is a change management consultant and international coach focused on intercultural alliances for organizations. Her clients include the private and public sector. She is an associate researcher in the cultural diversity unit at the University of Cape Town where she teaches a master's elective, and an associate at the University of Stellenbosch School of Public Management. Aiken earned her doctorate in philosophy at the University of Exeter and a professional doctorate in coaching at Middlesex University, both in the United Kingdom.

Neville Alexander became deeply involved in the antiapartheid struggle, after earning a doctorate in philosophy from the University of Tübingen. He cofounded the National Liberation Front. In 1964 he was convicted of conspiracy to commit sabotage and was imprisoned at Robben Island alongside Nelson Mandela until 1974. His book, *One Azania, One Nation* was banned during this time. He is director of the Project for the Study of Alternative Education in South Africa (PRAESA) at the University of Cape Town and an expert on South African language policy and planning.

Nasima Badsha is Advisor to the South African Minister of Education and Chief Executive of the Cape Higher Education Consortium. She was previously Deputy Director General in the Department of Education and has held various other positions, including Associate Professor at the University of the Western Cape, where she headed the Academic Development Centre and was Executive Assistant to the Rector; and Research Officer with the UCT's Alternative Admissions Research Project. She has served on the Council on Higher Education.

Deborah Loewenberg Ball is Dean of the School of Education and William H. Payne Collegiate Professor at the University of Michigan. Her research focuses on the necessary depth of teachers' mathematical knowledge, evaluates effective strategies of teaching mathematics, and designs interventions to improve both student performance and mathematics instruction. A recipient of awards and honors, she has served on national and international commissions and panels focused on policy initiatives and the improvement of education, including, most recently, the National Mathematics Advisory Panel.

Haroon Bhorat is Professor of Economics and Director of the Development Policy Research Unit at UCT and an expert in labor economics, poverty, and income distribution. Coeditor of the book *Poverty and Policy in Post-apartheid South Africa,* among other works, he has consulted for numerous departments of the South African government, as well as international organizations. He is currently a member of the South African Deputy President's Joint Initiative on Priority Skills Acquisition, and an economic advisor to President Kgalema Motlanthe.

Akua Campanella holds a 1996 bachelor's degree in literature from Tufts University and earned a master of social work from the University of Washington in 2008. In between she was a casting director in the entertainment industry and held acting workshops for elementary school children. While at Washington she facilitated Intergroup dialogue classes as a research associate for Dr. Ratnesh Nagda. In the summer of 2007, she traveled to Cape Town South Africa to cofacilitate an undergraduate exploration seminar on the Truth and Reconciliation Commission. She is currently a Bonderman Fellow.

Nancy Cantor is the eleventh Chancellor and President of Syracuse University, and Distinguished Professor of Psychology and Women's Studies in the University's College of Arts and Sciences. Dr. Cantor is an eminent social psychologist, and member of the American Academy of Arts and Sciences, and the Institute of Medicine of the National Academy of Sciences. While Provost at the University of Michigan she was closely involved in the *Grutter* and *Gratz* cases.

Mary Sue Coleman is President of the University of Michigan and Professor of both Chemistry and Biological Chemistry. She is a national spokesperson on the educational value of affirmative action and diverse perspectives in the classroom. She was previously Provost and Vice President for Academic Affairs at the University of New Mexico and President of the University of Iowa. Serving on various boards and executive committees, President Coleman is a trustee of the John S. and James L. Knight Foundation and the Gerald R. Ford Foundation.

André du Toit is Emeritus Professor of Political Studies at UCT. His main research and teaching interests are in the intellectual history of South African political thought; academic freedom; transitional justice; and the narrative interpretation of political violence in South Africa. Among his books are *South Africa's Political Alternatives, Afrikaner Political Thought, 1780–1850* (with Hermann Giliomee), *Political Violence and the Struggle in South Africa* (with Chabani Manganyi), *Towards Democracy: Public Accountability in South Africa,* and *Autonomy as a Social Compact.*

Zimitri Erasmus is a Senior Lecturer in Sociology at the University of Cape Town, where she teaches in the fields of "race," racisms and social identities, and qualitative research methods. Her research interests include the deployment of racialized identities during social transformation, processes of creolization, and strategies for antiracist practice. Erasmus is also the editor of *Coloured by History, Shaped by Place: New Perspectives on Coloured Identities in Cape Town*.

David L. Featherman is Professor of Sociology and Psychology at the University of Michigan and former President of the Social Science Research Council in New York City. Previously directing Michigan's Institute for Social Research, he is founding director of the Center for Advancing Research and Solutions for Society, an advanced study center pursuing team-led analyses and interventions into critical social problems.

Judith February is the head of the Political Information and Monitoring Service at the Institute for Democracy in South Africa (IDASA). Trained in law at the University of Cape Town, she is an expert on good governance, transparency, and accountability in South Africa. She is particularly interested in legal advocacy and the development and interpretation of socio-economic rights jurisprudence.

David J. Garrow is a historian and author of the book *Bearing the Cross: Martin Luther King, Jr., and the Southern Christian Leadership Conference*, which won the 1987 Pulitzer Prize for Biography and the Robert F. Kennedy Award. A Senior Research Fellow at the University of Cambridge's Homerton College, he writes frequently on the history of the United States Supreme Court and is a regular contributor to the *New York Times*, the *Los Angeles Times*, the *Wilson Quarterly*, and *The New Republic*.

Patricia Gurin is the Nancy Cantor Distinguished University Professor Emerita of Psychology and Women's Studies at the University of Michigan. She also directs the research of the University's Program on Intergroup Relations, a nationally recognized program using intergroup dialogues to foster students' cultural competence. A social psychologist, Dr. Gurin's work has focused on social identity and its role in political attitudes and behavior; motivation, and cognition in achievement settings; and the role of social structure in intergroup relations.

Martin Hall is Vice-Chancellor of the University of Salford, Greater Manchester in the United Kingdom. An anthropologist and archaeologist who has written extensively on southern African history, culture, and higher education policy, Hall was previously Deputy Vice-Chancellor at the University of Cape Town and Professor in the UCT Graduate School of Business, where he researched emerging enterprises in developing economies, and the relationship between knowledge systems and entrepreneurship.

Sylvia Hurtado is Professor and Director of UCLA's Higher Education Research Institute. She specializes in research on student educational outcomes, campus climates, the impact of college on student development, and diversity in higher education. *Black Issues in Higher Education* has named her one of the 15 most influential faculty in the academy. Dr. Hurtado has coordinated several national research projects, including a U.S. Department of Education–sponsored project on how colleges are preparing students to achieve the cognitive, social, and democratic skills to participate in a diverse democracy. She is working on a National Institutes of Health / National Science Foundation project on the preparation of underrepresented students for science careers.

Jonathan D. Jansen is Honorary Professor of Education at the University of the Witwatersrand and Vice President of the Academy of Science of South Africa. He was previously a Fulbright Scholar at Stanford University and former Dean of Education at the University of Pretoria. He spent many years as a high school science teacher. An expert on the leadership of transition and on comparative education policy in South Africa and the United States, his books include *Knowledge in the Blood: How White Students Remember and Enact the Past* and *Diversity High: Class, Color, Character, and Culture in a South African High School.*

Marvin Krislov is President of Oberlin College. He was previously the first person ever to simultaneously serve as both Vice President and General Counsel at the University of Michigan. He was recognized by the NAACP Legal Defense and Endowment Fund for his leadership in the defense of affirmative action. A Rhodes Scholar, Krislov clerked for U.S. district judge Marilyn Hall Patel of the Northern District of California before joining the U.S. Department of Justice. After several years in the White House Counsel's office he moved to the U.S. Department of Labor, where he served as Acting Solicitor. In addition to his duties at Oberlin, Krislov is a member of the American Anthropological Association's Project Advisory Board on Race and Human Variation.

Danielle LaVaque-Manty is a Lecturer at the University of Michigan's Sweetland Writing Center. She previously worked as a Researcher Specialist and Program Manager at UM's Institute for Research on Women and Gender.

Jennifer Lewis recently completed her Ph.D. in teacher education at the University of Michigan, after working for 10 years as a teacher in grades 2 through 8. As a postdoctoral fellow at Michigan, she currently teaches and does research in mathematics education and teacher education.

Glenn C. Loury is the Merton P. Stoltz Professor of the Social Sciences and Professor of Economics at Brown University. A prominent social critic and public intellectual, Loury has published hundreds of essays and reviews on racial inequality and social policy in scholarly journals and the popular media. He is a member of the Council on Foreign Relations, a former contributing editor at *The New Republic,* and a member of the editorial advisory board of *The American Interest.* His books include *One by One, From the Inside Out: Essays and Reviews on Race and Responsibility in America,* winner of the American Book Award, and *The Anatomy of Racial Inequality.*

Michael S. McPherson is President of the Spencer Foundation. He was previously President of Macalester College. He serves concurrently as a senior research associate at the University of Chicago's Harris School of Public Policy and as an adjunct professor at Northwestern University's School of Education and Social Policy. McPherson is Chair of the Advisory Board to the Murphy Institute of Tulane University, a member of the executive planning board of Project Pericles, and a trustee of Wesleyan University.

Nazeema Mohamed is employed as Transformation Director at the University of Witwatersrand (Wits). Prior to her appointment at Wits she served as Transformation Manager at the University of Cape Town. Her training and expertise is in higher education policy development with a focus on equity concerns. Mohamed has worked as a researcher, consultant, and manager in higher education. She served in the South African Government as Director of Policy Development in Higher Education.

Biren (Ratnesh) A. Nagda is Associate Professor in the University of Washington School of Social Work and Director of the University's Intergroup Dialogue, Education and Action (IDEA) Center. Born in Kenya, he has been a principal investigator for the Multiversity Intergroup Dialogue Research Project. He has also served as a visiting scholar at the Desmond Tutu Peace Center in Cape Town. Nagda has published widely on intergroup dialogue and is coauthor of the recently published *Intergroup Dialogues in Higher Education: Meaningful Learning about Social Justice* (Jossey-Bass).

Njabulo S. Ndebele, former Vice-Chancellor and Principal of the University of Cape Town, is an acclaimed literary critic, poet, and fiction writer. His 1983 book *Fools and Other Stories* won the Noma Award honoring the best book published in Africa. His other publications include an influential collection of critical essays, *South African Literature and Culture: Rediscovery of the Ordinary,* the novel *The Cry of Winnie Mandela,* and his latest essays *"Fine Lines from the Box."*

Sandra Day O'Connor recently retired as an Associate Justice of the Supreme Court of the United States. She authored the Court's now-famous *Grutter v. Bollinger* decision on affirmative action at the University of Michigan.

Naledi Pandor is Minister of Science & Technology of the Republic of South Africa, a member of the African National Congress's National Executive Committee, and of the South African Parliament. Before accepting her portfolio as Minister of Education in 2004, she served as Senior Lecturer in the University of Cape Town's Academic Support Programme, Deputy Chief Whip of the African National Congress in Parliament, chairperson of the National Council of Provinces, Chancellor of Cape Technikon, and a member of the Council of the University of Fort Hare.

Richard W. Riley is a partner in the law firm of Nelson, Mullins, Riley & Scarborough, LLP, and a board member of the Albert Shanker Institute. He was United States Secretary of Education during both terms of President Bill Clinton's administration. Riley began his career in politics as a member of the South Carolina House of Representatives. He then moved to the state senate before being elected to two terms as governor, a tenure marked by significant improvements in funding and support for education. He served as cochair of Senator Hillary Clinton's presidential campaign.

Elaine Salo is currently director of the Gender Unit, and a member of the Department of Anthropology, University of Pretoria. She worked previously as a senior lecturer at the University of Cape Town's African Gender Institute. She also served as lecturer in the Sociology and Anthropology Departments at the University of the Western Cape, and as a researcher at UCT's Southern African Labour and Development Resource Unit. Her research and publication focuses on youth, gender, popular culture, and globalization; gender, sexuality, and citizenship; and the cultural meanings of physical space.

Stuart Saunders earned his degree in medicine at the University of Cape Town in 1953 and did postgraduate work at Harvard University and the Royal Postgraduate Medical School at Hammersmith in London. He went on to head UCT's Department of Medicine, where he founded the Liver Research Group. As Vice-Chancellor of the University during the crucial years 1981 to 1996, Saunders oversaw an unprecedented increase in the enrollment of black students. He also served on the South African Minister of Education's National Working Group on the structure of higher education. He is now a consultant physician at Groote Schuur Hospital and now Senior Advisor for South Africa to the Mellon Foundation.

Stewart J. Schwab is the Allan R. Tessler Dean of Cornell Law School and the coauthor of *Foundations of Labor and Employment Law* and *Employment Law: Cases and Materials.* An expert on labor and employment law, he earned both his Ph.D. in economics and his J.D. from the University of Michigan, and then clerked for the Honorable J. Dickson Phillips of the

U.S. Court of Appeals for the Fourth Circuit and for Justice Sandra Day O'Connor.

Ian Scott is Director of the Academic Development Programme, Deputy Dean of the Centre for Higher Education Development, and Professor of Education at the University of Cape Town. He became interested in educational development while teaching in South Africa's Coloured schools during the 1970s. He then spent seven years as an editor and a multinational educational publisher and has served on task forces and undertaken research for various national higher education bodies. His research centers on equity and effectiveness in learning and teaching in higher education, with particular reference to policy development and comparative models of widening participation.

Matthew A. Smith is a Research Associate at the Spencer Foundation and a graduate of Stanford University. He is a specialist in philosophy of education and is a coauthor of a recent article in *Theory and Research in Education* entitled "Financial Independence and Age: Distributive Justice in the Case of Adult Education."

Crain Soudien is Director and Professor at the University of Cape Town School of Education. A sociologist and historian of education, Soudien has published extensively in the areas of race, culture, educational policy, comparative education, educational change, public history, and popular culture. He is currently President of the World Council of Comparative Education Societies, and was recently selected by Minister of Education Naledi Pandor to chair her ministerial committee on transformation and discrimination in public higher education.

Abigail J. Stewart is the Sandra Schwartz Tangri Distinguished University Professor of Psychology and Women's Studies at the University of Michigan. She currently directs the UM ADVANCE Project, a multilevel program designed to improve the campus environment for women and underrepresented minority faculty in all fields at the University of Michigan. Her research focuses on the psychology of women's lives and personality; race, gender, and generation; and research and interventions on gender and science.

Teresa A. Sullivan is Provost, Executive Vice President for Academic Affairs, and Professor of Sociology at the University of Michigan. She was previously Executive Vice Chancellor for Academic Affairs for the University of Texas System. Sullivan's research focuses on labor force demography, with particular emphasis on economic marginality and consumer debt. She is a fellow of the American Association for the Advancement of Science.

Jo Thomas reported for the *New York Times* for 26 years, working in Washington, Miami, London, Denver, and New York. She led the *Times'* Oklahoma City bombing investigation and shared the 2002 Pulitzer Prize for Public Service for reporting on the aftermath of the September 11 attacks. She retired from Syracuse University as Associate Chancellor and Professor of Journalism.

Marta Tienda is the Maurice P. During '22 Professor of Demographic Studies and Professor of Sociology and Public Affairs at Princeton University. She is coauthor and coeditor of numerous books, including *The Hispanic Population of the United States, The Color of Opportunity, Hispanics and the Future of America,* and *Africa on the Move.* She chaired the National Academy of Science's Panel on Hispanics and served as 2002 president of the Population Association of America.

Bruce Western is Professor of Sociology and Director of the Multidisciplinary Program in Inequality and Social Policy at Harvard's Kennedy School of Government. His work focuses on the role of incarceration in American social and economic inequality. His book *Punishment and Inequality in America* won the American Sociological Association's 2007 Albert J. Reiss Award for major contributions to the study of crime, law, and deviance and the American Society of Criminology's Michael Hindelang Award for the most outstanding contributions to research in criminology in 2008.

Judith A. Winston is a principal and cofounder of the legal and education consulting firm Winston, Withers & Associates, LLC. She has served as Research Professor of Law at American University's Washington College of Law and General Counsel and Undersecretary of the U.S. Department of Education under Secretary Richard W. Riley. She was also appointed by President Bill Clinton to direct the President's Initiative on Race. A member of numerous boards, she is the author of many articles on education, civil rights, employment discrimination, and women of color in the workplace.

Nan Yeld is Dean of Higher Education Development and Associate Professor of Education at the University of Cape Town. An expert in academic development and assessment, her research focuses on widening access to university study for students from educationally disadvantaged backgrounds. Yeld has been a Senior Africa Fulbright Scholar based at the Educational Testing Service and a Nelson Mandela Fellow at Harvard's W.E.B. Du Bois Institute for Afro-American Studies. She has been appointed by three successive ANC ministers of education to chair pivotal education policy committees.

Index